AF517392

Natural Language Processing
An Information Access Perspective

Kavi Narayana Murthy
University of Hyderabad

Published by
Ess Ess Publications
4837/24, Ansari Road
Darya Ganj
New Delhi-110 002

for

Sarada Ranganathan Endowment
For Library Science
Bangalore

This book has been printed from the camera ready copy prepared by the author using LaTeX

Natural Language Processing
An Information Access Perspective

First Published 2006

ISBN: 81-7000-485-3

Price: Rs.850/-

Published by
Ess Ess Publications
4837/24, Ansari Road, Darya Ganj,
New Delhi-110 002
Tel: 011-23260807, 41563444 Fax: 011-41563334
E-mail: info@essessreference.com
www.essessreference.com

For

Sarada Ranganathan Endowment for Library Science
702, 'Upstairs', 42nd Cross, III Block, Rajajinagar,
Bangalore-560 010
Tel: 080-23305109
E-mail: srels@vsnl.com

Printed in India at: Printline, New Delhi

Preface

The contributions of Dr. S R Ranganathan to the field of library and information sciences is well known. Sarada Ranganathan Endowment for Library Science (SRELS), founded by Dr Ranganathan in 1961 has been carrying out commendable work in promoting library and information sciences. SRELS has been working towards improvement of library and information services in India, training personnel in library and information sciences and applying research results in related areas. The endowment organizes three series of lectures: Sarada Ranganathan Endowment Lectures, Dr S R Ranganathan Memorial Lectures and Curzonco-Seshachalam Endowment Lectures. It also conducts workshops, projects, consultancy work. SRELS publishes the SRELS Journal of Information Management and has also published a large number of books. This book grew out of the Sarada Ranganathan Endowment Lectures I gave in August 2004 on Natural Language Processing and Intelligent Information Retrieval.

The aim of my lectures was to outline broadly the current state and future research directions in Information Retrieval (IR) and Natural Language Processing (NLP), highlighting the role of NLP in moving towards more Intelligent Information Retrieval. The book has expanded on this theme and included material on related areas such as Information Extraction, Automatic Text Categorization, Automatic Summarization and Machine Translation. The chapter on NLP includes relevant topics in linguistics as well as a brief outline of statistical techniques for machine learning. Included are sections on Corpora, Dictionaries, Thesauri and WordNets, Morphology, Syntax and Semantics. The orientation is towards Indian Languages although much of the material is also relevant for English and other languages of the world. The book reflects to a large extent my own experience in teaching and research in Artificial Intelligence, NLP and Text Processing over the last 15 years.

Language engineering is a highly multi-disciplinary field, borrowing as it does, from such varied disciplines as Linguistics, Psychology, Cognitive Science, Artificial Intelligence, Computer Science, Mathematics, Statistics, Physics and Engineering. No individual can claim expertise in so many areas. Yet we need to have some understanding and appreciation of the concerns, aims, terminology, definitions and methodologies of these various disciplines. While good specialized books exist, introductory books that give a balanced view from different perspectives are rare. There is an acute shortage of trained manpower in this fascinating and important subject. Perhaps one of reasons for this situation is the non availability of suitable text books. It is hoped that this book will be useful for beginners from varied disciplines.

This book grew out of a series of lectures and you will find the same informal, almost conversational style of presentation. This is not so much of a formal text book or a research monograph as it is a beginners' manual. No background is assumed. Anybody should be able to read the book without much difficulty. The aim has been to ensure technical correctness and soundness while still sounding simple and easy. This is especially difficult in a highly multi-disciplinary area, each area having several competing theories and view points. At times simplicity and understandability by un-initiated beginners coming from diverse backgrounds had to be given priority over being technically the most precise as per particular theories or models of language.

The primary goal of the book is not so much to describe state-of-the-art technologies and advanced research results as it is to provide a broad background to help prepare students and researchers coming from different backgrounds including computer science, library and information science, artificial intelligence and linguistics. The book aims to provide a balanced treatment of linguistic, statistical and technological material with an Indian language focus. Treatment is kept simple and mathematical jugglery is kept to a minimum. No background in any specific area is assumed. Style of writing is not very formal or terse. The focus is on the major lines of thinking, ideas and themes. Instead of giving ready made solutions in all cases, the book raises questions and issues, to get budding researchers to start independent thinking. The bibliography is limited to readily accessible text books - references to difficult-to-get research articles and the ever changing web-sites are avoided. Language Engineerings is a very active area of research and development and the interested reader will find good resources on the web.

There is enough material in the book to be used as a text book for a first course on the topic within library and information sciences, linguistics, computer science, artificial intelligence and other related disciplines. Parts of the book may also be found useful for more advanced courses. It is hoped that this book will be well received. Comments and suggestions to improve the book are welcome.

A second aim of the book has been to provide some assessment of the status of language technologies in India. It is important to stop once in a while and take a fresh, unbiased look at what all we have achieved and where we have not been very successful. An analysis of failures and deficiencies and a feeling that we can actually do much more, is absolutely essential for taking up fresh initiatives with new life and vigour. All disciplines make such an honest self-assessment at periodic intervals. In this spirit, I have taken the liberty of freely expressing my views and opinions, especially with regard to the status and progress of NLP in India. My views on linguistics must be viewed in terms of the limited interface linguists and engineers have had in India on topics of relevance here. Linguistics itself has changed substantially over time. There have been competing theories and view points. Focus areas, theories or models adapted and view points have varied substantially even within the Indian context. Generalizations and extrapolations can thus be dangerous. Comments on the current state of technology should be taken with care as technology keeps changing very fast. All views expressed are especially applicable to the Indian scene. If some of the statements appear a bit negative, it is because the assessment being made is with respect to the perfect, the ideal, with respect to what we could have achieved. It is not that all the good work that has been done is not appreciated. It should be taken in the positive sense that we have the capability to do much more. We can be world leaders. It is essential to have this optimism but at the same time we must plan our work based on the knowledge and understanding of the ground realities. This is the recipe to success. I hope this view will be appreciated and well received.

Kavi Narayana Murthy
caitra s'ukla pratipat, paarthiva naama saMvatsara
(chaandramaana yugaadi - 9 April 2005)

FOREWORD

When I agreed to chair on the occasion of Sarada Ranganathan Memorial Lectures 2004 delivered by my former colleague from Hyderabad University days, Professor Kavi Narayana Murthy, little did I know that this was going to become a part of a much-needed text in Natural Language Processing (NLP), which many of us have been asking one another to write but none was willing to spend so much time and care for the newcomers in the field, in the midst of numerous academic commitments. KNM has had probably a thought of doing something like this, useful for both linguistics as well as AI students for a long time, and this comes now as his wish-fulfillment. The perspective has, of course, been made very clear from the author's end, in case we want to know for sure about his angle of looking into it, and that is stated in the sub-title : 'The Information Access Approach'.

It is, therefore, not surprising that KNM would start from the information science knowledge explosion, and situate the text in that context. In fact, he begins with QA-system under which he deals with ELIZA and early NLP systems. This is followed by a lucid introduction to the two greatest utility works being done world-wide on information sciences, namely, 'Information Retrieval' and 'Information Extraction' systems. The other advantages of the latest developments in machine understanding of human language texts are creation of automatic summary as well as auto-categorization of text-types and sub-types.

It is obvious that many readers of this book would be interested in getting to know more about Machine Translation (MT) as well as Machine-Aided Translation (MAT), and the author has devoted a whole section on that area. He has identified the challenges before the machine translation enthusiasts as they exist today. An introduction to the field of speech technology is given after that. With this, it is easy for KNM to lay the foundations of NLP in the next section. How doing purely esoteric linguistics is different from doing computational linguistics has been brought about by him clearly in a section. Those interested in corpora are also going to benefit from this text book tremendously as there is a long section devoted to this area, besides introductory remarks in the earlier section. Under 2.4, a lot of loosely strung issues have been put together in a rather well-written and lengthy section.

The third chapter deals with the latest researches in 'Information Retrieval', a matter so very dear to all librarians and information science persons who were present during the talk. For those who are uninitiated, an introduction to the basic model of retrieval has been presented but the advance learners and persons on the job can also benefit from the description of an advanced IR model, which he calls the 'Intelligent IR'. There again, KNM brings out the role played by linguists and semanticists.

The best part of the book is that it has a very good reading list for those interested in NLP in its Bibliography section as well as a few very relevant appendices that go very well with the text.

I sincerely hope that like his lectures were well-appreciated by those who were fortunate enough to attend them in Bangalore, the text as put together here will also be highly appreciated by the readers of all times to come. On behalf of NLP community, let me thank KNM for a laudable effort, and he deserves a word of praise also from the library and information scientists.

Udaya Narayana Singh
Director, Central Institute of Indian Languages, Mysore
May 31, 2005

Acknowledgements

The origin of this book can be traced to the Sarada Ranganathan Endowment Lectures I gave at SRELS (Sarada Ranganathan Endowment for Library Science, Bangalore) during August 2004. I am indebted to SRELS for having given me an opportunity to present my views to such an august audience. The book has expanded from the topics covered in the lectures, based on my own experience in teaching and research in this field over the last many years. I am grateful to SRELS for coming forward to publish this book.

My special thanks go to Prof. A Neelameghan upon whose invitation and inspiration I undertook the job of writing this book. Although the idea of writing a book on NLP was there in me for a long time, it is only due to his encouragement that this book has taken shape so soon.

Prof. Udaya Narayana Singh, director CIIL, Mysore was kind enough to inaugurate my lectures at SRELS. His speeches are always as inspiring as they are informative. I am also grateful to him for writing an excellent foreword to this book.

A number of my colleagues, friends and students, coming from diverse backgrounds including linguistics, computer science, artificial intelligence, mathematics and engineering, have taken pains to go through the drafts and have made very valuable comments and suggestions. My sincere thanks go to G Uma Maheshwara Rao, S Rajendran, S Durga Bhavani, L Sobha, S Baskaran, Ramesh Kumar, G Bharadwaja Kumar and Hla Hla Htay.

I sincerely acknowledge the AU-KBC Research Centre, a small but very active privately funded research organization in Chennai, for inviting me as a visiting scientist and giving me an opportunity to sit and work peacefully. If I could complete the book in such a short period, it is because of the nice academic environment at the centre and the cooperation and support of Prof. C N Krishnan, the director, and all the scientists and researchers at the centre. My special thanks go to Dr Sobha and Mr. Baskaran for all the lively discussions we have had on NLP.

Although the idea of writing a book was there in my mind for a long time, finding time was not easy. I am thankful to the authorities of University of Hyderabad for giving me leave. Whatever little I have learnt during the last 15 years there is due to the close interactions I have had with experts from varied disciplines including linguistics, philosophy, mathematics and statistics. My colleagues at the Department of Computer and Information Sciences and my students have always been a constant source of inspiration. Not a single day passes without some lively discussion and debate on some research topic or the other in computer science or artificial intelligence.

The book is based largely on my notes, slides, scribblings, papers and reports written over the last many years. I have been greatly benefited by all the lectures and seminars I have attended and all the discussions I have had with many experts from varied fields. I would have surely borrowed many ideas and examples from many sources. It would be practically very difficult to acknowledge each one of them separately. There are few sections that have been influenced substantially from writings of others. The section Automatic Summarization has drawn partly from the papers and summaries compiled by Inderjeet Mani and Mark T Maybury. Parts of the section on morphology dealing with English morphology have been influenced by the book by Andrian Akmajian, Richard A Demers and Robert M Harnish. Acknowledgements and credits have been included at appropriate places in the text.

My wife Nalini and my daughter Arabhi have put up with many hardships and extended their fullest cooperation while I was away from home writing the book. I do not have words to thank my father Kavi Krishna Murthy who initiated me into Sanskrit and taught me the joy of working with languages. Nor do I have words to thank my mother who has in a sense taught me everything I know, not by teaching or preaching but by making me think.

Kavi Narayana Murthy

Contents

Chapter 1

The Age of Information and Technology

1.1 The Information Age

Modern technology enables us to store and process not only text and speech but also images (line drawings, half-tone pictures, colour photographs, animations and scanned pages containing handwritten or printed text, tables, pictures, etc), video, music, structured databases and presentation materials (slides, brochures, hand-outs, pamphlets) in various interesting combinations. Even the relatively small and economical hand held devices such as PDAs and cell phones now support voice, text, static images and video. Some cell phones come with a built-in camera while others include a music player. There is a confluence of information technologies, communication technologies and entertainment. We routinely create, store, maintain, process and disseminate large amounts of information whether it is for serious study or for routine office work or just for fun. The boundaries of space and time have melted away. We can access information from anywhere in the world. We are no longer confined to one office or one library. Today we live in the information age.

We have billions of pages of material on the Internet today. With the Digital Library initiatives whole libraries are getting converted to electronic form. Trillions of bytes of electronic data are getting generated everyday. But merely having some data or information somewhere is of no use. What is really required is an easy way to access relevant, timely, useful, and authentic information in a well presented manner. How do we know which documents are relevant, authentic and dependable? How do we fish out what we are looking for in this vast ocean of web pages? How do we categorize, classify, index and structure these largely unorganized collections of electronic documents on the Internet so that they become more easily accessible and hence more useful?

Technology enables us to create, store and process large volumes of information at great speed. But the speed at which we human beings can read and understand documents remains the same, irrespective of technological advances. We still take minutes to browse a page, possibly hours to read carefully and understand the content and may be days, weeks or even months to chew and fully digest the purport of a serious piece of writing. Thus we are in a situation today where we have more information than we can handle. Technologies believe (and wish to believe) that the solution to this information overload problem lies in more technology. We can develop technology that helps us to access relevant pieces of information from large collections of electronic documents so that we can take informed decisions within constraints of time. We can develop technology that helps us to locate, retrieve, categorize, summarize and translate the material we are interested in.

The field of *Information Retrieval (IR)* is all about locating relevant document from a large collection of documents - one of the most basic requirements in all walks of life today. At one point of time, the scope of IR was essentially one library but today we need to look at a world-wide interconnected mesh of billions of electronic documents. In this book we will explore this fascinating field of information retrieval in relation to other closely related areas. We limit ourselves to processing of text documents, leaving aside pictures, sounds, etc. Processing texts requires linguistic and statistical analysis of natural languages and we include a chapter on foundations of *Natural Language Processing (NLP)*.

It will be understood throughout this book that by documents we mean documents stored in electronic form in computer memory, not printed books or hand-written manuscripts. Also, we are looking for automatic or semi-automatic means of storing, processing and retrieving such documents, not the entirely manual methods. Manual methods can presumably give better quality results but they are tedious, time consuming and often error-prone and inconsistent. Necessary human expertise for manual processing is often not available or is too costly. As the amount of available information and the desire to quickly retrieve relevant documents increase, manual methods give way to automatic methods based on technology. In most situations manual methods are simply not practicable.

1.2 Technology for Accessing Information

The processing speed and memory capacity of computers have been increasing at mind boggling rates making it possible to electronically process information at extremely high speeds. But computers are dumb - they have no common sense, world knowledge or human-like thinking and reasoning abilities. Human beings are far superior to computers in reading and understanding texts but the speed at which they can do this is limited. While computer speeds are increasing, the speed of human processing always remains the same. The challenge is to make these dumb computing machines give human-like performance, only many times faster. Our aim here will be to give an idea about the tools and technologies being developed today to address this grand challenge.

There are several ways we can look at this problem of accessing relevant information from large collections of documents:

- A **Question Answering System** accepts a question in natural language, attempts to understand the user's requirements, accesses relevant information and presents it to the user in natural language. As you may guess, this is not going to be an easy task. Words have several senses, meaning depends upon context, natural language sentences have fairly complex structure, and you often need to read between lines to understand exactly what the user is looking for. Answering questions requires a good deal of intelligence.

- **Browsers** allow us to interactively navigate through a web of inter-connected documents, physically located in different computers spread across the globe. Here the role of the computer is limited to locating and taking you to the documents you ask for. You start by specifying a URL (Uniform Resource Locator) - an address of a website or a specific document you are looking for. You decide which links to explore further and which documents to read or download and save for future use.

- **Search Engines** and **Information Retrieval (IR) Systems** accept a query from the user and attempt to retrieve those documents in the collection that seem to match the user's needs as expressed in his/her query. The role of the machine is limited to drawing the user's attention to documents that are potentially relevant to his/her needs. The challenge is to understand the user's specific requirements and locate documents that are, hopefully, the most relevant. Search engines have become an integral part of our everyday use of computers.

- There are many search engines but no single search engine is good enough in all situations. **Meta Search Engines** combine the best of several Search Engines. They provide a common user interface, format queries as required for various search engines, fire the search engines serially or in parallel either as a foreground or as a background process, collect and collate results, store results in a local database for reuse, personalize and adapt to individual user's needs etc. Search engines are general purpose solutions while meta search engines can reside on your computer and they can be personalized to suit your needs. The challenge is to build user models as well as to decide which search engines to fire for what kind of queries. Collating retrieved results, removing duplicates etc. also require substantial amounts of intelligence.

- **Expert Systems and Recommender Systems** may use expert knowledge to make suitable recommendations to users. There are systems, for example, which use a variety of clues (also called heuristics), to suggest books that particular readers are likely to get interested in. The challenge is to make good models of users' needs and preferences and to locate documents that suit these needs, likings and dis-likings.

- **Document Filtering Systems** evaluate documents

according to some specified criteria and decide to exclude specific documents accordingly. For example an email filtering system could be designed to filter out junk mails. The challenge is to decide which documents are relevant and which ones are not.

- **Routing Systems** go one step further and automatically route the documents to appropriate agencies for further action. Here the system must also decide to which department or individual a document must be sent. This requires modelling these individuals and departments.

- **Information Extraction (IE) Systems** attempt to analyze given documents in depth and detail and extract structured information. For example, an IE system can process earthquake related documents and automatically fill specified fields such as date, time, location, magnitude on the Richter scale, extent of damage to life and property etc. in a database table or an XML form. The challenge is to locate specified fields accurately within the given texts

- A **Text Summarization system** produces abstracts or summaries of documents so that we can select appropriate documents by looking at the summaries instead of the whole documents. The challenge is to understand the essence of a document and produce appropriate summaries.

- A **Categorization system** classifies and groups together similar documents so that it becomes so much easier to locate relevant documents. The big question is how to quantify similarity. Computers can only work with quantified data, qualitative reasoning is best done by human beings.

- By embedding an **Automatic Translation** component, we may be able to handle multi-lingual and/or cross-lingual information processing. For example, a Hindi query can be translated into English, the web searched for relevant documents, the retrieved documents summarized and the summaries translated back into Hindi for presentation to the user.

All these technologies are closely inter-related. For example, we may retrieve relevant documents using IR and then summarize the retrieved documents. Text Categorization and Summarization can be used prior to indexing or searching.

Each one of these technologies is a big field in itself and all of them are very active areas of research today. There are many common threads and cross fertilization of ideas takes place regularly across these areas. We shall take a look at some of these technologies briefly in this book. Our aim would be to give basic ideas behind these technologies. Readers interested in more detailed or more technical material will find useful pointers in the Bibliography.

Throughout, we will see examples of the need for a more thorough and detailed linguistic analysis to overcome the current problems and challenges. Chapter Two will lead us through foundations of Natural Language Processing. We will get back to more on Information Retrieval in Chapter Three.

1.3 Question Answering Systems

The simplest way to find out something is to ask. If computers could understand our questions and give us appropriate answers that would perhaps be the simplest and easiest way to access information. After all that is what we do when we want to know something from somebody.

One of the fundamental goals of Natural Language Processing (NLP) is to build computer systems that can understand natural language. But no one knows exactly what is the meaning of *meaning.* We do not know how exactly meanings should be represented as a physical symbol system inside a computer. It is not clear exactly what we mean by *understanding* a text. How then do we know if somebody has understood something or not? We cannot dig into somebody's brain and see the changes before and after a sentence has been read and understood. The only way is to guage from external behavior. The best bet is to ask questions and see how he or she answers. This is what we do in tests and examinations. This is what we do in personal interviews. In fact this is by and large the only general way to ascertain the level of understanding of somebody on a given topic. Question-answering is a natural way to test understanding. Naturally, a lot of attention was given to building Question Answering systems during the early days of NLP.

Question-answering is a very powerful and flexible means for testing the level of understanding. We are free to select the number, nature and order of questions. We may probe deeper by asking follow-up questions. We may give a set of options to chose from. We may ask the candidate to fill gaps, match alternatives, define, describe or explain something, we may ask him to give examples and counter-examples. You might have seen a variety of questions in school examination question papers, entrance tests and personal interviews. We may prompt the candidate with clues and hints. We may ask difficult questions just to see how he reacts, rather than worry about what actually he says. Applied carefully, one can get a fairly clear idea of somebody's level of understanding through question-answering.

One may also ask a candidate to perform some task that presumably requires understanding and guage the level of understanding by his proficiency in performing the task. For example, we may ask the candidate to translate the given text into some other language. Such task based evaluations are difficult because the overall proficiency in performing the task depends not only on proper understanding of the given text but also on other factors such as proficiency in the target language for translation. Question answering remains the best bet.

Presumably, one has to understand the meaning of a text before he or she can answer questions relating to the given text. Naturally there was a great deal of interest in building question-answering systems in the early days of NLP. Here we sample a few of them just to get a taste of the nature of the problem and the range of ideas that have been tried out. We begin with a very simple yet highly successful system that was however never intended to be an NLP system nor was it designed to answer any questions at all. Yet this system has a simple and neat design and knowing this helps us to understand other NLP systems better.

1.3.1 ELIZA - The Rogerian Therapist

There are many approaches to improving mental health. Here we are talking about a particular approach called Rogerian Therapy and a system called ELIZA developed with this approach in mind. Empathy is the foundation of Carl Rogers' client-centered therapy (also known as Rogerian therapy). He asserted that empathy alone is healing. A client centered therapist strives to provide an environment of empathy, unconditional positive regard, and acceptance. Therapists are trained to accept the client where they are at the moment. Client-centered therapists consider diagnosis and treatment planning to be much less important than being supportive to the client. Instead they act as an understanding listener, helping the client by providing advice and alternate interpretations to past events only when asked.

Rogerian therapy involves the therapist's entry into the

client's unique phenomenological world. In mirroring this world, the therapist does not disagree or point out contradictions. Neither does he/she attempt to delve into the unconscious. The focus is on immediate conscious experience. Rogerian therapy is a process of freeing a person and removing obstacles so that normal growth and development can proceed and the client can become independent and self-directed. During the course of therapy the client moves from rigidly of self-perception to fluidity.

The ELIZA system was developed by Joseph Weizenbaum in 1966. ELIZA is a system whose sole purpose is to maintain a conversation with the client. It is not really required to understand what the user says nor is it expected to answer his questions. Such a system is very useful for recording and later analyzing the mind of patients with a mental problem. When allowed to talk in a free and conducive environment, such patients tend to come close to the source of their problem irrespective of what topic the conversation starts from. Psychiatrists are trained to analyze the conversations and guess the source of the problems and hence plan further investigations. Patients are always conscious of what the other person may think of whatever they speak. It can be expected that patients tend to be more free and forthcoming when they are talking to a dumb, faceless machine than with doctors or other people. Hence this system. Here is a transcript of a typical conversation with ELIZA:

```
Men are all alike.

IN WHAT WAY

They're always bugging us about something
or the other.
```

```
CAN YOU THINK OF A SPECIFIC EXAMPLE

Well, my boyfriend made me come here

YOUR BOYFRIEND MADE YOU COME HERE

He says I'm depressed much of the time.

I AM SORRY TO HEAR YOU ARE DEPRESSED

It's true. I am unhappy.

DO YOU THINK COMING HERE WILL HELP YOU
NOT TO BE UNHAPPY

I need some help, that much seems certain.

WHAT WOULD IT MEAN TO YOU IF YOU GOT
SOME HELP

Perhaps I could learn to get along with my mother

TELL ME MORE ABOUT YOUR FAMILY
```

FIG 1.1 Sample Transcripts from ELIZA. ELIZA's output is in all-caps.

Quite impressive, right? ELIZA was so successful that even its developers were said to have started confessing to ELIZA! There are many implementations that are freely available and the readers may find it interesting to play with versions of ELIZA. The gnu-emacs editor comes with a built-in version too. Source codes are also available and those interested in building similar toy NLP systems may find it useful to go through the code.

ELIZA is, however, an extremely simple system. The sole purpose of ELIZA is to maintain a conversation. Since ELIZA does not have to really understand what the user is saying, it does not have to linguistically analyze the input sentences in any great depth or detail. In fact ELIZA does not perform any of the usual NLP tasks such as dictionary look-up, morphological analysis or syntactic analysis. In fact a useful by-product of this simplistic approach is that ELIZA does not complain if you make spelling mistakes or your sentences are grammatically incorrect or incomplete. All that ELIZA does is to look for *keywords*. ELIZA has a set of prioritized keywords and for each keyword a set of input-patterns to match the input sentences against and a set of output patterns which it uses to generate responses. If many keywords are found, it simply uses the one with highest priority. If no keywords are found, ELIZA has a set of default outputs such as "please continue", "I see", "tell me more" and so on. To avoid giving a sense of monotony and repetition, it rotates among a set of alternative responses for a given keyword. Thus if you say the same thing again, ELIZA's response could be different. Many people have re-implemented ELIZA and the more sophisticated versions can detect if you are too curt and reserved or if you try to abuse the system. Some of them try to pull you back into what you were saying earlier to avoid digressing too far. The table below shows a sample of the kind of keyword based pattern matching system that ELIZA uses. Letters prefixed with a question mark are variables that can match parts of sentences.

Key	Priority	Pattern	Possible Outputs
alike	10	?X	In what way? What resemblance do you see?
are	3	?X are you ?Y	Would you prefer it if I weren't ?Y?
	3	?X are ?Y	What if they were not ?Y?
always	5	?X	Can you think of a specific example? When? Really, always?
what	2	?X	Why do you ask? Does that interest you?

TABLE 1.1 PATTERN MATCHING SYSTEM IN ELIZA

ELIZA's power is in its simplicity and generality - it can say something for any input whatever and what it says is usually reasonably well connected with the given input. This strength is also its weakness - its shallow, superficial analysis often leads it astray. The system is not scalable or expendable to applications that demand deeper and better understanding.

1.3.2 Early NLP Systems

A large number of NLP systems were developed in the 1960s and 1970s. Many of them were question answering systems. They were all toy systems by today's standards but it is instructive to take a peep at some of them. For the first time, researchers were trying to integrate linguistic analysis at various levels ranging from dictionaries and morphological analysis through rudiments of syntax to discourse analysis and build complete working systems. Here we take a quick look at a few of them.

STUDENT

The STUDENT system was developed by Daniel G Bobrow in the year 1964. This system was designed to solve algebra story problems from school text books. These problems are expressed in English sentences. STUDENT constructed from the given English sentences algebraic equations and solved those equations. The following transcripts from the system illustrate the nature of the task:

```
Q: The distance from Newyork to Los Angeles is 3000
miles. If the average speed of a jet plane is   600
miles per hour,  find  the time it takes  to travel
from Newyork to Los Angeles by jet.

A: THE TIME IT TAKES TO TRAVEL FROM NEWYORK TO  LOS
ANGELES BY JET IS 5 HOURS

Q: Bill's  father's uncle is twice as old as Bill's
father.  2 years from now Bill's father  will  be 3
times  as old as  Bill. The sum of thier ages is 92.
Find Bill's age.

A: BILL'S AGE IS 8
```

FIG 1.2 Sample Transcripts from STUDENT

The big thing is not solving these problems - simple solutions exist. The difficult part is in understanding the natural language sentences. Let us go through one example in some detail to get an idea of the nature of problems and solutions.

Q: If the number of customers Tom gets is twice the square of 20 percent of the number of advertisements he runs, and the number of advertisements he runs is 45, what is the number of customers Tom gets?

In order to simplify further processing, STUDENT breaks complex sentences into simple sentences called "kernel" sentences. Thus the given sentence is broken into "The number of customers Tom gets is twice the square of 20 percent of the number of advertisements he runs", "The number of advertisements he runs is 45" and "What is the number of customers Tom gets?". STUDENT works with objects such as numbers, variables and operators. It has to deal with precedence and associativity of operators. Algebraic equations can then be formed. For example, the expression "twice the square of the number of advertisements he runs" is formulated as

(TIMES 2 (EXPT (NUMBER OF ADVERTISEMENTS
HE/pro RUNS) 2))

STUDENT needs to know that "twice" is same as "2 times" an "of" is to be interpreted as "times" in some cases but not always, "is" means "equals" in some cases but not in every case. STUDENT needs to handle anaphoric references. "HE" refers to "TOM" in the above example. This looks simple but resolving anaphoric references is not always that easy. A definite noun phrase such as "the line" may refer to one of the previously mentioned lines and STUDENT needs to figure out which line we are talking about. We often use equivalent expressions and say "twice the sum of the length and width of the rectangle" or just "perimeter of the rectangle". General world knowledge such as "Distance equals Speed times Time" is also essential. Thus STUDENT needs some degree of syntactic, semantic and discourse level analysis as well as world knowledge and ability to perform logical deduction.

SIR

SIR (Semantic Information Retriever) was developed by Bertram Raphael in 1968. SIR was intended to be a prototype "understanding" machine. It could accept statements in natural language and answer questions based on them. SIR used simple pattern matching techniques. The following transcripts illustrate the system's capabilities:

```
Every keypunch operator is a girl.

I UNDERSTAND

Any girl is an example of a person.

I UNDERSTAND

Is a keypuch operator a person?

YES

Is a person a person?

YES

Is a person a girl?

SOMETIMES

Is a monkey a keypunch operator?

INSUFFICIENT INFORMATION
```

FIG 1.3 Sample Transcripts from SIR

These transcripts clearly bring out the differences between human beings and machines. We human beings have a great deal of world knowledge and we are capable of very sophisticated common sense reasoning. Machines lack both world knowledge and common sense reasoning. We do not need to be told that a girl is a person - we know it. We do not need to be given a rule which says an X is a X - we know it. But computers need to be told even such "obvious" things. This is why it has not been possible to build machines that show human like intelligent behaviour even till date.

Language is not a completely independent and autonomous faculty of the mind - knowledge representation, reasoning, learning are all inseparably tied up with the language faculty. There was a time when somebody could become a good painter if he had some imagination and skill in handling the brush. To become a successful painter today, one must know the physics of light, the chemistry of the paint, the biology of the eye, the psychology of colour and many other things. Language must be explored not only from the point of view of linguistics but also from the perspectives of psychology, cognitive science, artificial intelligence, statistics, mathematics, physics, computer science and engineering. We have created artificial boundaries of departments, disciplines and specializations for the sake of convenience but now they seem to have become major barriers for scientific exploration. Science today is highly inter-disciplinary. This is perhaps the most important lesson we have to learn from these early NLP systems.

PSP2

The PSP2 system was developed by the author in the eighties. PSP2 is a simple natural language question answering system in the domain of financial investments. It is a keyword based pattern matching system like most other early NLP systems, only the pattern matching is a bit more sophisticated. We first give sample transcripts and then summarize the salient features. Only the queries given by the user and the system's interpretation are given. After taking user's concurrence, the system gives out pre-stored responses. The spelling errors are all intentional.

```
User:     PSP?

System:   WHAT IS PSP2 INVESTMENT PLAN ALL ABOUT?

User:     How muhc should I ivnest?

System:   WHAT IS THE INITIAL AMOUNT OF INVESTMENT
          IN THE PSP2 PLAN?

User:     Is that the lest?

System:   WHAT IS THE MINIMUM AMOUNT OF INVESTMENT?
```

```
User:    Why?

System:  WHY IS THERE A MINIMUM AMOUNT FOR INVESTMENT
         IN PSP2?

User:    How many yearrs

System:  WHAT IS THE PERIOD OF INVESTMENT?

User:    is that the least?

System:  WHAT IS THE MINIMUM PERIOD OF INVESTMENT?

User:    How much iterest do I get?

System:  WHAT IS THE RATE OF INTEREST IN PSP2 PLAN?

User:    Can I take back my money whenver I want?

System:  IS THERE A FACILITY FOR PREMATURE
         WITHDRAWALS?

User:    Where should I sign on the check?

System:  TELL ME MORE ABOUT PSP2 CHEQUES.
```

FIG 1.4 Sample Transcripts from PSP2

PSP2 accepts free format natural language queries and produces natural language responses using a bank of pre-stored frequently asked questions and corresponding answers. These stored questions and answers are provided by human experts and can therefore be taken as accurate and reliable. The only issue is how to understand the users' queries and map them to the closest stored question. If this could be done correctly, the system can generate appropriate responses.

PSP2 answers questions posed by potential customers of a finance company. It would not be acceptable for PSP2 to give incorrect or inappropriate answers. The answers better be correct. Since the answers themselves are given by human experts and stored in the machine, this translates to the requirement that PSP2 must understand the user's question correctly. In order to be sure that the users' questions have been properly understood, PSP2 comes back and asks the user to confirm its interpretation. Contrary to initial expectation, this does not cause much of annoyance because the confirmation questions are reformulated by the system and the reformulations are often technically more precise. Thus "How many years?" is reformulated as "What is the period of investment?". Users may actually feel glad that their query has been accurately understood by the machine. The system's interpretations are usually correct but what if they are not? PSP2 generates a ranked list of matching queries and it can give several options in ranked order for the user to simply choose from. One or the other interpretation can be generally expected to be alright. Users are required to re-state their queries in different terms only if none of the possible interpretations match.

Pattern matching has to be more powerful here than the simplistic methods we saw in the case of ELIZA. There are many different ways the same thing can be expressed and PSP2 needs to handle unrestricted, free format queries. Order of keywords is important because "I am interested in withdrawing so and so amount" is not the same as "How much interest do you charge for the amounts withdrawn". Simply listing keywords such as "interest", "withdraw" and "amount" with priorities is not sufficient. PSP2 uses not just keywords but "patterns" of keywords. Patterns can specify mandatory, desirable and optional parts. Patterns can specify which parts are order-sensitive and which parts can appear in any order. Some key words may be required to appear next to each other while others may be permitted to appear with other words in between. Logical connectives such as AND, OR and NOT can be used. Patterns are constructed hierarchically, starting from individual keywords and gradually building more and more complex patterns according to specified rules. There is thus a "grammar" of patterns. In fact PSP2 comes with an auxiliary program called PATGEN to assist developers in interactively developing patterns according to the rules of the system.

There can be several patterns for each stored question. A given query may thus match several patterns in several queries.

Patterns are ranked according to degree of match. If nothing matches at all PSP2 has a set of default outputs. It may say for example, "I am sorry, I may not be able to help you this time. Please contact so and so". Also, as in the case of ELIZA there are multiple output formulations and outputs are selected at random, avoiding repetitions to reduce monotony.

PSP2 remembers the previous questions and corresponding confirmations. While performing pattern matching, patterns from previous questions are also included, appropriately weighted to ensure that patterns in the current query have more weightage than patterns in the past queries. More recent queries have higher weightage compared to queries in the distant past. This enables PSP2 to interpret queries in the context of previous conversation. Thus it can understand just a "why" as "why is the maximum period of investment only 9 years" or "why is there a limit on the minimum amount I can invest" based on the context of the previous conversation. Thus follow up questions need not be complete and self-contained in themselves. This ability to interpret queries in context makes interaction with PSP2 a lot more natural than other key-word based pattern matching systems we have seen before.

PSP2, like other early NLP systems, does not perform very detailed linguistic analysis of the input queries. Morphological analysis with dictionary look-up and a limited analysis of local structure is all that is performed. User queries need not be grammatically correct or complete. Handling ungrammatical inputs can be considered to be a virtue of these simple NLP systems, not easy to realize in much more sophisticated systems. However, this limited, shallow linguistic analysis is also a major source of weakness and brittleness of such systems. It is easy to fool the system and the system does grossly mis-interpret user queries now and then.

PSP2 also has a built-in spelling error detection and correction system. Non-keywords of course do not matter but PSP2 can tolerate spelling errors even in the keywords. The spelling errors in the transcripts above are intended, observe them carefully.

The power of NLP systems such as PSP2 comes from their simplicity. This simplicity is also their main weakness. Programs such as PSP2, STUDENT and SIR are simplistic, superficial, limited and ad-hoc. They cannot be scaled to real life, wide coverage, robust applications nor can they be easily adapted or retrained for different application domains. These systems surely generated enough initial interest and curiosity at their times. In fact such toy systems are being developed and used even today, albeit in a more sophisticated form with animated human faces and voice output. The only purpose they serve is to generate some curiosity. The big question remains - can machines really understand language at all?

1.3.3 Foundations of Story Understanding

During the seventies, Roger Schank and his team at Yale University were focussing on the foundations of story understanding. *Conceptual Dependency* (CD) theory, *Scripts, Plans and Goals* were some of the ideas that came out of this effort.

Conceptual Dependency is a system designed to represent the meanings of sentences by decomposing them into a small number of primitive "acts". In CD theory, sentences with identical meaning should have the same underlying conceptual representation, regardless of the differences in grammatical form or the language used. In this sense, CD was a kind of an inter-lingua. A basic premise of the Cd theory is that meaning arises from a combination of memory search, planning and inference. Only a small fraction of meaning is actually conveyed directly by the lexical items which explicitly appear in a given sentence. For example, if we read the sentence "John bought a television" we understand many things - that John probably bought the TV in a store, there was another person in the store, John gave him money, that person gave John the TV, the person who sold the TV no longer possesses that TV, John bought the TV in order to watch the shows probably for his own enjoyment, John will plug in the TV at home, and so on. Although we can never be sure about such inferences, understanding texts necessarily involves a large number of such inferences. We will have to make such assumptions and inferences, even if some of them need to be changed later on in the light of new information coming in. Note that our understanding of the sentence is going to be same or similar if the sentence were to read "A TV set was sold to John". CD theory proposed that any sentence in any language can be broken down and expressed in terms of eleven primitive acts. Each of these acts had an associated set of cases such as the actor, the recipient and the instrument. These case-frames encapsulated expectations for the conceptualizations being built. Such expectations are useful for word sense disambiguation, pronoun reference etc. too. The sentence above could be conceptualized in Cd as

```
(ATRANS
          ACTOR     John
          OBJECT    money
          FROM      John
          TO        individual)
(ATRANS
          ACTOR     individual
          OBJECT    TV
          FROM      individual
          TO        John)
```

Here ATRANS stands for transfer of possession. The other primitive acts in CD theory were PROPEL (the application of physical force - throwing, hitting, falling, pulling, kicking, etc.), PTRANS (transfer of physical location - driving, flying, taking a bus, walking, etc.), INGEST (AN organism taken something from outside environment and makes it internal - breathing, eating, smoking, etc.), EXPEL (opposite of INGEST - sweating, crying, defecating, spitting, etc.), MTRANS (transfer of mental information from one individual to another - speaking, reading, etc.), MBUILD (thought processes which create new conceptualizations from old ones - deciding, concluding, realizing, considering, imagining, etc.), MOVE (movement of a body part of some animate organism - waving, dancing, jumping, etc.), GRASP (the act of physically contacting an object, usually by MOVE arm/hand - grabbing, holding, hugging, etc.), SPEAK (vocalization), and ATTEND (the act of directing a sense organ - hearing, etc.).

CD theory was considered adequate for representing mundane physical actions. However, most actions are part of larger plans in service of higher-level goals, and much of the comprehension process involves recognizing what these plans and goal are. These goals were classified as S-GOALS (satisfaction goals for satisfying recurring bodily needs such as sex, hunger, sleep and thirst), D-GOALS (delta goals standing for a desire for a change of state - mental states (D-KNOW), physical proximity (D-PROX), or desire to gain control of something (D-CONT) or someone (D-SOCCONT) as in kidnapping), E-GOALS (entertainment goals such as E-COMPANY, E-TRAVEL and E-EXERCISE), A-GOALS (achievement goals such as A-GOOD-JOB, A-SKILL) and P-GOALS (preservation goals such as P-APPEARANCE, P-COMFORT, P-HEALTH, and P-FINANCES.).

For each goal, there are a number of plans which may be used to achieve it. For example, you wish to get control over some object, you may ASK, INFORM-REASON, BARGAIN, THREATEN, OVERPOWER or STEAL. Plans have preconditions. You have to be in physical proximity to ask or you must a communication device such as a phone. In order to steal some object, you must go near that object (not the owner!)

Detailed planning is however not always required. There are stereotypical situations where a lot of details are generally known. Taking a train involves going to the station, buying the ticket, reaching the platform, waiting for the train, entraining, looking for a seat, detraining at the destination station, exiting the station etc. Buying groceries, going for a movie, going to a restaurant or a marriage party can all be visualized this way. *Scripts* capture the full details of such stereotypical scenarios. Nobody writes down in minute detail all that happened and if at all one tries, that would be the most boring story. Writers write only the interesting and significant aspects and readers fill in the rest by their commonsense knowledge. Scripts can be used to do this filling in.

The Yale school made significant contributions along these lines and built many systems. But the big questions remained. How do we make computers understand language in a way we humans can do?

1.3.4 In-Depth Understanding

All the systems we have seen above are toy systems. They cannot be easily scaled up to real systems. None of them answer serious questions about the feasibility of developing real question-answering systems. Can we, even in principle, build systems that can answer questions like human beings can? Can we build systems that can read, understand and then answer questions? In early 1980s Michael Dyer was working on the ideas of in-depth understanding as part of his doctoral work at MIT. He built a system called BORIS (Better Organized Reasoning and Inference System). BORIS showed that under certain assumptions, it is possible for computers to demonstrate in-depth understanding and answer complex questions in a human-like manner. Let us look at samples of actual transcripts from BORIS:

```
Richard hadn't heard from his college roommate Paul
for years. Richard had borrowed money from Paul,
which was never paid back, but now he had no idea
where to find his old friend. When a letter finally
arrived from San Francisco, Richard was anxious to
find out how Paul was.

Q What happened to Richard at home?

A Richard got a letter from Paul

Q Who is Paul?

A Richard's friend

Q Did Richard want to see Paul?

A Yes. Richard wanted to know how Paul was

Q Had Paul lent money to Richard?

A Yes. Paul had lent money to Richard

Q Why didn't Richard pay Paul back?

A Richard did not know where Paul was

Q How did Richard feel when the letter appeared?

A Richard felt glad because Paul and he were friends
```

FIG 1.5 Sample Transcripts from BORIS

This sample transcript vividly brings out the depth of understanding by BORIS. It is not straight forward to answer questions such as what happened to somebody somewhere. Many things might have happened, some of them may be explicitly given to us in the story while some we can infer from our world knowledge of what "typically" happens in given kinds of situations. But everything that happened or could have happened would not be interesting. Something unusual, something special, something worth noting is what is expected out of such a question. Notice also that the story never says explicitly that Paul wrote the letter. Since we are talking of Paul and nobody else, we can infer that it must be Paul who must have written the letter. To say Paul was Richard's friend, BORIS would need to know what colleges are and what exactly college room-mate means. It is easier to answer questions on what happened to whom, where, when etc. literally but assessing mental states and reactions of people in different situations is a different matter. That BORIS could understand that Richard wanted to know how Paul was is surely a human-like response. BORIS knows that if X lends money to Y, that is the same as Y borrowing money from X.

The point is not whether the answers are correct or not. Often there are no correct or wrong answers, only more appropriate and less appropriate ones. If somebody asks you where is Taj Mahal what would you say? If you are in Europe you would perhaps say that Taj Mahal is in India but if you are in some part of India you would probably say that it is in Agra. If you happen to be already in Agra then you are perhaps expected to say how exactly to reach Taj Mahal from wherever you are. An precise description of the location in terms of latitudes and longitudes may be mathematically more accurate but it may not serve the purpose. Appropriateness of answers depends upon the situation and understanding situational context is as much a part of natural language understanding as all the linguistic processing. Speakers have mental models of listeners and vice versa. To answer somebody you first need to understand what exactly he or she wants to know. Literal interpretation of given texts does not constitute in-depth understanding.

With many more examples of this kind, Dyer in his thesis tries to convince the reader that in-depth understanding and human-like question answering behaviour is very much possible for computers. Then why is it that we still do not have computers that we can communicate with in natural language? Why are we still stuck with complex programming languages with so little expressive power? Why don't we still have "intelligent" computers assisting us in all walks of life?

In-depth understanding requires great amounts of world knowledge. It is all much more to do with commonsense reasoning than with merely linguistic analysis or straight forward mathematical logic. Dyer's purpose was to show that given all the required knowledge, represented in suitable structures, computers could be expected to give human-like performance in natural language understanding. If every piece of knowledge required was available, computers could perhaps think like us. But this "if" is a very big "if". Dyer could, over a period of several years, carefully hand-code all the required knowledge for demonstrating in-depth understanding in a limited set of stories. We cannot possibly hand-code such vast and complex knowledge structures for real applications spanning across a wide range of topics and situations. Nor can machines learn such knowledge structures automatically. Commonsense is what we have learnt automatically by mere contact with the real world. Commonsense is what cannot be explicitly taught or learnt. We still do not know how exactly we acquire commonsense knowledge. We still do not know how to make computers acquire commonsense knowledge.

BORIS demonstrated that in-depth understanding was possible provided all relevant knowledge could be obtained and properly represented in the computer. However, the big question that remains is how to make the computer obtain all relevant knowledge. Thus fully automated in-depth understanding has remained a distant dream even today.

1.3.5 Turing Test

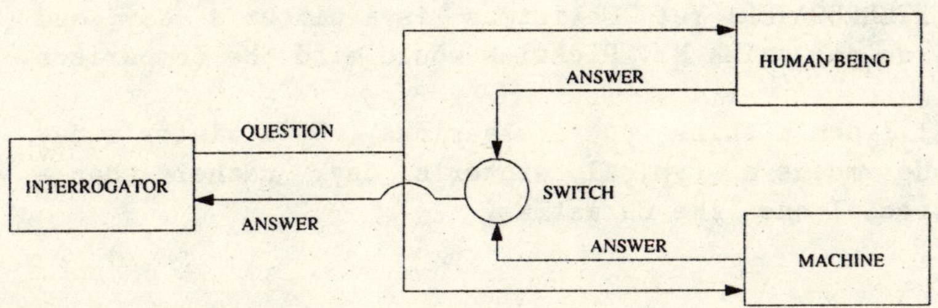

FIG 1.6 Turing Test

In 1950 Alan Turing devised a test for the thinking ability of machines. An interrogator asks questions and gets answers from either a human being or a machine, sitting in different rooms, and communicating only through typed messages. If the interrogator is unable to tell the man from the machine purely based on the answers he gets for his questions, we may conclude that the machine is at least as intelligent as the human being. The interrogator is free to ask any question and the machine is allowed to do whatever it wants to prove its case. For example, given a simple arithmetic problem the machine may take a long time and answer wrongly. Here is a hypothetical conversation given by Turing:

```
INTERROGATOR: In the first line of your sonnet which
reads  ‘‘Shall I compare  thee  to a summer’s  day’’,
would not ‘‘a spring day’’ do as well or better?

A: It woudn’t scan.

INTERROGATOR:  How  about  ‘‘a winter’s day’’?  That
would scan alright.

A:  Yes,  but  nobody  wants  to  be  compared  to a
winter’s day.

INTERROGATOR:  Would  you say  Mr. Pickwick  reminded
you of Christmas?
```

```
A: In a way.

INTERROGATOR: Yet Christmas is a winter's day, and
I do not think Mr. Pickwick would mind the comparison.

A: I don't think you are serious. By a winter's day
one means a typical winter's day, rather than a
special one like Christmas.
```

FIG 1.7 A Hypothetical Conversation

If the "A" in the above conversation were actually a machine rather than a human being, perhaps we can accept that the machine was intelligent and capable of thinking and understanding. Of course there is no machine today that can pass the Turing Test and nobody knows if we will ever be able to develop one. It is interesting to note that question answering based on natural language understanding and generation has been used as a test of human-like intelligence. Indeed language is at the very core of human intelligence.

NLP started off with simple ideas and toy systems. Over the years, researchers have discovered how complex natural languages are. Focus has shifted from building toy systems to developing large scale linguistic data resources, wide coverage grammars and parsers etc. Statistical analysis and machine learning techniques are being combined with linguistic approaches. Scalability and adaptability or trainability have now become very important issues. Many useful applications have emerged. Yet we are far from the ultimate goals of NLP - human-like understanding, generation and language learning by machines. There are no question-answering systems today that we can reliably use for accessing whatever kind of information we may need.

1.4 Information Retrieval

In this section we sketch the rudiments of modern IR systems. The ideas we describe here will form the background for more advanced techniques we will be looking at in Chapter Three.

1.4.1 IR Defined

Information Retrieval is a vast field concerned with the storage and retrieval of documents. Documents may include texts, images, video, speech, music and web pages in various combinations. Processing and retrieval of images, video, speech, music and rich multi-media documents has become an increasingly active area of research in recent times. Nonetheless, text remains the most basic, ubiquitous and the most widely used medium of representing and communicating information. Text documents take much less space to store and less network bandwidth to move across than pictures. After all, a picture is worth a thousand words! Here we will mainly look at the issues relating to storage and subsequent retrieval of text documents in response to user queries.

Of particular interest will be what is termed *ad hoc retrieval.* Here an unaided user formulates a query and requests for relevant documents. The system searches the collection and returns a possibly ordered set of potentially useful documents. For example, you may go to a search engine, type "computer" and press the search button. The search engine comes back and says it found so many million web pages that seem to be relevant to your query and it also displays the links to the top few that it thinks are the most relevant. A good system will be expected to return most of the relevant documents in the collection and few irrelevant documents.

A *Document* is a unit of text that is indexed and retrieved. A document may be an article, a research paper, a whole book, a chapter or section from a book, or even single sentences. In a traditional library setting, a document may be a book while on the Internet a document may be just a single web page. A *Collection* is a set of such documents. A *Query* refers to a short formulation of a user request in a suitable format.

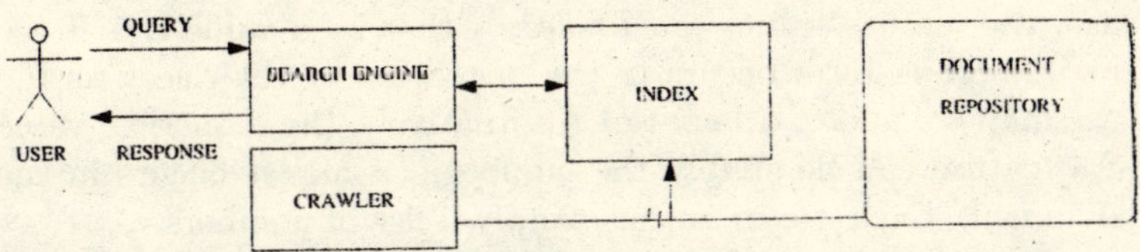

FIG 1.8 Information Retrieval

1.4.2 Documents as Bags-of-Words

The meaning of a text is indicated by the meanings of the words used as also by the syntactic, semantic and pragmatic structures into which these words are placed in a coherent framework. Nevertheless, it is very common in IR systems to take the extreme view that texts are merely unordered sets of words, without any regard to syntactic, semantic or discourse structure. Thus *'I eat, therefore I am'* and *'I am, therefore I eat'* will be treated as equivalent! This representation is called the *bag-of-words* representation and has been widely used, despite its obvious limitations. In the bag-of-words representation the document texts as well as the user queries are represented as unordered collections of words and word-like features such as phrases, together known as *terms.*

Queries may be simple or they may be structured query expressions involving Boolean operators such as AND, OR and NOT. You may ask, for example, for documents containing the terms "Data" AND "Mining" but NOT "Coal" OR "Gold". If exact match is expected, there are chances of getting too few or too many matching documents, especially when the document collections are large and heterogeneous. The queries may be simply too general or too very specific. Recent research has therefore focused on probabilistic models where documents are ranked according to their estimated relevance to the user query instead of looking for exact matches.

1.4.3 The Vector Space Model

One of the most widely used models for IR is the vector space model. Here documents as well as queries are represented as vectors of features. In the bag-of-words approach, features correspond to the terms - each term (word or phrase) is a potential feature. Features are given numerical values. In the simplest case, the feature values are *Boolean* - that is, a value is 1 if the corresponding term occurs in the document or the query as the case may be, and 0, otherwise. Alternatively, the numerical value of a feature can be simply the number of times it occurs in the document. Each vector is thus simply a list of numbers.

A vector of n such features can be geometrically viewed as a point in n-dimensional space. The geometric spatial proximity between two vectors is used as a metaphor for the semantic prox-

imity between the corresponding documents and/or query strings. This model is thus conceptually simple and appealing. The most relevant documents are the ones that include the most terms from a given query and thus spatially closest to the query vector. The example below illustrates these ideas in just two dimensions. If there were three terms, we need to consider vectors in three dimensional space and, by extension of this idea, if there are n terms, the vectors will be in n-dimensional space - difficult to get a mental picture but mathematically a simple extension all the same.

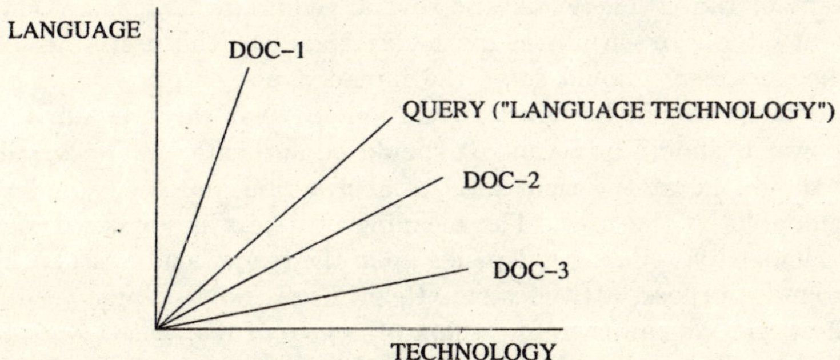

FIG 1.9 Vector-Space Model

The direction of the vectors is a good indicator of the semantic content of the corresponding documents, not the length of the vectors. Hence it is usual to *normalize* the lengths of all vectors to unity and consider only the directions.

1.4.4 Performance Evaluation

Performance of IR systems is measured in terms of *Recall* and *Precision.* Recall gives the proportion of relevant documents retrieved. Of course we may get 100% Recall by simply retrieving all the documents in a collection! Thus we must also look at the proportion of retrieved documents that are relevant. This latter quantity is called *Precision.* There is a clear trade-off between precision and recall. We can increase precision by being very choosy and retrieve only those documents we think are surely relevant. Recall comes down. Alternatively, we can try to retrieve as many hopefully relevant documents as possible, possibly bringing down the precision. The challenge is to maximize both Precision and

Recall so that we get most of the relevant documents and very few irrelevant documents.

1.4.5 Measuring Relevance

Performance measures are dependent on the notion of relevance. How do we know a document is relevant or not? A document's relevance must be measured in relation to a user's need at a given point of time. There may be several requirements. The document's topic or *aboutness* must correspond to the user's needs. The document should serve the intended use or purpose. The document should be novel in relation to what the user already knows. It should be recent. It should be authentic and accurate. It should be at the right level of abstraction and easily understandable by the user. The meaning of a text is not fixed and unchangeable. Meaning depends upon the reader's interest, background, purpose, attitudes etc. Relevance is not a simple yes-no question. We can therefore think of degree of relevance. No single document may be highly relevant but a combination of two or more may be.

Clearly, such a strong view of relevance is subjective and impracticable for automatic evaluation. Hence in practice a weaker definition involving only the topical relevance is used as an indicator of potentially useful documents. Topical relevance is necessary but not sufficient. It is easier to deal with and often a major contributor to total relevance. Topical relevance is more closely tied up with the document itself and not so much to idiosyncrasies of individual users. The relevance of documents is measured by simply counting the proportion of terms in the query which are found in the documents retrieved. The retrieved documents are ranked accordingly.

What we have seen in this section is the bare-bones description of a modern IR system. It is deficient in many ways and a large number of ideas have been proposed and used to go beyond this primitive design. Chapter Three of the book is devoted to addressing these concerns in some detail and Chapter Two provides the required background in Natural Language Processing.

1.4.6 Challenges in Information Retrieval

In his Turing Award lecture, Jim Grey defined the *Software Grand Challenge* as a *software that could answer questions as effectively as an educated person.* Answering questions, or even just retrieving relevant documents from which we can hopefully find answers to our specific questions, is not easy. There are three steps in the process and each one is a challenge - 1) understand exactly what the user wants 2) understand the contents of the documents so you know which document is relevant for what, and 3) develop automatic methods for matching the user requirements with the contents of the documents available in the collection.

A search for "veda" from Google got about 1,420,000 matches. The top ten included some relevant entries but also the following completely irrelevant entries: 1) "The Vestibular Disorders Association (VEDA)...", 2) "Veda Hille's Home Page...", 3) "Veda rent a car Sofia Bulgaria..." and 4) "Armour Home Electronics - HiFi, home cinema and whole house custom ...". A search engine has no clue as to whether I am looking for renting a car or I am a doctor looking for information about some types of diseases or I am actually interested in knowing about ancient Indian traditional knowledge sources. IR today is more like a blind man groping in darkness rather than like an intelligent being performing a systematic informed search or exploration.

We just saw that four out of ten of the top hits were irrelevant. That gives us only a 60% performance. An IR system giving sixty percent performance is useable and people do use it. The particular search example took only 0.23 seconds and the user can selectively dig deeper and get some useful information in a matter of minutes or hours. Imagine doing the same thing without such a technology. A machine translation system that gives 90% accuracy may be considered hopeless and utterly unuseable but an IR system which gives even 40% performance is still useful, although far from being completely satisfactory.

It appears, therefore, that IR requires a great deal of Natural Language Understanding. However, some researchers in the IR field have traditionally considered it neither absolutely essential nor always highly beneficial to carry out in depth linguistic analysis of documents or user queries. The challenge they have set for themselves is to achieve high levels of retrieval performance *with-*

1.5 Information Extraction

1.5.1 What is Information Extraction?

Handling large volumes of information represented as natural language texts has become essential today in various walks of life. Unlike databases which are structured into records, fields and so on, natural language texts show very little explicit structure. For a computer which really cannot read and understand the meaning of natural language sentences, texts appear to be simply sequences of words. If we could somehow make computers dig into the hidden structure of natural language texts, if not into the meaning and intentions, it would be possible to cull out useful pieces of information and present them in suitably structured ways. Let us consider newspaper articles about earthquakes. If a computer could read through such documents and tell us the place, the time, the magnitude of the quake on Richter scale, extent of damage to life and property etc. in a tabular form, it will open up a whole range of possibilitics that would otherwise require manually reading all those thousands of documents.

While Information Retrieval is concerned with location and retrieval of relevant documents, Information Extraction is all about eliciting relevant pieces of information from given documents and imposing a desired structure on them. The task is more complex since it requires, by definition, a thorough and detailed analysis of the full texts. There are many interesting and useful applications. Systems have been built to extract structured information from resume submitted by job seekers. There are systems to populate a relational databases from classified advertisements and brochures of electronic components. Here is another example:

Input to the system:

"14 April- A bomb went off near a communication tower in Delhi leaving a large part of city without energy. According to official sources, the bomb allegedly detonated by Pakistan militants, blew up a communication tower in northwestern part of Delhi at 06:50 P.M."

Output of the system:

Incident type:	Bombing
Date:	April 14
Location:	Delhi
Alleged Perpetrator:	Pakistan militants
Target:	Communication Tower

TABLE 1.2 Template Structure

Information extraction (IE) is a term which has come to be applied to the activity of automatically extracting pre-specified kinds of entities, events and relationships. The goal is identification of instances of a particular class of events or relationships in a natural language text, and extraction of the relevant arguments of those events and relationships. IE systems produce a structured representation such pieces of information extracted from the given texts. These structured databases can in turn be used for analysis using conventional database query methods and data-mining techniques, for generating natural language summaries, question-answering, intelligent information retrieval, text indexing and so on.

1.5.2 Information Extraction Tasks

In the mid 1980's a number of research sites in the United States were working on IE from naval messages, in projects sponsored by the Defense Advanced Research Projects Agency (DARPA). In order to understand and compare the behavior of such systems, a number of these message understanding (MU) projects decided to work on a set of common messages and then convene to see how their systems perform for some new, unseen messages. This gathering constituted an ongoing series of extremely productive message understanding conferences (MUCs), which have served as key events in driving the field of IE forward. Because of the complexity in information extraction task, MUCs divided IE into different tasks and then evaluated the performance of IE tasks separately. The IE tasks defined in MUC-7 are:

1. **Named Entity Task:** The "NE task" involves finding and categorizing certain classes of proper names that appear in

the text. A named entity task consists of three subtasks (entity names, temporal expressions, number expressions). Some examples are: Names of organizations, persons, locations, mentions of dates, times, currency and percentage.

2. **Coreference Task:** The "Co task" involves finding and linking together all references of the same object, set or activity. This task is important, because it helps in proper acquisition of attributes and relations between the IE task entities.

3. **Template Element Task:** The "TE task" builds on NE and Co tasks. The goal of this task is to find entities and identify certain features of entities.

4. **Template Relation Task:** The Template Relation (TR) task marks relationships between template elements.

5. **Scenario Template Task:** Scenario templates are the prototypical outputs of IE systems. They tie together TE entities into event and relation descriptions. This task requires identifying instances of a task-specific event, identifying event attributes, and construction of an object-oriented structure recording the entities and the relationships.

One of the advantages of this task orientation is that inputs and outputs of an information extraction system can be defined precisely, which facilitates the evaluation of different systems and approaches. Two important metrics for assessing the performance of an IE system are Recall and Precision. Recall measures the amount of relevant information that the NLP system correctly extracts from the test collection. Precision refers to the reliability of the information so extracted.

$$Recall = \frac{correct\ slot\ fillers\ in\ output\ templates}{slot\ fillers\ in\ answer\ keys}$$

$$Precision = \frac{correct\ slot\ fillers\ in\ output\ templates}{slot\ fillers\ in\ output\ templates}$$

A single scoring measure known as the F-measure is also used to rank IE systems. It is an approximation to the weighted geometric mean of recall and precision:

$$F = \frac{(\beta + 1)PR}{\beta P + R} \tag{1.1}$$

where P is precision, R is recall, and β is a parameter encoding the relative importance of recall and precision. When we give equal weightage to precision and recall, F-measure will be $2PR/(P+R)$.

1.5.3 Architecture of an IE System

Hobbs proposed a generic architecture for an IE system. The Hobbs system consists of the following ten modules:

- **Text Zoner** - turns a text into a set of segments.
- **Preprocessor** - turns a text or text segment into a sequence of sentences, each of which is a sequence of lexical items.
- **A Filter** - turns a sequence of sentences into a smaller set of sentences by filtering out irrelevant ones.
- **A Preparser** - takes a sequence of lexical items and tries to identify reliably determinable small-scale structures.
- **A Parser** - takes a set of lexical items (words and phrases) and outputs a set of parse-tree fragments, which may or may not be complete.
- **Fragment Combiner** - attempts to combine parse-tree or logical-form fragments into a structure of the same type for the whole sentence.
- **A Semantic Interpreter** - generates semantic structures or logical forms from parse-tree fragments.
- **A Lexical Disambiguator** - reduces the ambiguity of the predicates in the logical form fragments.
- **A Coreference Resolver** - identifies different descriptions of the same entity in different parts of a text.
- **A Template Generator** - fills the IE templates from the semantic structures.

The SIFT system developed by BBN, the LOLITA system developed by University of Durham, The SRA IE system, the Pinocchio IE Toolkit, The CICERO system, genescene and Proteus-BIO are some of the major systems developed for Information Extraction in the last few years.

The overall performance of IE systems remains very low till date. IE is an inherently complex task and more detailed and thorough analysis of the texts is essential to move further. Recent research in IE has again shown very clearly the need for deeper syntactic and semantic analysis of texts and resolution of anaphoric references.

1.6 Automatic Summarization

1.6.1 Why Summarization?

There is an ever increasing amount of electronic texts available today. Millions of pages of text are available for free reading from the World Wide Web and other on-line Resources. Developments in Information Technology have made it possible to produce such large volumes of information within a short period of time. The speed at which we can read and understand texts is, however, constant as always. How then do we make best use of all these available resources? How then do we take decisions as we are called upon to take in a reasonable amount of time based on as much of available information as we can? One solution lies in developing technologies for automatically summarizing available texts. Gists and summaries are shorter by definition and hopefully easier to get a hang of too. Tools which can quickly digest large quantities of information will enable us to consider a wider and potentially richer set of information sources to support decision making. Hence this relatively new field of Automatic Summarization.

Text summarization can be used as an application by itself or integrated in various interesting combinations with other technologies. Summaries help us to get a quick idea about the contents of a large book or report. We may use that to decide whether to read the report in more detail or not. Information Retrieval can be performed on summaries of documents rather than the original documents, hopefully giving faster and better results. Information Extraction can be performed on summaries rather than the original documents. Text categorization can be done on the summaries. Summaries can be used to filter out unwanted mails and to route the rest of the mails automatically to relevant departments. Documents retrieved from the web may be summarized and the summaries translated into other languages. Hopefully, translating the summaries would be easier and quality of translations would be better. A doctor may want to see case histories related to a particular case retrieved, summarized, the treatments compared and a report generated, all automatically. Imagine instructing your home computer to watch the TV news while you are away and give you a summary of what all is happening when you come back home. Imagine instructing your computer to search the web for relevant documents in various languages and produce a summary of what the Russians and the Japanese are saying about a particular move by the United States Government. Think of a system that can read aloud a summary of a given text for a blind person.

Summarization can improve the performance of other applications. Summarization involves size reduction and this in turn can give speed benefits to other applications. Hopefully, the data size reduction results in the essentials being retained and less important stuff eliminated. One way to view this is to say that noise is reduced. Eliminating or reducing noise can also increase the accuracy in many applications.

We are all familiar with summarization in our daily life. We often scan news headlines before or instead of reading the full news. Teachers produce outlines of notes and course materials to students. Minutes of a meeting summarize what all transpired in the meeting. Previews of movies give a quick advance view of the shape of things to come in the movie. Synopses of TV serials are telecast to let the users get a feel for the serials. Book reviews are summaries as retold by the reviewer. Newspapers and magazines publish Radio and TV guides for the coming week or month. Resumes and Obituaries are biographical summaries. Novels are often specifically abridged for, say, children to read. Weather forecasts and Market report bulletins are summaries too. Sound Bites consolidate on going debate on a particular issue. Chronologies and gists of history are a kind of summary. Summarization is itself not new. Automatic techniques for summarization are.

Alta-Vista Discovery uses Inxight's summarizer for filtering web based IR. Orcale's Context (data mining of text databases), Microsoft Word's AutoSummarize, British Telecom's ProSum are some of the commercial implementations.

1.6.2 Approaches to Automatic Summarization

Summarization can be viewed as a reductive transformation of source text to summary text through content reduction by selection and / or generalization of what is important in the source. Text Summarization has been defined as the process of distilling the most important information from a source(s) to produce an abridged version for a particular user(s) and task(s). The primary aim is to automatically produce a gist. There is no manual intervention. The appropriateness of the summary so produced is often task specific and depends on the specific needs of the users. What is appropriate in a given situation may not be the best for another situation.

Human beings have an incredible capacity to produce excellent summaries. This is possible because we are intelligent, we have common sense and world knowledge, we have superb reasoning power and we understand the meaning and intention of the document before we try to summarize. Computers are deficient in these respects and hence building automatic summarization systems is a challenge.

The input to a summarization system may be a single document or several. Texts can be in one language or several. Traditionally, summarization is performed on text documents but multi-media documents containing images, audio, video etc. may also be considered. Output produced may be a stand-alone document or it may be linked and presented in the context of the source such as by highlighting the selected parts. In some cases coherent, connected sentences may be generated as summary while in others it may be fragmentary, say just a list of phrases. Generic summaries can be produced for wide readership or a user's specific need as expressed in a query, area of interest or topic may be used to generate user-specific summaries. A summary can be *indicative* of the topic of the original document, *informative* in the sense of summarizing the essential information content of the given source document, or a *critical* evaluation of the source. The required compression ratio (ratio of the size of the summary to the size of the original text) can be specified by the user. Typical compression ratios range from 1% to 30%.

Summarization involves reduction in size. Reduction is achieved by one of three methods:

1. *Selection* of salient or non-redundant information

2. *Aggregation* of information - from different parts of the documents, from different linguistic descriptions etc.

3. *Generalization* of specific, detailed information with more abstract information

Thus we may aggregate terms - different inflected forms may be aggregated into their root forms, spelling variations can be normalized, synonyms and different representations of the same entity can be collapsed. Computing, computation, computers, computerization are all morphologically related forms of the same root. Defence and Defense are same. A pachyderm is an elephant. The morning star is the same as the evening star. First February 2005 is the same as 01/02/2005. Ministry of Communications and Information Technology is the same as MCIT. Particular regions of the text may be eliminated as redundant. A sequence of statements describing an object or event may be generalized to name the object or event. Thus a whole paragraph may be replaced with "negotiation of terms and conditions".

The process of summarization can be broadly divided into three phases for facilitating our understanding:

1. *Analysis* of given text

2. *Transformation* into a summary representation

3. *Synthesis* of appropriate natural language summary report

Summarization has been attempted by selection, aggregation and generalization at various levels of linguistic description:

1. *Surface Level:* Here shallow, superficial analysis leads to selection of terms and other surface features which are then combined to produce the summaries. There are several kinds of surface level features:

   (a) Features based on frequency of occurrence of terms

(b) Features based on location - position within the document, position within a paragraph, depth of nesting of sections, specified sections

(c) Features based on background information - terms present in the title or headings, terms present in user queries

(d) Features based on cue words and phrases - "to summarize", "in conclusion", "in particular", "more importantly"

(e) Features based on domain specific "bonus" and "stigma" terms - "bear" and "bull" are bonus terms in economy and business domain

2. *Entity Level:* Here entities and relationships are extracted and some internal representation of the source text is built in terms of these entities and relationships. The internal representation may model the essence of the text as patterns of connectivity such as by using a graph. Summaries are then produced from these internal representations. Some of the features that can be used are:

   (a) Similarity - vocabulary overlap

   (b) Proximity

   (c) Co-occurrence

   (d) Thesaural Relationships - synonyms/antonyms, hypernyms/hyponyms, part-of

   (e) Co-reference

   (f) Logical relationships - agreement, contradiction, entailment, consistency

   (g) Syntactic relationships - subject, object, object of preposition etc.

   (h) Semantic relationships - predicate-argument relations

3. *Discourse Level:* Here global and hierarchical structure of the text and its relation to communicative goals are identified. Such structures include

   (a) Format - Hypertext Markup, Document Outline

(b) Discourse Segments and Themes

(c) Rhetorical Structure - argumentation, proof, narrative, etc.

A summary may be an *extract* or an *abstract.* In the former case, parts of the original document, say important sentences, are *selected* and presented as a summary. For example, in any coherent writing, it is usually possible to identify one or two sentences in each paragraph which contain the essence of the whole paragraph. Replacing the paragraphs with these extracts will result in a condensed form of the original text that, hopefully, retains the essential information. Extraction is therefore identification and "lifting" of important parts of the source text. The output is therefore linguistically close to the original source and follows the same general order. An abstract, on the other hand, is *generated* from salient pieces of information identified from the original text. Extracts are usually easier to obtain than abstracts, as can be expected. Generation of natural language sentences is itself a very complex task.

1.6.3 Summarization in Relation to Information Extraction

Text summarization is related to Information Extraction. Text summarization is an open approach to extracting information in that there is no prior assumption or expectation of what kinds of information are important or what kinds of things to look for. What is important for a source text is marked by the text itself according to some general, linguistically-based importance criteria. In contrast, Information Extraction is a closed approach in that you already know what is important and you look for just those pieces of information in the source text. Thus the source text is viewed as a specific instantiation of some previously established generic content. Thus summarization is intended to let the important information emerge naturally, as appropriate for each case while information extraction is intended to find individual manifestations of specified important notions, regardless of source status. In information extraction one view of what is important is assumed and imposed regardless of what the original intentions of the author were or what the readers of the document would naturally find important. Summarization is "text extraction" while information extraction is "fact extraction". Summarization has the advantage of generality but delivers relatively low-quality output because the weak and indirect methods used may not be very effective in identifying important material and presenting as a coherent, well organized text. The information extraction approach can deliver better quality output in substance and presentation as far as the selected material is concerned, but with the disadvantages that the required type of information has to be explicitly and effortfully specified and may not be important for the source text itself. Thus the two approaches are complementary and both views can be applied for summarization as well.

1.6.4 Summarization in Relation to Other Technologies

Text summarization is also related to other areas of language engineering. Information retrieval, information extraction, text categorization translation etc. may be performed on summaries instead of original texts. Or summaries can be produced after retrieving relevant documents or after translation.

1.6.5 Evaluation of Summarization Systems

Automatic summarization is an inherently hard task. We have to characterize a source text as a whole, we have to capture its important content, where content is a matter of both information and its expression, and importance is a matter of what is essential as well as what is salient.

Automatically generated summaries cannot be expected to be as good as human generated summaries. However, automatic summarizers work much faster and thereby enable us to consider more documents in a given amount of time.

1.6.6 Summarization in the Context of Indian Tradition

It is interesting to relate current interest in technology for automatic summarization with the Indian scene, especially with regard to our ancient tradition. Brevity was considered an essential quality and every effort was taken to write briefly and precisely. Many of the greatest works, which are widely read, discussed and debated for thousands of years now, are very small in size. The *bhagavadgiita* has only 700 verses. baadaraayaNa's *brahmasuutras*, which purports to explain all of the upanishadic thought in a coherent way, is just 555 aphorisms. pataMjali's *yoogasuutras* consist of 195 aphorisms. *maaMDuukyoopanishat*, considered to be the essence of all upanishadic thought, is just 12 mantras. s'aMkara's *aatma SaTkam* is six verses. His *saadhana paMcakam* is just five verses. People could remember entire texts by heart. There was in fact not much need for writing. Summarization makes no sense.

In fact the need was the opposite. Some of the works were so cryptic, they had to be explained in more detail. Commentaries had to be written. Interestingly, some of the commentaries also required further elaboration and explanation and one finds several layers of commentaries. The original text itself remains small and can often be completely memorized. This book could be written in just a few pages. But that would not be very easy for most readers today to read and understand. Understanding short and cryptic statements require more effort and seriousness on the part of the readers. (In fact this book has actually been written point by point and then expanded.) It looks like we are in a situation today where we tend to write too much and then see the need for producing summaries.

We find a plethora of ideas on summarization in the mimaaMsa and other s'aastras. We can learn a lot about proper way of organizing and structuring our thoughts and hence the documents we create. One of the basic requirements for any cohesive piece of writing, however small or big it may be, is that it should be possible to express its purport in just one sentence (*eekavaakyata*). If you cannot express the gist in one sentence, either you have not understood the writing properly or the writing itself is incoherent. Ramayana, which runs into 24,000 s'lokas, has been summarized into a few pages, into one page, into one small paragraph and into a single statement.

1.7 Automatic Text Categorization

1.7.1 Why Text Categorization?

Over the past decade, there has been an explosion in the availability of electronic information. As the availability information increases, the inability of people to assimilate and profitably utilize such large amounts of information becomes more and more evident. One of the most successful paradigm for organizing this mass of information, making it comprehensible to people, is perhaps by categorizing the different documents according to their subject matter or topic.

Automatic text categorization has many applications. Information Retrieval systems and Search Engines will greatly benefit if the documents in the collection are already categorized. It would then be possible to limit the search to relevant classes of documents, thereby enhancing both the speed and the performance. Text Categorization system can be used for automatic filtering and routing of documents. For example, junk mails can be detected and removed and mails can be routed to different departments based on their topic. There are tools that collect news from various newspapers and other sources on the web, perform news aggregation and suitably re-organize the results. Automatic text categorization can be of great value to such systems. Identification of topic also helps in many other areas such as word sense disambiguation by narrowing the space of possibilities and bringing things into sharper focus.

1.7.2 Approaches to Automatic Text Categorization

Before the 1990s, the predominant approach to text classification was the knowledge based approach. Rules and heuristics based on experience were used to place documents in appropriate classes. When performed on a small scale, as in the case of individual libraries, classification experts manually read the title, front matter, cover page material, table of contents etc. and decided where exactly to place the book in a predefined classification scheme. This takes time and effort but the quality of work done would be, hopefully, very good. When one is faced with the problem of classifying a large number of documents, these same rules, guidelines and heuristics can be codified into computer programs and categorization performed automatically. Hence the name knowledge based approach.

With the increasing availability of large scale data in electronic form, advances in machine learning and statistical inference, there has been a clear shift over the last decade or so towards automatic learning from large scale data. In the Machine Learning approach, a general inductive process (also called the learner) automatically builds a classifier for a given category by observing the characteristics of a set of training documents already classified under a specified set of classes. The inductive process gleans from these labeled training data, the characteristics that a new unseen document should have in order to be classified under a given category. The classification problem is thus an activity of supervised learning.

A Machine Learning program automatically learns to distinguish between different classes or categories based on examples. Learning here is basically generalizing from examples. The machine must figure out which features are more discriminative and which ones are not. Accordingly the features are weighted. All useful features are considered but the more discriminative one will carry higher weightage. Under suitable assumptions, it is possible to prove that what the machine does is about the best possible, given the features and the training data as the basis. The performance of a machine learning system can only be improved by using better features or by increasing the quantity and quality of training data.

The aim of Automatic Text Categorization is to classify documents, typically based on the subject matter or topic, without any manual effort. A text categorization program can automatically categorize thousands of documents in a few minutes. There is no way manual classification can match that speed. In terms of accuracy of classification, automatic systems can achieve accuracies of 95% or even higher, depending upon the specificities of the task. Manual classification can in principle be fully correct but in practice one must make allowance for some errors.

Automated text categorization can be defined as assigning pre-defined category labels to new documents based on the likelihood suggested by a training set of labeled documents. Given a set of documents with the associated category labels, the system looks for discriminating features that help to set the various categories apart. This process is called training. The system *learns*, so to say, how exactly documents within a class are similar and documents in different classes are different from each another. Once the system has been trained, it can look at new documents unseen before and classify them into one of the set categories.

The similarities and differences between documents of various classes are expressed in terms of *features*. In the simplest case, features are the words in these documents. The assumption is that there are words that occur frequently in certain classes but not in the others. Words like *election, mandate, constituency, party, legislature, parliament* are more likely to occur in the political arena than in sports. Of course there can be politics in sports, there can be elections and parties in sports domain too. That is why is not a good idea to try and fix such terms manually. Given a set of representative training documents, the system automatically learns those features that have sufficient discriminative power and other features that occur more or less equally in all categories are ignored.

The big advantage is that the machine learning system can easily adapt to any new kind of classification problem whereas manual methods will require starting all over again if the nature of the classification task changes. For example, if the set of categories is re-defined or changed significantly, all it takes for an automated system is a few minutes of re-training. In fact, once such a learning system has been developed, it can easily be adapted and customized for a wide range of tasks. It would be possible, for example, to take a system trained for classifying news articles in Telugu language and apply it to classify computer programs based on the programming language used. Almost all the human effort that would have gone into creating a completely manual classification system for Telugu news articles would become practically useless if asked to classify computer programs.

We have given a broad definition of Text Categorization above. There are several variations to the basic theme:

- In *Document Pivoted Categorization* a given document is to be assigned category label(s) whereas in a *Category Pivoted Categorization*, all documents that belong to a given category must be identified. This distinction is more pragmatic than conceptual. Thus if all the documents are not available to start with, document pivoted categorization may be more appropriate while category pivoted categorization may be the preferred choice if new categories get added and already classified documents need to be re-classified.

- In *Hard categorization*, the classifier is required to firmly assign categories to documents (or the other way around) whereas in *Ranking Categorization*, the system ranks the various possible assignments and the final decision about class assignments is left to the user. This leads us to the possibility of semi-automatic or interactive classifiers where human users take the final decisions to ensure highest levels of accuracy.

- Constraints may be imposed on the number of categories that may be assigned to each document - exactly k, at least k, at most k, and so on. In the *single label* case, k = 1 and a single category is to be assigned to each document. If k is more than 1, we have the *multi-label* categorization.

- The text categorization problem can be reduced to a set of *binary classification* problems one for each category - where each document is categorized as either belonging to a given category or not.

- If only unlabeled training data is available we may have to use unsupervised learning techniques to perform *Text Clustering* instead of classification into known classes. Here the aim is to determine the similarities and differences among the various documents and find out a natural way of grouping them so that similar documents are grouped together.

1.7.3 Text Representation

Classification systems represent documents in terms of sets of features. Feature sets form a compact and effective representation of the whole data. Typically a vector space model is used - each data item can them be visualized as a point in the D-Dimensional feature space where D is the number of features.

Each word in a text is a potential feature. In the domain of text categorization, words and word-like features (such as phrases) are called *terms*. Documents are treated as bags of terms. Feature dimensions are thus often very large, running into tens of thousands. *The curse of dimensionality* is that the number of training data samples required grows exponentially with the number of features. Choice of the right subset of potential features is a major concern. A variety of dimensionality reduction techniques are used in pattern recognition. The discriminating power of features is evaluated and the least discriminating features can be discarded without much loss. Concepts such as *Mutual Information* and *Information Gain* have been applied to evaluate the discriminating power of features. *Principal Component Analysis* is a standard technique for identifying the feature dimensions with maximal variance. Similarly, *Singular Value Decomposition* is a technique that rotates the feature space so as to align the most discriminating features along the axes of the rotated feature space. Interested readers are directed to books on Pattern Classification or Machine Learning for more details.

Commonly used pre-processing steps include

- *Stop word removal* - eliminating function words and other very frequently occurring, less discriminative terms
- *Morphology or Stemming* - replacing fully inflected words with their root/stem forms
- *Chunking* - grouping together words into phrases

These pre-processing steps help to obtain more discriminative features and/or to reduce the number of features. It may be noted that these methods are to a large extent language specific.

1.7.4 Feature Weighting

Numerical weights need to be computed for the index terms before machine learning techniques can be applied. Here are some of the basic ideas for term weighting:

- *Term Attributes:* Attributes of the terms such as their syntactic categories can be used to weight the terms.
- *Text attributes:* The number of terms in a text, the length of the text etc. can be used.

- *Relation between the term and the text:* Relative frequency of the term in the text, location of the term in the text, relationship with other terms in the text etc.
- *Relation to corpus:* Relation between the term and the document corpus or some other reference corpus can also be used.
- *Expert Knowledge:* Expert knowledge is a potential source but is rarely used.

The most common approach is to consider the frequency of occurrence of terms in a given document in relation to their frequencies of occurrence in other documents in the collection. This scheme is known as the *tf-idf* scheme. Here is how tf-idf weights can be computed for given terms:

- *Term Frequency:* Words that occur more frequently in a given category are likely to be more significant to the specified category and are thus given higher weightage. Since the occurrence of a rare term in a short text is more significant than its occurrence in a long text, log of the term frequency is used to reduce the importance of raw term frequencies in those collections that have a wide range of text lengths. Anaphoric references and synonyms reduce the true term frequency. In morphologically rich languages, poor morphological analysis or stemming also adds to this effect.
- *Inverse Document Frequency:* Terms that occur in almost all documents are useless for classification. Therefore, terms that occur in smaller number of documents are given higher weightage.
- *Inverse Category Frequency:* Inverse Category Frequency could be more appropriate than inverse document frequency since the distribution of documents into categories may be skewed. A log can again be taken to weigh this factor down so that it does not become over-dominating.
- *Product of tf and idf:* Term frequency and Inverse Document Frequency are inter-related. Terms that occur frequently in a particular class but not very frequently in other

classes are the most significant. Hence a product of tf and idf is often used.

- *Length Normalization:* Long and verbose texts usually use the same terms repeatedly. As a result, the term frequency factors are large for long texts and small for short ones, obscuring the real term importance. Term frequencies can be normalized for length of texts by dividing them by the total word count in the document, or better still, by the frequency of the most frequently occurring term in the document.

- *Cosine Normalization* The directions of the feature vectors rather than their lengths are considered to be better indicators of the various classes. In cosine normalization, each term weight is divided by a factor representing the Euclidean vector length. Thus all vectors become unity length vectors.

1.7.5 Text Classification and Clustering

Once texts are represented in terms of features and the weights of the features are computed, any of the standard classification and clustering techniques can be applied. The section 2.3.3 gives a brief description of some of these techniques. In particular, there we will show how the Bayesian Learning approach can be applied to the task of automatic text categorization. Models are built from labelled training data and then applied to classify new unseen documents. When there is no labeled training data set available, it is also possible to automatically cluster or group together similar documents. A suitable measure of similarity must be defined. Often the term *distance* is used as a measure of dissimilarity. Clustering techniques work by attempting to reduce the intra-cluster distances while maximizing the inter-cluster distances. See section 2.3.3 for more on this.

A number of automatic text categorization systems have been developed and put to use for English and other major languages of the world. Work on Indian languages has started only recently. A categorization system developed recently by the author could classify News Articles in Telugu into broad categories such as Sports, Politics, Economics and Business and Cinema with nearly 95% accuracy. The system was trained on a preclassified set of about 600 documents and tested on about 200 previously unseen documents.

Developing automatic text categorization systems requires a large amounts of pre-classified training data. Also, the performance of the system may deteriorate if the classes considered are fine grained or there is a lot of overlap. Performance also drops down when the distribution of training documents in various categories is non-uniform and highly skewed. To classify library books into the standard categories, for example, would require a much larger collection of training documents. One may have to resort to multi-level or hierarchical classification.

We have seen that practical text categorization systems treat documents as unordered collection of words, use these words as features and count frequency of occurrence to weigh these features. Linguists will be shocked to know that today's text categorization systems treat "India beat Australia" and "Australia beat India" as identical - both have the same three words. There is hardly any linguistic analysis of the texts concerned. Speed is not the only criteria in all situations. More intelligent text classification systems will surely require a deeper linguistic analysis of the document texts. Also, the feature dimensions are extremely large and dimensionality reduction is an important issue.

It is interesting to note that NLP started with big goals like natural language understanding and generation but only toy systems could be built then. Nowadays much larger applications that give reasonably good performance in real life situations are being built but with only the most superficial and rudimentary linguistic analysis of the language. Future may perhaps lie in an intelligent combination of deep linguistic analysis and statistical methods based on large scale training data.

1.8 Machine Translation

Machine Translation (MT), also known as automatic translation throws open great opportunities. While human costs are going up, machine costs are coming down. Human translators are not always available where and when needed. You can make multiple copies of an MT system and use it simultaneously at many places whereas one human expert can only be at one place and can only do one thing at a time. The machine does not get bored or tired, and it does not complain if asked to work 24 hours a day. With increasing globalization and need to communicate with people in different languages, translation loads are increasing every day and we will never be able to meet the demands only through human translators. MT can, in principle, save a lot of time, effort and money. The crucial question is can we build MT systems with adequate performance to meet these demands.

Automatic Translation was perhaps the first and the most prominent application of NLP. Interest in Machine Translation is almost as old as modern digital computers. Computers can store and process large collections of textual data efficiently and so they should be able to translate texts from one language to another without much difficulty. After all, a text is simply a sequence of words and if we are able to choose the right words and place them in the right order, we should be able to perform translation automatically. That would save a great deal of time, effort and money. Such was the optimism with which work on Machine Translation started right in the nineteen fifties and sixties.

1.8.1 Machine Translation is Hard

It was soon discovered that translation is an inherently complex task and a great deal of fundamental research and development work was essential before we can start building useable systems. Let us see why machine translation is a hard problem:

- *Lexical Ambiguities*: Every language has many words that can mean more than one thing. Words may also belong to more than one grammatical category. The English word "like" can be a verb, an adjective and a preposition. We use our common sense, world knowledge and context to disambiguate between different usages as in *'I like mangoes'*, *'I like citrus fruits like oranges and sweet lemons'* and *'unlike poles attract each other and like poles repel one another'*. Note that *a dictionary simply lists all possible grammatical categories* - it does not tell us in any great detail, how to figure out the actual grammatical category when the word is used in a particular context. A large number of words in English are both nouns and verbs. Identification of the correct grammatical category is essential to figure out the correct meaning. POS tagging systems are far from perfect.

- *Word Sense Disambiguation*: Knowing the correct grammatical category or part-of-speech is not sufficient. Words can have several meanings or senses even within given grammatical categories. Human languages strike a balance between having too many words so that each idea can be expressed precisely using a specific word made just for that purpose but difficult to remember so many words, and, overloading words with too many different senses, thereby making it easy to remember and use the words but so much more difficult to resolve the ambiguities and understand them correctly. A large number of words in any language tend to have several senses. *Following* Swamy Vivekananda's ideals in your life, *following* a thief who is just running away with your purse and *following* a lecture in a classroom are all very different kinds of *following*. Is *capital* a capital city, the financial capital or an upper case letter of the alphabet? Simple words like *have, give* and *go* have dozens of meanings. When we hear *'Mary had a little lamb'* somehow our mind does not even seem to get many of the *possible* meanings. Contrast with the meanings we get if we place the same sentence in different contexts: *'I had dosa for breakfast. Mary had a little lamb!'* or *'Mary was expecting. Mary had a little lamb!'* Machines tend to get a large number of *possible* solutions and are left clueless as to which one is the right one. We may say context helps but characterizing this notion of context in a precise way is a challenge in itself. *Word Sense Disambiguation* has remained a hard nut to crack. People use world knowledge and commonsense. Machines have serious difficulties with things that are so simple and commonplace for us. They have neither commonsense nor human like abilities to reason out things.

- *Idioms and Phrases*: Idioms and phrases are sources of difficulty for machines. Machines have no clue unless these are listed in a dictionary. Dictionaries of idioms and phrases meant for human users tend to list only those items that are potentially confusing to human beings, obvious ones may be left out. Nothing is obvious for machines. How does the machine know that *tooth powder* is not powder of the tooth unless it is told in so many words? How does the machine understand that *heavy water* is not just water that is heavy? How does the machine understand that a *water meter cover adjustment screw* is a screw meant for adjusting the cover of a meter meant for measuring the flow of water? In what way is *water pump* different from *cast iron pump*? Some soaps say *for dry skin* and others say *for healthy and beautiful skin.* A vast majority of all that we say requires non-literal interpretation.

- *Expressions*: Non-literal usages and figures of speech can add to the confusion especially because they vary widely across languages. In Kannada you say something like *'a dream fell to me'* to mean I dreamt a dream. You say something like *'He told words of advise to his legs'* to mean he fled. You say something like *'not possible in my hand'* to mean I cannot. In English night falls but day breaks. Each language has its own set of idiosyncratic usages. Studies have shown that a large percentage of all texts need non-literal interpretation. Traditional dictionaries rarely list all such usages.

- *Lexical Substitution*: Even if the machine is able to get the correct sense of words in the source language text, selecting appropriate target language words is not an easy job. There may be several nearly synonymous words and choice of the most appropriate word requires thought and care. One famous example is the English sentence *'The spirit is willing but the flesh is weak'* which when translated into Russian and back to English by a machine came back as *'The vodka is fine but the meat is rotten!'*. The spread of senses of words in the source and target languages may show subtle variations and a wrong choice may introduce unintended twists and misinterpretations. We see this in translated advertisements and commercials everyday. A well meaning Indian Language guideline has been translated into English as *'Give way to traffic on the right!'* (instead of *make way*).

  It is also possible that there is no direct equivalent at all in the target language. This happens especially with scientific and technical terminology and domain specific terms. Many strategies can be adapted. We may retain the source language word as it is (example: *phone, car, bus, radio* in Indian languages). We may borrow and/or extend a word from another language such as Sanskrit (example: *vidyut* meaning lightening in Sanskrit for electricity). We may coin new words using words of another language(example: *aakaas'avaaNi* literally meaning sky-speech for broadcasting radio). We may extend or stretch the meaning of available words (example: *fan* is used for electric fans as also for the age-old hand-held fan, *motor car*, nowadays only *car* as an extension of the horse-carriage, *mouse* for the pointing and selecting device on the computer because it looks like a mouse and is connected by a long wire like the tail of a mouse, *notebook* to mean a compact note-book sized computer). We may use acronyms as words (example: *LED, CD, LASER, RADAR*. We may use part of an expression to mean the whole (example: *radio* to mean radio receiver, *transistor* to mean transistorized radio receiver). We may coin new words by compounding etc. (example: *plywood, new-wood, go-cart, laptop*). But we must remember that a coined word is like a counterfeit note - it has no currency. Until and unless the word comes into regular usage, it will continue to affect communication.

We may also use various interesting combinations of these techniques(example: The word *xray* was coined in English after the discovery of this new kind of ray and this word is often translated in Indian languages as *ksha-kiraNa* where the part *ray* has been translated into its equivalent word *kiraNa* in the usual way but the prefix *ksha* is not usually used to represent an unknown quantity but the English *'x'* often is.). The ordinary word *window* has been borrowed into the realm of graphical user interfaces on computer screens with the idea that each window opens a window to a new world. But notice that opening one window in front of another existing window still shows you the same world through both of these windows, not a new world. Perhaps *curtain* could have been a much better term to use. Thus while many strategies can be used for any situation demanding a word in general and translation in particular, each of these strategies has its own drawbacks. A wrong choice will only add to the confusion. The ultimate question is whether the translated material is well received and easily understood by the readers. Human translators face serious difficulties.

Machines cannot do better.

- *Structural Ambiguities*: There are also structural ambiguities in language which are difficult for machines to disambiguate. Attachment of prepositional phrases and subordinate clauses is particularly hard without commonsense understanding. *'I saw a man on the hill with a telescope'* could mean several things. Perhaps there was a telescope erected on top of the hill we are talking about. The man on the hill was possibly carrying a portable telescope in his hand. Or the man on the hill was sighted by me using a telescope. Similarly, in *'I gave the book to the boy who had come home after taking bath'*, there are two possible interpretations depending upon whose taking bath we are talking about. *'mothers with babies 6 months old'* and *'mothers with babies more than 40 years old'* are both correctly understood by humans because we *know* babies cannot be 40 years old and mothers cannot be 6 months old. Machines have serious difficulties.

- *Syntactic Parsing*: There may be substantial differences between the structures of source and target language sentences. Complete syntactic parsing of source language sentences and appropriate mappings to target language structures may be necessary. Suitable mappings are difficult to find at times. Further, source language may encode less information than what is required in the target language. Similarly the source language may have more explicit information than required for translating into target language. Should this extra information be simply thrown out? For example, Hindi requires grammatical gender information even for the words that are neuter gender in English.

  The performance of parser-based translation systems is limited by the performance of the syntactic parsing systems. Today even the best available parsers are not good enough.

  The situation is much worse in the case of Indian languages. There are no wide coverage computational grammars for any Indian language yet. There are no syntactic parsers.

- *Anaphoric References* Pronouns such as *it, he, her, they, them* as also definite noun phrases such as *the second one, the cover* may refer to items already mentioned somewhere in the discourse. Referents may be in the same sentence, in the previous sentence, or several sentences before. Resolving such anaphoric references is essential for understanding the texts but may or may not be essential for translation. In some cases substitution of appropriate pronouns and definite noun phrases in the target language may carry forward identical interpretations from source language to target language.

Discourse Structure It is not sufficient to work with one sentence at a time. Sentence by sentence translation does not always work. Discourse level analysis is essential to ensure good translation.

Thus machine translation requires many steps and the errors accumulate and compound. The performance demands on the individual modules will be very high in order to obtain reasonable performance for MT as a whole. MT remains a tough problem.

The best known event in the history of machine translation is without doubt the publication in November 1966 of the report by the Automatic Language Processing Advisory Committee (ALPAC 1966). Its effect was to bring to an end the substantial funding for MT research in the United States for some twenty years. More significantly, perhaps, was the clear message to the general public and the rest of the scientific community that MT was hopeless. For years afterwards, an interest in MT was something to keep quiet about; it was almost shameful. To this day, the "failure" of MT is still repeated by many as an indisputable fact.

The report said (page 16): "There is no emergency in the field of translation. The problem is not to meet some nonexistent need through nonexistent machine translation. There are, however, several crucial problems of translation. These are quality, speed, and cost." Quality, speed and cost remain the most important yardsticks even today.

1.8.2 Deploying Machine Translation

Whenever we talk of machine translation, the first thing that comes to the mind is translation of literary works. However, literary works exploit higher levels of human cognition to bring out the effect and subtle emotions and superficial analysis of sentences will not be sufficient to produce good translations. MT was never intended for literary translations. Translation of literary works is best performed by human experts. They can do it, they enjoy doing it and there is no need to replace that with any kind of automatic device. Contrast this situation with, say, Information Retrieval from a large collection of documents, a task that human beings just cannot do, nor will they enjoy doing. Machine translation is a very different kind of an application compared to many other areas of language engineering.

A layman can get direct benefit from an IR system or a summarization system. All of us can use these applications in our daily life. But who wants machine translation? Common people have no daily requirement for translation at all. If you are thinking in terms of an application meant for direct use by ordinary people, machine translation is a non-existent, imaginary task.

Automatic translation makes more sense in those areas where it is routine, tedious and boring for people and people really wish to avoid doing it manually. Such situations include translation of manuals for scientific instruments, machinery and consumer products, routine paper work in government offices etc. However, in situations such as these, the people who need translations are not expert translators themselves. Their proficiency in language may not be very high. They would therefore be expecting a fully automatic, high quality translation which is very difficult to achieve even under restricted conditions.

With today's technology MT makes sense only when viewed as a combined man-machine effort. Human translators who need to routinely translate large volumes of textual material may find some of the MT tools useful and time saving. The final responsibility for quality of translation must lie with the human expert, not with the machine. The time has not yet come for stand-alone MT.

One way MT systems can find real uses today is in applications in which MT becomes an embedded component. Users do not get to see the quality of translation directly. Only the overall performance of the integrated system is perceived by the user. MT is thus getting embedded into Information Retrieval systems, leading to cross-lingual IR. Performance of such systems is currently still very low.

1.8.3 Approaches to Machine Translation

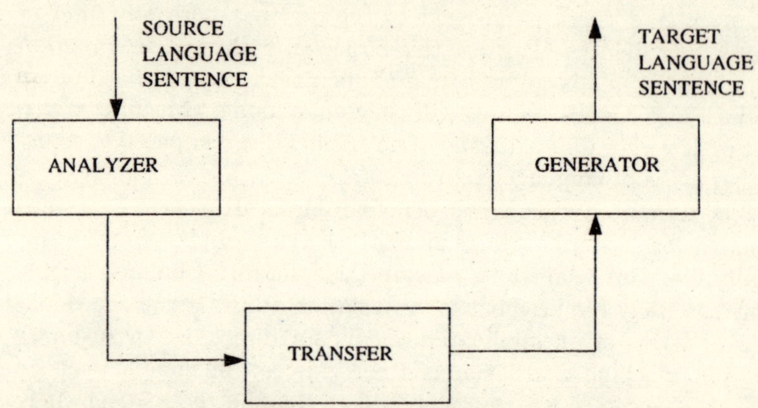

FIG 1.10 Machine Translation

Fully automatic high quality translation has not been possible so far between any pair of languages of the world in general. Languages are rich and varied - there are a large number of words, words take on various morphological forms, there is a lot more to sentence structure than merely a sequence of words, words have many meanings and meanings of sentences are not always simple combinations of meanings of words. It is not possible to obtain good translations without sufficiently detailed and thorough analysis of the given texts. Superficial analysis may be sufficient to give good enough performance in other areas but translation is a different story.

Some researchers are concentrating on developing larger and better dictionaries, better grammars and analyzers, better rules for translation, and so on. Others are trying to build large scale parallel corpora so that statistical machine learning techniques can be employed to automatically *learn* such rules. Still others are working on developing a database of examples of translated pieces so that new texts can be translated by analogy with already translated examples. Many others are focusing on human aided translation and translation support systems. Thus we can talk of

Rule Based Translation, Example Based Translation, Statistical Machine Translation, Human Aided Machine Translation and so on.

- Translation is ideally a meaning preserving transformation from one language to another. This requires analysis of the source language text to determine the meaning and generating appropriate natural language sentences in the target language. Semantics is largely language independent and it should be possible to represent the meaning of the source language texts in a truely language independent meaning representation. This approach is termed the *inter-lingua approach.* The UNL project is a recent attempt in this approach. The inter-lingua approach is theoretically neat and it has the practical advantage that only n analyzers and n generators would be required to build translation systems between all pairs of n languages. However, finding such an ideal inter-lingua representation itself has turned out to be very hard. Also building analyzers and generators that work with truely language independent representations is not easy. In fact one may argue that the inter-lingua translation is actually two translations, one from source language into the inter-lingua and the other from the inter-lingua to the target language.

- Many systems therefore do not go for a true inter-lingua but posit a level of analysis and representation that to a large extent captures the semantics. The representations will still be instantiations in a given language. Thus translation involves analyzing the source text to produce an internal representation of the meaning instantiated with the source language terms, a transfer from this source language instantiation to the corresponding target language instantiation, and finally generating target language text from those representations. This approach is called the *transfer approach* is more practical.

- In principle, deeper the analysis, better the understanding and hence better the translation. However, in practice, analyzing the semantics of the source language is extremely hard. It will also be very difficult to generate natural language sentences from a deep semantic representation.

> Structure is a function of meaning and in many systems only structural analysis and generation is performed, presuming that the structural analysis (that is, parsing) and generation are good enough to capture and preserve meanings. Some systems do not even do syntactic parsing, only superficial analysis in terms of morphology and local word grouping is performed. These systems are said to follow a *direct approach.*

One can argue that translation is merely a set of formal operations to transform from one code system to another and so there is no need to understand the meanings at all. Given two sets of symbols and a set of rules to operate upon strings of symbols from the two sets, anybody should be able to do translation from one language to another. This may sound like a good philosophical argument but in practice it does not take us anywhere. The only known examples of good translators are the human beings and we human beings read, understand and only then translate. There are no working systems to prove mechanical transformation ideas and no one has any clue how to go about building such a system.

1.8.4 Challenges in Machine Translation

Great progress has been made in the area of machine translation and some systems have even be deployed for regular use in limited domains. Also, crude, first-cut translations are available and are being used by Search Engines. Nonetheless, do not expect high quality automatic translations to become available in the near future. Wherever quality is important (and quality is almost always important) you can only expect semi-automatic, human aided translation systems.

Some of the major areas of focus in automatic translation today are 1) detailed analysis of sentence structure 2) identifying the correct sense of words in context, 3) combining human judgement and commonsense with statistical learning techniques and 4) building high quality lexical resources in large scale.

1.8.5 Machine Translation in India

There has been a great interest in India in Machine Translation and a lot of work has been done over the last 15 years. In fact

MT has been given so much of attention that many equate NLP to MT. Some groups have concentrated on translating from one Indian language to another, exploiting as they do the commonalities in linguistic structure and interpretation based on common social context. Others have started working on translation between English and Indian languages. Demonstration level systems are now becoming available but there are still no real life applications.

The MAT System

Here we briefly describe MAT - a small machine assisted translation system that was developed by the author for the Government of Karnataka, a southern state in India. MAT is used for translating English texts into Kannada, the official language of Karnataka. MAT is a parser based translation aid, suitable for translating between positional languages like English and Indian languages, which are characterized by a relatively free word order and a very rich system of morphology. MAT is based on the UCSG (Universal Clause Structure Grammar) theory of syntactic analysis developed by the author. The primary goals of the MAT project were to explore the feasibility of parser based translation between English and Indian languages and to develop a prototype machine aided translation system for translating the budget speech texts of the Government of Karnataka with the primary goal of saving time and effort. Quality of translation was ultimately the responsibility of the human translator.

It is now fairly clear that fully automatic high quality translation is difficult to realize in practice. Either we lose out on quality or we will have to involve the human translator in the process somewhere. MAT is a machine assisted translation system that provides for a full spectrum of possibilities - from fully automatic generation of raw translations suitable for manual post editing, through semi-automatic translation to almost fully manual translation using the facilities provided by the system. The basic idea is to make the best of both the human and machine capabilities to achieve good translations with minimum time and effort. Apart from a very powerful post editing tool, MAT also comes with dictionaries, a thesaurus, morphological analyzer/generator and several other useful tools.

MAT is a parser based translation system. Each sentence in

the source text is parsed syntactically using the UCSG framework before translating. This makes MAT suitable for translating between languages that show a significant variation in sentence structures. MAT was developed especially for translating between English and Indian languages but it can be applied to other languages too.

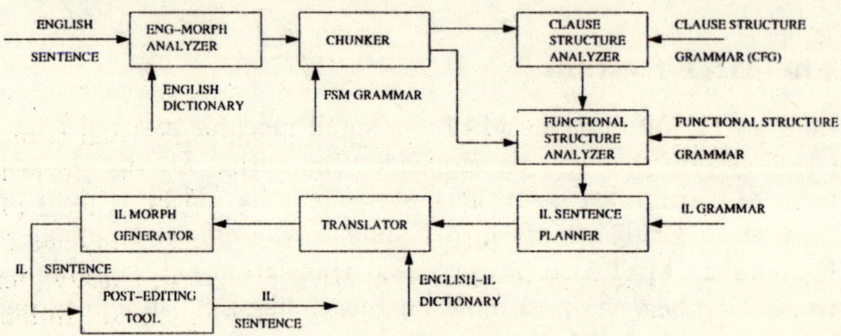

FIG 1.11 Architecture of the MAT System

In MAT, the parser and translator can be run in one of the three modes called *non-interactive*, *interactive* and *custom* modes. In the non- interactive mode, the system neither asks the user for any help nor does it pause to display intermediate results. This is the simplest and the fastest mode - a full 100 page text can be processed in less than a couple of minutes on a personal computer. In the interactive mode, the system stops to ask the user for help in dealing with unknown words, unresolved ambiguities, etc. It also stops to show the parse structure of each sentence. The user can select the correct parse if there are several of them, and translation proceeds after getting confirmation from the user. This mode is very useful for researchers and system developers. We can also expect better quality of translation. In the custom mode, the user can customize the system interface by specifying the kinds the questions the system may ask the user, the intermediate results that should be displayed and/or sent to log file etc. This mode is ideal for testing and development as also for getting a feel for how exactly the system works. A time limit can be specified to instruct the system to skip a sentence if it is taking too much time. Performance of the system is displayed continuously and a summary and a histogram are displayed at the end.

In MAT, like the parser, the translator also works from whole to part, rather than from left to right. After a sentence has been parsed by the UCSG parser, we would know the number, type and inter-relationships amongst the various clauses in the sentence and the word groups that take on various functional roles in each of these clauses. Keeping this structure of the sentence in mind, a suitable structure for the equivalent sentence in the target language is first developed. Where it is not feasible to make more or less direct transfer of structure, sentence transformation rules can be called to restructure the source sentence so that it becomes amenable for translation. This makes it possible to deal with languages with vastly different sentence structures.

After having fixed the overall structure of the target language sentence, the individual clauses are mapped. Finally, the various word groups are mapped. In each word group, the head and the modifiers are identified and transfered, keeping in mind the L-grammar of the target language.

For each word, a suitable target language equivalent is obtained from the bilingual dictionary. The MAT system provides for incorporating syntactic and some simple kinds of semantic constraints in the bilingual lexicon for word sense disambiguation. For example, the word 'rise' is mapped differently into Kannada in the following three sentences:

I *rose*	naanu *eddenu*
The moon *rose*	caMdra *huTTitu*
The prices are *rising*	belegaLu *heccuttive*

Kannada, the target language in the current experiments, is morphologically very rich. Words in Kannada often take as many as 6 suffixes. In many cases, a whole word group in English translates into a single highly inflected word in Kannada. The MAT system includes a morphological analyzer/generator for Kannada. Using the Kannada morphological generator, appropriate word forms are generated in each case.

Finally, the target language sentence is generated by placing the clauses and the word groups in appropriate linear order, according to the constraints of the target language grammar. For example, in Kannada the subject has to agree with the verb not only in number but also in gender. So gender feature is extracted from the subject of the English source sentence and used in the morphological generation of the Kannada verb so that, for example, 'she came' becomes 'avaLu baMdaLu' and 'he came' becomes 'avanu baMdanu' in Kannada. See transcripts given at the end for more examples.

In case a complete parse with satisfactory rating was not obtained for whatever reason, the word groups with or without the functional roles assigned to them are available for semi-automatic translation. The user picks up parts of the sentence, interactively calls the translator module to translate the part and finally assists the machine in assembling the target language sentence.

The post-editing tool displays the source text and the corresponding translated target language text one sentence at a time. Using the tool, the translator can move around pieces of text easily. He can also delete, insert and edit words at will. More significantly, he can call the thesaurus on line and substitute selected words by their equivalents. *Morphological analysis and generation are done on the fly* so that the correct word forms are substituted automatically. Thus *toMdarege* can be substituted with *kaSTakke* by mapping the root *toMdare* to *kaSTa*, with appropriate morphology at both ends. Substitution can be called on both the target and source language words. One can also specifically call the morphological analyzer, look at and modify the feature list and then re-generate a new word form. Further, it is also possible to call the translator to translate selected parts of a text. These unique advanced features make it possible to translate full sized English texts with a minimum of effort. As a last resort the user can manually retype the correct translation. High quality translations can be obtained irrespective of the complexity of sentence structures employed and the inherent limitations of the parsing technology. Overall, the post editing tool makes the life of the translator so much easier and gives significant time savings too.

There are separate monolingual dictionaries for English and Kannada as also a bilingual English-Kannada dictionary. A unique feature of this system is that the bilingual dictionary can be used as a kind of thesaurus too. You can get all *related words* for a given word.

There is also a morphological analyzer cum generator for Kannada. Kannada words can be analyzed for their internal structure. Specific word forms can also be generated from a given root word. Further, it is possible to get a full paradigm, that is, a systematic listing of all the forms of a given word. Both noun and verb morphology are included.

When tested on Budget Speech texts, MAT system 1.0 could parse and translate only about 40 percent of the sentences fully automatically. The translations so produced by the machine are usually in more or less acceptable form. However, Some sentences may need substantial editing and in a few cases, the outputs may have to be rewritten completely. Where automatic translation fails, semi-automatic translation is possible - user selects parts of the sentence, calls the translator to produce translations for the parts, and finally assembles the parts into the complete target language sentence. Thus MAT is far from a large scale, robust, highly automatic machine translation system.

Here are some transcripts from the MAT system 1.0. Clause structure in parse output is indicated through indentation. The first parse produced by the parser has been shown here. Translations shown here are raw translations - no post editing has been done. Note how the order of clauses have been changed during translation as required by the target language grammar. Gloss in English has been added manually.

```
1 :  Efforts are being continued to obtain more funds for providing
 relief to the victims. : 14

F_Structure 1 :

Sent 1 : Parse No. 1 : Clause 1 : Rating 0 : Passive : efforts are
being  continued  to obtain more funds for providing relief to the
victims

   2 : subj : empty :: EMPTY :: [] :: []
      3 : subj : empty :: EMPTY :: [] :: []
1 : obj : 2 :: 2 :: [] :: []
   2 : cause :  3 :: 3 :: [] :: []
1 : subj : np :: efforts :: [ng,[n,pl,(rt,effort)]] :: []
1 : vg : vg :: are being continued :: [vgf,[v,aux,be,(rt,be)],
                                       [v,aux],[v|_]] :: []
   2 : vg : vg :: to obtain :: [vgf,[v]] :: [[(nf2,infinitive)]]
   2 : obj : np :: more funds :: [ng,[a,cmp,(rt,much)],
                                  [n,pl,(rt,fund)]] :: []
      3 : vg : vg :: for providing :: [vgf,[v]]
                                      :: [[(nf2,infinitive)]]
      3 : obj : np :: relief to the victims :: [ng,[n],
                             [prep,(semf,[space,time])],
```

```
        [det],[n,pl,(rt,victim)]] :: []

KANNADA:
toMdarege       oLagaadavarige                parihaaravannu
difficulty-dat be-subjected-to-people-dat relief-acc

odagisalu    heccina nidhigaLannu paDeyalu    prayatnagaLu
provide-inf more     fund-pl-acc  obtain-inf effort-pl

muMduvarisalaaguttive.
continue-passive2-pres-p3-pl

2 : The Government knows that the people of Karnataka will welcome
 this. : 11

F_Structure 1 :

Sent 2 : Parse No. 1 : Clause 1 : Rating 0 : the government knows
that the people of karnataka will welcome this

1 : obj : 2 :: 2 :: [] :: []
1 : subj : np :: the government :: [ng,[det],[n]] :: []
1 : vg : vg :: knows :: [vgf,[v,p3,sl,(rt,know)]] :: []
   2 : cls_link : sentinel :: that :: [] :: []
   2 : subj : np :: the people of karnataka :: [ng,[det],[n,pl],
                                                [prep],[n,prp]] :: []
   2 : vg : vg :: will welcome :: [vgf,[v,aux,modal],[v]] :: []
   2 : obj : np :: this :: [ng,[pr,sl,nom,acc,dem]] :: []

KANNADA:
karnaaTakada janaru idannu svaagatisuttaare
Karnataka-of people it-acc welcome-non-past-p3-pl

eMdu  sarkaara tiLiyuttade.
that  govt.    know-pres-p3-sl
```

The Status of MT in India

Now we make some general remarks on the status of MT in India. Small successes here and there notwithstanding, the general picture is bleak. No systematic survey of the MT needs in our country has been made. Who are the potential users of MT, what kinds of translation tasks do they have, what kinds of challenges are involved in those tasks, what kinds of languages and domains of specialization are involved, what are the user expectations, how well does the current state of MT technology match the user needs - these are all largely unexplored questions. No feasibility studies have been made. Users are not involved. Formal specifications are not written. No formal designs are worked out. There are no benchmark standards for testing and evaluation. There are no ground truth data for performing a systematic evaluation. In most cases developers themselves do the testing. Testing is done on training data and training on test data. Experts working on machine translation have no experience in translating. Nor are expert translators interested in machine translation research. No wonder we are so weak in both research and product development.

1.9 Speech Technologies

Speech is one of the most natural and efficient means of communication. Working with texts and graphical user interfaces requires typing skills and hand-eye coordination, whereas speech is a hands-free mode of communication. Even illiterates would be able to communicate with computers and reap the benefits of modern science and technology. Future surely lies in speech technologies.

Speech technologies are especially relevant for a country like India which has an oral tradition that goes back to thousands of years. Entire libraries have been learnt by heart and preserved accurately all these years without ever writing them down. In contrast we find that even recent writings such as those of Shakespeare are already into several versions. Even after writing was invented, it was considered the sign of a weak mind to write things down in India - only accountants were using writing. The oral tradition continues even today. If all available copies of the works of Shakespeare are destroyed today, his works will be lost for ever. On the other hand if all available copies of the vedas are destroyed beyond recovery, nothing will be lost - there are people who know the whole thing by heart. We can simply sit and write them down again.

The western notion of illiteracy is questionable. Illiterates are not necessarily uneducated. The greatest scholars in India were illiterate and they preferred to be illiterate. It is not really true that speech is transient and ephemeral and writing is permanent and safe. What we have in our minds and finger tips is what actually matters in life. What is the use of all the knowledge that resides in a library or the Internet?

1.9.1 Automatic Speech Recognition

Speaking as well as listening and understanding come so very naturally to human beings that we may tend to think that these are simple and easy tasks. In fact these are extra-ordinarily complex tasks. Unlike in written text, there are no clear cut word boundaries or even sentence boundaries. Speech signals show substantial variability across speakers. Even the same word spoken by the same speaker can be very different in terms of the signal characteristics. External noise can cause serious problems. While significant progress has been made in automatic speech recognition over the last fifty years, we still have a long way to go to achieve human like capabilities.

Speech understanding requires all aspects of NLP including syntax, semantics and pragmatics and in addition requires the capability to decode information encoded in speech signals. A speech signal is a composite of the linguistic message being conveyed, the language and dialect used, style, speakers identification including parameters such as sex, age, health and emotional status, as also background noise which may include speech sounds of other people speaking nearby. Automatically extracting the linguistic message while filtering out all other irrelevant aspects from such a composite signal is not an easy task. While the aim in *automatic speech understanding* is to understand the meaning and intentions conveyed by a given speech utterance, *automatic speech recognition* tries to look at a supposedly simpler task of extracting the message content and representing it in text form, without necessarily having to understand the meanings or intentions.

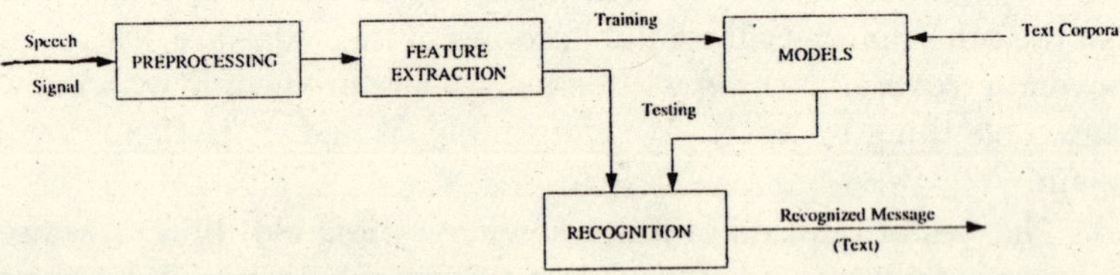

FIG 1.12 Speech Recognition

People do not seem to recognize speech to produce a text representation and then process that text in their brains to understand speech. Understanding seems to be a direct process without need for an intermediate text representation. In fact the very act of trying to represent speech as text incurs both loss and distortion of information. Thus there is no guarantee that speech recognition is actually simpler than speech understanding. By saying we do not need to understanding meanings, we are also losing all the constraints that come from semantics. Any way, the decision to go for speech recognition rather than speech understanding is a purely practical, engineering decision. Let us now see in broad terms how this can be done.

Speech sounds are produced by the vibration of the vocal cords caused by the air flow pumped by the lungs, and subsequent manipulation of the sounds by the articulatory movements of the tongue, lips etc. in the vocal tract to produce different kinds of sounds. Electronic, mathematical or computational analogues of this source-filter system have been developed to find out how we can distinguish different sounds from one another. Finding an appropriate set of features to characterize and distinguish between different speech sounds while accounting for the large inherent variability in natural speech across speakers and contexts is still a largely unsolved problem. It has not been possible so far to build speech recognition systems that handle unlimited vocabulary and spontaneous speech of any arbitrary speaker in open domains. Nevertheless, under restricted conditions, it is possible to develop automatic speech recognition systems that perform fairly well.

Initial attempts therefore restricted one or more dimensions of variability. Isolated word recognition systems did not have to worry about identifying word boundaries. Small vocabulary systems exploited reduced possibilities of confusing one word with other similar sounding words. Domain specific systems exploited the limited space of possibilities in structure and meaning within carefully controlled application domains. Speaker dependent systems avoided problems due to variations from speaker to speaker. Some systems can be easily adapted to the voice of individual speakers and once that is done, they can perform fairly well for that speaker. Speaker adaptive systems have been used as dictation machines - you can speak into your computer instead of typing from the keyboard. In fact there are applications where you do not want anybody other than the authorized user to have access to the system. You do not want your military aircraft to accept voice commands from strangers, right? Thus speaker specific systems have their uses too.

It is now possible to build speaker independent continuous speech recognition systems with vocabularies going into tens of thousands of words. Current systems are, however, still quite brittle. Performance may deteriorate rapidly due to external noise, change of microphone and other devices used etc. Humans can recognize correctly even in the midst of noise as in a cocktail party or automobile or a factory environment. We can easily handle multiple speakers and mix up of languages. There is a lot that still needs to be done in the area of speech technologies.

We recognize that the main differences between different speech sounds are in the frequency components and the way they change with time. Features based on such observations are extracted from a large training data collected from many speakers. Inherent variability is handled by building probabilistic models. Since boundaries between linguistic units such as words and sentences are almost impossible to recognize accurately, language models are built for sub-word units and then extended for whole sequences of words based on the statistical analysis of large text corpora. Tools to perform all these complex tasks are now freely and publicly available. There are also commercial products fine tuned for specific applications such as dictation machines to replace typing.

In future we may see more and more of speech based interfaces to computers. Information retrieval via speech may become a reality soon. Speech recognition is a complex multi-disciplinary area and it is beyond the scope of this book to provide a detailed account. Good books are available for the interested reader.

1.9.2 Speech Synthesis

Machines that read out given texts, called Text-to-Speech (TTS) systems, are in some sense easier to develop since several dimensions of variability have already been removed in expressing the message in text form. Speaker's voice qualities or external noise are no longer relevant when text is given as input. Sentence and word boundaries are usually quite clear. However, there are issues that need to be taken care of. There can be words which are written with the same spelling but pronounced differently and the other way around - *project (n)* versus *project (v)* and *their* versus, *there.* 1999 may have to be read as *one thousand nine hundred and ninety nine* in some situations and as *nineteen ninety nine* in others. Thus *Text Normalization* forms the very first step in TTS. Some languages such a English use an alphabetic, spelling oriented writing system and mapping from written spellings to appropriate pronunciations is an important task. Indian languages use a phonetic writing system and hence there are really no such things as spellings. Only a few relatively simple rules of mapping are sufficient to take care of deviations from true phonetic representation.

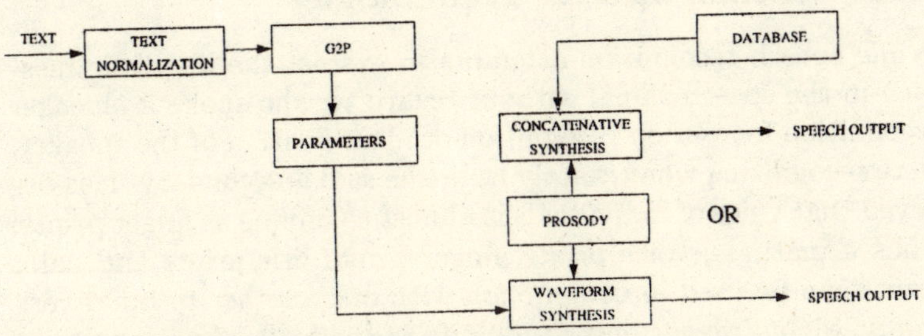

FIG 1.13 Text to Speech Synthesis

There are basically two different ways speech sounds can be actually generated. In waveform generation approaches, a speech signal waveform is actually constructed from features corresponding to the sounds to be produced. Different kinds of resonances (called formants) are set up in the vocal cavity when we speak different sounds. Formant synthesizers produce different speech sounds by simulating these resonances. Articulatory synthesizers attempt to model the speech production processes and synthesize speech using those models. Alternatively, one may record bits and pieces of sounds and concatenate them to produce whatever sequences of sounds need to be generated. Choice of the right level of recorded units and smoothing at the junctures are two important considerations. It is found that splitting in the middle of linguistic units can be better than splitting at the boundaries themselves, since the middle portions are generally more stable and maximum variations and co-articulation effects occur at the boundaries. For example, diphones, consisting of latter half of previous phone and initial half of current phone, have been found to be useful. Some systems work with several levels of sound units and intelligently select the most appropriate units.

To make the sounds produced by TTS systems more natural, it is essential to include prosodic features such as stress, duration and intonation. Systems without good prosody sound very dull and machine like. Developing high quality, natural sounding TTS systems is in fact quite difficult. Interested readers may refer to any of the good books available on the subject.

1.9.3 Other Speech Technologies

While speech recognition attempts to extract the linguistic message in the speech signal without regard to who spoke it, speaker recognition focuses on recognition or identification of the speaker. Here recognizing what exactly he or she said is secondary. It is believed that voice of individuals is almost as unique as finger prints. Thus signatures, voice prints, finger prints, iris prints and palm prints can be used in conjunction with one another to build very robust biometric systems to identify individuals. A speaker may be asked to speak out pre-specified passwords or the system may dynamically prompt the user each time with a different password. We have just have to accept or reject a candidate or we may have to find the correct identity of the individual. Speaker recognition and identification have applications in various forms of security and access control.

We may tend to think that written texts are more authentic since speech sounds themselves are ephemeral. However, it is easier to tamper with written texts (or even replace them with fake ones) than manipulate speech files. Thus recorded voice may in future be accepted as a better and more authentic proof than written documents. Technologies to record and carefully preserve such proofs will be of immense value.

If speech can be compressed to read faster, it will save space and give a quick view. Similarly if speech can be slowed down, we can carefully listen and use that for, say, transcription. Secretaries need not learn short hand. Note that a speech signal cannot be simply compressed or expanded linearly in time - that would change the speech quality or even render it unintelligible.

Separating the speech of individual speakers in a multi-party conversation has many uses. You can then store, index and retrieve different speakers' speech separately.

In multi-lingual environments, one may have to first recognize the language even before speech recognition is attempted. This is very important in countries like India where people speak many different languages. Language identification from short speech samples is an interesting and challenging problem in itself.

There are interesting applications of speech technologies to music recognition, understanding and synthesis. Machines that compose and sing can be built. Machines that teach music can be conceived. Even models of creativity in music can be explored. Information retrieval in the music domain is a fascinating field by itself.

Speech is a technologically complex area requiring insights from diverse disciplines. Acoustics, Signal Processing, Pattern Classification, Machine Learning, Linguistics, Computer Science are all involved. It is beyond the scope of this book to go into the details of speech technology. Interested readers will find many good books and articles for further exploration.

1.10 Human and Machine Intelligence

The common belief that machines are dumb, they can only follow the instructions we have given them, and therefore can never be more intelligent or better than us is to a large extent a myth. Computers can remember large volumes of data and process the data at great speeds. It is relatively easy to accept that machines can beat us easily when it comes to simple tasks such as counting, searching and sorting. Can you remember an entire telephone directory in your mind and search for entries in a fraction of a second? It is harder, however, to realize that much more complex tasks that appear to require a good deal of intelligence can also be broken down into simple tasks and we can build machines that outperform ourselves even in these complex tasks. You might have heard of chess playing programs that can beat even grand masters. These programs derive their "intelligence" from their ability to consider much larger number of options and look ahead many more steps than people can do. Playing chess is generally considered to involve a good deal of intelligence and computers can do this task quite well. It is possible to break this complex task into a large number of very simple tasks - tasks such as counting, searching and sorting, and chess playing programs can be built that beat the developers themselves. Sure, the developers have programmed the machine and the machine does "blindly" follow the instructions given by the developers. The crucial point is what kind of instructions are given. If you program a machine to play a particular instance of a chess game, it can play that particular instance of the game but pretty much nothing else. On the other hand, if you program the machine to observe how others play and learn from that, then the machine can actually beat you one day. The point is that it is possible to program machines not just to store and routinely process data but also to ask questions, seek answers, think logically, draw inferences, explore possibilities, try alternatives and evaluate decisions. It is possible to break even these sophisticated tasks that appear to require human-like intelligence into simple tasks such as comparison or addition. Computers can be made intelligent.

Computers can in fact do many more things than we may initially imagine. Text categorization programs can learn to consider the combined effect of lakhs of words occurring with various frequencies in different categories of documents and automatically categorize documents into different classes accordingly. Automatic summarization programs use a variety of heuristics to select the most salient parts of a document and produce a summary. Information retrieval systems sift through millions of documents and retrieve relevant documents based on occurrence of given key words. All of these can be done automatically with no manual intervention, at fairly high levels of performance and at great speed. Computers are much more than computing or calculating machines. Is not a wonder that some people continue to use computers as type-writers?

We *can* build intelligent computers. Then why is it that there are so many tasks that computers cannot do well today? Building intelligent machines requires breaking those complex tasks into simple tasks that computers are good at. For many tasks, we still do not know how to break them into simple tasks. We all can recognize somebody by their face but we do not know how exactly we do this in our brain. Our understanding of this process is not detailed and precise enough to express it as a computer program. Similarly, we all can understand spoken and written language and we can think creatively, but we do not know how exactly we do such things. In fact it is easier to build computers that behave like expert doctors or engineers than to build computers that can understand language like what every two year old kid can do. Tasks that are very simple and natural for us can be very hard for computers.

Human beings have common sense. They also have world knowledge. We can all understand the famous fox and crow story because we know that the fox is an animal, animals are living beings, living beings need food, if you don't eat food you feel hungry, hunger makes you look for food, if you cannot go to the food then you must make the food come to you, a fox cannot climb trees, a crow normally sits on trees, and a thousand other things and we are able to interconnect all these pieces of common sense knowledge with logical reasoning. We do all these long chains of reasoning so fast and almost unconsciously. Computers are very weak in common sense, they do not have world knowledge and their reasoning abilities are not as robust as ours.

Human intelligence is very broad and generic. We can know many things, learn many things and perform many tasks. A single person can be a good singer, a good driver and a good doctor. While the same computer can be programmed to many things, if we talk in terms of computer programs, usually one program specializes in only one task. It is built to do that task and we only see how well it can do that particular task.

We have knowledge. We also have meta knowledge - we know what we know and what we do not know well. We know where we are good and where we are weak. We can solve problems and puzzles. We can also learn generic strategies and methods to solve such problems and puzzles. We can theorize, we can "think on our own", we can be creative. Today's computers are still very weak in these terms.

Nevertheless, computers are superior to human beings in many ways. They can remember vast amounts of uncorrelated data, we cannot. They can count, search, sort, perform arithmetic computations at lightening speed and great accuracy, we cannot. There are infinitely many valid C programs and infinitely many invalid C programs but a C compiler can validate the syntax of any arbitrary C program, understand it and translate it into an equivalent machine language code, all in a few seconds. Human beings can develop such programs, they can develop the grammars upon which these compilers are based, but they cannot match the machine when it comes to the task of compilation itself. We must accept that there are tasks at which computers are far superior to us.

It is interesting to explore exactly what kinds of things machines can do better than us. We can write a C compiler but the machine does the compilation better. Computers can execute programs with great speed and accuracy, we cannot. We can develop new programming languages but we are in fact not very good at writing programs ourselves. Computer programming is difficult because it requires you to think like a dumb machine and it is not easy for intelligent human beings to think like a machine. Even experts can rarely write a program correctly the first time. This is not because they do not understand clearly what is it that they want to do but it is because writing computer programs is an inherently difficult task. The human brain is designed for communicating with natural languages, not with computer programming languages. It is easy to explain what a program should do in English but is not so easy to express the same thing in a programming language. It is easy for us to draw an approximate circle but difficult to draw an exact circle. On the other hand it is straightforward to write a program to make the machine draw a perfect circle. It is much more difficult to make it draw an approximate circle. The machine does not know what you mean by "approximate circle" - it expects you to define it precisely! The computer has been of great help to me in writing this book - I have written, erased, placed it back, re-arranged, re-written many many times. I could not have done all that with equal convenience and speed sitting with paper and pencil. But the machine could not have written this book by itself. The critical factor, therefore, is to understand what kinds of things machines are good at and exploit them for our benefit. Machines can indeed do many more things than we expect of them.

In terms of speed, automated systems are far superior to manual methods in most tasks. Computers can process thousands, lakhs or even millions of documents in the time it takes us to go through just a few pages. In terms of accuracy, automated methods give comparable or superior performance today in certain areas such as Information Retrieval, and Text Categorizations when the data is very large. On the other hand, people are often much better compared to machines when it comes to tasks such as translation or question answering. But we must remember that even when automated systems give good performance, their scope is often limited and they may be brittle - even a small change in the conditions may bring down the performance drastically. For example, today's speech recognition systems are not robust against such simple looking variations as change of microphone or even moving the head a little away from the microphone while speaking. Human beings are generally more robust than machines in most cases.

The question therefore is not whether people are better or machines are better. Each of them have their own strengths and weaknesses. The challenge is to properly understand the strengths and weaknesses of the two and build man-machine synergies that can produce the best results with minimal effort.

1.11 Shape of Things to Come

So far we have seen several interesting and useful applications of human language technologies. Our treatment has been introductory and informal. The focus has been on what kinds of things can be and have been done. In the process we have got some feel for the need for thorough linguistic and statistical analysis of language, techniques for representing and reasoning with knowledge, computational methodologies for making the machines learn from data, and large scale linguistic data resources that permit effective learning and generalization by machines. We have made progress but there is still a long way to go. There are many serious issues and problems yet to be solved. The field of NLP or Language Engineering is both fascinating and challenging.

There are many other possible application areas for NLP. We use natural languages for communication among ourselves but we can also imagine using them one day to communicate with machines. It takes a substantial amount of training to learn and use artificial languages such a computer or robot programming languages but comparatively little training is required to use human languages we already know. Natural Languages form a common standard - we all know and use these languages. Communicating with human languages is more natural and simpler compared to using artificial, abstract, formal languages. Natural languages are, or can be, concise. Compare "who makes more than their manager" to the equivalent query in, say, SQL. Natural languages are also complete - we can express almost anything and everything we wish to, whereas programming languages are highly restricted in their expressive power. Many of them do not even allow you to make statements or ask questions. We "teach" others, not "program" them. Programming is unnatural, difficult and highly error prone. Thus natural languages hold promise, at least in principle, as replacements to computer programming languages. Imagine a day when you could just talk to your computer and your computer could understand what you said and answer back in speech or written language.

Let us stretch our imagination further and think of possible technologies of the future. But beware, today's science is only yesterday's science fiction. Some of things we are talking about here have already been attempted and you may even find limited successes here and there. But by and large they are largely unsolved problems as yet.

What if we could do simultaneous translation into many languages in real time? You have seen human experts doing this in important international meetings. What if we could do speech understanding rather than speech recognition? Computers are getting embedded into all kinds of devices and you can think of talking not only to your computer but also to your refrigerator, washing machine, TV, car or your home robot. What if we could combine speech recognition and speech synthesis with automatic translation to build speech-to-speech translators? You speak in Tamil over phone and I would hear it in Hindi. I speak back in Hindi but you hear the Tamil version. Language barriers would melt away. A vast majority of our Indian population who are currently deprived of the direct benefits of information technology would be able to access information through speech in their own language. Knowledge of English would no longer be essential. You could get information from your phone, there is no need to have access to a computer or know how to use it effectively. What if could combine intelligent information retrieval systems with automatic summarization systems or Information Extraction systems? What if we could integrate these with Expert Systems and Decision Support systems? What if we could build intelligent assistants and robots for use at office, home or factory? What if you can instruct your TV, in spoken language, to watch all the major news channels during the day and give you a summary of the important happenings, keeping your own interests in mind, when you come back home from the office late in the evening? What if you could go to your computer and just say, "Hey, this man here seems to have had a heart attack. Help!", and the computer searches the Internet, finds out about what to do and what not to do till help arrives, advises you on first aid, calls an ambulance, finds out hospitals where suitable facilities are available, selects a few good ones based on distance, cost or whatever and fixes appointments with good doctors, all on its own? What if the embedded computer in your car take over control when you are too drunk, unconscious or otherwise in bad shape, inform your kin or a doctor, and safely drive you home? What if the computer embedded in your shoe inform you when you over exert or automatically call the doctor when things go really bad?

People grow as per the demands they place on themselves, to aim low is crime. Students and budding researchers must be encouraged to think and stretch their imagination. All ideas must be encouraged to start with however foolish or idiotic they may appear to be. Some will surely lead to progress. Only one needs to combine imagination with proper knowledge of ground realities. Only then will knowledge really expand and grow. Often scientists and engineers glorify some aspects and hide the other side. We need to stop once in a while and take stock. Industrial revolution was supposed to automate manufacturing so that quantity and quality improvements can be obtained at reduced cost and the time so saved can be be fruitfully used by people for human development in general. Don't we find people putting in many more hours today than before just to earn their bread? Have dams really helped us to control floods and promote irrigation? Farmers are committing suicide.

Mere imagination will not help us to move forward. Imagination and creativity must be combined with proper knowledge and deep understanding. There are real theoretical, conceptual, engineering and pragmatic issues and problems. By the time you have completed reading this book, you will hopefully have some idea about these issues and hence your own calculated judgements about the shape of things to come.

Chapter Two will be devoted to the foundations of NLP. We will get to know more about linguistic data resources and the analyses of data from linguistic and statistical points of view. A brief introduction to some of the machine learning techniques is included.

Chapter Three will take us back to Information Retrieval. In the light of our understanding of language and technology for language, we will be able to say more about the issues, problems, solutions and ideas that is shaping Information Retrieval today.

This is only an introductory book. Each of the topics included here is a vast area by itself. You will need to dig deeper into areas of your interest to get a deeper and more thorough understanding. The aim of this book is only to help you get started.

Chapter 2

Foundations of Natural Language Processing

2.1 Introduction

2.1.1 Language, Communication, Technology

If there is one thing that sets human beings apart from all other living creatures it is Language. Language and thought are closely related. Language enables us to articulate our thoughts and communicate with fellow human beings. Man is a social animal. It is communication through language that binds this society together. It is the language faculty that makes us what we are today. If it were not for language, perhaps the human society could not have developed to this extent. To understand the importance of language, try spending just one day without using language in any way. Asking somebody to shut up is a big punishment.

Language manifests itself most naturally in the form of speech. Speech is a natural, efficient and direct means of communication between human beings. Technology such as the Tape Recorder, Radio, the Television, the Telephone make it possible for people to communicate with one another across space and time - you can speak at one place and at one time and be heard at another place or at a later time.

Language can also be codified in other ways. Speech, by its very nature is transient. Writing, that is creating graphical shapes on a two dimensional surface, is more permanent. Scribing, engraving or embossing on any kind of a surface including stone, palm leaves, parchment, metal, cloth or paper qualifies as written form of language. Speech is an all-in-one representation, encoding as it does the message being conveyed, the language, the speaker's identity, his or her emotional status, environmental conditions and so on. Written text is limited - a lot of useful information is lost when we write down things. Yet writing has played a major role in shaping the destiny of mankind. In fact our knowledge of our history owes in a large measure to the development of writing. Writing gives us an opportunity to carefully plan, organize and structure our thoughts and thus communicate more effectively. Speech is direct and real-time. The written form of communication, on the other hand, is not limited by the real-time processing constraints. Hence writing can be more detailed, more elaborate. Written texts can be preserved for long periods of time, reproduced in large quantities and read by many people at the same time at different places.

Printing technology enabled effective dissemination of knowledge and gave a big push to human development. Now the modern computer and communication technology is making it ever so much more easier to create, store, modify, reproduce and disseminate documents in electronic form. A single CD can store the equivalent of several hundred full length books. Modern technology has revolutionized the way we communicate. The impact technology will have on society at large is difficult to guage.

Technology now makes it possible to scan text documents and create images of these texts. This technology goes a long way in preserving ancient manuscripts. It is easier to make several copies of electronic documents and store them in many different media and at many different places for ensuring safe custody. Preserving palm leaves etc. is more difficult. Technology, known as *Optical Character Recognition* also exists for recognizing the written shapes and converting the scanned images into electronic text. Text is much smaller in size compared to images and texts can be easily edited.

Thus language processing can be viewed at the levels of speech, text and scanned images. NLP has traditionally focussed only on text documents. While there is an increasing trend towards processing of multi-media documents, text processing continues to be the major focus. We shall limit ourselves mainly to processing of text documents in this book.

2.1.2 Natural Language Processing and Computational Linguistics

This chapter deals with the fundamentals of language processing that are essential for realizing Intelligent Information Retrieval as well as other applications of language and speech technologies. Natural Language Processing (NLP) forms the backbone of every human language technology application. NLP is concerned with natural or human languages - languages which we human beings use for day to day communications, as against artificial languages such as computer and robot programming languages.

The terms *Natural Language Processing* and *Computational Linguistics* have been used interchangeably and we shall do the same here. There is no real difference between the two except perhaps that linguists sometimes tend to prefer the latter term - in *Computational Linguistics*, *Linguistics* is the head of the phrase and *Computational* is only an adjectival modifier. Computers, like mathematics, are generic and powerful tools and mere use of computers to carry out linguistic studies will not qualify as a distinct branch of study in itself. Computational Linguistics or NLP is different from Linguistics in that the primary aim is to build computational models of various aspects of human language faculty. Such models need to be simple, elegant and efficient, yet very precise, detailed and exhaustive. The models built must stand the test of large scale real life data - language as people use it. NLP also includes various applications dealing with natural languages and the tools and technologies for realizing such applications.

Of late there is an increasing emphasis on corpus based statistical approaches either in conjunction with or as an alternative to, purely linguistic analysis. There is a confluence of ideas from such varied disciplines as Linguistics, Statistics, Mathematics, Engineering, Computer Science, Artificial Intelligence, Cognitive Science, Logic, Philosophy and Psychology. Machine Learning and Pattern Classification Techniques have become the main stream methodologies. Thus the term *Language Engineering* has become more appropriate. Sometimes we also use the term *Language technologies.* The term *Human Language Computing* is also in use.

Natural Language Processing started off as a part of Artificial Intelligence (AI), a discipline with two broad goals - 1) to understand the nature of human intelligence and 2) to build intelligent systems. Language faculty is at the very core of human intelligence. Whether language precedes and causes thought or the other way round is debatable but the close relation between language and thought is indisputable. Without language faculty, we perhaps could not have been *intelligent* at all. Naturally NLP became a major focus area within AI. The primary goal of NLP was to understand how exactly we human beings understand, generate and learn languages. Language faculty was to be explored not in isolation but in close relationship with other cognitive processes such as speech, vision and learning. Also, computer systems were to be designed that could process and communicate with human languages. Speech perception, understanding and synthesis were also major areas of focus. However, early work in NLP was mostly limited to handling written texts and was thus largely disjoint from speech technology research. Of late we can see a closer integration of NLP and speech technologies. There is also a trend towards multi-modal communications involving speech, language and gestures.

We begin this chapter with elements of linguistic analysis essential for NLP and take up corpus based statistical approaches in the second half. The treatment is introductory. Interested readers will find pointers to more advanced and detailed material in the bibliography.

2.1.3 NLP: An AI Perspective

There are three major concerns in NLP:

- *Natural Language Understanding (NLU)*: How do we understand what we read or hear?
- *Natural Language Generation (NLG)*: How do we synthesize Natural Language utterances to convey whatever we have in mind?
- *Natural Language Acquisition (NLA)*: How do we acquire or learn a language?

The Producer-Comprehender Model

We use language to communicate information as also our ideas, feelings, emotions and attitudes. This communication through language can only happen between active, cognitive processors such as human beings and, hopefully, computers. We don't speak to walls, right? There can be no proper communication if one or both the parties are sleeping or otherwise inattentive. We shall use the term *producer* to refer to a person or entity that produces speech or written text material for others to comprehend. Similarly, one who listens or reads will be termed a *comprehender*. The producer and the comprehender must be active cognitive processors. We can model communication between one producer and one comprehender without loss of generality - communication among several entities can always be modelled in terms of several one-to-one communications.

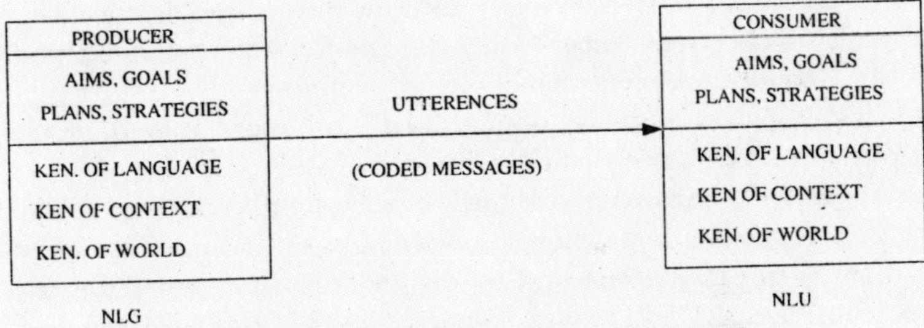

FIG 2.1 The Producer-Comprehender Model

The producer starts with his own aims, goals, plans and strategies. If he decides to communicate and use language for that communication (he can also communicate through gestures or even through silence), then he constructs natural language utterances and speaks or writes them out. Similarly, the comprehender has his own aims, goals, plans and strategies. He tries to understand the received messages accordingly. The speech or text samples themselves are actually just codes - they encode the messages to be conveyed - information, feelings, attitudes, whatever. Thus language is merely a coding system and language in use is a simple linear sequences of symbols. The producer generates these codes and the comprehender decodes them.

For effective communication, the producer and comprehender

must have a common language, that is, a common set of codes. The knowledge of language includes vocabulary, grammar, etc. The knowledge of language as possessed by any two persons is very unlikely to be exactly the same. I may know some words or expressions that you do not know and vice versa. However, there must be a large overlap between the knowledge possessed by the two parties. If 90% of the words I use are unknown to you, you just can't understand anything. For effective communication, we have to assume that knowledge of language we have is largely common.

Effective communication through natural language also requires common sense and world knowledge. We rarely say everything and if we try, we will only produce the most boring, dry and uninteresting output. Human beings have excellent ability to fill up the gaps and we only need to state the unusual, special or interesting aspects. We all understand, even kids understand the story "the wily fox tricked the vain crow into dropping the meat by praising its lovely voice". Why did the fox want the meat first of all? How does praising somebody get you food? If we start saying that fox is an animal, animals need food, meat is food, crows sit on trees, foxes cannot climb trees, earth and meat have masses, gravity attracts masses, if one mass is very small compared to the other, the smaller mass moves towards larger, if the crow opens its beaks, the meat falls and so on and on, that would be the most boring story you would have ever heard. But all these and more steps of commonsense reasoning based on world knowledge are essential to understand even simple sentences in natural language. A great deal of common sense, world knowledge and ability to draw inferences intelligently are essential for natural language understanding.

Also, knowledge of the context is essential for proper communication. If you enter a room where people are talking it will take a while before you get to know what they are talking about. The same utterances may mean very different things if placed out of context or in different contexts. Try placing "Mary had a little lamb" in the contexts of "I had sandwiches for breakfast", or "Mary was expecting"!

It is important to realize that speakers say and listeners understand based on their own aims, plans and strategies. You may say something to literally mean what you said but you often say something with different intentions. You may want to tell a lie. You may want to cheat. Your best friend has come home after a long gap and you want him to stay longer but he is in a hurry. You say "it is raining". Both of you know very well that it is not raining. You have communicated your desire to keep your friend at home longer and your friend has understood it. You may be teaching in a classroom and some students may be trying to understand the meaning of what you say. Others may in fact be analyzing your style and mannerisms. Some may be just looking for faults. Some may be thinking of something else. Communication through language is much more involved than many think.

A teacher needs to know what his/her students already know, their general mental abilities, their proficiency in language etc. A university teacher may find it very difficult to teach school kids because he/she is used to different kinds of models of his listeners. Every speaker has a mental model of the listener. If somebody asks "where is Taj Mahal?", you answer "in India", "In Agra", "go straight and take a right turn" or whatever depending upon your impression of what the user wants to know and the context where the question is being asked. When a teacher asks a question he/she may be wanting to test the students' knowledge and when a student asks the same question he/she may be genuinely interested in knowing the answer. Of course a student may be testing the teacher too. We communicate through language under the assumptions of the mental models of the other party.

NLP is concerned with building models of the minds of the producer and comprehender as also with the mechanisms of coding and decoding of language utterances. Mental models include aims, objectives, goals, plans, strategies, attitudes, representation and processing of knowledge of language, knowledge of the world and common sense as also reasoning and logic.

Natural Language Understanding is concerned with the mental models of the comprehender that explain how the meanings and intentions encoded in language utterances are understood.

Natural Language Generation is concerned with the mental models of the producer that explain how language utterances are produced to express specified ideas, emotions, attitudes or pieces of information. Note that this is not the same as simply generating some arbitrary but grammatical sentences from a given grammar. Sometimes linguists use the term "generation" in connection with abstract grammars that can generate all and only the grammatically valid sentences.

While we are speaking and listening, we are also simultaneously learning new ideas and concepts as also elements of language. *Natural Language Acquisition* is concerned with mental models of the comprehender that explain how knowledge of language itself can be acquired, refined and perfected as we keep analyzing natural language utterances. There are significant differences between first language acquisition and second language acquisition. Learning language by being taught is different from learning language by merely interacting with the community of speakers of that language. Natural language acquisition deals with all forms of language learning.

The aim in all cases is to build computational models - models that are amenable for detailed inspection, models that can be tested on real life data. The models need to be both exhaustive and very detailed and precise. Samples are not sufficient.

Although understanding, generation and acquisition have all been the primary goals of NLP, we find that over the last 50 years or so maximum attention has been given to natural language understanding, generation has received relatively less attention and language learning has not received much attention at all. In fact an analysis view point is presumed in many cases by default. Thus while talking about syntax, NLP researchers tend to take the syntactic analysis view point rather than that of synthesis or generation. Linguists, on the other hand, are more used to thinking of grammars as abstract characterizations of the constraints of a language for producing all and only valid structures.

NLP involves a deep understanding of human cognition and intelligence. For the sake of convenience, the language faculty is often studied independently of other cognitive tasks but we must remember that this is only a restricted view taken for convenience and not the complete and accurate picture in itself. NLP is concerned more with the mental models of the producer and the comprehender than merely with the details of the code - the linear sequence of symbols, the message that is physically communicated through a medium from the producer to the comprehender. It is unfortunate that many have given too much of attention to the details of the code itself rather than to the mechanisms of producing and interpreting the codes. For example, syntacticians have often spent all their life analyzing the intricacies of structure of sentences rather than worry about what those sentences really mean and how particular syntactic structures encode given meanings and intentions. The central element of language is meaning and intention. It is unfortunate that phonology, morphology and syntax have come to be considered the "core" of linguistics rather than semantics. A lot of time, effort and energy has been spent on superficial details rather than the real, core problems and issues. The available body of knowledge in linguistics and NLP today is thus heavily skewed and inevitably, this books reflects the same. We will be raising some critical issues with semantics but we may not be able to give satisfactory solutions in all cases.

2.1.4 NLP Over the Decades

We have seen the origins of NLP within Artificial Intelligence during the mid fifties. The primary aims were a) computational modelling of human language production and comprehension and b) building intelligent systems with natural language capabilities. Many NLP systems were developed mainly to demonstrate ideas, problems and possible solutions. They were all toy systems by today's standards. One of the major application area was machine translation.

One of the important lessons learnt during the initial period was that languages are richer and more complex than we may initially tend to think and a much more thorough and deeper analysis of all aspects of languages is essential. Evaluation of NLP systems came to focus. During the seventies and eighties, much more sophisticated systems were built. Linguistic data resources had expanded and tools and technologies had also matured to some extent. Slowly signs of saturation started showing up. There were barriers that were difficult to cross. Performance of systems could not be improved even with great effort. It took great effort and time to develop and improve linguistic knowledge but the incremental improvements in performance obtained got smaller and smaller.

The early nineties saw a major paradigm shift. The limitations of the knowledge based approach had been well understood. It had been shown that natural language understanding and generation could be done if all the required knowledge could be made available but knowledge acquisition became the real bottleneck. Experts were hard to find, hand-crafting knowledge structures was extremely tedious, time consuming and costly and after all that, saturation points would be reached beyond which it is difficult to progress. Focus shifted to machine learning techniques to automatically 'learn' to solve a problem by looking at a large collection of examples. Computing power and memory had increased manifolds and machine costs had drastically come down. What could once be tried out only on big machines could now be attempted on a desk top PC. Focus shifted to development and statistical analysis of large scale linguistic data resources and suitable machine learning techniques. It is easier to find people who can generate linguistic data than people who can provide expert knowledge. Commercial companies started working on NLP problems. NLP had moved from the research laboratories to the market place.

The strengths and weaknesses of purely statistical approaches have now been clearly understood. It is now generally believed that a combination of linguistic and statistical approaches may be essential. New application areas have emerged. At one point of time NLP had become almost synonymous with Machine Translation, especially in our country. Now Information retrieval, Information Extraction, Automatic Categorization, Automatic Summarization, Text Mining have all become major application areas for NLP. There is an increasing confluence and synergy between text and speech technologies. People have started talking about multi-lingual and multi-media applications. There is an increased awareness of the importance of language and speech technologies at all levels. Many large funded research projects have been initiated all over the world. In India the Government has been showing a keen interest in developing technologies for Indian languages. There are scores of universities and research organizations that have been working on various aspects of language technologies. Teething problems have been largely overcome and attention has shifted to applications that can have serious impact on our society.

We have come a long way. However, if you look back carefully and analyze our achievements and failures, you will find that almost all the critical problems have remained unsolved. We have not been able to build systems that understand, generate or learn natural languages. It is in fact unfortunate that so much of attention is being given to very superficial analysis of language and the core is almost forgotten. Semantics has taken a back seat even in linguistics. Not everything can be done by simply counting words. Perhaps the time has come to rethink and re-plan the NLP agenda.

2.1.5 Linguistics versus NLP

Many still think that computational linguistics or NLP can be done by putting together a linguist and a programmer. Just as China plus Philosophy does not yield Chinese Philosophy, Computational Linguistics or NLP is not merely computers plus linguistics. Computers are powerful tools, like mathematics, and have applications and uses in almost all branches of study. Computational, linguistic, statistical and engineering concepts need to be closely integrated in order to synthesize a new field of study called computational linguistics, NLP or language engineering. The purpose of this book is to give a flavor of such an integrated multi-disciplinary field. Understanding or at least appreciation of the concerns, aims, assumptions, jargon, definitions and methodologies of various disciplines concerned is important. People who are trained to think and work like that are in short supply. If this book helps in any way to develop such trained manpower, that would be considered a success.

Computational linguistics or NLP provides a computational view point for linguistics. There are many things that are obvious for human beings and the focus will naturally be only on the unusual, special situations when all this is for human consumption. People have world knowledge and commonsense and this forms a tacit assumption when dealing with people. The goal of NLP, on the other hand, is to make the computer, the idiot box that has no commonsense, world knowledge or human-like reasoning power, to perform language processing tasks with human-like performance. A few examples are not enough. Exhaustive sets of data, rules, guidelines and principles need to be provided to handle special, unusual situations as also the run-of-the-mill cases. Explaining in simple language is not sufficient, we will have to write detailed and precise program code.

Let us take a specific example. One of the primary goals of modern generative linguistics lead by Noam Chomsky is to understand how children, exposed to such small and imperfect samples of language use, can learn the structure and properties of their native language, whatever that may be, so easily within just a couple of years. From a computational point of view, an acceptable solution to this problem would be a computational model of child language acquisition which can be experimentally tested. We should be able to give controlled input and observe the outputs as well as the changes that take place in the internal structure of the model to see what exactly constitutes learning and how the child is actually learning with each input sample. We cannot open up somebody's brain and see before and after changes as a sentence is being processed by the brain. But with a computational model such a detailed probing would be feasible. For example, if we build a neural network model, we can see the changes taking place in the various synaptic weights with each iteration. The individual numbers may not make much sense but we can surely get a global picture of whether the system is learning, at what rate it is learning, has a saturation point been reached etc. Despite the great deal of effort that has gone into building linguistic theories of human language learning, it has not been possible to come anywhere near a mathematical or computational model or theory of language learning.

NLP throws upon both challenges and opportunities. NLP forces us to go into each aspect in great detail and with great precision. This exercise in itself brings out many interesting problems and issues that were never known or considered with any seriousness. Linguists, for example, have never taken the problem of segmenting a running text into sentences very seriously especially for languages such as English where there are fairly clear cut sentence boundary markers such as the period, the question mark and the exclamation mark. A detailed study shows, contrary to initial expectation, that segmenting texts into sentences and sentence fragments is not a completely trivial task. In fact this leads to a serious discussion and debate on what really constitutes a sentence and how do we deal with sentence segments. A number of sentences, sentence groups, and/or sentence fragments can be embedded inside a given sentence forming a list. An NLP researcher needs to worry about distinguishing between a full stop, a decimal point and the dot used in acronyms and abbreviations whereas linguists rarely find such things interesting enough to merit scientific inquiry. Although we have tried to drive home the problem by taking a down to earth example here, the nature of difference in the orientation of linguistics and NLP is the same at all levels of abstraction.

NLP forces linguistic theories, models, ideas and hypotheses to be tested on large scale, real world data. This helps to validate the theories, find places where they fail, pick up counter examples and refine the theory or model accordingly. The NLP approach also makes available large scale data which can be used to build theories and models. Manual methods are tedious, time consuming and hence limited to small data sets. They are also prone to human biases and misinterpretations. Testing on large scale real world data often throws out new insights.

Any aspect of human language processing can be modeled and tested in NLP as long as the data and rules to handle all cases are covered exhaustively in detail and in precise enough terms for a computer to follow. Priorities for development may be dictated by concerns of practical need etc. but there is really no area of linguistics that NLP cannot touch.

NLP attaches great importance to computational efficiency in terms of memory space and computation time. Linguistics attaches great importance to simplicity, elegance and economy of expression but efficiency in terms of computational space and time is usually not a major concern except in certain areas such as psycholinguistics. The fundamental assumption in AI is that human beings are intelligent and doing things in a simpler, more elegant, faster and more efficient way is an important element of human intelligence. In this sense, if an NLP approach shows a much more efficient method of solving a particular problem, linguists cannot afford to ignore the implications. After all, linguistics is all about human language faculty and how it intelligently handles language.

Application orientation also often helps in fixing priorities and plans of action in a more systematic and justifiable manner. It helps, for example, to make clear distinctions between open ended pure research, applied research with clear cut aims an objectives with reference to specified applications and developmental activities leading to data generation, products, services etc.

2.2 A Layered View of Computational Linguistics

Linguistics recognizes that there are several appropriate levels of linguistic representation such as phonemes, morphemes, words, phrases, clauses, sentences and discourse segments. A word is a minimal meaningful unit at a particular level of abstraction while a sentence is also a minimal meaningful unit but at a different, higher level of abstraction. Linguistic theories postulate and show that certain kinds of units are appropriate while others are not. Thus whether words can be understood in terms of lower level units called morphemes would be a fundamental question in linguistic theory. Linguistics provides tools and techniques of scientific inquiry into human languages at each of these appropriate levels of description.

We can also cut words or sentences into arbitrary parts but such parts may not have any linguistic significance. For example, the individual characters of which a word is made, carries no linguistic significance. The length of words expressed in terms of number of characters it includes or the length of a sentence in terms of the number of words in it are generally considered to be of no consequence in many areas of linguistics. However, quantities such as these can have considerable statistical significance and statistical models of language often exploit such quantities as useful features.

Modern linguists have also taken a layered view of language and each level of linguistic description is studied more or less independently of other levels. That is, the interactions between layers are presumed to be separable from the core of a given level itself so that the core and the interactions with the neighboring levels can be explored separately to characterize any particular level. For example, Chomsky claims "autonomy of syntax" by saying that syntax can be studied more or less independently of other levels of linguistics. Syntax is presumed to be loosely-coupled with other levels, not tightly and inseparably coupled.

The above stratified view of language raises certain basic questions. For example, can we understand the meaning of a sentence in terms of the meaning of the words in the sentence? Or is a sentence an atomic unit of meaning and breaking it into words artificial and unhelpful? Such questions have been scientifically explored in great depth and detail within the Indian tradition dating back to several thousand years. In fact whether there are identifiable units such as words and sentences is a question that deserves careful consideration. As opposed to the stratified model, one can posit a holistic view of language and claim that we process and understand language all in one go, not layer by layer. Do we perform a dictionary look up and morphological analysis first and then perform syntactic analysis and finally get into semantics in our minds to understand the meaning of an utterance? Or do we do all these things together, in a closely integrated fashion? On the one hand these are questions of implementation strategies. At the same time, these are basic questions relating to layered or modular view as against a holistic view. Most practical systems take a layered view since it is easier to work level by level, from simpler to more complex, rather than try to do everything in one go. Here we will take the layered view and look into the structure and function of words and then sentences .

We begin our study of language at the level of words and then move on to the level of sentences. Our primary focus is only on texts and so we will not cover phonetics or phonology - the study of the basic sound units in a language at the physical and abstract levels respectively. We will also not get into discourse level analysis. A lot can be done at the level of words and sentences, discourse level analyses are a lot more complex, our knowledge and understanding at the discourse level is relatively less at the moment, and many applications can be developed even without getting into a detailed analysis at the discourse level. However, we will be exploring statistical analyses techniques in the latter half, some of which work on entire texts.

2.2.1 Dictionaries

Knowledge of language is essential for meaningful communication through language. Words of a language, and the phonological, morphological, syntactic and semantic information associated with them, forms a very important part of the knowledge of language. Knowing the words is an extremely important part of knowing a language. Dictionaries are storehouses of such information and therefore, they have a key role to play in NLP. Also, theoretical linguistics has come to assign an increasingly central role to the lexicon.

Longman's dictionary of contemporary English (1987) defines a dictionary as 'a book that gives a list of words in alphabetical order with their meanings in the same or another language and usually with their pronunciations'. According to Random House Dictionary of the English Language (College Edition), a dictionary is 'a book containing a selection of the words of a language usually arranged alphabetically, giving information about their meanings, pronunciations, etymologies etc.; a lexicon'. These definitions suggest that a dictionary is essentially a list of words of a language, typically sorted alphabetically, giving the associated meanings. Pronunciation, part-of-speech and other grammatical features, etymology, usage, examples, pictures and so on may also be optionally provided.

Dictionaries can be built for specific purposes and the contents and organization would vary accordingly. Thus we can talk of a dictionary meant for second language learners, a dictionary of technical terms in a specified domain, or a dictionary for pedagogical purposes. We can have a dictionary of phrasal verbs and a dictionary of idioms. A children's dictionary may contain only the most frequent and basic words. The term 'lexicon', on the other hand, is used in a technical sense in linguistics. A lexicon contains a complete inventory of all the words in a language along with associated information conforming to the specifications of a given theoretical framework. This information would be organized as required by the theory. The term lexicon is also used in NLP to stand for a dictionary considered to be one of the components of an NLP system. Although a lexicon is different from a dictionary, these two terms are sometimes used interchangeably.

Electronic Dictionaries

Dictionaries in the form of printed books are not of much direct use in NLP. Only dictionaries in electronic form can be used by computer programs. Computer programs can be written to search and automatically process such electronic dictionaries. Programs also exist for assisting the very development of electronic dictionaries. Electronic dictionaries greatly enhance the flexibility, convenience and speed of access by human beings too. Understandably, therefore, the development of large computerized lexical knowledge bases has emerged as probably the most urgent, expensive, and time consuming task facing linguistics and NLP today. And this is all the more relevant and exigent in the Indian context where, what is already available is very little compared to what is needed.

One might think of electronic dictionaries as simply electronic counterparts of printed dictionaries. The same information is stored in magnetic medium in computer processable forms and used in a similar way. People 'look up' the dictionary by making suitable requests to a computer program and in turn get the program to display on the screen or print onto paper the information requested by the user. The computer can hold huge amounts of information and can turn the pages for you very fast. While all this is true, electronic dictionaries are in fact much more powerful. The following paragraphs show how.

We go to a dictionary to look up the meaning of a word or its correct spelling or pronunciation. Sometimes we may be interested in knowing more about the grammatical properties, usage, etymology etc. We can use electronic dictionaries for all these purposes. We can also do many more things that would be difficult with printed dictionaries. How do you extract all words that are both nouns and verbs? How do you make a list of 5 letter words? Or bisyllabic words? Or words with a Sanskrit origin? With printed dictionaries one will have no option than to scan through the whole dictionary manually, a task that can be extremely tedious and time consuming. With an electronic lexical database, one could script a few lines of code and get all these done in seconds.

A researcher interested in morphology may like to extract and or reorder the words in the dictionary in the right to left (reversed) alphabetical order so that for example, all '-ing' ending words would get grouped together and words ending with '-ed' would form another cluster. This can be done very easily and very fast on a computer. Electronic lexical databases, properly designed and organized, can also be easily 'reconfigured' to suit different needs. For example, one can create graded dictionaries for children, with vocabularies limited to what can be considered adequate for various age groups. Clearly, large scale lexical databases are extremely important and useful linguistic resources for any language.

Electronic dictionaries are also directly usable by computer programs. Electronic dictionaries form an integral component of almost every activity in computational linguistics and NLP - word processing and text critiquing systems, spelling error detection and correction, grammar checking, office automation, morphological analysis and synthesis, parsing and generation, machine translation, question answering systems, story understanding, natural language interfaces to databases, computer aided instruction, information retrieval, speech synthesis, speech recognition, automatic indexing and abstracting, concordance and other statistical analyses, vocabulary studies, stylistics, psycholinguistic studies, taxonomical studies etc.

We have seen that electronic dictionaries can be very useful for people as also for NLP applications. Yet another dimension of the relationship between dictionaries and computers is the use of computers in developing dictionaries. Dictionary development is a huge and complex task requiring great skill and expertise on the part of the lexicographer. Classical dictionaries have taken decades to develop. At one point of time words used to be written down on cards, cards sorted manually, then word frequencies counted manually and duplicate cards removed and so on. Today computers provide assistance at practically every stage of dictionary development. To give an idea of this, we may start with large and representative collections of electronic texts, extract words and perform a type-token analysis (each distinct word form is a type and each occurrence of a type is a token), perform morphological analysis to extract root words, select words, identify parts of speech (POS) using POS tagged corpora or through morphological analysis, use a KWIC (Key Word in Context) Concordance program to extract sentences containing a given key word and decide meanings etc. from these sentences, select examples of usage, and format the entries in the dictionary as required. All these steps can be done semi-automatically. The machine performs more or less routine things like searching, sorting as also more sophisticated tasks such as morphological analysis or word sense discrimination. Human experts take intelligent decisions using their common sense and world knowledge. A number of powerful tools exist to assist lexicographers in their tasks. Good dictionaries can be developed much faster today than was possible before the age of computers.

The structure and contents of a dictionary in printed form are frozen at the time of its publication. On the other hand, the content, organization as well as formatting of electronic dictionaries can be changed easily. An electronic dictionary can grow and quickly respond to changes. You do not have to wait for the next edition of the dictionary to be printed. Users may also be allowed to alter the dictionary as needed.

A variety of tools exist for developing, formatting, printing, maintaining and using electronic dictionaries. Statistical tools for corpus analysis are invaluable for developing dictionaries from corpora. The internal physical representations may vary widely depending upon applications and whether the dictionaries are to be used from web site or CDs or as databases stored in the hard disk of a computer. XML has emerged as the preferred exchange format. A DTD (Document Type Definition) defines the structure of the dictionary so that other applications can use the dictionary. Web enabled dictionaries require server side and/or client side scripts to interact with the users, search the dictionary, format the search results for display etc. Efficient algorithms exist for fast searching. There are tools for verification and validation. These tools make it possible to develop, maintain and use large dictionaries and other lexical resources effectively and efficiently.

We have seen printed dictionaries that include line drawing and maps but electronic dictionaries may be enriched in many ways that printed dictionaries do not allow. We can include monotone or colour photographs as also animations to illustrate some action 'by doing and showing it'. We can incorporate speech output to illustrate correct pronunciations. We can include maps that you can zoom into.

Our focus here will be electronic dictionaries designed for NLP applications. There are three main issues in the design of dictionaries:

- What kinds of words are listed in the dictionary?
- What information should the entries provide?
- How should that information be organized and structured?

Let us explore each of these in turn.

The Contents of a Dictionary

A dictionary consists of lexical entries and the associated information. What kinds of lexical entries should we include in a dictionary? What kind of grammatical, semantic or other kinds of information should be include for these lexical entries? Let us look at these issues one by one.

The content of a dictionary and its organization critically depend on the ways in which NLP applications use the dictionary. Spell checkers often use merely a list of words. For a syntactic parsing program, the grammatical category and other grammatical features of words may be sufficient and the dictionary may not even contain information on pronunciation, etymology or meaning descriptions. However, for a full-fledged natural language understanding system, meanings and even usage may be extremely important.

This question of content is also closely tied up with theoretical frameworks. In LFG, the lexicon is expected to have separate entries for 'hand', 'hands', 'handed', and 'handing', in spite of the fact that these words are morphologically related according to very simple and regular rules. In the Tree Adjoining Grammar, the lexicon contains sets of trees for each entry. Small's theory of word expert parsing places a heavy demand on the dictionary too. The lexical entries (word experts) are complicated programs with coroutine structure, the specification of which requires not only the detailed knowledge of the architecture of the parser, but also acquaintance with a specialized language for writing word experts, besides being able to judge what constitutes linguistically relevant information and how to represent that procedurally, and readiness to bring in arbitrary amounts of more general and common world knowledge. No division is made between syntactic, semantic or pragmatic knowledge. Connectionist parsing systems require a qualitatively different kind of a lexicon due to the highly distributed nature of their knowledge sources.

Dictionaries are treasuries of words but what exactly is a word? Generally speaking, entries in a dictionary may include single words (man, intelligence, Delhi), sub-word units which are less than words, morphemes which can not occur in isolation (-ed, -ment, -es), supra-word units consisting of combination of parts of two or more words such as blends and abbreviations (can't, TV, laser) and super-word units consisting of compounds and phrases (can not, white house, civil war, kick the bucket).

Should we store both the words "table" and "tables" in the dictionary? All countable nouns have plural forms. Should we list singular and plural forms of all such nouns? To answer such questions we may have to turn to psycholinguistic theories or computational considerations. It is unlikely that people store all the singular and plural forms of nouns in their mental lexicon since plural formation in English is quite regular. It would be a more intelligent strategy to store, say, only the singular forms and derive the plural forms using a rule. Suitable mopho-phonemic rules may be used so that "car-cars", "bus-buses", "mango-mangoes", "bush-bushes" are all handled properly. What about "child-children"? Here one may argue that the regular rule does not seem to apply and it may be best to store the plural form directly in the dictionary rather than make a rule that works just for this one word. What about "formula-formulae", "thesis-theses", "radius-radii", "datum-data"? Are these regular rules applicable to many instances or exceptional cases? How productive should a hypothetical rule be before we can accept it as a rule? Linguistic theories have argued in different ways and many different models have been proposed. It is not easy to obtain reliable psycholinguistic evidence in all cases. The computational bases to answer these questions are perhaps more easy to understand and apply. Memory space and computation time are the two basic computational resources and a strategy is considered intelligent if these resources are used efficiently. It takes space to store the words and it takes space to store the rules too. It takes time to search for a word in the dictionary and it takes time to apply a rule. Practical wisdom dictates that only the most productive rules need to be used and all other irregular forms can be directly stored in the dictionary. Many applications store all derived forms directly in the dictionary and use only a handful of inflectional morphology rules for plurals of nouns, past tense of verbs, degrees of comparison for adjectives etc. in the case of English. The morphology of Indian languages, especially that of Dravidian languages is extremely complex and research is still going on to find optimal solutions.

What seems adequate for human users is not always good enough from an NLP point of view. Most dictionaries meant for human users list only the root words, not the regular inflections.

For example, the entry "baker, n" may give a fairly clear idea to a human user but the fact that "baker" is a noun form obtained from the verb "bake" is implicit here. Generalizations are lost unless somewhere we note that "weaver", "teacher", "player" are similar. How do we understand the meaning of new word, say "gorker"? Where do we store the fact that a "sleeper" in the context of railways is a piece of wood used below the rails to hold them in place, and not simply one who sleeps. How do we understand "waiter" in the context of a restaurant? What is common to "car driver" and "screw driver" and what makes them different? "hand-writing" and "hand-written" are fine but there is no such thing as "hand-write". Lexical semantics has somehow not received the attention it deserves within the NLP community.

A large dictionary is not always better than a smaller one. Think of a dictionary based spelling error detection and correction system. Any word found in the dictionary will be taken to be a valid word. If a word is not found in the dictionary, it is taken to be a spelling error and similarly spelled words from the dictionary are given out as possible corrections. If you type "lave" instead of, say, "leave", a large dictionary that includes the rare word "lave" will not even detect your mistake, let alone helping you to correct it.

What grammatical information should we include? There seems to be general agreement about such notions as 'noun' and 'verb'. But exactly what information a dictionary should give is to some extent theory bound. For example, should the lexicon give transitivity, case frames or sub-categorization frames, or argument structures for verbs? Should the lexicon say that 'soldier' is '+ human '? What all semantic features should the lexicon include? How should the lexicon denote the selectional restrictions? How exactly should the lexicon represent the fact that 'play' is either a noun , or a verb in first person (singular or plural), or second person (singular or plural), or third person (plural but not singular)? How should the lexicon capture the generalization that other verbs also behave the same way? What defaults can a lexicon use to avoid saying the same thing over and over? The answers to some of these questions depend on the links between the lexicon and morphology and other components that may make use of the lexicon.

The information that we wish to incorporate directly into the dictionary is dependent on what kind of programs use this information. English plurals are often formed by adding an 's' as in 'books' and 'dogs'. But 'books' is pronounced with a final [s] and 'dogs' is pronounced with a final [z] sound. Similarly, in Hindi fronting of short /a/ when followed by /h/ is a regular and automatic as in /kahna/ [k ^{e} hna], /pahcan/ [p ^{e} hcan] etc. Since these phenomena are quite regular and automatic, we might use a general rule to handle this and leave no explicit indication whatever in the lexicon. The adjective 'electric' is pronounced with a final /k/ but its noun form 'electricity' is pronounced with an /s/ ending as in 'city'. This phenomenon is less regular and non-automatic - it might be necessary to indicate explicitly in some way in the lexicon, how 'electric' and 'electricity' must be pronounced.

In fact a dictionary is a list of exceptions. Words are actually association between sounds and meanings. These associations are arbitrary and not rule governed. Hence the dictionary lists words and their meanings. Spellings are also quite arbitrary in English and an English dictionary must spell out each word. If something is very regular and users or computer programs can be expected to know it, there is no need to list such things in the dictionary. We need to list those pieces of information which are unpredictable and idiosyncratic with respect to the rules or knowledge available elsewhere in the system. A dictionary really stores only the exceptions.

The problems are more complex when we come to meanings. Firstly, printed dictionaries meant for human use give meaning descriptions using natural language sentences. This causes a chicken and egg problem in NLP. The purpose of an NLP program may be to 'understand' natural language sentences but, in order to do so, the NLP system is required to 'understand' the meaning descriptions given in the lexicon!

In monolingual dictionaries, the meanings are given in the same language as the language whose words are being described. Hence, use of such dictionaries requires that the users be already familiar with that language to some extent. Bilingual dictionar ies provide descriptions and/or give equivalents for words of one language in another language. We can also have multilingual dictionaries where for each word of one language, equivalents may be given in several other languages. In any case, since today's computers do not understand any natural language, meanings given in natural languages are essentially useless for computers.

Most printed dictionaries adhere to the general principle of reducing complex concepts into a composite of primitive ones, avoiding straight cases like (the apocryphal) "recursion : see recursion"! Dictionary builders may be simply told to use the simplest words in describing the meanings of other words or they may even be given a pre-specified list of simple words to use for the purpose. Many dictionaries claim that they use only a small number of simpler words (sometimes even giving a listing of such words), that these words have been used only in their 'central' meanings, that only easily understood derivatives are used in the meaning descriptions and syntax used is simple. This reduces the chicken and egg problem to the boot strapping problem. But where do we start? We still need to be sure that the description language is 'understandable'. We will have to specify what is meant by 'central' or 'core' meaning and exactly what morphologically derived forms are used. One may have to think of mapping the meaning descriptions given in natural language sentences onto some system of formal semantics and represent the meanings in a certain scheme of knowledge representation. Various issues in knowledge representation including representational adequacy and parsimony arise. These problems remain largely unsolved.

We may take the stand point that computers need not understand the meanings of words or sentences to perform well in a given task domain. A typical example of such a scenario is machine translation. A dictionary meant for machine translation simply lists the source language terms and their equivalents in the target languages. Elaborate descriptions, explanations and examples are avoided and more or less one-to-one substitutable equivalents are listed. Either a single most common, most neutral, most widely applicable equivalent can be given, hoping that it fits fairly well in most contexts, or a list of possible equivalents given in order of their presumed effectiveness in various contexts. MT proceeds by simply substitution of equivalent words hoping that meanings will be preserved.

Most NLP applications today do not attempt to go to meaning level at all. Dictionaries need not contain meanings then. Pragmatic knowledge is also usually not included in a dictionary, but the distinction between lexical semantic knowledge and general pragmatic knowledge is hazy.

From a computational point of view, completeness and consistency are desirable. We cannot include "November" and exclude "December". The list of function words and other closed-class words must be complete. Redundancy should be minimized. Circular definitions must be avoided. A detailed analysis by computer points to many places where such requirements have not been met in many good printed dictionaries. For example, in one dictionary 'body' is defined as 'the whole of a person' and used in a different sense in defining 'parliament' as 'a law-making body'. In another dictionary a 'box' is defined as 'a container' and then a 'container' as 'a very large, usually metal box'. Circular definitions of higher path lengths are very difficult to detect.

Lay users as well as students of NLP often have a very simplistic view of dictionaries and lexicography. Developing lexical resources is considered a lower job, more akin to typing work, and nobody wants to work on these areas. There is always a fancy for big tasks such as machine translation or speech recognition. If significant progress has to be made in any of the applications of NLP, lexical resources must be given great attention. One of the purposes of this section has been to show that there is more to it than meets the eye when it comes to dictionaries.

Structure and Organization of a Dictionary

The most common organization of dictionary entries is a alphabetically sorted list of entries. Such a dictionary arranged in alphabetical order makes it simple and efficient to look up a given word. Efficient data structures and algorithms exist for searching in sorted lists of items. Data structures such as height balanced binary search trees (also called AVL Trees), height balanced m-ary trees (such as B-Trees, B+ Trees and B* trees), splay trees, TRIE etc. have been used. Readers may refer to any good text book on Data Structures and Algorithms for more details on these topics.

However, alphabetically sorted arrangement is neither essential nor possible in all cases. Not all languages use an alphabetic system of writing. Languages such as Japanese and Chinese follow an ideographic writing system where written symbols correspond more or less directly to meanings. For such languages, it would be natural to classify words into semantic classes and organize the dictionary accordingly. An ancient example of this is the *naamaliMgaanus'aasana* also known as *amarakoos'a* - a collection of nouns in Sanskrit organized into 27 major *vargas* or classes based on meaning. All words relating to plants are in one group and words relating to earth are in another. If you know something about a word, you can locate it in the dictionary to know more about it as also about many other words semantically related to it. It is interesting to note that amarakoos'a is in verse form and it was expected that every student gets the whole dictionary by-heart!

In fact a dictionary organized in terms of semantic classes could be called a thesaurus. We use a thesaurus for searching for the most appropriate word for a given situation. The idea can be extended further to build networks of words inter-related along many dimensions of relationships. Such a structure is called a WordNet. We will see more on Thesauri and WordNets in later sections.

The most appropriate organization of a dictionary depends upon the ways we intend to use it. If you wish to look up the dictionary for spellings, you do not necessarily know the correct spellings to start with and hence simple direct search would not work. You will need a tool that can find out words closely related to the given word in terms of spellings or pronunciation. Then you could search for 'seperate' to know the correct spelling as well as pronunciation or meaning of the word 'separate'. You could type-in 'paradime' to locate 'paradigm'. If you expect frequent searches for words of given grammatical categories, organization in terms of different major grammatical categories may be a better choice. Organization based on frequency of occurrence of words may be better suited in other situations.

Computationally, we must ensure that searching and processing are efficient in terms of memory space and computation time. Algorithms for searching and other kinds of processing are closely tied up with the organization and structures used.

Building electronic dictionaries

There are two major sources of information for building electronic dictionaries for NLP applications. We may use existing dictionaries as a starting point or we may use corpus based methods. We sketch both of these alternatives briefly here.

One might think of starting a new lexicographic project to create an electronic dictionary from scratch. It is obvious that creating a dictionary is an enormous task in terms of manpower, time and financial support required. It also takes a great deal of lexicographic experience to do a good job of it. If one is interested in developing a dictionary for a given NLP application, it may not always be a very good idea to start from scratch. The complexity of the dictionary building task is often under-estimated by computer scientists. It is not merely a typing job.

A better alternative is to depend on the dictionaries already available in the book form and attempt to extract and reorganize the required information. This way we are making use of the enormous amount of thought, research and experience that has gone into making these dictionaries. The information these dictionaries contain is likely to be highly reliable and authentic.

Using printed dictionaries requires typing - a time consuming, tedious and error prone task. Alternative methods of converting printed pages into electronic texts include OCR (Optical Character Recognition) and ASR (Automatic Speech Recognition). You can scan the printed pages and use an OCR system to convert the scanned images into editable texts. Similarly, you may read aloud the contents of the printed dictionary and the ASR system will recognize your speech and give you the content as electronic text. Both OCR and ASR systems are far from perfect, especially when applied to dictionaries and a substantial amount of effort will go into editing and proof reading. OCR systems have started appearing and ASR systems are still in the research stage for Indian languages.

Earlier, dictionaries were available in "Machine Readable" form, typically as typesetting tapes. These tapes could be read into the computer using a suitable device driver program. Machine Readable tapes of dictionaries are, however, basically designed only for typesetting and printing the dictionaries, not for building electronic dictionaries. This makes the process of creating an electronic version of the dictionary more complex. Nowadays, dictionaries are available in electronic form either for downloading or for interactive search from a website or in CD form. Thus there may not be any need for starting from printed texts.

Printed dictionaries are usually meant for human beings - intelligent beings with common sense and world knowledge, capable of understanding natural languages. Such dictionaries are very different from the dictionaries we need for NLP specific applications. A great deal of thought and care is required in extracting the required content and in restructuring and reorganizing this content. Available printed dictionaries are very useful resources but rarely directly usable. Substantial effort is required to develop dictionaries for NLP applications. For example, elaborate descriptions, examples and explanations are not useful for a dictionary meant for machine translation. Substitutable equivalents are required instead.

In the case of Indian languages, the lexical databases we have today are still very meager. We have nearly 150 different languages in our country and in many cases we do not even have vocabulary lists, let alone dictionaries. We do not have, even in the printed form, the required monolingual, bilingual or multilingual dictionaries. Some of the printed dictionaries available are very old and outdated. There are no thesauri even for many major languages. It is only in very recent times that electronic dictionaries and other lexical resources have started appearing. Large, comprehensive, dependable, uptodate dictionaries in electronic form suitable for NLP applications are badly required today.

Dictionaries can also be developed starting from corpora. Some of the best dictionaries for English have been developed using the corpus based methods. Large and representative corpora are useful at practically all stages of dictionary development. Corpora assist in extracting words, grammatical categories and features, contexts, meanings and word senses, usage, etc. A number of computational tools exist for analyzing corpora and extracting, filtering, sorting and checking the relevant pieces of information.

Corpora in Indian languages have started appearing. About 3 Million word corpora are now available for the major languages. These corpora are not sufficient for many applications. A 35 Million word corpus now exists for Telugu. Large scale corpora will hopefully become available in all the major languages of India soon. There will still be challenges to be overcome before good dictionaries can be developed. Indian languages, especially the languages of the Dravidian family, are characterized by an extremely rich system of morphology. What kinds of words must be listed in the dictionary and what kinds of word forms can be obtained by rules of morphology is not yet very clear. Exactly what kind of grammatical information we should provide for a given word or even the set of POS tags to use are open questions today.

2.2.2 Thesauri and WordNets

Thesaurus

In very general terms, a thesaurus is a treasury or a storehouse; hence, a repository, especially of knowledge; often applied to a comprehensive work, like a dictionary or encyclopedia. More specifically, a thesaurus is a book containing a classified list of synonyms, organized to help you find the word you want but cannot think of.

Roget's thesaurus describes a thesaurus as 'the opposite of a dictionary. You turn to it when you have the meaning already but don't yet have the word. It may be on the tip of your tongue, but what it is you don't yet know. It is like the missing piece of a puzzle. You know well enough that the other words you try out won't do. They say too much or too little. They haven't the punch or have too much. They are too flat or too showy, too kind or too cruel. But the word which just fills the bill won't come, so you reach for the Thesaurus'.

We go to a thesaurus when we have an idea, some concept or a meaning in our mind but we are unable to get the just the right word that fits our need. We have some word on hand but we somehow feel that there should be a better word, a word that says more precisely what we wish to say, a word that is best for the current context. A thesaurus usually contains an index from where we can start. We look up the the index for the tentative word we have with us, a word that approximates what we wish to say but not quite exactly. The index tells us which locations in the thesaurus we need to see. We go to those locations and hopefully we will get the word that we are looking for. At times, we get more ideas and we may want to continue searching from the words we just got and we may go on several rounds in this fashion.

The content of a thesaurus is, therefore, very similar to that of a dictionary - words and meanings. A dictionary is typically organized in alphabetical order so that you can quickly locate the word of interest and then you can get the correct spelling, pronunciation, meanings, usage, etymology and other such pieces of information associated with that word. A thesaurus, on the other hand, is organized in terms of an ontology - a hierarchy of concepts, and the words are structured into groups that convey a specific meaning. The difference between a dictionary and a thesaurus, therefore, is more of structure and organization rather than that of content. In other words, dictionaries are typically semasiological in direction, i.e., name to notion or form to content, whereas thesauri are typically onomasiological i.e., notion to name or content to form.

Both the dictionary and the thesaurus contain words of a given language and the meanings. Given this, it makes a lot of sense to consider a dictionary and a thesaurus as simply two different views of the same data, rather than as two entirely different entities. Why should we store the same words, once structured as a dictionary, and then again structured in a different way as a thesaurus? Especially when we are talking of electronic dictionaries and thesauri, it appears to be a good idea to store the words only once and provide two different indexing mechanisms, one to use the words as a dictionary, and another to use the same words as a thesaurus. We have seen that *amarakoos'a*, the Sanskrit dictionary, is actually organized in terms of semantic groups. All you need is an efficient indexing mechanism so that you can also look up words based on spellings rather than meaning classes.

Constructing a thesaurus is not an easy job. It requires, like other lexicographic works, an in-depth and thorough understanding of words, their meanings and behavior. It also requires a great deal of time and effort even with all the modern information technology tools we have today. Developing a suitable ontology is itself a huge task. Whether we see the world through the language we use or we look at the language in terms of our real world experiences is not a point for debate here but surely the two are closely related. Any attempt to classify the words of a language and impose a structure on them amounts in some sense to an attempt to classify and structure the whole world. There is no single best way to do this and whichever way you do this, there is something to gain and something to lose. Striking a good trade-of among various competing possibilities is a difficult challenge. Once the ontology is designed, selected or adapted, the entire set of words in the language needs to be grouped into semantic classes so that they can be placed suitably in the hierarchy. Developing thesauri takes a lot of time and effort. No wonder there are no thesauri at all for many languages even till date. For example, Kannada, a language spoken by more than fifty million people and with vast and rich literature dating back to at least 9th century AD, had no thesaurus till date.

Given this scenario, technology for automatic construction of thesauri is of great current interest. An automatically constructed thesaurus may not be as good as one that is carefully handcrafted by lexicographers. But it can serve an immediate need. Also, a thesaurus so generated can be viewed as a raw material for linguists and lexicographers to do further research and development. The contents of a thesaurus is similar to the content of a dictionary, only we also need some way of grouping together semantically related words. Here we show how a thesaurus can be automatically constructed from a suitable bilingual dictionary. We show some examples from a Kannada thesaurus constructed by us recently.

To construct a thesaurus automatically, the data needed include the words of the language, the grammatical categories and other relevant features, and the meanings. Different words may have same spellings and a word may have many meanings. It is important to keep these things in mind while developing a thesaurus. Perhaps the best single source of all these required pieces of information is a bilingual dictionary of equivalents. Target language words given as equivalents to a given source language word could be expected to be semantically closely related if not synonymous. Thus by a suitable indexing technique, we should be able to extract related words and hence form a thesaurus. The following skeleton of an algorithm shows how such an indexing can be obtained:

ALGORITHM:

INPUT: A BILINGUAL DICTIONARY OF EQUIVALENTS

OUTPUT: A THESAURUS

#First Create a Reverse Index:

For each entry in the dictionary with head word W
For each the categories i = C_1, C_2, ... C_n
For each of the meanings j = M_1, M_2, ... M_p
For each synonym k = S_1, S_2, ... S_q
index(i,j,k) = W
Create the thesaurus index:
For each word W
For all HW = index(i,j,W)
synset(i,j,W) = synset(i,j,W) Union (i,j,X) for all index(i,j,X) = HW

Note that the algorithm keeps the synsets separately for each category and each meaning and thus users should be able to locate the word they are looking for without mixing up different grammatical categories or different senses of a given word. The algorithm can be implemented efficiently using suitable data structures and hashing techniques. It takes only a few minutes to generate the complete thesaurus on a desktop personal computer. The thesaurus so generated may then be enhanced, enriched and refined further.

We show below examples from a thesaurus for Kannada generated automatically from an available English-Kannada dictionary. The dictionary itself was developed for the purposes of machine aided translation and as such gave more or less substitutable equivalents. Several possible equivalents were listed in the dictionary to give maximum choice for the users of the machine translation system. These semantically related words have been grouped together to construct the thesaurus. No in-depth analysis has been performed, only simple re-grouping of words.

nooDu :

Synset	Category	Sense
paris'iilisu	v	LOOK
diTTisu	v	LOOK
kaaNu	v	LOOK
tooru	v	LOOK

mane :

Synset	Category	Sense
kaTTaDa	n	BUILDING
sadana	n	HOUSE
gRha	n	HOUSE
nivaasa	n	RESIDENCE
vaasasthaana	n	RESIDENCE
vaasa	n	HABITATION
iruvu	n	HABITATION
biiDu	n	HABITATION
vasati	n	HABITATION

cikka :

Synset	Category	Sense
svalpa	a	LITTLE
koMca	a	LITTLE
tusa	a	LITTLE
giDDa	a	SHORT
kuLLa	a	SHORT
mooTu	a	SHORT
saNNa	a	SMALL
puTTa	a	SMALL
kiriya	a	SMALL
kSudra	a	SMALL
puTaaNi	a	TINY
kaDime	a	LESS
eLeya	a	YOUNG
hareyada	a	YOUNG
yauvanaavastheya	a	YOUNG
yuvakanaada	a	YOUNG

FIG 2.2 Examples from a Machine Constructed Kannada Thesaurus

Here the different meanings and usages are indicated by English words. This was a natural choice since the starting point was an English-Kannada dictionary.

Clearly, the words we get from this thesaurus are not always exactly synonymous. The whole idea of a thesaurus is to provide a tool to the user to explore the semantic space of words by offering terms that are related in some way to the given word. Users are often not looking for exact synonyms, they are in fact looking for terms that that fit the particular usage on hand.

WordNet

WordNet is an on-line lexical reference system whose design is inspired by psycholinguistic theories of human lexical memory. English nouns, verbs, adjectives and adverbs are organized into synonym sets, each representing one underlying lexical concept. Different relations link the synonym sets. WordNet was developed by the Cognitive Science Laboratory at Princeton University. Similar efforts are now going on for many other languages of the world.

WordNet groups together words into synonym sets called synsets. Various types of relationships between synsets are depicted. Some of these relationships are:

- *Hypernym:* The generic term used to designate a whole class of specific instances. Y is a hypernym of X if X is a (kind of) Y. A rose is a kind of a flower.
- *Hyponym:* The specific term used to designate a member of a class. X is a hyponym of Y if X is a (kind of) Y.
- *Meronym:* The name of a constituent part of, the substance of, or a member of something. X is a meronym of Y if X is a part of Y. A finger is a part of a hand.
- *Holonym:* The name of the whole of which the meronym names a part. Y is a holonym of X if X is a part of Y.
- *Troponym:* A verb expressing a specific manner elaboration of another verb. X is a troponym of Y if X is to Y in some manner. Limping is a kind of walking.

Here is the search result for the word "table" from WordNet:

The noun "table" has 6 senses in WordNet.

1. table, tabular array - (a set of data arranged in rows and columns; "see table 1")
2. table - (a piece of furniture having a smooth flat top that is usually supported by one or more vertical legs; "it was a sturdy table")
3. table - (a piece of furniture with tableware for a meal laid out on it; "I reserved a table at my favorite restaurant")
4. mesa, table - (flat tableland with steep edges; "the tribe was relatively safe on the mesa but they had to descend into the valley for water")
5. table - (a company of people assembled at a table for a meal or game; "he entertained the whole table with his witty remarks")
6. board, table - (food or meals in general; "she sets a fine table"; "room and board")

Clearly, WordNets are very useful lexical databases. Many word sense disambiguation programs use the WordNet as the primary basis for defining sense classes as also for determining word senses based on the information and examples contained in this lexical database. Some work has been initiated for developing WordNets in Indian languages too.

The more recent Berkeley FrameNet project aims at creating an on-line lexical resource for English based on frame semantics and supported by corpus evidence. The aim is to document the range of semantic and syntactic combinatory possibilities (valences) of each word in each of its senses, through computer-assisted annotation of example sentences and automatic tabulation and display of the annotation results.

FrameNet is in its name obviously modeled after WordNet, and the intention has always been for FrameNet to be both a dictionary and a thesaurus, much in the sense that WordNet is. A major difference is that the FrameNet database is founded on corpus attestations, and that it includes examples, taken from the corpus, of each sense and each grammatical variant of each word in each sense, going far beyond the *'Someone __s something'* patterns found in WordNet. It also differs from WordNet in recognizing relationships among words in a single frame that are of different parts of speech.

Ontology

The term ontology is used in different disciplines with somewhat different connotations. Philosophers have been using this term for a long time, and AI researchers have borrowed and used the term in a somewhat different sense. Ontologies, as used in NLP and related disciplines is simply an organization of concepts and their inter-relationships. The crucial point is that an ontology is defined in terms of concepts, not words of a particular language. Concepts are generally independent of language and hence a given ontology is expected to be useful for various languages. Oftentimes the concepts are represented using words of a particular language but they are concepts, not words nonetheless. The organization of words in a hierarchical structure in the Roget's thesaurus could be considered an ontology.

One may think of a general ontology of the whole world or smaller, specialized ontologies that are relevant for particular domains of applications. There is no single perfect way of describing the world, or a sub-world for that matter. There is thus always a question of which way of structuring the concepts is the best? For NLP applications, the criteria would naturally be in terms of the applicability and suitability for specific applications. A structure restricts and limits the focus of attention and guides our search. If the structure is well designed, it takes us to the right places with minimal effort and thus useful. If the structure is not good, it may lead us away from the goal, confuse us or prevent us from reaching the goal quickly. Thus design of ontologies is a complex mix of science and art.

2.2.3 Morphology

Morphology is the study of structure, properties and formation of words. We are all familiar with the notion of a word - *apple, eat, good* are English words. We can similarly name words in other languages. Words form one of the most fundamental units of linguistic structure. As children we learnt to speak single words and as we grew up picked up thousands of words and a variety of information associated with those words. The list of all the words of a given language is referred to as its *lexicon*.

When we hear somebody speak our language, we can recognize the words as they speak. When we read printed text, we can see the words neatly laid out on paper separated by spaces. Existence of words seems obvious. Yet, if you listen to a language that you do not know, you will hear only a continuous blur of sounds and you find it hard to recognize individual words. You tend to think the speaker is speaking too fast. Recognizing individual words from a continuous stream of sounds when somebody speaks is an extremely complex task. The ability to recognize words constitutes a major part of language comprehension. When you "know" a language, you have mastered the art of recognizing words without effort. You will have in fact understood many properties associated with words albeit unconsciously.

What is a word?

Is there a need at all to give a formal definition of a word? Let us see. *Apple* is surely a word but what about *apples?* A dictionary of English language is very likely to list the 'word' *apple* but is very unlikely to list the 'word' *apples.* Should we define words based on their listing in a dictionary? Do we then say *apples, eating* etc. are not 'words'? Should we consider *compute, computer, computing, computability, computerize, computerization, computerizable. computerizability* as unrelated and independent words in their own right? In that case, are we not losing the inter-connections among their meanings and thus a good deal of generalization? Is *ice-cream* one word or two? The notion of a word is more complex than we may initially tend to think. Let us try by giving some definitions for a word and see the implications.

1. A Word is a Sequence of Characters

Look at printed text. A word is simply a sequence of characters separated by spaces. A character is any letter of the alphabet, a punctuation mark or any other special symbol such as

', %, (, $

This definition is not very precise. What exactly do we mean by spaces? In computer typed texts, a space can be a blank space or a tab space. We may not actually have a space at the beginning or end of a line of text and so the invisible *newline* character must also be considered a kind of space. The beginning of a text file and the end of a file also function as word separators or terminators. A good definition must therefore list the set of possible delimiting characters.

Words are usually made up of only alphabetic characters and so we may have to treat all punctuation marks and other special symbols as delimiters. Quote marks are not part of the words but then do we consider *Rama's* as one word or two? Is *'s'* a word? Hyphens may have to be included as part of words but one must not confuse hyphens with dashes or the minus sign!

It is also important to make it clear that a word is a sequence of non-delimiting characters - otherwise we will be allowing spaces inside words. However, if you wish to treat compound words like *ice cream* as single words, then spaces must be allowed. When do we allow spaces and when not?

It is clear that there can be no ideal or perfect definition. Different applications require different treatments. If one were tokenizing a C program, the set of delimiting and non-delimiting characters can only be decided based on what constitutes a valid token in C language. Given a set of delimiting and non-delimiting characters, however, it is possible to efficiently segment texts into words. The following diagram shows how:

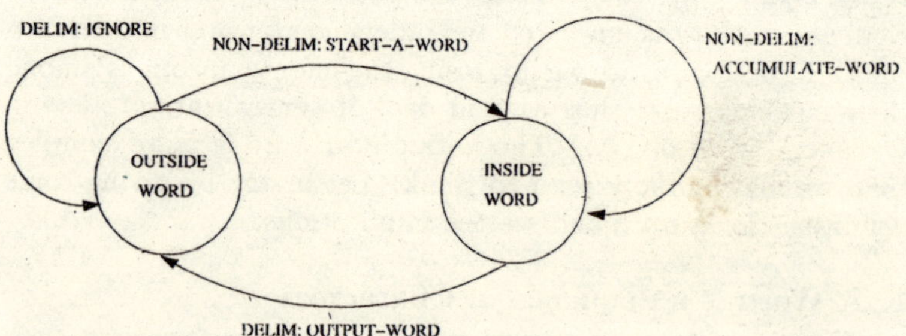

FIG 2.3 Tokenization into Words

Finite State Machines:

Let us digress a bit into Finite State Machines. A Finite State Machine, or a Finite State Automaton as it is also called, is a finite set of states interconnected by directed labelled arcs. One of the states is designated as the start state and some of the states may be designated as terminal states. Such a machine can be used to recognize strings that belong to a particular language. We start from the start state and for each symbol in the given string, we make a transition from the current state to a new state to which there is an arc labelled with that symbol. When we have finished reading all the symbols in the given string, if we end up in any of the terminal states, we say the machine accepts the given string. Otherwise the string is rejected. The machine is therefore an abstract characterization of all the strings of a language and can therefore be called a grammar. Every finite state machine defines a grammar. Languages recognized by finite state machines are called Regular languages.

Note that the above diagram for tokenization into words is not exactly a finite state machine. It has a finite number of states, in fact just two states. The starting state is "outside word". There is no terminal state. Thus there are no strings accepted by this machine. The arcs are labelled with DELIM and NON-DELIM and can be understood as sets of arcs, one for each specified delimiting and non-delimiting symbol in the alphabet. The arc labels are augmented with actions to be taken while making the transition. No such augmentation is permitted in a Finite State Machine. Nonetheless, formulating the problem along these lines helps us in making good designs and implementations. We may, for example, have a single variable called "current-state" and allow it to take one of the two values "INSIDE WORD" and "OUTSIDE WORD". The variable is initially assigned the value "OUTSIDE WORD". Each token in the input is either a DELIM or a NON-DELIM and we can only be in one of the two states. Thus there are only four possibilities to consider. Accordingly state transitions are made, that is, the value of the current-state variable is set. Actions such as START-A-WORD, ACCUMULATE-WORD and OUTPUT-WORD can be written as separate functions and called during the appropriate state transitions. We thus have a very simple, neat and generic solution that can be easily understood and adapted to a variety of tokenization requirements.

It is possible that there is more than one arc going out from a given state and labelled with the same symbol. Further, we may allow ϵ arcs, arcs that allow us to make a state transition without consuming any input symbol. The machine is then called a Non-Deterministic Finite State Automaton (NDFA or NFA). If there is no such non-determinism, the machine is called a Deterministic Finite State Automaton (DFA). For every NFA there is an equivalent DFA and hence NFAs are not in any sense more powerful than DFAs. We can start with either a DFA or an NFA based on our convenience and convert the NFA into an equivalent DFA as and when desired. There is also a procedure by which an equivalent minimal DFA (that is, a DFA with minimum number of states) can be constructed for any given DFA. Also Regular Expressions are equivalent to Finite State Machines. We thus have a powerful set of techniques to help us define grammars precisely and recognize strings of the corresponding languages efficiently. Recognition of strings using a DFA can be done with linear time complexity and hence about the fastest one can do.

Finite State Machines capture Regular Languages. Natural languages have been shown to be not regular but it is possible to divide the problem so that some parts become Regular. Many important aspects of structure at the level of words and some aspects of structure of sentences can be captured using Finite State Machines. In particular, linear precedence, repetition, alternatives and optional items can be handled elegantly using Finite State Machines. Finite State Machines form a sound theoretical basis for dealing with these aspects of structure of natural languages. Systems designed and implemented based on the principles of these Finite State models can be simpler, neater and more efficient in terms of both grammar development and the recognition or parsing algorithms. A lot of work done so far in Indian languages are completely ad-hoc, based on hoch-poch pieces of program code. There is no point in going for such ad-hoc programming when good theoretical models exist. Readers are advised to refer to books on Theory of Computation for more details of Formal Languages, Grammars and Machines.

Finite State Machines are Regular Expressions are equivalent. Many good operating systems and programming languages provide support for regular expressions. Many basic tools including text editors allow regular expression based searching, replacement, matching, filtering etc. You can do with a few simple commands what would otherwise require a lot of programming. All students and researchers interested in NLP must be encouraged to master these basic tools. To give just one example, we can take a sentence as input and break it into a list of words by using a single simple command in Perl:

```
$words = split(/\s+/,$line)
```

Here the line is split into words using one or more white space characters as delimiters. You could of course replace the regular expression
$s+$ with any other regular expression to perform a different split. If something could be done in one line, how do we justify hundreds of lines of hoch-poch program code that is not based on any sound theoretical principles? There is too much of ad-hocism in NLP in India today.

Let us get back to the question of what constitutes a word. The above definition of a word based on spelling treats structurally and semantically related words as independent words in their own right. *'eat', 'eats', 'eating', 'eaten', 'ate'* are all different, independent words. Significant generalizations in language are lost. There are languages where words are written together without intervening spaces. Not all languages use alphabetic or syllabic writing systems. Some use ideographic system. The notion of a character, then is not as simple as we may initially imagine. As such, this definition of word is far from perfect.

2. A Word is a What is Listed in a Dictionary

A dictionary lists the words of a language and for each word provides associated information such as pronunciation and meanings. We often refer to a dictionary to know the meaning, pronunciation or to confirm the spelling.

Dictionaries normally do not list all the inflected forms of words. There may be too many of them. Readers are expected to possess some knowledge of the morphology of the language. Only a few peculiar or potentially confusing cases may be explicitly mentioned. Morphological generalizations are implicit in a dictionary. The word *'baker'* may be listed and its meanings given but the generalization regarding forming nouns by adding *-er* to verbs, the nature of semantic relations between the associated words, exceptions and deviations from this canonical semantic relation etc. are not within the scope of dictionaries. A dictionary does not help to guess the meanings of new words either. Words of a language are under constant change. New words get in, existing words get new shades of meaning, some words go into the oblivion. Proper names, acronyms etc. may not be listed in the dictionary. No two dictionaries agree fully. Using dictionaries as a basis for defining words is also far from perfect.

3. A Linguist's Definition

There are many facets to a word. Consider the word *apple*. The word apple has to be spelled a-p-p-l-e. Only this particular string of alphabets constitutes a valid spelling for the word - any other sequence of alphabets is at best a spelling error. The word apple has a specified pronunciation, a specified sequence of sound units. Then there is a meaning. An apple is a kind of fruit with so and so properties. A grammatical category may also be associated. As we shall see, grammatical categories are also meanings, only very broad and general meanings applicable to a whole class of words.

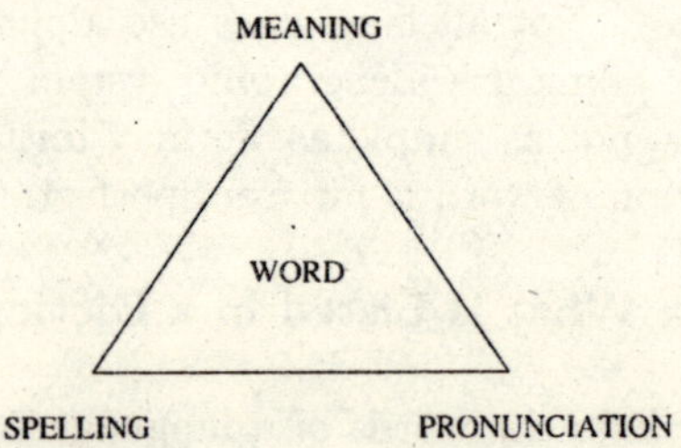

FIG 2.4 Words: Meanings, Spellings and Pronunciations

Note that a few words may have more than one permitted spelling. *Grey and gray* are both acceptable. So are *defence and defense.* British and American spellings may vary - *colour, color*

Sometimes words having the same spelling may have completely different meanings: The word *bark* has two entirely different meanings, one as a verb and the other as a noun. The word *bank* has several very different meanings - bank of river, bank as a financial institution, a bank of filters - all of them being nouns. *Project* as a verb and *project* as a noun mean very different things. In this case in fact the pronunciations are also different. Spellings are not the most important aspects of words. Spellings are required only for writing down words. Words exist even if we never write them down. Not all languages of the world have a script. Sounds are more fundamental than spellings. It is worth noting that Indian languages have always given primary importancc to sounds at all levels, even at the level of scripts.

The mapping between spellings and sounds can be highly systematic or largely ad-hoc. English spellings are quite chaotic. Although with some experience one can get a general feel for how to spell words, there are many exceptions and there is no other go than to simply memorize all cases. Indian scripts are phonetic in nature and what we write is to a very large measure the same as what we speak. Thus there are hardly any spelling rules.

There are a few onomatopoeic words in many languages where the sounds themselves signal the meaning - *buzz, hiss etc.*. Nevertheless, the mapping between sounds and meanings in general is also largely arbitrary. Why should a chair be spelled c-h-a-i-r or pronounced as chair? Why not as l-i-m-b-a-g-o or r-i-c-h-a? There is no logic or rule or principle. People at some point of time have chosen some arbitrary sounds to represent objects or whatever they want to talk about and we have to simply accept that. Language is a means of communication and if we wish to communicate effectively, we must all follow a common code. Sounds being completely arbitrary, we should not consider sounds as the most fundamental aspects of words.

Of the three basic properties of words namely spellings, pronunciation and meanings, linguists consider meaning to be the primary aspect. Words have totally different sounds and spellings in different languages, yet we are able to find equivalences because they signal the same thing, they mean the same thing. Meanings form the core aspect of words, not spellings or pronunciations. The most important aspect of the word *apple* is its meaning. Why is apple spelled that way or pronounced that way? Why not some other spelling? Why not some other sound sequence? Pronunciations and spellings are arbitrary. Linguists therefore define words as *(arbitrary) mapping between sounds and meaning.*

Thus it is more appropriate to think that there are several different words, with different meaning, that so happen to have the same spelling and pronunciation *bank*. It is not that the word *bank* has two or more different meanings, rather two or more different words have one spelling. Different words with same spelling and/or pronunciation are called *homonyms* (for "same name"). Further, the term *'homograph'* is used when the spellings are the same and the term *'homophone'* is used when the pronunciations are the same.

It is also possible for one word to have many closely related meanings or senses. Consider the word *play*. This word can mean, among other things (sampled from Merriam-Webster Dictionary), a game or sport; the conduct, course, or action of a game; a particular act or maneuver in a game as the action during an attempt to advance the ball in football, the action in which cards are played after bidding in a card game, the moving of a piece in a board game (as chess); one's turn in a game (it's your play); a recreational activity - especially the spontaneous activity of children; absence of serious or harmful intent (said it in play); the act or an instance of playing on words or speech sounds; an act, way, or manner of proceeding (that was a play to get your fingerprints); a operation or activity (other motives surely come into play); a brisk, fitful, or light movement (the gem presented a dazzling play of colors); free or unimpeded motion (as of a part of a machine) or the length or measure of such motion; scope or opportunity for action; the stage presentation of an action or story; a dramatic composition (drama). There are many meanings but the meanings are all related in some way. Here it would not be appropriate to think that there are many different words all spelled as p-l-a-y. Instead, it is better to think that this one word p-l-a-y has so many related meanings. The phenomenon of one word having several related meanings is termed *polysemy*. Many of the most common, simple, frequently used words are highly polysemous. Look at any dictionary to find out how many meanings these simple words have. It is a wonder that we are able to get the correct sense without any difficulty. Computers have serious difficulties in identifying the correct sense of a word even when the context is known.

Words are *arbitrary mapping between sounds and meaning*. This definition is also not entirely satisfactory. Phrases and sentences are also sound sequences with meaning. Also there are 'words' which do not appear to have any definite meaning. What is the 'meaning' of the word *it* in *it is raining*? Should contractions be treated as one word or several? What about compound words? Linguistics offers techniques to answer such questions in a scientific and systematic manner. For example, notions such as *internal stability* and *external mobility* are used. If it is one word, it must not be possible to insert something in between. If it is one word, it must always move as a single unit.

The concept of a word is not as simple as we may tend to think in the beginning. It is generally agreed, however, that there are units called words in most languages of the world. We can talk of words. We can, hopefully, find words in spoken and written language. We can work with words as units of structure and meaning. We can consider bigger units made up of several words and subword units that together make up individual words. Words are a reality.

Words, Phrases, Compounds

We have defined words as mappings between sounds and meanings. This definition does not help us to develop algorithms or computer programs to break a given sentence into its constituent words. The goal of many NLP applications is to start from given texts and then analyze the text to explicate structure and hence meaning. We do not know the meanings to start with, meanings are hopefully what we can get to at the end of the whole process. We need to start by breaking sentences into words, then perform a dictionary look-up or morphological analysis and may be some syntactic analysis before we can think of meanings. It is common practice in NLP, therefore, to use our first definition based on spaces as delimiters to initially tokenize given sentences into words. Let us call the 'words' so obtained as *tokens* to distinguish between meaning based definition of words. If we wish to identify words as meaning units, we may have to either group together several such tokens into one or break one into several as required. Dictionary and morphology provide guidance in this process. A clear distinction between phrases and compounds is essential to identify words in texts.

i) Compounds:

Sometimes two or more tokens form a single unit of meaning and hence a single word. Examples of such multi-token words are *'white house'* and *'high school'*. The two tokens in these examples cannot be treated as independent units in their own right because the meaning of the group is not simply a combination of the meanings of the individual tokens. A white house is not simply any house which is white and a high school is not any school which is high in altitude. The two tokens in each of these cases form single units of meaning and hence single words. Such multi-token words are called *compound words* or simply *compounds*. A compound is a word that consists of more than one free morpheme. The Sanskrit term for compounds is *samaasa*. Sanskrit has a very productive mechanism for compound formation. A vast majority of words found in any text are complex compounds consisting of several words. If you simply tokenize a Sanskrit text and look up the tokens in any standard dictionary, you will find that a majority of the tokens will not be found in the dictionary at all. Only if you can understand the meanings and appropriately break the compounds into the constituent parts, you will be able to locate those parts in a dictionary. There are many types of compounds in Sanskrit based on how meanings can be understood. Interested readers may refer to any book on Sanskrit grammar for more details of compound formation in Sanskrit.

Whether we write the words of a compound as tokens separated by spaces or as one token is a matter of convention. You will generally find a lot of variations. Some English compounds are written with spaces in between, some are written as single tokens and sometimes the constituent parts are joined by hyphens. *Rowboat, devil-may-care* are also compounds, the former written as one token and the latter hyphenated.

The most important point to note about compounds is that the meaning of the whole is a complex function of the meaning of the constituent parts. If we treat *white house* as any *house* that is painted *white*, we have composed the meanings of the words *house* and *white* to get the meaning of the word *white house* in a simple, straight forward way. Since by *white house* we normally mean a special building where the President resides, not any house which is painted white, *white house* is not a simple sequence of two independent words but a single compound word. In compounds, meaning is not compositional.

In endocentric compounds, one of the constituents forms the head and the meaning of the whole compound is dictated by the meaning of the head. The grammatical category of the compound is also the same as the category of the head. A *doghouse* is a house, built for a dog. House is the head. Dog is only a modifier. In exocentric compounds, on the other hand, there is no head and the meaning of the compound is outside the meaning of its constituent parts. In Sanskrit these exocentric compounds are called *bahuvriihi* compounds. *bahu (much) + vriihi (rice)* means a rich man, a man owning much rice, so to say.

Identifying the correct meanings of compound words in a language like Sanskrit requires great skill and knowledge of commonly accepted conventions. Thus the compound word *das'aratha* has the two constituent parts *das'a* meaning ten and *ratha* meaning chariot. How do we combine these two meanings to correctly identify the meaning of the compound? Does *das'aratha* mean one who possesses ten rathas? Or does it mean one who built ten rathas? Or one who can simultaneously steer ten rathas? It could be any of these but the intended and generally accepted meaning is "one who has great expertise in steering a chariot and can steer the chariot in all the ten directions - North, East, South, West, the four directions in between these, and up-wards and down-wards"! The compound *tiloottama* has the parts *tila* meaning a tiny black coloured oil seed and *uttama* meaning better. Does this word mean one who is slightly better in colour than the dark oil seeds? Does this mean one who is bettered by the black oil seeds? The intended meaning is very different from any of these. *tiloottama* is a woman who is so beautiful that she is more beautiful by at least a small amount (as indicated by the tiny oil seed) than any other highly beautiful lady you can find on earth. Essentially it means the most beautiful lady. The oil seed is only used to imply a small quantity, an iota. From these examples it should be clear that analyzing the meanings of compounds is a difficult task even for human beings.

ii) Phrases:

Not all sequences of words are compounds. A *red ball* can be understood as a ball that is red in colour. Meanings are compositional and there is no compound formation. Should we then treat sentences as simply a single linear sequence of words or are there intermediate levels of description between words and sentences? In fact words can be grouped into higher level units called *'phrases'* based on structure or meaning. Phrases are typically contiguous sequences of two or more words in a sentence.

It is generally accepted that *phrases* are groups of words which behave as syntactic units. Thus we can talk of noun phrase and adjective phrase. *All sequences of words* and *intermediate levels of description* are examples of phrases found in this very paragraph. Phrases are syntactic units. Thus a noun phrase may act like the subject or object of a verb in a sentence. It is the whole noun phrase, not its individual constituent words, that fill the role of the subject or object. That is why they are treated as units.

For the sake of uniformity, we may include a single word also in the definition of a phrase. Thus a phrase is a word or group of words forming a syntactic constituent with a single grammatical function. The words in a phrase are typically but not necessarily contiguous in the surface sentence.

The constituent parts of a phrase are less tightly integrated than the constituents in a compound. Thus it may be possible to remove a part of phrase to get another valid phrase and we may also insert some more words in between. Thus *all sequences of words* is a phrase and so is *sequences of words* or just *sequences. Intermediate levels of description* is a phrase and so is *intermediate levels of linguistic description.* It is much more difficult to manipulate compounds this way.

English has a large number of phrasal verbs. *'Look after', 'look out', 'look into' and 'look up'* mean quite different things. *'Put up with'* has three tokens. The particles used in phrasal verbs are usually prepositions too. If *'Rama went after Sita'* did he simply go after Sita went or did he really go after Sita? How o we understand *'he looked up the dictionary'* and *'he looked up the chimney'*? Distinguishing between phrasal verbs and verbs followed by prepositional phrases can be tricky.

We must observe that the term *phrase* has been used in several different senses in different disciplines. Modern syntacticians have used rules such as $S \rightarrow NP \quad VP$ to indicate that a sentence typically has a Subject and a Predicate and the Subject can be a noun phrase and the Predicate, a verb phrase. Note however that the term phrase as used here can imply complex structures defined recursively. Thus while an NP can be a simple noun phrase consisting of a head noun optionally modified by one or more adjectival modifiers and an optional determiner, an NP can also include whole clauses, say, relative clauses. These clauses are more like the S above and may in turn consist of their own NP and VP. Similarly, the VP is not just a verb optionally modified by auxiliary verbs but the whole predicate possibly including several NPs, and other clauses. Phrases and Clauses are different levels of description, clauses being higher, bigger, sentence-like units composed of phrases. Mixing up phrases and clauses is unnecessary and unwise. A lot can be gained by separating phrases from clauses.

Dividing a complex problem into simpler sub-problems is a wise move indeed. The division must be into roughly equal sized parts and, more importantly, the parts must all of the same type. Only then does this divide-and-conquer strategy give us any real benefits. The assumption is that solving the constituent sub-problems and then combining the results will be more efficient than solving the whole problem in one go. This is a piece of traditional wisdom universally followed in all engineering disciplines. Sorting two arrays of 50 items and merging the results can be faster than sorting an array of hundred items. But sorting an array of 99 items and another array of one item and then combining the results hardly gives us any improvement. In fact the task of combining the results of the parts will be an added overhead

Note that our $S \rightarrow NP \quad VP$ rule violates these basic requirements of a good divide-and-conquer strategy. Although widely used in linguistic theories today, this treatment of structure of sentences appears to be fundamentally flawed. NPs are typically much smaller than VPs. In fact the VP is the whole of the sentence, except for the one NP depicted in the rule. Thus the constituents are rarely roughly equal in size. Note also the VPs may, and often do contain NPs but NPs do not contain VPs (except indirectly through an S). Hence the NP and VP cannot be of the same type. The NP here typically fills one functional role - the Subject, whereas the VP fills several - Verb, Object, Indirect Object etc. Division of a sentence into one NP and one VP does not seem to make much sense at all. In what way is 'object' less important than the 'subject'? Why not treat sentences as 'subject verb' or 'subject verb object'?

Obsession for phrase structure rules and tree structures has lead to unnecessarily complicated theories that seem to be preoccupied with solving non-existent, unreal problems. Instead of helping to uncover the underlying meanings, these syntactic theories have only further obscured semantics. There is hierarchical structure in syntax but not where modern generative linguists see. A tree structure is helpful to depict the nested structure of part-whole relationships. There is no semantic part-whole relationships between determiners, adjectives and nouns in a noun phrase. Neither the determiner is inside the adjective nor the other way round. There is no point in writing trees where one is not a part of the other in terms of meaning. On the other hand, there are indeed semantically oriented nested modifier-modified structures within noun phrases but the syntactic rules that linguists posit do not even attempt to capture these semantic relationships.

Old habits die hard. Linguists will naturally oppose all this vehemently. Nevertheless, breaking a sentence into one NP and one VP is neither essential nor the wisest thing to do. There are alternative, perhaps better ways of doing things, if only we are ready to unlearn all we have learnt and bring in some fresh thinking. To see the truth, often one must learn to think like a non-stake holder. That is not easy. Linguists have been using rules of this sort so widely and for so long now that they would find it extremely difficult to think any other way. We are stuck up with NPs and VPs and you may have to learn to live with them too. But do not hesitate to think independently. What experts say is not always correct. If everyone always follows what elders say, there would be no development.

Instead of raising a controversy over the definition of the term *phrase* NLP researchers simply prefer an alternative, less confusing terminology. Simple, non-recursive, non-nested sequences of words are called *chunks* or *word groups.* Each chunk or word group has a head. Chunks are categorized based on the category of its head. Thus we can talk of noun groups, verb groups adjective groups and so on. Note that a noun group will never include verbs and a verb group will never include nouns or whole noun groups. In simplest terms, a noun group is a noun, optionally modified by adjectival modifiers and an optional determiner.

Similarly a verb group is simply a main verb optionally modified by auxiliary verbs. A sentence is a sequence (or a set, in the so called word order free languages) of such chunks or word groups. A noun group typically fills one thematic role such as Subject or Object. A verb group fills the role of the Verb in the sentence or clause.

iii) saMdhi or Conflation:

In many languages of the world, noteworthy among them being Indian languages, we can join or conflate several words into one for the sake of convenience of pronouncing and writing together. This is known as *saMdhi* or conflation. There are no changes in meaning and saMdhi must not be confused with compounding. Words in a saMdhi can be broken into constituent parts by saMdhi rules clearly specified for each language. Thus *naanu* (I) and *iiga* (now) can be conflated to form *naaniiga* in Kannada. The meaning remains the same. The grammar remains the same. Only the rules of saMdhi formation will have to be incorporated into the system. It is of course possible to combine saMdhi and samaasa.

iv) Multiword expression (MWE):

Multi-token words and multi-word expressions are of great current interest. Here is a starter extracted from an on-going project from Stanford University. Any phrase that is not entirely predictable on the basis of standard grammar rules and lexical entries is termed a *'Multiword expression (MWE)'*. Here are some examples: *alive and well, all aboard, all of a sudden, as good as gold, at all, beat around the bush, behind someone's back, bite the bullet, bull market, by and large, enough is enough, first off, fly off the handle, good morning, in effect, in retrospect, kick the bucket, kith and kin, let the cat out of the bag, on an even keel, on show, out of action, pack one's bags, plain truth, the be all and end all of NP, to and fro, wide awake, you can't have your cake and eat it too* . MWEs are characterized by qualities such as Institutionalization / conventionalisation (process of an expression becoming recognized and accepted as a lexical item, through consistent use over time), Lexicogrammatical fixedness (formal rigidity, preferred lexical realization, restrictions on aspect, mood, voice, etc.), Semantic/pragmatic non-compositionality (there is a mismatch between the semantics/pragmatics of the parts and the whole), Syntactic irregularity (the expression cannot be parsed based on the simple morphology of the components), Non-identifiability (when first exposed to the expression, the meaning cannot be predicted from its surface form), Situatedness (the expression is associated with a fixed pragmatic point), Figuration (the expression encodes some metaphor, metonymy, hyperbole, etc, even if the nature thereof is underspecified), Proverbiality (the expression is used to describe and implicitly, to explain a recurrent situation of particular social interest by virtue of its resemblance or relation to a scenario involving homely, concrete things and relations), Informality (the expression is associated with more informal or colloquial registers) and Affect (the expression encodes a certain evaluation of affective stance towards the thing it denotes). Identifying and analyzing multiword expressions is a topic of current research interest. Interested readers will find many good resources on the web.

Traditionally, linguists discriminate between the following types of languages with regard to morphology:

- Isolating languages (e.g. Mandarin Chinese): there are no bound forms, e.g., no affixes that can be attached to a word. The only morphological operation is composition.
- Agglutinative languages (e.g. Ugro-Finnic and Turkic languages): all bound forms are either prefixes or suffixes, i.e., they are added to a stem like beads on a string. Every affix represents a distinct morphological feature. Every feature is expressed by exactly one affix.
- Inflectional languages (e.g. Indo-European languages): distinct features are merged into a single bound form (a so-called portmanteau morph). The same underlying feature may be expressed differently, depending on the paradigm
- Polysynthetic languages (e.g. Inuit languages): these languages express more of syntax in morphology than other languages, e.g., verb arguments are incorporated into the verb.

This classification is quite artificial. Real languages rarely fall cleanly into one of the above classes, e.g., even Mandarin has a few suffixes. Dravidian languages are inflectional as well as agglutinative. Moreover, this classification mixes the aspect of what is expressed morphologically and the means for expressing it.

There is a lot more to it than meets the eye:

By now you must have understood that even a simple looking task such as breaking sentences into words is really a very complex task. It is easy to build demonstration systems to give a false impression of progress and success. You might have heard people claim that they have solved all problems. Researchers must learn to see through the hype and propaganda and get straight to the ground realities. NLP is not easy. NLP should not be compared with telephones or cars. NLP requires working with meanings, NLP requires working with complex issues of human cognition. NLP can only be compared with other similar tasks that are also linked to human cognition. Have we been able to understand how we learn? Have we been able to understand how we understand speech? Have we been able to understand how we can recognize a person by his/her voice, hand-writing or a momentary glance at his/her face? May be but in a very limited way. NLP is no different. Fantastic results should not be expected. Do not fall for false claims.

It is also not a very good idea for every young researcher to jump into machine translation, information extraction, speech recognition or other such big tasks. We need to do a lot of ground work before we can see real successes in such large tasks. The computational dictionaries and morphological analyzers we have today for Indian languages are all far from perfect, far from adequate. It takes many years of real hard work to prepare a good dictionary. Developing a dictionary, for example, may not carry the same kind of appeal and respect that bigger tasks carry but if nobody takes up the basic, enabling technologies how can we ever achieve success in the big tasks? Let us hope budding researchers are able to get out of hype, understand ground realities and put in some serious effort on real core problems rather than go after name and fame.

Properties of Words

Words are arbitrary pairings of sound sequences and meanings. *Phonetics* and *Phonology* deal respectively with the physical and logical (or abstract) characterizations of sound units in a language. *Semantics* deals with the meanings of words and other larger units of language. Apart from these aspects, words also carry several other pieces of information with them. Associated with each word is some idea of how that word can be used in phrases and sentences. The word *eat* begs questions on who eats and what is eaten. *Syntax* deals with the structure of phrases and sentences. Words also tell us something about their own internal structure. Consider the word *unrecognizable.* We recognize that this word is related to *recognize* and *recognizable.* We recognize that there is no such word as *unrecognize.* We have some idea of the parts of words and how they are related to one another. *Morphology* is the study of structure and formation of words. *Pragmatics* deals with the actual usage of words, expressions and sentences in different contexts. Knowing words forms a major part of knowing a language.

There are also some properties of words that native speakers of a language may not know - how the same words are used to mean different things by different groups of people (the words *flat* and *bonnet* have very different meanings in British and American English), how words have changed over time (*deer* used to mean any animal), how words of one language are related to words of other languages (*man, mother, father, brother, daughter, two, three, September, October, November, December etc.* are related to the Sanskrit words *maanava, maatR, pitR (hence paternal), bhraatR, duhitR, dwi, tri, sapta, aSTa, nava, das'a* (hence *deca, deci* etc. too), *bandicoot* is from the Telugu word *pandikokku, juggernaut* has come from the commotion that goes on during the ratha yaatra of Lord *Jagannath* at Puri, *bank* has come from the French word *bunk* meaning a low piece of wooden furniture - behind which the money lender used to sit, and so on.)

Sometimes we know the meanings but we do not know the right words. Many people would have seen the short valance or small cornice for concealing curtain fixtures but they may not know that this is called *pelmet.* Similarly we would have come across words and we may even be using them without knowing the precise meanings. Dictionaries and thesauri are excellent sources of information about words. We must all inculcate the habit of looking up dictionaries to find out the correct meanings of words we use.

Is there any relation at all between *medical case*, *legal case*, *lower/upper case letters of the alphabet*, *jewel case*, and *suit case*? Is there a primary, nuclear meaning for the word from which we can link up and explain the meanings of other cases? Let us hypothesize. A case is really just a box but not any box. A case is a box made for a particular purpose. A jewel case is made for keeping jewels just as a suit case is made for keeping a suit. Then we can perhaps explain that legal and medical records are physically or metaphorically arranged in different cases (boxes, files, folders), and we can locate and access a particular case through a logical organization of records in different cases/files/folders. During the letter press times, the letters were kept in boxes and the lower case letters were physically kept at a lower height and upper case letters at a higher level. Lower case letters are more frequent and hence this organization into lower and higher cases was practically more convenient for picking up and composing in the letter press.

This is all just a hypothesis, we are not at all asserting here that this is in fact the case. How then do we convince ourselves that we are really right in our hypothesis and not confused by coincidences or imagination? Etymology holds the answer. Etymology is the scientific exploration of the history of a linguistic form (such as a word) shown by tracing its development since its earliest recorded occurrence in the language where it is found, by tracing its transmission from one language to another, by analyzing it into its component parts, by identifying its cognates in other languages, or by tracing it and its cognates to a common ancestral form in an ancestral language

Sanskrit words, just as in the case of other languages, often have several meanings or senses. Thus the word *hari* is used to denote Lord Vishnu as also to refer to a lion and to a bee. One way of looking at this is that the word *hari* has several senses and we need to use Word Sense Disambiguation techniques to disambiguate between the various possible meanings based on the context in which the word is used. However, this is not the way it is looked at in Sanskrit. The word *hari* is derived from a root *har* that means to take away. Lord Vishnu takes away all our sins and is therefore called *hari*. A lion also takes away something, your life. Thus a lion can also be called *hari* when used to denote its killing instincts. Similarly a bee takes away nectar from flowers and when this connotation is intended, we may call a bee *hari*. Thus the correct understanding of the senses of words is based on an appreciation of what the root means and how to interpret that in a given situation. This is not really a WSD problem as we usually formulate it. It is not that one word has several meanings. One word has only one meaning but its interpretation varies according to context. Exploring words is a fascinating topic in itself.

To know one word completely is to know practically everything. To know the meaning of the word *car* completely, you will need to know its structure and function. That means you must know about the engine, the body, the parts that make up these, their structure, function and inter-relationships. To know ignition subsystem you need to know thermodynamics, fluid dynamics and chemistry. To understand electrical subsystem you need to know all about electricity. To know a car you need to know mechanics, physics, material science, electrical engineering, chemistry, paints, plastics, rubber, ..., practically everything in the world. This is what Indian philosophy says. To know one word completely is to know practically everything. No one knows even one word completely! Yet we are all so arrogant!

How many words?

Words are finite but unbounded - new words get coined and some go into the oblivion. The numbers change but not drastically. Compare this with sentences. The total number of possible sentences is potentially infinite. No reasonable limits can be put, no reasonably complete list of all possible sentences can be made. Lists of words can be made. Dictionaries do exactly this.

There are several hundred thousand words in English. We use a small number in daily life. About a 1000 are the most frequent. A typical book may contain of the order of 5000 different words. The British National Corpus has about 100 Million tokens but only a few lakh types. (Each distinct word form is called a *type* and each occurrence of a type is called a *token*.) About 1,20,000 most frequently occurring types in this corpus give 95% to 98%

coverage. That is, given any arbitrary English text, about 95% or so of all the words in that text could be generally expected to be available in the specified word list. Of course if the text on hand is a very special kind, the numbers may go down. These are very rough figures, mentioned here only to give you some idea of the magnitude of the numbers involved.

We cannot expect any dictionary to give 100% coverage. Any real text is likely to contain proper names, acronyms, loan words from other languages, special symbols and notations, domain specific terminology etc. In many practical applications, standard dictionaries have to be supplemented with domain specific or task specific dictionaries.

Standard dictionaries of Indian languages tend to contain much smaller number of words - most dictionaries have only between 15,000 and 35,000 entries. These dictionaries tend to include words mostly from literature, not from all the major walks of modern life. You should expect a large mismatch between words found in a standard dictionary and words used in newspapers and other media. Many words used in the media today may not be found in the well known dictionaries and many words found in these dictionaries may never be used in the media language. Thus building electronic dictionaries for modern language technology applications in Indian languages needs a lot of thought and care.

We can obtain an idea about the number of types we have in a given language by performing a growth rate analysis on a text corpus. The figure below shows the growth rate of types against tokens for major Indian languages based on corpora of about 3 Million words in each language. These corpora were developed with support from the Department of Electronics, Government of India (now called Department of Information Technology) and distributed by the Central Institute of Indian Languages, Mysore. The corpora were divided into equal sized sections and type-token analysis performed on each section. The cumulative number of types is plotted against the cumulative number of tokens.

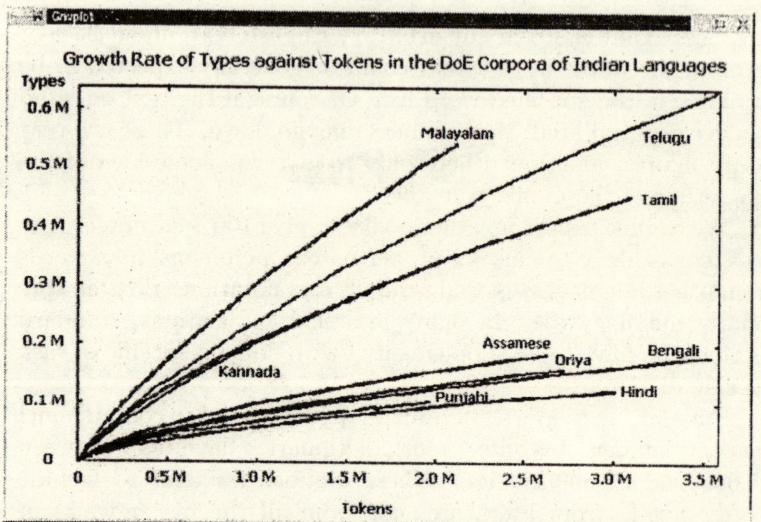

FIG 2.5 The Type-Token Growth Rate Curves for Indian Languages

It can be seen that the curves show clear signs of saturation (slowing down, flattening) for Indo Aryan languages whereas the curves for Dravidian languages show rapid growth even at the right edge. This shows that the available corpora already include most of the word forms in the case of Indo Aryan languages while many possible word forms have possibly not occurred even once in the corpora of Dravidian languages. We need much bigger corpora for Dravidian languages. It may also be observed from the curves that the number of types in Indo Aryan languages are of the order of 1,00,000 to 1,50,000 words, comparable to that of English. The number of types in Dravidian languages are at least an order of magnitude bigger. Morphologically, Dravidian languages are among the most complex languages of the world, comparable only to languages such as Finnish and Turkish.

Since words are arbitrary mappings from sounds to meanings, they cannot be derived from any more basic representation - words will have to be somehow *stored* in our mental lexicon. Computers do the same. The numbers seem to be small and today's computers should have no difficulty in listing all the words and permitting efficient search. Several good data structures and indexing techniques exit for efficient indexing of dictionaries.

However, dictionaries may list only the root forms of words and expect the morphological component to handle the inflected words. Taken together, the dictionary and the morphology must be capable of handling all word forms including inflected, derived, conflated and compound forms in various combinations. What aspects are handled by the morphological component and which types of word forms are directly listed is dictated both by theoretical considerations and simplicity and efficiency of practical implementations.

Structure of Words - Morphemes

Look at the words:

dog	dogs
cat	cats
tree	trees
cow	cows

We can see that the words in the second column are plural forms of the corresponding words in the first column. When we find a large number of examples of a particular phenomenon, we tend to generalize and make a rule - you can add an -s to an English noun to make a plural form. The words in the first column cannot be broken down into smaller parts in any meaningful way, the words in the second column can be considered to be made up of two parts - a root and the -s suffix. Such *minimal units of word building are termed 'morphemes'*. Thus dog is a base morpheme and -s is a plural morpheme. The meaning of the word dogs is in some intuitive sense, related to the morphemes it is made up of. Note that arbitrary substrings of words cannot be considered as morphemes even if they occur quite frequently. *-ceive* is not a morpheme although it occurs with many words such as *receive, perceive, conceive, deceive.*

Morphemes that can occur independently are called *free morphemes* and morphemes which can only occur in conjunction with other morphemes are called *bound morphemes.* Dog, cat, tree, cow are all free morphemes and -s is a bound morpheme. Bound morphemes that occur as *prefixes* or *suffixes* are called *affixes.*

Thus -s is a suffix and un- as in 'uneasy, unethical and unrealistic' is a prefix. In some languages, an affix may also occur in the middle of another morpheme in which case it is known as an *infix* Contracted forms like *'ll, 's, 're* are also bound morphemes. Morphemes to which affixes are attached are called *base or stem morphemes.*

At one point of time, morphemes were defined to be minimal meaningful units. It has since been realized that the meaning of a morpheme may vary based on suprasegmental features such as stress and tone, as also with the immediate context in which it occurs. That is why we have defined morphemes as simply appropriate units for word formation and avoided any direct reference to the notion of minimal units of meaning. A morpheme may be realized as one or more *morphs.* The morphs of a morpheme are called its *allomorphs.*

The morphological component must include the list of morphemes allowed in the language, the legal combinations of such morphemes, the changes that take place when morphemes are joined to form words, and the associated changes in meaning if any. We will then be able to construct complex word forms from the constituent morphemes, break words into the constituent morphemes, and understand the meaning of the whole in terms of the meanings of the parts.

There is some psychological evidence to show that morphemes are real. We think in terms of morphemes and the way they combine to form words. For example, when we work with new or foreign words, possibly not already stored in our mental lexicon, we seem to be applying the rules of word formation based on morphemes we know. There is also some psychological evidence to show that we do not always apply rules to construct or analyze words - we seem to be storing the words directly at times although we could have analyzed those words using the rules we already know. At least the most frequent word forms seem to be directly stored in the mental lexicon. One way is to think that the rules come first and then all the forms generated by such rules. The other way to think is that words are initially simply stored and as we keep seeing many similar examples we naturally generalize by learning the rules. There have also been some studies regarding automatic acquisition of morphology from training data.

Word Formation

Words in a language can be broadly classified into *Open Class* and *Closed Class* words. Closed class words include grammatical or *function words* such as articles (example: a, an, the), prepositions (example: of, in, from, with), conjunctions (example: and, but), quantifiers (example: all, some, any, each, every), demonstratives (example: this, that). Closed class words are usually small in number and fixed - new words cannot be coined or added easily. On the other hand, open class words include the *content words* - nouns, verbs, adjectives and adverbs. There are usually a large number of words in this class and new words keep getting added to language.

There are situations where function words are dropped and only content words are retained. This happens in telegraphic language, in early stages of child language, in the speech of people with aphasic brain syndrome, in classified advertisements, certain styles of poetry, in news headlines and wherever there is need to reduce a message to its essentials. Many applications in language engineering routinely remove these so called *stop words*. Stop words tend to be small and frequent.

Words connect sound sequences and meanings. New words can be created by inventing new sound sequences and pairing them with meanings, by changing the meaning of existing words, and by augmenting or modifying the sound sequence of an existing word. Let us now examine some of the mechanisms that languages provide for creating new words.

- Acronyms (a word formed from the initial letter or letters of each of the successive parts or major parts of a compound term) tend to become words in their own right. Examples: 'radar' (radio detection and ranging), 'laser' (light amplification by stimulated emission of radiation)

- Abbreviations such as 'PC' (Personal Computer) and 'CD' (Compact Disk) tend to get full word-hood

- Clippings such as 'Prof', 'Fax', 'Photo' tend to get full word-hood

- Orthographic Abbreviations such as 'Mr.', 'Dr.', 'MB' become words. Here the pronunciations may not necessarily be altered.

- New words can be created by blending existing words - 'infomercial' from information and commercial, 'edutainment' from education and entertainment, 'brunch' from breakfast and lunch etc.
- Generification: Xerox, the name of a company has now come to mean photocopying.
- Giving new grammatical categories to words: to skill your employees, to ponytail the girl, to PERT the project
- Metaphorical extension: Let me chew on those new ideas
- Compounding:

  Compound words are formed by joining together two (or more) words.

  The part of speech of a compound is the same as that of its *head*, which in English is usually the rightmost word. Compounds are sometimes written as a single orthographic word without spaces, sometimes the individual words are separated by hyphens and in other cases the words are written with intervening spaces just as in the case of phrases. English is not very consistent at this. Hyphens tend to get lost over time as the compound sets in firmly. Multi-token compounds are more often written with spaces in English and without spaces in German.

  Compounds differ from phrases along several dimensions. Some compounds have a characteristic stress pattern associated with them. In noun-noun compounds in English, the stress is usually on the first word. Thus *high*chair is a compound meaning a chair specially designed for kids and high*chair* is a phrase meaning any chair that is high. Words in a phrase can be inflected - we can say *higher chair*. We can incorporate modifiers into phrases - we can say *a very high chair*. Compounds are much more tightly integrated. We cannot say *a very white house* while referring to the residence of the president.

  It is not always straightforward to predict the meaning of a compound. *Alligator shoes* are made of alligator hide and *horse shoes* are iron shoes worn by horses.The meaning of the head of a compound is usually central to the meaning of the whole compound.

Sanskrit has a wide variety of compounds. Compounding is a very productive mechanism for word formation, so much so that in many places compounds are more frequent than simple words. Tokens tend to become very long and complex (example: nijas'ookas'aMkuutpaaTanakSamamiva = nija + s'ooka + s'aMku + utpaaTana + kSamaM + iva). A thorough understanding of saMdhi and samaasa is essential to understand a Sanskrit text.

- Derivation:

  New words can be derived by combining base morphemes with affixes. For example, the suffix -er can be added to verbs to make new words that have the meaning one who does X or an instrument that does X where X is the meaning of the verb: *sing-singer, dance-dancer, write-writer, drive-driver* etc. The study of how affixes combine with stems to derive new words is known as *derivational morphology* and affixes such as the -er agentive suffix are known as derivational affixes.

  Word formation follows systematic principles of morphology. There are rules by which complex words are built from simpler words and morphemes, and, conversely, these same rules can be used to analyze complex words into simpler ones.

  Derivation is usually associated with

  - Category Change
  - Semantic Change

Sing is a verb and singer is a noun meaning one who sings. -able derives adjectives from verbs and the derived adjectives mean 'able to be Xed' where X is the meaning of the verb. ion derives nouns from verbs. The sound often changes to sh from t. The stress of the derived word is always on the vowel just before the -ion irrespective of where the stress originally was. -able can be combined only with transitive verbs. The subject of V+able is always the object of V. Word formation rules state predictable information about complex words. That is how we understand the meanings of novel words.

Backformation

The words pedlar, beggar, hawker, stoker, scavenger, editor, swindler, burglar, sculptor existed long before people thought they were the agentive nouns derived from verbs by adding -er and created the verbs to peddle, to beg, to hawk, to stoke, to scavenge, to swindle, to edit, to burgle, and to sculpt. The words resurrection, preemption, vivisection, electrocution, television, emotion and donation existed and people created the verbs to resurrect, to preempt, to vivisect, to electrocute, to televise, to emote and to donate. One fine day, people may take the words handwriting and handwritten and create a verb to handwrite. This is called backformation, the process of using a word formation rule to analyze a morphologically simple word as if it were a complex word in order to arrive at a new simpler form. Ironically, the word backform has been backformed from the word backformation!.

Morphological rules and analyses are not merely abstract theories. Speakers produce and hearers understand new words using these rules and analyses. NLP researchers are naturally concerned more about simplicity and efficiency considerations but some understanding of the theoretical underpinnings is essential to curtail ad-hocism and arbitrariness in design and implementation.

Indian languages exhibit a rich and complex system of word formation. Sanskrit has perhaps the most elaborate system of forming words. We will not be able to give a detailed account of Sanskrit morphology here, readers are advised to consult any good grammar book. We shall only show through examples how knowing the meaning of a small number of roots guides us in knowing the meaning of more complex words. The root *jnya* is to know. *Jnyaana* is knowledge, *ajnyaana* is ignorance, *vijnyaana* is discrimination (and hence science), *prajnya* is consciousness, *jnyeeya* is the thing that is knowable, *jnyaatr* is the the knower, *jnyaani* is a knowledgeable person, *ajnyaani* is an ignorant person, *vignyaani* is a scientist. Note how the English equivalents are all morphologically completely unrelated to one another.

khaga is a bird because it *khee gacchati* goes in the sky. *paadapa* is a tree because it *paadeena pibati* drinks from the foot (absorbs food and water from the roots). *s'asa'* is rabbit. *s'as'aaMka* is one who bears the symbol of rabbit, namely the moon. *s'as'aaMkaaMka* is one who bears the symbol of moon, namely lord s'iva. Even simple words have meanings that can be understood in terms of even more simpler components. Many roots are actually single syllables. In comparison it appears that English requires us to blindly memorize a much larger number of arbitrary associations. Sanskrit sentences are small in size but convey a lot of meaning. One word in Sanskrit equals many words in English. One example will suffice: *agajaananapadmaarkaM (= agaja (aga (a + gaM = immovable, that is, mountain) + ja = born) + aanana = face + padma = lotus + arkaM = sun) = one who makes the face of paarvati (daughter of mountain king) bloom with happiness like the sun does to the lotus, that is Lord gaNees'a, son of s'iva and paarvati.* English translations are usually much larger in size. They are more like explanations than translations. Some of the greatest Sanskrit books written thousands of years ago and widely read and discussed even today are just a few dozens of lines.

In India we have the tradition of praying God by chanting his one thousand names (*sahasranaama*). Giving one thousand different names would not make any sense in a language which does not permit a lot of meaning to be encoded in words containing just a few letters. Every one of the thousand names is actually a prayer in itself, full of meaning. Each name is often just one token. Try *John, Peter, Bob, Bill, ...!* Perhaps the study of morphology and lexical semantics is more interesting and revealing than studies of syntax, at least in Indian languages.

Inflectional Morphology

Inflectional affixes result in certain changes in grammatical features without significantly changing anything else. In English, the main inflectional affixes are 1) the plural suffix -s and 2) the possessive suffix 's added to nouns, 3) the third-person-singular suffix -s, 4) the past tense suffix -ed, 5) the progressive suffix -ing, and 6) the past participle suffixes -en or -ed for verbs, and, 7) the comparative suffix -er and 8) the superlative suffix -est for adjectives. All these affixes are suffixes. Some derivational suffixes, on the other hand, are prefixes. Derivation often changes the grammatical category while inflection does not. Inflection is added after derivation if any and there can be no more derivation once an inflection is in place. Meaning changes are minimal, regular and highly predictable in inflection while this is not always so in derivation. A railway sleeper is a piece of wood (or other similar object) placed below the rails to hold the rails together, not just someone who sleeps. A waiter in a hotel is not just someone who waits (you may have to wait for the waiter instead, especially if it is a five star hotel!). Note the the inflectional suffix -ing adds a progressive sense to a verb whereas the derivational suffix -ing derives a noun from a verb. Inflected word forms that are bound by grammatical features such as personal endings are called finite forms and can be placed in tabular form of word sets known as *paradigm tables.*

Indian languages have a richer system of inflectional morphology than English. Telugu nouns are inflected for case, gender and number. Verbs are inflected for aspect, tense, gender, number and person. Apart from these, a Telugu verb may also incorporate aspectual auxiliaries, negation, causation etc. Exhaustive studies have not yet been made for many of our languages. Some experts have estimated that there can be as many as 1,80,000 different word forms that can be obtained from a single verb root in Telugu!

Meaning of Complex Words

The main justification for analyzing the structure of words in terms of the constituent morphemes comes from the assumption that the meaning of the word as a whole can be understood in terms of the meaning of its parts. Let us examine to what extent this assumption of compositionality of meaning is actually valid. Curable means able to be cured and inflatable means able to be inflated. Things are not always so simple. If a theory is questionable, it is not just that questions can be asked about that theory. Questions can anyway be asked about any theory. If you say a theory is questionable, you mean it is dubious and suspect. If a bill is payable by so and so date, it means you better pay it before the specified data. If a book is readable, it is well written. Morphology can only point to the general nature of semantic relationships between a complex word and its constituent parts. Morphology is only a guide, not a complete solution. We cannot expect to write down a set of rules that can help us to correctly analyze the meaning of any given word. It is not easy to write computer programs to analyze the meanings of words. It is not easy to automate language understanding.

New Meanings for Old Words

Native Speakers often take an existing word and extend its meaning in a recognizable way. Although no new word is added, the language is enriched just the same. For example, many terms used in ocean navigation have been extended to the realm of space exploration - ship, docking, navigation, floating, captain, crew, deck, etc. Although the situations are drastically different, people see enough similarities to make analogical or metaphorical extension. Here objects, ideas or events from one realm are described with words from a different realm of objects, ideas and events. Words like chew, swallow and digest are used in the mental realm. Indeed people show great creativity and imagination in extending the existent language into new realms of human experience.

We generally tend to extend from simpler to more complex, from general to specific, from old to new, from physical to abstract. Spacial words have been extended to temporal domain - in, on, ahead, before, etc. The terms hot and cool have been extended and applied to all kinds of domains. Meanings can also be narrowed down. The meat, which once used to stand for any edible solid food item, is now used only to refer to edible solid flesh of animals. Deer used to mean any animal but now it refer to just that one species. (Interestingly, the equivalent Sanskrit word *mRga* is used to denote either the deer or any animal) There are also cases where the connotations reverse over time, from good to bad for example, especially in slang words.

Electrical engineers know bus, conductor and driver although no passengers. Computer science uses trees, roots, leaves, nodes, branches, forests but not fruits or flowers. Analogy works to some extent but not always. Computer scientists cut off the root of a tree to obtain a forest! Mechanical engineering has adapted terms like spring, crank, eccentric, nut, bolt, screw, dog. Civil engineers talk of plan and elevation. Every subject has its own set of technical terminology some of which may also exist with very different meanings in the common vocabulary of a language.

Languages influence one another. Words of a language are borrowed by another language and gradually assimilated into the language. Languages change with time. Languages change to some extent from place to place too. The English word 'man' has come from the Sanskrit word 'maanava' or 'manuja' meaning born from 'manu' the first human being in each cycle of creation. As such, it is neutral to gender. The words 'maanava', 'manuja' and 'manuSya' are applicable to both men and women, especially in plural. Etymologically, therefore, there is no gender bias in using the word man.

Computational Morphology

There are many competing theories of morphology in linguistics. Among the descriptive models of morphology of the twentieth century, Item and Process model was considered as the precursor of modern generative phonology. Item and Process model believes that all surface stem alternants are derived from either one of the existing surface stem alternants or a hypothetical stem set up. In this model the stem is represented in the lexicon as invariant. In contrast to Item and Process model, the Item and Arrangement model allows all surface stem alternants to be represented in the lexicon. A third model known as Word and Paradigm model allows full listing of paradigms in the lexicon.

Here we have only tried to show that morphological rules and analyses seem to be real in the sense people appear to understand and use them in practice. It would be wrong, however, to think that there exist simple known rules to handle all kinds of words that we come across in various applications. A waiter in a hotel is not just any person who waits (customers wait for food etc. too). Cooker is not one who cooks but the vessel we use for cooking. Analysis of words is not always straight forward. Synthesis is also very complex. The noun form of create is creation but noun form of state is statement, not station. Computational models of morphology aim to produce exhaustive yet simple, elegant and computationally efficient solutions to morphological analysis and generation. Computational models do not guarantee correct interpretations of meanings. Instead the aim is to produce appropriate analyses for all words of a given language.

From one point of view, morphology is just a question of storing all word forms versus deriving some from a smaller, more basic set of stored words. Computationally, this translates into the usual trade-off between time and space. It takes space to store all forms of all words and it takes time to search for a given word in a large list. It also takes some space to store the rules of morphology and more importantly, it takes time to select and apply the rules. A practical solution has to find a good compromise. The productivity and uniformity of rules is the key factor. In the case of English, where there about 300 affixes for derivation, one widely used approach is to simply store all derived forms and handle only the few cases of inflection through rules. There are many idiosyncrasies in the rules of derivational morphology and it is simpler to simply store all the derived forms. Thus friend, friendly and friendliness are all directly stored in the dictionary but friends is not stored.

Several computational models have also been proposed for morphological analysis and generation. In the next section we shall briefly sketch one such model.

Morphology of Indian Languages

Indian languages in general and Dravidian languages in particular, exhibit a very rich system of morphology. While the English verb *eat* gives rise to only a few variants such as *eats, ate, eaten and eating*, the corresponding verb in Telugu can give rise to a very large number of variants. It is estimated that a single verb root may give rise to as many as 1,80,000 different possible word forms. Words in Dravidian languages like Telugu and Kannada are long and complex, built up from many affixes that combine with one another according to complex rules of saMdhi. For example, the single Telugu word *nilabeTTukooleekapootunnaaDaa?* essentially means something like "Is it true that he is finding it difficult to hold on to (his words/some such thing)?" Obviously the trade-offs are very different compared to English.

Morphology includes inflection, derivation, conflation (saMdhi) and compounding. Compound formation in modern Indian languages is not very productive. Compounds are largely frozen forms and can even be listed in the dictionary. The rules of external saMdhi are also fairly simple and well known. However, the juncture where saMdhi takes place is unknown and hence a search is involved in analysis. Nouns may be inflected for case and number and as such not too complex although more complex than that of English. The most challenging part is the verb morphology. Verbs may be inflected for aspect, tense, gender, number and person. There are also a number of forms which are independent of gender-number-person variations. These are called non-finite forms as against the finite forms that are determined by personal endings.

To illustrate the nature and complexity of morphology of Indian languages, here we give a brief sketch of Kannada morphology using a computational model known as *Network and Process Model*. Kannada is one of the four major literary languages of the Dravidian family, spoken mainly in the state of Karnataka, South India. Kannada is mainly an agglutinating language of the suffixing type. Nouns are marked for number and case and verbs are marked, in most cases, for agreement with the subject in number, gender and person. This makes Kannada a relatively free word order language. Here we take examples from the inflectional morphology of Kannada verbs. We exclude prefixation, external saMdhi and compounds in our discussions here. We give a brief account of the Network and Process Model and then give examples of Kannada inflection using this model.

In the Network and Process model, morphology is divided into two distinct but related components respectively called the *network* and the *process*. The network component includes three aspects:

- the various affixes (morphemes) that take part in the morphological processes in the language
- the associations between the affixes (morphemes) and the grammatical features (and hence meaning)
- constraints on the selection and ordering of affixes (morphemes) in various combinations

When morphemes combine, often there are complex morphophonemic changes at the juncture as specified by the rules of saMdhi. The saMdhi processes are dealt with in a separate component called the *process*. As we shall see soon, this division into the two components offers certain unique advantages over other possible approaches.

i) The Network Component:

Consider the structure of a finite verb in Kannada. In its simplest form, a finite verb form includes the root, a tense suffix and a gender-number-person suffix, taken in that order. For example

```
maaDu        + utt              + aane
Root:(do)    Tense:non_past     GNP: m,sl,p3

= maaDuttaane
  ((he) does)
```

It may be noted that the gender, number and person are all encoded into a single atomic suffix. Further, note that while Kannada has three persons, three genders and two numbers, not all combinations have distinct suffixes. Thus the suffix 'aare' indicates third person masculine or feminine plural - it is partly neutral to gender. Similarly, in first and second persons, there are no gender distinctions. Also, the gender-number-person suffixes show variations across the three tenses - there are three separate sets of suffixes, one for each tense. For example, the n-sl-p3 suffix is 'ide' in the past tense, 'ade' in the non-past, and 'udu' in the future/habitual. Thus the selection of a particular gender-number-person suffix is conditioned by the selection of the tense suffix and vice versa. Likewise, there are constraints on the selection of auxiliary verbs in the non-finite forms. For example, aspectual auxiliaries like biDu (lit. leave or let go), nooDu (lit. see), koDu (lit. give) and haaku (lit. put) occur only after a past verbal participle and other aspectual auxiliaries such as aagu (lit. become) and toDagu (lit. start) occur only in an infinitival context. The network component provides a simple and efficient scheme for incorporating such constraints. Figure 2.6 gives a sample of the network for the inflectional morphology of Kannada verbs. The first line lists all the states, the second line gives the start state and the third line lists the set of final states. The subsequent lines are triplets indicating state transitions. The first component gives the source state and the last component gives the destination state for the transition. The middle component gives the labels and the associated feature bundles.

```
0 10 20 40 50 51 52 60 70 100
0
100

0   - ASPECT:phi,iru(perfective)                      -  40
40  - TENSE:PAST:id                                   -  50
40  - TENSE:PRESENT:utt                               -  51
40  - TENSE:FUT:uv                                    -  52
51  - AGR:GNP1                                        -  60
52  - AGR:GNP2                                        -  60
53  - AGR:GNP3                                        -  60
60  - CLITIC:(question,doubt,surprise...)             -  70
70  - VOCATIVE:ammaa,appaa,ayyaa,aNNaa,akkaa,...      - 100
0   - CONCESSIVE:ruu                                  - 100
0   - CONDITIONAL:re                                  - 100
0   - IMPERATIVE:phi                                  - 100
0   - PLURAL-IMPERATIVE:i                             - 100
0   - HORTATIVE:ooNa                                  -  60
0   - PAST-VERBAL-PART:i/u                            -  10
10  - ASPECTUAL-AUX1:biDu,nooDu,koDu,haaku...         -   0
0   - INFINTIVE:alu                                   -  20
20  - APSCTUAL-AUX2:aagu,toDagu...                    -   0
0   - CAUSATIVE:isu                                   -   0
```

FIG 2.6 Kannada Morphology

A network consists of a set of states interconnected by labelled arcs. The states are given labels for convenience of reference. The states in figure 2.6 are represented by numbers. The arc labels are the affixes. Each affix also carries the associated grammatical feature bundles. There is a well defined start state and one or more well defined terminal states. To generate a complete word form from a given root, we start at the start state and move through a sequence of states until we reach one of the terminal states. During each state transition, we attach the affix on the corresponding arc label to the stem. If the affix attachment is done according to appropriate saMdhi rules as specified in the process component, we get the correct word form. Some examples are given below to illustrate this process of generation:

```
nooDu    + 0       + utt              + aane
Root:(see) Aspect:0 Tense:non-past GNP:m,sl,p3

= nooDuttaane
((he) sees)

tinnu    + i                + haaku        + i
Root:(eat) past_vbl_part. aspectual aux. past_vbl_part.

 + iru        + id        + anu        = tiMduhaakiddanu
   Aspect:Perf. Tense:past GNP:m,sl,p3 ((he) had eaten)
```

For analysis, we start from a terminal state and look for suffixes that match the labels of arcs leading to those states. By a series of affix stripping steps, we get to the root which can then be checked against the lexicon. Computationally, it is usually more efficient to work from right to left for analysis since the number of suffixes is much smaller than the number of roots. The branching factor is much smaller if we work from right to left than the other way round. Further, we work directly at the level of affixes and stems/roots, not at the level of individual letters. This adds to the efficiency of this model.

Formally, the network component is an extension of the well known Finite Automata. The major extension is in terms of the incorporation of a separate process component that combines the affixes and/or root/stem according rules of saMdhi rather than simply concatenating the strings. We thus have an augmented simple (non-recursive) state transition network. The network used here is a non-deterministic finite automaton. It is well known that for every non-deterministic finite automaton, there is an equivalent deterministic finite automaton. Recognition/generation algorithms for deterministic finite automata are of linear time complexity and hence about the fastest possible.

The network component is itself inherently bi-directional and can be used for both analysis and generation. Changes made to the network are automatically and immediately reflected in both the analyzer and the generator, saving the burden of having to build and update the two separately, ensuring consistency. This makes it possible to build an analyzer, test it on large scale data and refine accordingly. The corresponding generator is also automatically obtained without any extra effort. Observe that it is much easier to test an analyzer than a generator on large scale data.

Note that it is impossible to select, say, the past tense and a GNP suffix from the non-past set. All kinds of selectional constraints (syllabic pattern, phonological constraints, etc.) are naturally and elegantly incorporated into the augmented network. An arc is taken if and only if the conditions specified therein, if any, are satisfied. Observe that unlike ATNs, the networks used here are non-recursive and hence far simpler and far more efficient.

Networks are efficient in representation too. Common subparts can be collapsed. Loops can be represented easily. For example, from state 10 in figure 2.6 we can go back to state 0. Thus we can generate and analyze word forms such as 'maaDisikoMDubiTTuhoodanu' (maaDu + isu + i + koLLu + i + biDu + i + hoogu + 0 + id + anu). Also, networks have simple visual representations, making it easy for people to read and understand. This helps in grammar development.

ii) The Process:

Here we are concerned with the saMdhi processes that take place between affixes and/or root/stem. While in some languages the rules of saMdhi may be fairly simple and straight forward, there are languages where the saMdhi processes are quite involved. The Network and Process model incorporates a general and powerful process component.

The most common saMdhi process in Kannada is the deletion(loopa) of final vowel. If a vowel initial suffix combines with a vowel final stem/root, the last vowel of the stem/root is deleted. Thus, maaDu + id → maaDid. It must be noted, however, that Kannada has really no consonant ending words at all. Even in the case of loan word such as car, an enunciative vowel -u is added to make it 'kaaru'. A large number of Kannada words end with -u. However, the final -u in many words is only an enunciative vowel and is not real. Thus the root is 'maaD' and it is simply concatenated with 'id' to form 'maaDid' - there is really no loopa taking place. None the less traditionally the citation forms in dictionary include the enunciative vowel and a loopa saMdhi may have to be carried out in the process component.

In some cases, aagama saMdhi also occurs. For example, 'bare' + 'itu' → 'bareyitu'. Kannada does not permit vowel sequences. Hence wherever two vowels join and the first one is not enunciative and hence not deletable, a glide is inserted between the two vowels. Similarly, an -a ending human noun gets an 'n' inflectional increment: 'huDuga' + 'annu' → 'huDugananu'. The process component checks for the relevant conditions and applies the appropriate saMdhi rules for analysis or generation as the case may be.

For example, the dative case suffix in Kannada is 'ige' with the following variations: Neuter nouns ending with -a take 'kke' and -e and -i ending words get 'ge'. Thus we get

```
mara   (tree)     =>  marakke
taayi  (mother)   =>  taayige
taMde  (father)   =>  taMdege
muugu  (nose)     =>  muugige
huDuga (boy)      =>  huDuganige
```

Note that although the suffix in question is an vowel initial suffix, the final vowel in the root is not lost in the last example and an inflectional increment gets in between. Without the increment, we would have obtained huDugige which confuses with the dative case of huDugi (girl).

In the Network and Process model, one has the freedom to divide the work between the network and process components as appropriate. For example, the process component can be used as a base for incorporating all exceptions and idiosyncratic variations. This strategy of capturing the variations inside the process component has the advantage that the network needs to show only the default, major, unmarked, basic cases and thus simpler and more economical. The rule is segregated from the exceptions.

The division of labour between the network and the process components seems to be justified on several counts. The network component is declarative in nature. On the other hand, the processes of making and breaking saMdhi are more procedural. The order in which the various constraints are checked differs from analysis to generation. While generating a word form from a given root, we would know the grammatical and semantic features of the root to start with. When we are analyzing a complete word form, these aspects can only be verified after a tentative analysis is produced and a possible root is hypothesized. Hence the process component needs parallel procedures for making and breaking saMdhi. On the other hand, the network component is inherently bidirectional.

Lemmatization and Stemming

We have seen that morphology of Indian languages is quite complex. It has not been possible so far to develop high performance morphological analyzers and generators for many of our languages. Systems developed so far are far from adequate. Even simple applications such as spelling error detection and correction require the full power of morphological analysis and generation. Is there a way out?

For many applications, it is the root that contains the maximum useful semantic content and the rest of morphemes indicate grammatical features etc. which are relatively less relevant. For example, an Information Retrieval system would be substantially benefitted if all words could be replaced with their roots. This would reduce the sparseness introduced by the variations due to morphology. The crucial part is the meaning of the root.

Lemmatization is the process of extracting the root of a given word, without necessarily performing full morphological analysis. Lemmatization involves the reduction of corpus words to their respective headwords (lemmas). For example, the inflected forms "speaks" and "speaking" resulting from a combination of a single root with two different suffixes (-s and -ing) are brought back to the lemma "speak". Lemmatization is a process wherein the inflectional and variant forms of a word are reduced to their lemma - their base form, or dictionary look-up form. When one lemmatizes a text, one replaces each individual word in that text with its lemma. A text in English which has been lemmatized, then, would contain all forms of a verb represented by its infinitive, all forms of a noun by its nominative singular, and so forth. In languages other than English, this process would involve similar, though not exactly the same, principles of reduction.

Ideally, the words "am", "are", and "is", would appear as "be", and the words "car", "cars", "car's" and "cars"' would appear as "car". The phrase "the boy's cars are different colours" would appear in a lemmatized text as "the boy car be different colour". In practice, lemmatization may not, however, observe the rule of the common root in all cases, particularly in the case of irregular verbs.

Morphological analysis naturally leads us to the root but full morphological analysis can be difficult and unnecessary. There may be several morphemes and several levels of saMdhi within a word. The aim here is only to extract the root and complete morphological analysis may not be necessary for that. Thus lemmatization can be viewed as a short cut to full morphological analysis.

One may go a bit further and not even insist that we obtain correct roots. We will only be looking for common initial portions (assuming that the morphology is mainly suffixing in nature). Thus we may reduce *computer* and *computing* into *comput* - the common initial part, also called the *stem*. Note that *comput* is not a valid word at all. Yet, by reducing all related morphological forms to a common stem, we can expect improvements in the performance of NLP applications such as Information Retrieval systems. Stemming reduces the data sparseness and tightens the statistics we derive from training data.

Morphological analysis is complex and time consuming and even for languages such as English, lemmatization and stemming have been widely used to build practical NLP systems. Porter's stemmer and Lovin's stemmer are good examples for English.

Practical stemmers are far from perfect. Once a stemmer stemmed *stockings* to *stock* and when a customer was searching for stocks in the share market, the search engine retrieved a lot of documents relating to silk stockings!

As we have stated already, we do not have comprehensive, authentic, reliable, readily usable electronic dictionaries and thesauri for most of our languages in India. Morphological analyzers available are incomplete, imperfect, untested. Good spell checkers are not available. As of this writing, we do not even have good lemmatization of stemming systems for many Indian languages.

There are no benchmark standards. There is no standard test data. There are no standard testing and evaluation procedures. Researchers would not like to admit but there is a lot that needs to be done on a priority basis if we have to reach a state of global leadership in language technologies.

2.2.4 POS Tagging

We have seen that words may belong to more than one part-of-speech (POS) category. A dictionary simply lists all possible grammatical categories for a given word. It does not tell us which word is used in which grammatical category in a given context. Grammatical categories, as indicated by POS tags, are rough indicators of meaning. Thus *book* when used as a noun refers to a bound collection of pages whereas the same word used as a verb indicates the activity of reserving a ticket, a seat, etc. *Shop* as a noun refers to the store where we go and buy things and the same word when used as a verb refers to the activity of going to a shop, buying things, paying money etc. Thus knowing the grammatical category of a word in context is helpful in ultimately determining the meaning.

Of course words may have several meanings even within given grammatical categories. *Bank* as a noun may refer to the bank of a river or the financial institution where we deposit money or a bank (that is, an array) of batteries, filters etc. *Banking* may refer to the activity of transacting with a bank or the slope intentionally provided on highways near bends to compensate for the centrifugal force of vehicles while they turn. Simple verbs like *have*, *give* and *go* have dozens of senses. Knowing grammatical categories is not sufficient to know the correct meanings or senses of words but it is a useful first step. Grammar is nothing but gross, overall meaning. Nouns are things, verbs are actions or states and adjectives are properties or attributes of objects. Once a fire broke out in an army camp and the commander shouted "fire" only to find all the soldiers immediately picking up their rifles and firing! If we can distinguish between broad categories of meanings, even that much is useful.

POS taggers usually use richer sets of tags than just major grammatical categories. 50 to 80 tags are not uncommon for English. Important sub-categorizations can be brought out in defining the tag set. The Claws-5, Claws-7 and Penn Tree Bank tag sets are some of the well known tag sets for English. See Appendix for the C5 tag set used in the example given here.

POS tagging is the process of taking plain text as input and automatically marking or tagging each word with the grammatical category most appropriate to that word in the given context. The following is an example of a piece of BNC (British National Corpus) text with c5 part-of-speech markers (taken from Captain Pugwash and the Huge Reward):

```
<s c="0000002 002" n=00001>
When<AVQ-CJS> Captain<NP0> Pugwash<NP0> retires<VVZ>
from<PRP> active<AJ0> piracy<NN1> he<PNP> is<VBZ>
amazed<AJ0-VVN> and<CJC> delighted<AJ0-VVN> to<TO0>
be<VBI> offered<VVN> a<AT0> Huge<AJ0> Reward<NN1>
for<PRP> what<DTQ> seems<VVZ> to<TO0> be<VBI> a<AT0>
simple<AJ0> task<NN1>.<PUN>

<s c="0000005 022" n=00002>
Little<DT0> does<VDZ> he<PNP> realise<VVI> what<DTQ>
villainy<NN1> and<CJC> treachery<NN1> lurk<NN1-VVB>
in<PRP> the<AT0> little<AJ0> town<NN1> of<PRF>
Sinkport<NN1-NP0>,<PUN> or<CJC> what<DTQ> a<AT0>
hideous<AJ0> fate<NN1> may<VM0> await<VVI> him<PNP>
there<AV0>.<PUN>
```

POS taggers are far from perfect. The Claws tagger used to tag the BNC corpus gives two-tag combinations such as AVQ-CJS when it is not quite sure which of these two is the correct one. All it says is that the first tag in a two-tag combination is generally more likely to be correct than the second. If the tagger is unable to do even that, it issues an UNC (unknown) tag. POS taggers may not be able to distinctions between *homonymy* and *polysemy*. POS taggers generally may have difficulties in handling compounds, phrases etc. Taggers are not perfect and there may be tagging errors. Hence automatically tagged corpora must be used with care.

Dictionaries give us allowed sets of tags for words. Choosing one of the possible tags has to be done based on context. In

English words that follow the word "the" may be expected to be nouns or adjectives. Context imposes restrictions and we must exploit these restrictions to tag each word with the most likely tag. You may think of formulating context based linguistic rules. Can you get "was" after "the"? But a minute's reflection will convince you that there are too many possibilities and hard linguistic constraints cannot be found in most cases. Purely rule based WSD is not practicable. The only way is to use statistical knowledge. The category of the current word can be fixed based on the previous words. The technology used for this is based on Hidden Markov Models (HMM).

HMMs are statistical models based on simple notions such as probability of a sequence starting with a given symbol, probability of a symbol following another symbol and probability of symbols arising from different states. The probability of a sentence starting with "the" may be higher than the probability of a sentence starting with "been". Similarly, the probability of a noun or an adjective coming after a determiner may be higher than the probability of finding an auxiliary verb such as "was" after a determiner. "Pen" can be used as a verb but it is used more often as a noun. HMMs combine such basic notions of probability into a mathematically sound model. One cannot sit down and manually compute all the required probabilities for all possible words and sequences of words in a language. Algorithms exist that can automatically and efficiently compute all the required probabilities from training data. Algorithms also exist for evaluating given sequences with respect to given models and for determining optimal state sequences. See section 2.3.3 for a brief introduction to HMMs.

In the HMM formulation for POS tagging, the sequence of words in a given text would be considered as the observable states of the HMM and the sequence of associated POS tags would be considered to be the hidden states. There is an algorithm to find the optimal state sequence called Viterbi algorithm. This algorithm gives us the best possible tag sequence for a given word sequence. Note that whole sentences are tagged in one go, we do not tag one word at a time.

HMM based POS-taggers have been used quite successfully for English and other positional languages. Practical taggers use more sophisticated models. For example, tri-tag based models would consider three-tag sequences as states and consider sequences of such states.

A HMM model is built from training data. Training data here would consist of dependable POS-tagged text corpora. How would one get a POS-tagged corpus in the first place? We may have to tag a small corpus manually. Using this small manually tagged corpus as a training corpus, a HMM based POS-tagger can be built. This tagger is run on a larger corpus to produce a larger POS-tagged corpus. Since the tagger was built from small data, its performance will perhaps be not very good. Manual checking may be required to obtain accurately tagged corpus that can then be used as training data to build even better taggers. This sort of boot-strapping is common to many statistical approaches.

Suppose we tag every word blindly with the most frequent tag for that word irrespective of the context in which it has occurred. For English you will find that the tagging so generated would be about 85% correct! It appears that POS tagging is an easy job. This is just the nature of the language and the task and this level of performance can be taken as a *base line.* Performance of taggers would be judged relative to this base-line.

We have noted earlier that dictionaries usually simply list possible grammatical categories without worrying about which category is correct for a given situation. It must also be noted that dictionaries usually list only the root forms of words, not all the inflected forms. Irregular forms may be listed but all the regular inflections are rarely listed. For languages such as English that show extremely simple inflectional morphology and fairly strict word order, HMM models are naturally well suited.

Indian languages, especially the Dravidian languages are characterized by a very rich system of inflectional morphology that is also closely tied up with rich derivational morphology. Words carry a great deal of grammatical information within themselves and word order is not the main channel for expressing syntactic constraints. Sanskrit takes this to the extreme - almost any permutation of a given sentence is grammatically valid and all permutations convey exactly the same primary meaning. *Sentences are actually unordered sets of words, not really sequences.* This gives tremendous amount of flexibility to the composer in Sanskrit and poetry flows out so fluently and effortlessly. In fact it is easier to write in verse form than prose in Sanskrit. A large portion of all works in Sanskrit is in verse form. Modern Indian language lie in between Sanskrit and English in this regard but perhaps much closer to Sanskrit than to English. Any system that heavily depends on word order would be inappropriate. Morphology should be the major criterion. HMMs are perhaps not the best models for Indian languages.

HMM models may not be very suitable for Indian languages. Morphology of Indian languages has not yet been worked out fully. Preliminary tag-sets have been defined and used to build taggers for some Indian languages but there is still a long way to go. The grain size of the tag set is itself a major issue. If we include only the major categories that would be too coarse and although taggers may be built easily, tagged corpus so generated will be of very limited use. If, on the other hand, we attempt to capture all the fine variations depicted in the morphology of the words, the tag set would become very large and POS tagging will essentially boil down to morphological analysis. Should we have a hundred thousand tags? If one were to postulate morphological analysis at run time for any given application, generating and storing POS-tagged corpora would no longer serve any serious purpose.

Perhaps a hierarchical design where tags are not simple atomic symbols but composites indicating hierarchical refinements would be most appropriate for Indian languages. This would also enable development of more and more refined tag sets and POS taggers in a phased manner. An an example of this concept, the tag v for verb could be revised to include v-i and v-t for v-intransitive and v-transitive and this could further be refined to show more detailed sub-categorizations and so on.

2.2.5 Syntax: Grammars and Parsers

Languages exhibit complex structures and a detailed and systematic analysis of the structure of natural language sentences is invaluable in determining the meaning of the sentences. *Form follows function.* Knowing the structure will, hopefully, help us in knowing the meaning. Syntax is a branch of linguistics which deals with the problem of analyzing the structure of natural language sentences and producing structural descriptions. These structural descriptions can then be analyzed further by semantic and pragmatic components to obtain the meaning and the intentions behind the sentence thereby capturing the communicative aspect of language in its broadest sense.

Study of language can be roughly grouped into three levels - word level, sentence level and discourse or text level. Topics such as dictionaries, thesauri, WordNets, lexical semantics and morphology are primarily word level aspects of language. Syntax is mainly a sentence level phenomenon. Sentence level semantics is also a very important aspect. Discourse analysis and pragmatics requires going beyond individual sentences. The three levels are not water tight compartments and this grouping is only a very gross classification. There are certainly important interactions between levels and the topics may span across the levels. Nevertheless this stratification helps us to get a feel for where we stand. A lot of work has been done in Indian languages at the word level although we might still be far from perfect or even satisfactory levels of performance. On the other hand, very little has been done in syntax. There are hardly any computational grammars or parsers for Indian languages. Even such basic issues as sentence boundary identification have not been addressed in any serious measure. The sentence level forms a very important barrier and if we do not make an all out effort to pass through this stage at the earliest, there is a real danger that we will be left behind and we will not be able to compete with others in the world. Computational syntax has somehow not received the due attention it deserves in India. Given this, our treatment of syntax here will be a bit more elaborate and detailed. Young researchers are well advised to take computational syntax of Indian languages seriously.

People do not communicate using isolated sentences but with coherent pieces of discourse. Most syntactic theories, however, limit themselves to analyzing one sentence at a time, isolating inter-sentence interactions for a separate detailed study. Firstly, this is possible because sentences have their own internal syntactic structure that is for the most part independent of how and where the sentence is used. Secondly discourse level grammars have not matured to a stage where one can employ discourse grammars directly in practice for syntactic analysis of whole discourses in one stretch. We therefore generally presume that the input to the syntactic analyzer is one isolated sentence.

It is not easy to provide a precise definition of what a sentence is. Sentences are generally considered to be sequences of words that give complete meaning. Firstly this presupposes that there are identifiable things called words. Secondly it is not very clear what exactly we mean by complete meaning. If you remove some words from a sentence, it will usually appear incomplete but it is possible to remove some words such as optional modifiers, without giving a sense of incompleteness. Also, a single sentence taken from a paragraph surely does not convey the complete meaning conveyed by the whole paragraph. What do we mean by complete meaning? Phrases and clauses may also be meaningful sequences of words. We cannot perhaps hope to give a very precise definition. We have to assume that sentences are identifiable units of language, larger than words, phrases and clauses but smaller than paragraphs or discourse segments. We have to assume that such identifiable units of linguistics description exist in human languages. Similar statements have to be made about words.

Boundaries between sentences are not always explicitly clear. In English, sentences are terminated by a period, a question mark or an exclamation mark. However, the dot in decimal numbers is not a period marking a sentence boundary nor are the periods in Mr. and A. P. J. Abdul Kalam sentence boundaries. Sentences start with upper case letter but proper names also use upper case letters. Lists of proper names and abbreviations can be maintained. If a sentence end with etc. we should have actually used two dots, one for marking the abbreviation and one for marking the end of the sentence but we do not do this. Identifying sentence boundaries in English is relatively easy but not entirely trivial. There are systems built just for the purpose of breaking paragraphs into sentences and 99% plus accuracies have been obtained for English. There are no such systems for Indian languages as yet. There are also languages of the world where there are no explicit sentences boundary markers. Linguistic theories are usually oblivious to these issues but if one were to build practical NLP systems, these questions become very important.

Consider the following:

```
In order to make good for the revenue deficit I
propose to increase the tax on the following items:

  1. toilet soaps and tooth paste

  2. ready made garments (pure cotton and khadi shirts
     will however be spared. Cotton mixed garments will
     be taxed at rates as shown in table 5.4.)

  3. soft drinks, soft drink concentrates and essence;
     soda and other aerated drinks (see appendix I
     for a complete list.)

  4. furniture made up of

       a. wood (ply wood, new-wood and particle
                boards are exempted)

       b. wrought iron or steel

at the rates indicated in table 5.4 below.
```

As can be seen, items in a list may include sentences, sentence fragments or several sentences, and several such items may actually be part of one big sentence introducing the list. What are the sentences here? Where do they begin and where do they end? Should we allow nested structures of sentences or should we treat paragraphs as simple linear sequences of sentences. Headings are often not full sentences nor can be treated as parts of any other sentence. Should we allow sentence fragments? How do we define such fragments?

Boundaries between words are also not always explicitly clear. In English, words are usually separated by spaces. However, there are compounds written by convention as two or more tokens separated by spaces but linguistically to be treated as single words (example: white house, wrist watch). There are also contractions and abbreviations which are written as one token but to be treated as several (example: laser = light amplification by stimulated emission of radiation, radar = radio detection and ranging, won't = will not). The situation is more complex for some languages of the world. Languages like Sanskrit and German have very productive compounding processes and tokenizing by spaces will not do. There are also languages where there are no explicit word boundary markers at all. Note also that neither word boundaries nor sentences boundaries are clearly observable in spoken language even for English. Despite all this, we presume here that units such as words and sentences exist and it is possible to delimit discourse into sentences and view sentences as sequences of words. Syntax looks at one sentence at a time. A syntactic analyzer, also known as a parser, takes one sentence at a time as input and produces a description of the internal structure of the sentence.

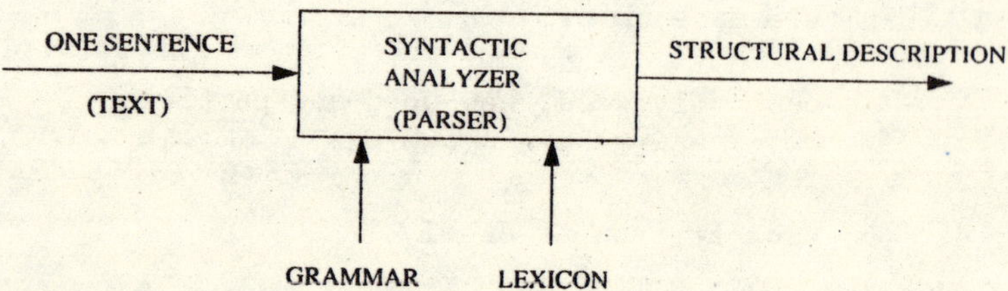

FIG 2.7 Syntactic Analysis

Syntax deals with the characterization of the structure of natural language sentences and as such can be applied for natural language understanding as well as for natural language generation. In keeping with the tradition, we have taken the analysis view point here. Needless to say, the same frameworks can also be applied for generating syntactically valid natural language sentences.

In a sense, the structural descriptions produced by the syntactic analyzer can themselves be viewed as raw representations of meaning, albeit broad and general, only waiting to be refined and perfected by subsequent semantic and pragmatic components. These structural descriptions produced by syntax only aim to capture the raw structural information content in the sentence. The structure of a sentence is analyzed in terms of meaningful parts and subparts and the relationships among these parts. The smallest parts are the words which can be mapped on to grammatical categories. Although we normally deal with grammatical categories like noun and verb as uninterpreted symbols within a syntactic framework, it should be emphasized that these categories are also essentially semantic in nature - nouns represent *things*, verbs represent *actions* and *states*, etc. When we say that 'book', 'beauty' and 'London' are all nouns, we are emphasizing what is really common between all these entities - that they are all *things* in a broad sense. Thus grammatical categories are *general meanings*, very general of course. When we need to make somewhat finer distinctions, we use the notion of sub-categorization. We divide nouns into proper nouns and common nouns, verbs into intransitive, transitive and bi-transitive verbs and so on, often making much finer distinctions than these, leading to a more detailed semantic classification. In any case, syntactic analysis is a kind of *understanding* wherein very gross, general meaning is captured. The syntactic structures that are obtained in such an analysis are representations of such very abstract and general meaning. A fundamental requirement of a syntactic analyzer is that it preserves and explicates as much of the meaning in the given sentence as possible but avoids distortions of meaning at all costs.

Syntax as an Independent Module

Syntactic analysis is a step towards the final goal of understanding or generation and it is not appropriate to deal with syntax completely independent of the final goals of NLP. What kind of analysis needs to be made and what kind of structural description should be produced are therefore dictated by the needs of the subsequent semantic and pragmatic processes. *Autonomy of Syntax* is to be interpreted to mean that syntax can be taken up and studied as an independent component within the overall system, not for its own sake, not as an end in itself.

Some researchers have argued that human mind does not process sentences in separate levels such as syntax, semantics and pragmatics and hence a good computational model must also employ an integrated holistic approach to language understanding. Others have argued and even attempted to provide evidence for the psychological reality of independent modules. It should be noted that our current understanding of semantics and pragmatics is in no way as clear and complete as our knowledge of syntax and hence even if integrated processing may finally turn out to be the ideal approach, a modular approach may be the best for the time being.

We would like to emphasize that integrated or modular processing approaches should not be confused with implementation strategies. The question is not really whether syntax, semantics and pragmatics should all be done parallelly or one after the other - this is more of an implementation strategy. The real question is whether it is reasonable to break the task into separate and independent modules. The degree of interaction between various modules is the dictating factor. The proponents of the integrated processing approach believe that the different parts interact so much and in so many complicated ways that it is not reasonable to break the task into separate modules. Others believe that it is possible to break the task into nearly decomposable modules. By *nearly decomposable* we mean that the interactions between the modules are minimal, localized and clearly understood so that we can treat the modules essentially independent of one another and take care of the interactions separately.

Of course if relevant semantic and pragmatic information was available, it could help the syntactic analyzer. Is this worth the effort and is it practically possible in all cases? To illustrate the nature of this situation, we will use an analogy. Expanding contractions such as *can't* and *won't* is essentially a morphological level (that is word level) process. However to expand the contractions in the following sentences

1) He's a nice boy

2) He's done it!

one has to get into the level of syntax. Analyzing individual words is a step towards analyzing the structure of the whole sentence. If analyzing words requires syntactic analysis, we are into a kind of a chicken and egg situation. More interestingly, we will have to get into the level of discourse analysis if we have to determine whether the *we're* in the following sentence is *we are* or *we were* since the tense can be determined in this case only based on discourse coherence.

3) We're eagerly waiting for the arrival of our new car.

Should we do discourse analysis before, or at the same time

when we are trying to find out what the words in a sentence are? We may feel it is much better to simply note down that *we're* can be either *we are* or *we were* and proceed with morphological and syntactic analyses. If the effort involved in solving a problem is too much, it is wiser to see if the problem can be left unsolved at this stage, hoping that at a later stage the necessary information would become more readily available. Postponing the solution of a problem can make it much more simpler, thereby more than compensating for the extra effort involved in keeping track of the unresolved problem all that way along. This is the sense in which we take *autonomy of syntax*. We should deal with syntax as independently as possible and simply postpone decisions that require extensive or costly processing at the semantic or pragmatic levels.

It is not always possible or desirable to try to obtain all the required information to resolve an ambiguity then and there. Obtaining all required information, even when theoretically possible, can be extremely costly in itself thereby more than compensating for the gain in being able to make the current decision correctly. Consequently, total determinism as claimed by some researchers may not a feasible goal. Yet it is highly desirable to try to attain determinism to the maximum extent possible. Determinism means being able to take the right decisions at the right time and is therefore both theoretically and practically highly desirable. This requires NLP to be viewed in terms of requirements, availability and flow of information and breaking the problem into modules accordingly.

In fact compilers for computer programming languages follow the same strategy. Programming languages are largely context free but there are aspects that are not context free. The requirement that there be one to one correspondence between the formal and actual parameters in function definitions and function calls translates to a cross-serial dependency that context free grammars and stack based push down automata cannot handle. Similarly, the requirement that variables are declared before they are used cannot be captured using context free rules. What compilers do is to ignore these non-context free aspects and go ahead with parsing using context free grammars. All the aspects that were ignored are taken care of in the next phase which is generally known as semantic analysis (although there is hardly any semantic analysis done in the true sense).

Capturing semantics of modifier-modified relationships, analysis of anaphoric references to determine exactly what refers to what and the nature of the semantic relation between the reference and the referent, attachment of prepositional phrases and subordinate clauses are examples of issues that a purely syntactic framework cannot hope to adequately model. These are all issues that lie in the border between syntax and semantics. Syntax often provides biases that can be used as default or preferred solutions but syntax may not be able to give definite solutions in all cases. A syntactic theory must, therefore, either ignore these aspects altogether or admit that what it provides is at best a partial and imperfect solution.

Most syntactic theories take the modular approach and propose an independent syntactic module. It is assumed that it is possible to deal effectively with the structure of natural language utterances using only a bare minimum of semantic and pragmatic information.

Grammars

Languages manifest as linear sequence of symbols in text or speech form. Not all sequences of these symbols are meaningful. We need to restrict the set of all possible sequences of symbols and include *all* the valid sequences and *only* the valid ones. In other words, we need to impose constraints on the possible sequences of symbols. Such a set of constraints, expressed as rules, or principles or whatever, is called a grammar. A grammar of a language is a formal specification of the valid structures in that language. Thus we may think of grammars at various levels - morphology is the grammar at word level, syntax is usually concerned with grammars at the sentence level, discourse grammars define valid discourse elements and so on. In syntax, we are naturally concerned with grammars at the sentence level.

We have defined syntactic analysis as a process of mapping a given sentence to a description of its structure. The inputs to the syntactic analysis process, also called the parsing process, include the given sentence and the knowledge of language, in particular, the lexicon, morphology and the syntactic grammar of the language. The goal of syntax in linguistics is to characterize a grammar that accepts all valid sentences and only the valid sentences. The search is for such a grammar that is simple, elegant and psychologically plausible.

Computational grammars, that is grammars meant for automatic processing in NLP applications, need to be detailed, precise and exhaustive. Syntacticians often give only samples and then get into theoretical discussions on the abstract characteristics of grammars. What we need are descriptive grammars that are very detailed and precise so that computer programs can correctly interpret and apply them. Developing wide coverage grammars has proved to be a very difficult task. The best available grammars, even for languages such as English, are far from perfect today. When it comes to Indian languages, although so much is talked about in theory, there is no computational grammar for any of our languages.

Process View and the Importance of Efficiency

It is a central working hypothesis of the linguistic theories that a non-processing characterization is desirable. Grammars can then be developed independent of how they are going to be used by parsers and generators. Details of the algorithms can be kept separate from the basic characterization of the knowledge of language. Grammars can be viewed as a specification of a space of grammatical possibilities that does not say anything about how to search that space. While this division of knowledge into *what* and *how* is a boon to the grammar writer, who can write his rules without worrying about the details of the parser, a purely abstract specification oriented view of grammar can be a very bad choice in NLP.

While linguistics has typically dealt with characterization of structures, the science of computation deals with theories of processing. NLP attempts to build computational models of the processes of understanding and synthesis. Computational paradigm is based on the belief that by developing theories of the processes involved, we will have a clear and revealing way of explaining the structure. The structures follow from the processes. A procedural view point is desirable.

One should be careful not to confuse between idealization and proceduralization. One should not mix up the issue of procedural versus nonprocedural approach with the distinction between competence and performance. Chomsky argues for a model of competence and against a performance model by talking about memory limitations, changes in intention during speech, and even physical states such as coughing, sleepiness or drunkenness. Nobody may want to build a model of performance that includes coughing and sneezing. Idealizations are done in all approaches. This is not any significant argument against the procedural view at all.

Ignoring all purely physical and psychological influences of actual performance, the remaining *knowledge of language*, the characterization of the mental competence of a speaker, also has a procedural part in it that has got to be dealt with explicitly. The knowledge of language includes not only rules, constraints and principles but also the procedural aspects of what rules, constraints or principles are applied, how, when, in what order, etc. We have seen that when people speak, they start from their aims and goals, they build up their strategies, decide the structures and words and construct natural language utterances. Similarly understanding language requires many steps. A procedural view point is both natural and essential for NLP.

It should be emphasized that knowledge does not always have to be declarative and nonprocedural. The *procedure* for multiplying two numbers is very much a part of the *knowledge* of most of us. There was a time in the history of AI where the arguments for and against procedural and declarative representations of knowledge had taken almost the shape of a controversy. It is universally agreed now that both kinds of representations of knowledge have their due share. There is no clash between the two, one complements the other.

There is no guarantee that a good purely declarative competence model automatically leads to efficient performance. A model cannot be judged purely based on the structure of the declarative grammar that it employs. A model would be good only if both the declarative and procedural components are good. We all agree that human beings are efficient processors of language and linguistics is concerned with making good models of human language cognition. How then can linguistic theories ignore the efficiency of performance? It is not enough if grammars are simple and elegant, they must also be efficient. Grammars must be *designed* for efficient processing. Efficiency is a term applicable to procedures not abstract declarative knowledge.

Thus our aim in NLP should be to develop simple and elegant grammars that are also amenable for efficient parsing. We cannot characterize grammars independent of how they are going to be used. Parsing techniques and grammars are closely tied up. Data structure and algorithms are two sides of the same coin. We have seen that developing grammars is a challenging task. Thus ease of grammar development is also a key issue.

Modern linguists within the generative tradition believe that there is a single universal grammar underlying all human languages. Children all over the world pick their language with more or less equal ease and within more or less the same amount of time. How do we explain this? There must be underlying universal principles and all the differences we see across languages of the world must be superficial differences that can be handled by setting values for some parameters. The parameters themselves must also be universal. A great deal of research has gone on within this tradition over the last 50 years or so. However, neither the universal grammar itself or its instantiations into any specific language seem to have been developed into an exhaustive, detailed and precise enough description which can be applied within a computational framework for any given language for NLU or NLG. We will not be getting into details of these theories here. Instead, we will focus on grammar formalisms that can be implemented more directly on computers.

Grammar Formalisms

Every grammar defines a language but a given language can be generated by many different grammars. All possible grammars of a language will not in general be equally simple, natural and amenable for efficient parsing. Also, grammars can be expressed in a variety of ways. Grammars can be formulated as regular expressions, finite state automata, phrase structure rules, trees and tree operations, principles, constraints, etc. How do we design good grammars?

We need a meta language, called a *grammar formalism*, to specify how exactly the grammar of a language is written. A grammar formalism is a meta language - it is a language for expressing grammars. A grammar formalism specifies the kinds of grammars that can be written, defines the structure of grammars and hence the formal properties of the syntactic system employing those grammars. A grammar formalism also suggests the nature of processing that is involved in syntactic analysis and the kinds of structural descriptions produced. All grammars written within a grammar formalism will have similar properties imposed on them by that grammar formalism. Thus instead of talking about the desirable properties of individual grammars of specific human languages, we can talk about these common properties at the level of the grammar formalism itself. Hence the design of a good grammar formalism can be taken as the central problem in syntax. Let us now see what constitutes a good grammar formalism.

What Constitutes a Good Grammar Formalism?

i) Simple Grammars:

NLP requires exhaustive, detailed and precise grammars. Computers have no commonsense and no rule can be taken for granted, however simple or obvious it may appear to be for us. Writing such exhaustive and precise grammars is not a simple task. Complexity grows exponentially with the size of the grammar. A good grammar formalism requires only a small number of simple grammar rules thus simplifying the grammar writing task. A simpler grammar would also be a better choice as a cognitive model than a grammar that employs unnecessarily complex contrivances. For example, a grammar formalism that altogether eliminates the need for long distance dependencies will surely be better than a grammar formalism that posits some complex mechanism to deal with such dependencies.

A smaller and simpler grammar also makes the parser more efficient because at each step there are only a few alternatives to consider. An efficient parser is required not only because of practical needs for fast processing but also from theoretical point of view. An efficient syntactic system is a better candidate as a model of human language processing than an inefficient one. Since computationally less powerful grammars will in general lead to more efficient parsing, the search in NLP is for the least powerful grammar that is sufficient to deal effectively with natural languages. We should not use a bull dozer if that could be done with a hand tool. We should not use context free grammars if that could be done with regular grammars. Some of the early grammar formalisms including the transformational grammar proposed by Noam Chomsky and the Augmented Transition Network (ATN) grammars proposed by computer scientists were computationally more much more complex than needed. Many of the major grammar formalisms proposed by linguists continue to be that way even today. Positing an unnecessarily complex mechanism is unwise and wasteful. Computer science provides many powerful tools for analyzing the formal complexity of grammars and the corresponding parsing systems.

Academicians and researchers have a tendency to first look for what is most interesting, rather than what is most useful. Intellectuals are motivated by love of complexity. We take pride and derive personal satisfaction in doing complex things. We even have a tendency to do simple things in a complex way. The Red Queen in Lewis Carrol's Alice in Wonderland said, "I could have done it in a much more complicated way", with immense pride. A lot of time and effort is often spent on a few rare, odd exceptional examples rather than lay primary emphasis on simple, commonly used structures. Priorities get distorted.

ii) Universality:

It has been well recognized that despite superficial differences, human languages share certain common underlying principles. Linguists are on the look out for a universal grammar - a grammar that uncovers these underlying universal features. Linguists view universal grammar as an in-born biological endowment of the human mind. They worry about things that are pre-wired into the human brain and things are learnt after birth. If a grammar could be made universal and language independent, every effort must be made to move towards that end.

From a purely practical point of view, however, we need not make any reference to the human mind at all and deal with language as people use it, not with the hypothetical language or grammar that may be there inside the mind of humans. Use of the term 'universal' then only implies the identification and separation of language independent aspects of grammar from the idiosyncratic features of individual human languages. A grammar that is largely common across human languages is theoretically very desirable even without any reference to the human mind. Recognition of these universal common properties of human languages helps us in building grammars and parsers for various human languages with a minimum of effort, with a minimum of duplication of work. A Grammar developed for one language can be easily adapted for another language. Perhaps common grammars can be developed for a whole family of languages.

A good grammar formalism should lay primary emphasis on the universal aspects of grammar and relegate the treatment of idiosyncratic features of specific languages to a secondary level. The idea is to concentrate more on the rule rather than on the exceptions. It is not as important to deal with the idiosyncratic, peculiar and infrequent constructions in specific languages as it is to deal with the more basic, common and frequent constructions elegantly and efficiently. Knowing the rule from the exception is extremely important for getting insights into the true nature of human languages and for discovering the universal nature of our languages.

iii) Good Structural Descriptions:

Let us now turn to the structural descriptions produced through syntactic analysis. One of the most commonly used representations of syntactic structure is the tree. The children of a node in a tree are also trees by definition. Thus trees show the nested, part-whole, or hierarchical relationships between different constituents. Trees used in NLP and linguistics are ordered trees - the linear order of the nodes in the tree is significant. Trees thus show linear as well as hierarchical structure of sentences. Many grammar formalisms use tree structures to depict the syntactic structure of sentences. A tree structure produced by a syntactic analyzer, also called a parser, is called a parse tree. Here is an example:

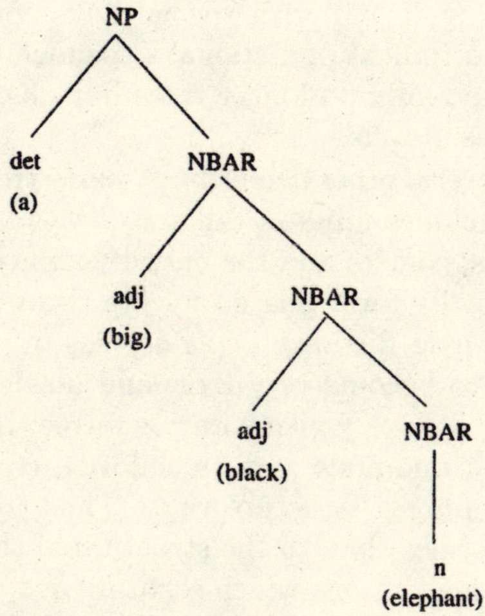

FIG 2.8 A Typical Parse Tree

In many languages, the linear ordering of nodes is sometimes significant and sometimes insignificant. These languages are called relatively free word order languages. Indian languages belong to this type. In a Telugu sentence, for example, all possible permutations of nouns are syntactically valid but typically the verb comes at the right end. Also while the nouns in a clause can come in any order, all of them must necessarily come before the nouns in the following clause. Linear order is important in some cases and insignificant in others. Trees are either ordered trees or unordered trees. Interpreting trees as ordered in some places and unordered elsewhere is not easy. Trees originate from phrase structure rules which imply strict order or constituents. Phrase structure rules and the tree structures they produce are not always the best choices.

Apart from depicting the linear and hierarchical structure of sentences, a syntactic analyzer must also determine the roles played by the various constituents in the sentence. The functional structure of a sentence depicts the assignment of functional or thematic roles to the various constituents in the sentence. Role assignment depends on functional structure constraints such as linear position, morphological inflections, agreement, subcategorization and selectional restrictions. A noun phrase may be the subject of one clause and the object of another embedded clause.

Trees cannot depict functional dependencies. So trees are often annotated and augmented with special links connecting various nodes in order to indicate functional dependencies. The resulting structures are really no longer trees but much more complex structures such as graphs.

Trees have several other demerits. A parse tree is a monolithic structure that includes units at different levels. A tree is a mess of words, phrases, clauses and the entire sentence. Consequently, parts which logically form one group are thrown far apart. All the problems of long distance dependencies originate from this. Also, trees tend to become very large and unwieldy for long and complex sentences. Every elementary subtree, that is, a subtree that includes just one node and its children, corresponds to one application of a phrase structure rule. Thus trees are closer to phrase structure rules than to the structure of the sentences. We need structural descriptions which separate out and vividly show linear, hierarchical as well as functional structure inherent in the given sentence. Trees are not the most suitable structures for depicting the structure of natural language sentences, although they are widely used.

We will now briefly sketch the merits and demerits of existing grammar formalisms. Linguistic grammar formalisms can be viewed as extensions of basic phrase structure grammars, more specifically, Context Free Grammars (CFG). Let us first understand the strengths and weaknesses of Context Free Grammars. This would help us in understanding other grammar formalisms clearly.

Context Free Grammars and Natural Languages

In the 1950s, there were major developments taking place in the field of computer science, including the development of high level programming languages. Grammars and parsers needed for compiling these programs received a great deal of importance. In his papers in 1956 and 1959, Noam Chomsky laid out the foundations of formal properties of grammars. Chomsky classified grammars based on string rewriting rules into four classes of formal complexity called Type 0 or Unrestricted Phrase Structure Grammar, Type 1 or Context Sensitive Grammar, Type 2 or Context Free Grammar and Type 3 or Regular Grammar. Context Free Grammars (CFG), the second least powerful in the Chomsky Hierarchy, were found to be ideal for dealing with programming languages efficiently. Since then a great deal of formal studies have been made on CFGs within computer science and very efficient parsing algorithms have been developed. Linguists often fail to make clear distinctions between these different formal types of grammars and simply use the term "phrase structure" rules. What they most often mean are the Context Free grammar rules. See books on Theory of Computation for more on types of grammars and their formal properties.

Context Free Grammars:

Formally, a language is nothing but a set of strings built from a given set of symbols. If the symbols are words, then a language could be viewed as sequences of words, namely sentences. A grammar specifies which sequences of words are valid or invalid. In other words, a grammar is nothing but a specification of the membership function for the set called language.

A Context Free Grammar is a 4-tuple (N,T,P,S) where N is a finite set of non-terminal symbols, T is a finite set of terminal symbols, disjoint from N, S is a special, designated symbol from N called the Start Symbol, and P is a finite set of Production Rules (or Productions), of the form $A \rightarrow \alpha$

where A is any non-terminal symbol and α is any sequence of terminal and non-terminal symbols. Unless the language itself contains the empty string, α can be required to be non-empty. Terminal symbols are the symbols that actually occur in the language and the non-terminal symbols are used for the purpose of defining the structure of the language. Here is an example grammar G:

```
NP -> det NBAR
NP -> NBAR
NBAR -> adj NBAR
NBAR -> n
```

Here NP and NBAR are non-terminal symbols and det, adj and n are terminal symbols. The string *det adj adj n* can be generated from this grammar. The set of all possible strings that can be generated from this grammar G is the language L(G) accepted by this grammar. Note that the language accepted by a CFG can be finite on infinite.

We could have added rules like

```
det -> the
det -> a
det -> an

adj -> big
adj -> small
adj -> black
adj -> white

n -> cat
n -> dog
n -> elephant
```

to directly generate sentences such as *the big black elephant* or *a small cat* or *dog*. However, it is conventional to stop at preterminal level and insert actual words through a lexical insertion process using a dictionary. This makes the grammars so much smaller.

Parsing:

The process of analyzing the structure of a given sentence using a given grammar is called parsing. Parsing can be done either *top-down* or *bottom-up*. In top-down parsing, we start from the start symbol S and repeatedly substitute non-terminal symbols by the corresponding sequences on the right hand side of matching rules until the given sentence is generated. Note that there may be several rules for each non-terminal symbol including S. Thus parsing using CFGs is essentially a non-deterministic process. In the bottom-up approach, we start from the given sentence and repeatedly substitute substrings with the corresponding left hand sides of the matching rules until the start symbol S is derived. Note that there may be many substrings that match the right hand sides of rules. Top-down or bottom-up, parsing using CFGs is inherently non-deterministic in nature. There are also parsing techniques such as chart parsing where the top-down and bottom-up parsing strategies are combined for practical advantage. Whatever the case, parsing in CFGs has an asymptotic worst case time complexity of $O(n^3)$ in general. Deterministic subclasses of CFGs exist in some cases for which the time complexity will be linear. Such special subclasses have been exploited for building grammars for programming languages but they cannot be extended easily to natural languages.

Phrase structure grammars are string re-writing grammars. We start with a string and repeatedly rewrite the string until we derive the string we are interested in. Each application of a rule to rewrite a string is called a step of derivation. The parse tree shows the end result of this process of derivation. The parse tree for the sentence *a big black elephant* is shown in figure 2.8 above. Note that the root of a parse tree always corresponds to the start symbol, the intermediate nodes correspond to non-terminal symbols, the leaf nodes correspond to the terminal symbols and any node with its child nodes constitutes one application of a rule. The node corresponds to the left hand side of the rule and the children, read left to right, correspond to the right hand side of the rule.

Strengths and Limitations of CFGs:

The merits and demerits of CFGs for dealing with human languages are now fairly well understood and it is generally accepted that CFGs do not form a good model for natural languages. Yet the study of CFGs is significant in NLP for four reasons. Firstly, significant portions of natural languages *are* context free although the whole may not be. Since our aim is to develop a grammar formalism of the least powerful type, it is important that we understand the strengths and weaknesses of CFGs. We should not employ more powerful grammars where CFGs suffice and we should clearly understand the reasons for using more powerful grammars where really required. Secondly, most of the linguistic grammar formalisms also incorporate CFGs in some form or the other, at some stage or the other. Understanding CFGs helps us in understanding these grammar formalisms. Thirdly, some of the important syntactic phenomena like long distance dependencies, cross serial dependencies and parsing of relatively free word order languages are also directly related to the powers and limitations of phrase structure rules in general and CFGs in particular. Lastly, development of other grammar formalisms can be fruitfully viewed as attempts to overcome the weaknesses of CFGs and various ways of reacting to their limitations. Keeping these points in mind, we first take up a detailed study of CFGs for natural languages.

There is a direct relationship between the generative capacity - the kinds of sentence structures which a grammar can generate or parse, and computational complexity. The most general grammar takes the largest amount of computational resources (processing time and/or memory space), and the least general grammar can be parsed with the least computing resources. It is important to note that these differences in computational complexity are not small differences. They are orders of magnitude differences. It has been natural in NLP, therefore, to look for the least powerful grammar that is sufficient for dealing with natural language sentences. Using more powerful grammars than required is wasteful, inefficient, unintelligent and thus unacceptable by both theoretical and practical considerations.

We might therefore ask ourselves whether regular grammars, the simplest type of grammars within the Chomsky Hierarchy, can be used to describe human languages. Regular grammars can handle all finite languages and also some infinite languages characterized by repeated substrings. Natural languages are commonly taken to be infinite, they involve arbitrarily deeply nested structures, not mere repetition of subparts. Regular grammars are not sufficient to capture the whole of natural languages. A formal proof exists and is based on the fact regular sets are closed under intersection. We will omit the proof here and take it for granted that regular grammars are insufficient for natural languages.

The next question would therefore naturally be whether context free grammars can be used. There are deterministic subclasses of CFGs which can be parsed in deterministic linear time. Even parsers based on general CFGs have a worst case time complexity of $O(n^3)$ where 'n' is the number of words in a sentence. Thus parsing with CFGs can be quite efficient. In the sixties, CFGs were actually widely applied to the study of natural languages. Context-free grammars were very popular as models for natural language in spite of formal inadequacies of the model for handling some of the features that occur in natural languages. The question of context freeness of natural languages has received a lot of attention. There have been many papers arguing for or against context freeness of natural languages. See the book entitled "The Formal Complexity of Natural Language" for example. As the editors of the book rightly note in the beginning of part two of their book, almost all the arguments given to demonstrate the non-context freeness of natural languages have hinged around peripheral, rare and certainly not the run-of-the-mill language phenomena. Also, as Gazdar and Pullum have pointed out in their paper in that book, many of these arguments are neither technically nor empirically sound. They contend that nobody has yet given a real proof that natural languages are not context free.

Whether natural languages are fully context free or not, is not really very important. The point of importance is, all these arguments and counter-arguments notwithstanding, *natural languages are largely context free.* We may recall that computer programming languages also have some features that are certainly not context free and yet context free grammars have been applied very fruitfully to deal with these languages very efficiently. We need to clearly understand which aspects of the syntax of natural languages are really context free and which aspects are not. We will then be able to apply more powerful grammars only where they are really required. Parsing with CFGs will be very much faster than parsing with more complex grammars. CFGs have to be used for whatever aspects they are necessary and sufficient.

From the history of the theories and models of natural language syntax, it appears that as soon as the limitations of a particular type of grammar are realized, researchers tend to jump to the next higher level of complexity. CFGs were insufficient and hence computer scientists developed ATN grammars. At the same time linguists developed the Transformational Grammars. Both of these have Type 0 power - much more than needed and much more than can be computationally handled efficiently in practice. A much better strategy to use, perhaps is to think of an appropriate way of breaking the problem into subproblems and employing the least powerful grammar that is essential for each. Natural languages are largely context free. In fact, there are aspects of natural language syntax that do not even require context free power, regular grammars are sufficient. Different strokes for different folks is the right approach.

In a formal sense CFGs have sufficient weak generative capacity to deal with almost all aspects of natural languages. Natural languages are largely context free. In a practical sense, however, CFGs have several disadvantages. Let us now look at specific syntactic phenomena to highlight these limitations of CFGs.

i) Functional Dependencies:

Languages enforce certain dependencies between the constituents in a sentence. Examples of this are grammatical agreement requirements and selectional restrictions. Thus 4) is grammatical but 5) is not, 6) is grammatical while 7) is not.

4) The students write the test
5) *The student write the test
6) The student read the paper
7) *The paper read the student

If we have to enforce these dependencies using (only) CFGs, we will be faced with two problems. For one thing, we will be forced to introduce new categories since CFGs, like all other phrase structure rules, can only generate strings of terminal symbols. (Note that we normally take grammatical category symbols as the terminal symbols when we write grammar rules, assuming that words are inserted by a lexical insertion process.) There would be singular-nouns and plural-nouns, singular-verbs and plural-verbs. There will be nouns that denote *things that can read* and nouns that denote *things which can be read.* This would cause an explosion of rules leading to very large rule sets. There would be separate rules for singular sentences and plural sentences. Computationally the syntactic system becomes extremely inefficient. Secondly, and more importantly, a simple requirement like agreement between subject and verb, which can be given in one simple statement in English, is being turned into a multitude of otherwise unrelated categories and rules. Simple generalizations are lost.

A word should be associated with a particular category purely based on its own intrinsic properties. A grammatical relation between two independent words is an intrinsic property of neither of these words. The phrase structure rules have no direct way of specifying these relations. Thus CFGs, why, all types of phrase structure rules for that matter, are unsuitable for dealing with dependencies between different constituents in a sentence. Also, the structural descriptions which CFG rules naturally generate, namely trees, cannot depict functional dependencies directly. It should be emphasized that we are not asserting that CFGs are insufficient. CFGs do have the necessary generative capacity to generate valid and only valid strings as far as such dependencies are concerned. But that is simply not the right way of doing things. Functional dependencies must be separately and explicitly specified in the grammar and clearly depicted in the structural descriptions. CFGs and trees are not the best way to do this.

ii) Relatively Free Word Order Languages

Linear order of words and phrases in a sentence may be significant - changing the order may render the sentence ungrammatical or anomalous.*I drank filter coffee* is not the same as *I drank coffee filter*. Grammars must therefore impose constraints on linear positions as required in a given language.

A sentence is a sequence of words in English and it looks almost unimaginable to view a sentence as an unordered set of words. However, there are languages of the world where order of words is the least important aspect of structure. All permutations of words in a Sanskrit sentence are grammatically valid and mean exactly the same thing. A sentence could be viewed as a set of words, not really a sequence. It is worth noting that English was also a relatively free word order language at one point of time.

There are also a number of human languages where there is considerable, though not unlimited scope for changing the order of words in a sentence without significantly altering its basic meaning (to be more precise, without altering the functional structure of the sentence). Modern Indian languages are examples of this. All of the following Telugu sentences mean essentially the same thing

8)

raamuDu	baDiki	siitatoo	veLLaaDu
Rama	school-to	Sita-with	went

9)

baDiki	raamuDu	siitatoo	veLLaaDu
school-to	Rama	Sita-with	went

10)

siitatoo	raamuDu	baDiki	veLLaaDu
Sita-with	Rama	school-to	went

The strong point of CFG is that it can effectively deal with both the linear and hierarchical structure inherent in human languages. This ability to deal with linear structure comes back as a weakness when we have to parse sentences in relatively free word order languages. Here a variety of word orderings are allowed and *linear order is not to be considered significant.* CFGs however, have no way of getting rid of their hold on linear order. A CFG rule such as

s → np1 np2 vp

asserts two independent things. Firstly it asserts that s has three constituents named np1, np2 and vp. Secondly, it also asserts, unfortunately, that np1, np2 and vp have to come in that linear order. A CFG rule cannot assert the hierarchical structure alone, without implying the order of constituents. Thus the above rule is completely different from

s → np2 np1 vp

Since both of these orders can be equally valid in some languages, we must have both the rules in the grammatical system. For rules with more number of symbols in the right hand side, many permutations may be possible and we need to include one rule for each possibility. We are in the unhappy state of being forced to take something irrelevant seriously. Having one rule for each possible permutation is like imposing a serious restriction and then having one case for each way of relaxing that restriction. Context free grammars are not the ideal for all languages. We multiply the number of rules thereby making our parser very inefficient. Note again that CFGs *are sufficient* in the formal technical sense of generative capacity but practically just unusable.

iii) Long Distance Dependencies and Movement:

Linear order of words and phrases in a sentence may be significant - changing the order may render the sentence ungrammatical or anomalous. There are valid syntactic constructions, however, where there are deviations from the usual order. Therefore these formalisms based on CFGs need to posit a *normal* or unmarked order and view syntactic constructs which deviate from the normal order as involving *movement.* The grammar is expected to specify what constituents move from which place to which place and under what conditions.

Some movements are local or bounded, as in the case of auxiliary shift in simple yes-no questions (example 11) and subject-object inversion in passives (example 12).

11) Can the company sell Pentiums now?

12) My Pentium was replaced by someone

Other types of movements take place across arbitrarily long distances and are termed *long distance dependencies.* Relative clauses (examples 13 and 14) and wh-questions (examples 15, 16, and 17) in English are examples. In these constructions a constituent from within a clause will have been removed from its normal position and moved to a different position. Long distance dependencies have been one of the serious problems for syntactic systems and various grammar formalisms have developed special techniques for dealing with them.

13) The machine which the company sold _ to me was defective

14) The machine which the company, which I believe everyone trusts,
sold _ to me was defective

15) Which computers does the company sell _?

16) Which computers does the company which I believe

everyone trusts
sell _?

17) Which computers do you think the company which I believe everyone
trusts sells _?

Historically, the concepts of movement and other kinds of transformations were introduced in order to account for the fact that sentences superficially looking different often have roughly the same meaning. So a *deep* structure, something closer to meaning than the surface structure of a sentence, was taken as the starting point and other related structures were obtained through transformations. It was soon shown that many of the supposedly meaning preserving transformations did in fact risk meaning changes and linguists had to give up the idea of linking deep structure to meaning. Linguists forgot the meaning aspect but stuck to the notions of deep and surface structures, now renamed D-Structure and S-Structure, and movement continued to be the primary mechanism of going from the D structure to the S structure. In the more recent minimalistic approach, the concepts of deep and surface structures have been completely abandoned with.

The notions of movement and other transformations are direct consequences of the employment of phrase structure rules and the corresponding ordered trees for describing the syntax of natural languages. As we have already seen, a tree is a mess of different levels of meaning units - words, phrases, clauses and sentences. In terms of linear position, the parts of a single meaning unit can be widely spaced apart. Long distance dependencies are only one type of functional dependencies and CFGs cannot effectively deal with any kind of dependency between two constituents.

If we could view sentences as sets, rather than as sequences of words (or phrases or clauses), there would be no question of any distance, long or short. Meaning of sentences is not best described in terms of length or distance, whether expressed in terms of number of intervening structures, words or in inches or meters. It looks like we are trying to solve non-existing problems.

Western grammar formalisms have been strongly influenced by languages like English where linear order constraints are very significant. Linear order has become such an all important and dominating core aspect of western linguistic models that these models have to bring in highly unnatural and unnecessary complications to deal with languages where word order is least important. If you want to work with Indian languages, the first thing you must learn to unlearn is this obsession with phrase structure rules and tree structures. Forget about word order. Forget about movement. Forget about distance. Forget trees.

iv) Cross Serial Dependencies:

CFGs can handle constituents that come linearly one after the other as well as constituents that are properly nested one inside the other. By proper nesting we mean that an inner constituent must end before the outer constituent closes. That is a last-in, first-out property must be satisfied. In English, we find some examples of cross serial dependencies, as illustrated by 18)

18) Manmohan Singh, A P J Abdul Kalam, and Rajasekhara Reddy are the Prime minister of India, the President of India and the Chief Minister of Andhra Pradesh respectively.

The 'respectively' construct 'A, B, C are D, E, F respectively' links A to D, B to E and C to F in a cross serial manner:

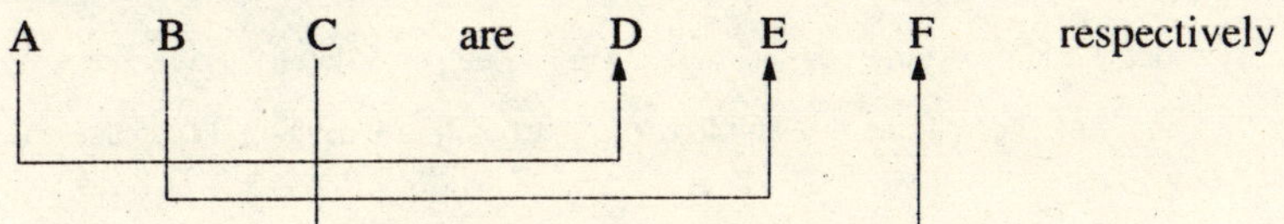

Cross serial dependencies occur in programming languages too. One example is in the requirement that the arguments must match one-to-one in a function definition and function call. Compilers simply ignore this aspect while doing the syntactic analysis of the source program and postpone the checking to a later phase. We could do the same thing for constructs like 'respectively' in English by simply taking 'A,B and C' and 'D, E and F' to be single composite constituents. It would be all right to postpone a few complex aspects to a later stage of analysis. The only thing a CFG grammar will not be able to do is to identify the links between the items in the two sets, rest of syntactic analysis can go on without any problem. The 'respectively' construct is perhaps the only example of cross-serial nesting in English. This is not a major problem.

There are languages such as Dutch, however, where we come across an infinite set of grammatically correct sentences with cross serial nesting. A way of directly dealing with them would therefore be preferable. Let us look at some examples from Dutch. Both the examples and the discussion that follows are based on Bresnan-et-al, 1982.

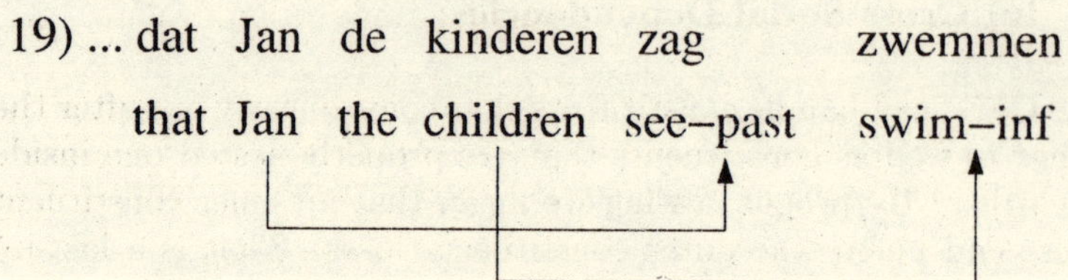

that Jan saw the children swim

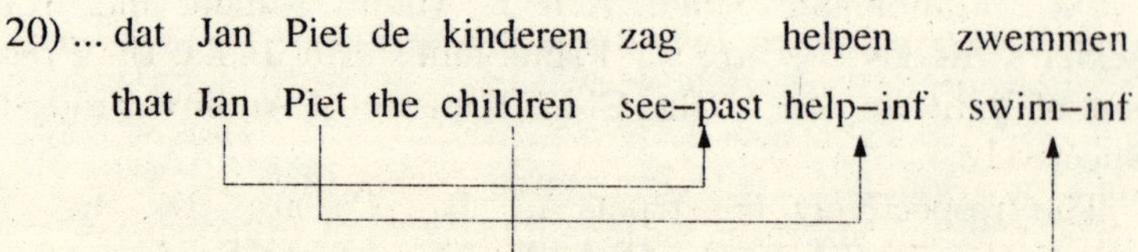

that Jan saw Piet help the children swim

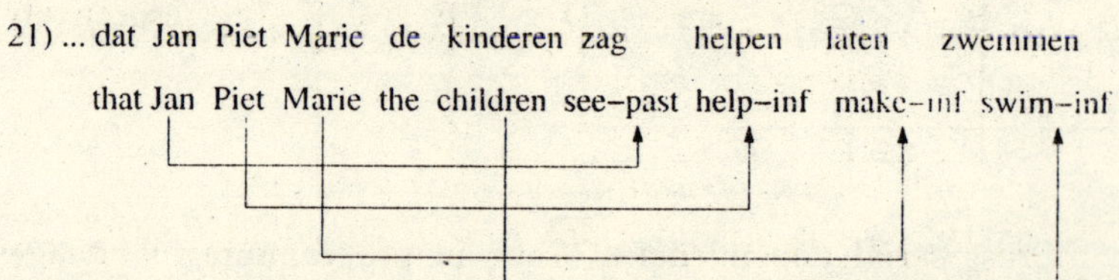

that Jan saw Piet help Marie make the children swim

There are restrictions on cross serial nestings in Dutch. The number of nps should match the number of verbs. The first np and the first verb must satisfy the basic agreement requirements. The final nps and the last verb must satisfy the subcategorization restrictions. Only a verb that is subcategorized for both a np and an infinitival complement without the complementizer *'te'* can be inserted in this cross serial fashion. There are only a finite number of such insertable verbs but they can be repeatedly used and hence there is no limit on the depth of such a nesting. It is to be noted that within these restrictions, all arbitrary permutations of the nps in the np sequence and all arbitrary permutations of the verbs within the verb sequence produce grammatical sentences:

22) ...dat Jan Marie Piet de kinderen zag helpen laten zwemmen

...that Jan saw Marie help Piet make the children swim

23) ...dat Jan Marie de kinderen Piet zag helpen laten zwemmen

...that Jan saw Marie help the children make Piet swim

24) ...dat Jan Marie de kinderen Piet zag laten helpen zwemmen

...that Jan saw Marie make the children help Piet swim

The point to note is that only the agreement between the first np and the first verb and the subcategorization restrictions between other nps and the final verb are to be encoded in the grammar. Hence it is possible to develop a CFG which can generate all these constructs. However, such a CFG will not assign linguistically correct structural descriptions to these sentences. That is, it is possible to get a CFG that sufficient to handle Dutch in terms of its weak generative capacity but it has been shown that Dutch is not strongly context free. This time we have a real restriction, CFGs are not sufficient as far as strong generative capacity is concerned.

If universality in the theoretical sense is not the main concern and the set of languages we wish to deal with do not show cross-serial dependencies in any serious measure, we may still go ahead and claim that CFGs are good enough in this limited sense of generative capacity.

v) Unbounded Branching

CFGs capture repetition through recursion. In many situations what we want is mere repetition and not recursion. For example, items in conjunction should really be all at the same level. Since there is no *a priori* bound on the number of items in conjunction, either we have to use recursive rules or make the number of rules potentially infinite. A sequence of a's can only be captured by one of the recursive rules

$A \rightarrow a\ A$

or
A → A a
along with the base rule
A → a
or by the potentially infinite set of rules
A → a
A → a a
A → a a a

and so on. Computational grammar formalisms require that the rule sets be finite and hence in general imposing nonexistent hierarchical structure through recursive rules is inevitable. CFG rules are suitable for dealing with recursion but not for handling repetition. It is worth noting that regular expressions, equivalent in computational complexity to the much simpler regular grammars, can directly and effectively deal with repetition.

Towards Better Grammar Formalisms:

In summary, CFGs impose *more structure* than really exists in some cases and *less structure* than required in others. CFGs impose linear structure when not appropriate, as in the case of relatively free word order languages. They impose too much of hierarchical structure in cases such as unbounded branching. As far as dependencies between different constituents are concerned, CFGs are unable to capture the required structural constraints effectively.

What then is good about CFGs? CFGs are excellent for handling situations where both linear and hierarchical aspects of structure are involved and nothing else is important. If hierarchical structure is not involved, we may not even require CFGs and if linear structure is itself not significant, CFGs are no good. CFGs are not the best in any situation where any kind of direct dependency between different constituents is involved. It should also be noted that going beyond CFGs and using more powerful phrase structure rules is not necessarily going to solve all these problems.

Given these strengths and limitations of CFGs, both linguists and computer scientists have endeavored to develop better grammar formalisms for handling natural languages. It would be instructive to view each of these grammar formalisms in terms how exactly they have attempted to overcome the deficiencies of CFGs and improve further. Despite the fact that several grammar formalisms have already been developed, the search for better formalisms continues. Theoretically, the available grammar formalisms are not fully satisfactory in explaining the human language faculty in all its ramifications. Computationally, the belief and hope that simpler and more efficient techniques exist, provides motivation for further search for better and better formalisms.

We will now make a brief survey of several important grammar formalisms that have made a significant impact on NLP. We start with Augmented Transition Networks (ATN) and give a sample grammar of English, adapted from Terry Winograd. This should serve two purposes. Firstly, readers will get an idea about the nature of a descriptive grammar for a language. Secondly, it should give some idea about the broad nature of issues involved in developing and using computational grammars. A set of sample sentences is given in the Appendix and the readers are strongly advised to try out each of these sentences on the grammar given here. In the latter part, we shall briefly summarize the salient features of several other grammar formalisms including the Lexical Functional Grammar (LFG), Generalized Phrase Structure Grammar (GPSG) and the Tree Adjoining Grammar (TAG). Our aim here is not to provide an exhaustive and in-depth coverage of grammar formalisms. We will be selective and very brief. Interested readers will find a good deal of literature on all aspects of syntax.

Augmented Transition Network Grammar

Augmented Transition Networks were developed in the early 1970s around the same time that linguistics was also taking a new shape with Noam Chomsky leading the generative linguistics programme with his Transformational Grammar (TG). While the concepts behind ATN existed for some time before, it was Woods who gave a formal shape to ATN. As is clear from his work, ATN came up as an alternative to, and improvement over, Chomsky's TG. While claiming equivalence to TG in power, Woods argued that ATN offered a number of advantages including perspicuity, sufficient generative power, efficiency of representation, ability to capture regularities, efficiency of operation and flexibility for experimentation. Surprisingly, linguists are hardly aware of ATN grammars.

We have seen that Context Free grammars are more powerful than Regular Grammars. Regular grammars are equivalent to Simple Transition Networks (more commonly known as Finite State Machines or Finite State Automata). CFGs are in fact equivalent to Recursive Transition Networks, state transition networks which can call one another recursively. Some of the arc labels can be labels of other networks. ATNs are obtained by augmenting RTNs with Initializations, Conditions, and Actions. Each time an arc is taken, initializations linked to that arc are performed first. The arc can be taken only if the specified conditions are met and if an arc is taken, the actions specified are performed.

A sample ATN grammar for English given below. There are basically three Finite State Networks, one for the sentence level, one for noun phrases and one for prepositional phrases. Note that these are not the usual Finite State Machines - some of the arcs are labelled with the names of other networks. Thus the networks are recursive. The arcs are associated with initializations, conditions and actions, together referred to as augmentation. The S network sets the agreement requirements while processing the subject noun phrase and cross-validates these while passing through the verb. This is essentially how ATNs take care of functional dependencies. The recursive transition networks, equivalent to CFGs, capture the linear and hierarchical structure. The augmentation deals with the functional dependencies. Study the networks and the associated arcs carefully.

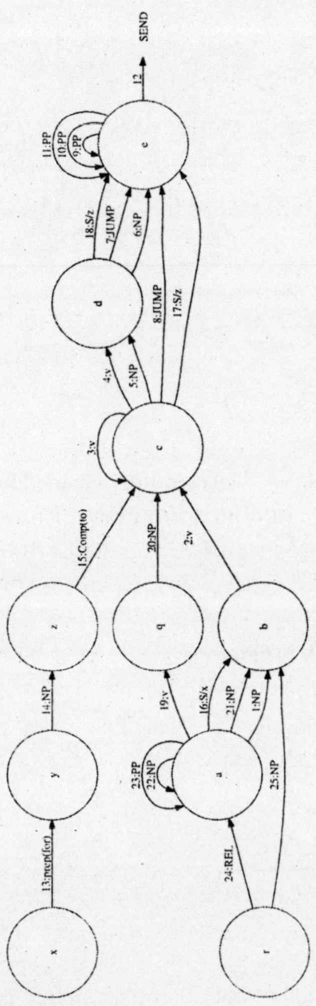

The start state is 'a'. Subject, Direct Object, Indirect Object. Main Verb, Auxiliaries, Modifiers and Question Element are the *Roles.* Voice ([Active] / Passive) and Mood ([Declarative] / Interrogative / Imperative / Relative / wh-Relative) are the *Features.*

FIG 2.9 The S Network

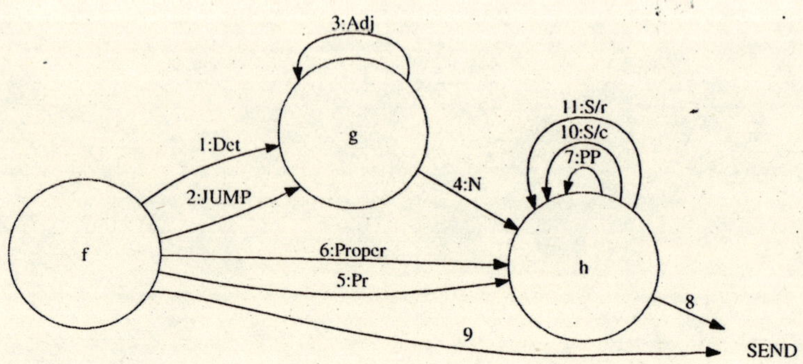

The start state is 'f'. Determiner, Head, Describers and Qualifiers are the *Roles*. Number (Singular / Plural), Person (First Second / Third) and Question(Yes / [No]) are the *Features*.

FIG 2.10 The NP Network

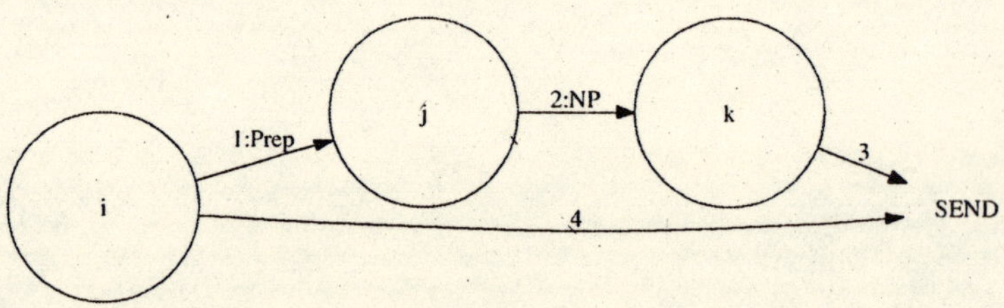

The start state is 'i'. Prep. Object and Preposition are the *Roles*.

FIG 2.11 The PP Network

The augmentation on the arcs are given below. Study each one carefully.

Arc	Augmentation
$S-1:_a NP_b$	C: Question of * is No and Mood ≠ Interrogative A: SUBJ = *
$S-2:_b V_c$	C: (Type of * is MODAL) or (Form of * is Past) or (Form of * is 3P-SL-Present and No. of SUBJ = SL and Person of SUBJ = 3rd) or (Form of * is Present and ((No. of SUBJ = PL) or (Person of SUBJ = 1st or 2nd))) A: Main-Verb = *
$S-3:_c V_c$	C: Type of Main-Verb = BE/DO/HAVE/MODAL A: Append Main-Verb to Auxiliaries; Main-Verb = *
$S-4:_c V_d$	C: Form of * is Past Participle and Type of Main-Verb is BE A: Voice = Passive; Append Main-Verb to Auxiliaries; Main-Verb = *; OBJ = SUBJ; SUBJ = a Dummy NP
$S-5:_c NP_d$	A: OBJ = *
$S-6:_d NP_e$	A: OBJ2 = OBJ; OBJ = *
$S-9:_e PP_e$	A: Append * to Modifiers
$S-10:_e PP_e$	C: Voice is Passive and SUBJ is a Dummy NP and WORD in Prep of * is 'by' A: SUBJ = Prep-OBJ of *
$S-11:_e PP_e$	C: WORD in Prep of * is 'to' or 'for' and OBJ2 is EMPTY A: OBJ2 = Prep-OBJ of *
S-12: $_eSEND$	C: OBJ2 non-EMPTY and Transitivity of Main-Verb is Bitransitive. OR OBJ2 is EMPTY and OBJ is non-EMPTY and Transitivity is Transitive. OR OBJ and OBJ2 are EMPTY and Transitivity is Intransitive
S-13: $_xPrep(FOR)_y$	C: WORD in * is 'for'
$S-14:_y NP_z$	A: SUBJ = *
S-15: $_zCOMP(to)_c$	C: WORD in * is 'to' A: Main-Verb = a Dummy Verb with Type = MODAL
$S-16:_a S/x_b$	A: SUBJ = *
$S-17:_c S/z_e$	I: SUBJ = SUBJ of ↑ A: OBJ = *
$S-18:_d S/z_e$	I: SUBJ = OBJ of ↑ A: OBJ2 = OBJ; OBJ = *

$S-19:_a V_q$	C: Type of * ≠ Non-Aux and Mood = Declarative or Interrogative A: Main-Verb = *; MOOD = Interrogative
$S-20:_q NP_c$	C: SAME AS C FOR S-2 ARC A: SUBJ = *
$S-21:_a NP_b$	C: Question of * is YES and MOOD is Declarative A: SUBJ = *; Question-Element = *; MOOD = Interrogative
$S-22:_a NP_a$	C: Question of * is YES and MOOD is Declarative A: Question-Element = *; HOLD = *; MOOD = Interrogative
$S-23:_a PP_a$	C: Question of Prep-OBJ of * is YES and MOOD is Declarative A: Question-Element = Prep-OBJ of *; HOLD = *; MOOD = Interrogative
$S-25:_r NP_b$	A: SUBJ = *
$NP-1:_f DET_g$	A: DET = *; No = No of *; Question = Question of *
$NP-3:_g ADJ_g$	A: Append * to Describers
$NP-4:_g N_h$	C: No is EMPTY or No = No of * A: Head = *; No = No of *
$NP-5:_f Pr_h$	A: Head = *; No = No of *; Person = Person of *; Question=Question of *
$NP-6:_f Proper_h$	A: Head = *; No = No of *
$NP-7:_h PP_h$	A: Append * to Qualifiers
$NP-9:_f SEND$	C: HOLD is an NP A: Empty and Return HOLD
$NP-10:_h S/c_h$	I: MOOD = Relative; SUBJ = a copy based on ↑ Main-Verb = a Dummy Node with WORD = 'be' A: Append * to Qualifiers
$NP-11:_h S/r_h$	I: MOOD = Wh-Relative; HOLD = a copy based on ↑ A: Append * to Qualifiers
$PP-1:_i PREP_j$	A: Preposition = *
$PP-2:_j NP_k$	A: Prep-OBJ = *
$PP-4:_i SEND$	C: HOLD is a PP A: Empty and Return HOLD

Table 2.0 Augmentation of the ATN Networks

Here a * refers to the most recent node and ↑ refers to the node from which a recursive call was made. HOLD is a special register used to hold information for reuse later. HOLD is used to handle long distance dependencies. OBJ is the Direct Object and OBJ2 is the Indirect Object. The notation S/x is a call to the S network but starting with node x rather than the default start node of the network. SEND arc indicates the termination. The SEND arc enables final checks to be made using the same standard augmentation procedures applicable to any of the arcs. Notice how subject-verb agreement, dative shift, passive voice, relative clauses, yes-no questions and wh-questions are handled. We will not give detailed descriptions of all the networks and the augmentation here. Readers are advised to apply this grammar to the sentences given in the appendix and see how the whole thing works or why exactly it does not work in cases where it does not.

ATN parses a sentence from left to right, simulating a nondeterministic machine either by using backtracking or through pseudo-parallelism. Nondeterminism appears in NLP because the information required to take the right decision may not be locally available at that point of time. Hence we will be left with only two options - keeping track of all the possibilities simultaneously, or making an arbitrary guess, proceeding sequentially and backtracking to earlier choice points if forced later on. In both cases extra effort is expended in trying unfruitful paths. ATN blindly searches all the possibilities applying the conditions on the arcs to prune search. Since actions on one arc may affect the result of applying a condition on some other arc later, wide coverage ATN grammars tend to become very complex and difficult to write.

ATN handles long distance dependencies using its *hold mechanism.* Constituents which are obtained earlier than required are *held* in the hold register until a place is reached where that constituent is required but found to be missing. The ATN grammar never made any cognitive claims and was hardly known in linguistic circles. However, the hold mechanism seems to promise psychological reality also.

ATN, like most other grammar formalisms, takes linear position of constituents in a sentence too seriously. This is natural, as ATNs are only augmentations of Recursive Transition Networks, which are themselves equivalent to CFGs. The positional aspect is so much a part of the entire mechanism that it is not very suitable for dealing with relatively free word order languages.

An ATN grammar can be viewed as a specification of a space of grammatical possibilities which says very little about how to search that space. While this division of knowledge into *what* and *how* is a boon to the grammar writer, ATN parsers are susceptible to becoming very inefficient. Unrestricted augmentation can make ATN as powerful as the Turing Machine. In general ATN is extremely powerful, much more powerful than needed, thus running the risk of becoming extremely inefficient. In this respect, ATN is not any better than TG or other formalisms proposed by linguists.

While several experimental NLP systems have been built using ATN and the ATN mechanism is still being used effectively to solve limited parsing problems, ATN is no longer a serious candidate as a good grammar formalism for NLP. We have given a sample grammar for English here only to illustrate the nature of computational grammars and issues in parsing.

Lexical Functional Grammar

Lexical Functional Grammar was developed in the early 1980s by Kaplan and Bresnan. As the name suggests, LFG attaches a high degree of importance to the lexicon. While being sensitive to computational viability, LFG took a distinct linguistic flavour and has been making serious cognitive claims also. Thus LFG has come to be considered seriously in many schools of linguistics and, at least on some points, LFG is deemed to offer serious competition to the more recent theories within generative linguistics including the Government and Binding theory.

LFG incorporates two levels of processing. To begin with, phrase structure rules (CFGs) are used to obtain a tree structure. The tree structure captures the linear and hierarchical relationships and is called the constituent structure or C-structure. Then the functional structure or F-structure is obtained by unifying feature bundles.

There are parallels between LFG and ATN. LFG shares many of the merits and demerits of ATN. The CFG rules that generate the C-Structure of LFG are equivalent to the unaugmented part of the ATN. The Functional Descriptions of LFG parallel the augmentation in ATN. Thus in an abstract sense LFGs and ATN are equivalent and LFG grammars are as powerful as the ATN grammars, just too powerful.

LFG uses the less natural and less intuitive "double shafted arrow" mechanism for dealing with long distance dependencies. LFG chose this direct linking of functionally dependent constituents instead of step by step linkage through transitive chains of functional identifications under the pretext that this may require the introduction of otherwise unmotivated functions at intermediate F-Structure levels.

LFG uses the single operation of unification instead of the two separate operations of setting and checking the values of the feature dimensions as in ATN. This makes the LFG grammar somewhat easier to write. However, unification in LFG implies that a large number of feature structures are built and then rejected. Also unification itself is a costly operation.

LFG also takes linear position too seriously and thus fails to deal effectively with relatively free word order languages.

Generalized Phrase Structure Grammar

GPSG was designed to be a notational extension of CFG. GPSG is thus weakly equivalent to CFG and under many views of strong equivalence, it is even strongly equivalent to it. GPSG uses meta rules to accomplish many of the things that are handled by transformations in the TG framework. In GPSG a grammar is defined by giving a finite set of CFG rules and a finite set of meta rules which allow you to extend the list of CFG rules by the application of the meta rules. The meta rule concept is a very useful notational device and it can make the life of the grammar writer much simpler. There are restrictions on the application of meta rules and hence the overall system complexity is limited. Nevertheless, GPSG is essentially CFG and hence it carries with it all of the merits and demerits of CFGs except for providing notational convenience.

Tree Adjoining Grammar

Tree Adjoining Grammars have been around since the mid 1970s. The significance of TAG is that it directly takes up the issue of the least powerful grammar that is needed to handle natural languages. Taking for granted that CFGs are not sufficient, the proponents go on to show that TAG, which is only mildly context sensitive, is sufficient to deal with natural languages. TAG has been shown to be sufficient to handle both subcategorization dependencies and filler-gap dependencies. In fact TAG grammars can also deal with crossed dependencies which CFG cannot handle. TAGs permit polynomial time parsing with a worst case time complexity of $O(n^4)$, just n times worse than CFGs at their worst. While still not the ideal, this is a very significant improvement over the worst case complexity of TG, ATN, and LFG. While GPSG may claim a worst case time complexity of $O(n^3)$ based on its equivalence to CFG, the $||G||^2$ term within the constant factor, where $||G||$ represents the number of grammar rules, can become large enough to make it worse on the whole.

In other grammar formalisms, recursion in the CFG or equivalent component first builds up structures some of which get filtered out later when dependency constraints are applied. In TAG, however, dependencies are defined initially on bounded structures (trees) and recursion simply preserves them. This leads to perhaps one of the most significant aspects of TAG namely its elegant way of handling long distance dependencies. In a sense there are no long distance dependencies at all since all dependencies originate within bounded structures which only get expanded later.

TAGs use ordered trees and thus have the same kinds of problems as other grammar formalisms we have seen above when it comes to handling free word order languages. With the more recent work in TAG however, the new quasi-trees are coming closer to the kaaraka charts of the paaNinian grammar.

Dependency Grammar

A phrase structure grammar, for example, is defined in terms of constituents. The head of a constituent is not linked directly to the other words in a phrase structure constituent. This makes the word order very important. In Indian languages as also in languages like Italian and Russian, which allow a lot of variation in the word order, a phrase structure grammar is not very appropriate. Dependency grammars attempt to get around the word order limitations of constituency based grammar formalisms.

In a dependency grammar, each word is linked directly to other words that it relates to. A link is a directed relation that connects a dependent word with its head. Thus there is no need for any non-terminals.

The term "Dependency Grammar" stands for a diverse collection of approaches to natural language syntax sharing the following fundamental characteristics: The distinction between heads and dependents; the immediate modification of a head by a dependent (i.e. without intervening nonterminals like in phrase structure grammars); and the naming of the relation between a head and a dependent. Approaches can be differentiated mainly according to whether they consider grammatical or semantic relations (example: "subject" vs. "Actor" or "agent"), and whether the grammar describes tree-structures or graphs.

Categorial Grammar

Categorial grammar is a term used for a family of formalisms in natural language syntax motivated by the principle of compositionality and organized according to the view that syntactic constituents should generally combine as functions or according to a function-argument relationship.

Categorial Grammar is a lexical approach in which expressions are assigned categories that specify how to combine with other expressions to create larger expressions. An analysis of an expression proceeds by inference over the categories assigned to its individuatable parts, trying to assign a given goal-category to the expression. In the type-logical variant of categorial grammar, a semantic representation is built compositionally in parallel to the categorial inference.

A categorial grammar shares some features with the simply - typed lambda calculus. Whereas the lambda calculus has only one function type $A \to B$, a categorial grammar typically has more. For example, a simple categorial grammar for English might have two function types

`A/B`

and

`A\B,`

depending on whether the function takes its argument from the left or the right. Such a grammar would have only two rules: left and right function application. Such a grammar might have three basic categories (N,NP, and S), putting count nouns in the category N, adjectives in the category

`N/N,`

determiners in the category

`NP/N,`

names in the category NP, intransitive verbs in the category

`S\NP,`

and transitive verbs in the category

`(S\NP)/NP.`

Categorial grammars of this form (having only function application rules) are equivalent in generative capacity to context-free grammar and are thus often considered inadequate for theories of natural language syntax. Unlike CFGs, categorial grammars are lexicalized, meaning that only a small number of (mostly language-independent) rules are employed, and all other syntactic phenomena derive from the lexical entries of specific words.

Another appealing aspect of categorial grammars is that it is often easy to assign them a compositional semantics, by first assigning interpretation types to all the basic categories, and then associating all the derived categories with appropriate function types. The interpretation of any constituent is then simply the value of a function at an argument. With some modifications to handle intentionality and quantification, this approach can be used to cover a wide variety of semantic phenomena.

Indian Theories of Grammar

Extensive studies of the structure of languages have been made in the Indian tradition. The most famous of them all is the grammar system given by paaNini more than 2000 years ago. More than merely writing a grammar of Sanskrit, paaNini has given us a whole science of grammar. Here we can only very briefly mention some of the salient features.

Syntactic analysis mainly concerns itself with the assignment of functional roles, here called *kaaraka roles*, to the various constituents in a given sentence. The verb has its expectations or *aakaaMksha* and the noun phrases have the required properties *yoogyata* to occupy different kaaraka roles. Thus this theory is similar in its spirit to the Case Grammars as given by Fillmore and many others who followed in the west. In a way, Fillmore's case grammar is a rediscovery of what paaNini and other ancient Indian grammarians had already said long before.

Parsing can be viewed as satisfying the constraints of aakaaMksha and yoogyata. In Indian languages information required for doing this is encoded primarily in the surface case markers, here called *vibhakti*. In modern Indian languages, vibhakti is indicated by morphology as well as post-positions. The concept of vibhakti can be extended to include linear position, so that positional languages such as English can also be handled. *sannidhi* or occurring together, is also a useful feature.

In Sanskrit as also in modern Indian languages grammar is much more to do with morphology than with syntax. Word order is not the most important issue and words carry substantial amounts of morpho-syntactic information with them. Syntax becomes so much simpler.

paaNini's grammar of Sanskrit is so detailed, precise and methodical that it is almost like an algorithm. The system is so perfect, it is extremely difficult to find a fault. Everything just works. Perhaps there is no other system anywhere in the world that can match this level of completeness and perfection.

UCSG

UCSG (Universal Clause Structure Grammar) was developed by the author during the early nineties. UCSG uses a divide and conquer strategy. The grammar is divided into three nearly independent modules. We apply the least complex grammars that are sufficient for each of the modules thereby leading to very efficient parsing. Also, grammars for the modules can be written separately and grammars become easy to write. By appropriately dividing the problem into modules, we also get to see where exactly relatively free word order languages differ from positional languages and what is really common between the two classes. This would enable development of syntactic systems that work both for positional languages such as English and relatively free word order languages exemplified by modern Indian languages.

Grammars can be viewed as sets of constraints on the structure of sentences. There are constraints on linear position of constituents, hierarchical nesting of constituents one inside the other and functional dependencies between different constituents in a sentence. We find that these three primary kinds of structure inherent in human languages, namely linear, hierarchical and functional structures, lend themselves naturally for analysis by three independent modules. The three modules in UCSG are called linear (L), hierarchical (H) and functional (F) components. Both the grammar and the parser are divided into L, H and F parts. Correspondingly, there will be three levels of syntactic representation called L-Structure, H-Structure and F-Structure. While other grammar formalisms also tackle linear, hierarchical and functional aspects some way or the other, the division of labour into these three separate modules, especially the introduction of an independent H level is the highlight of the UCSG formalism.

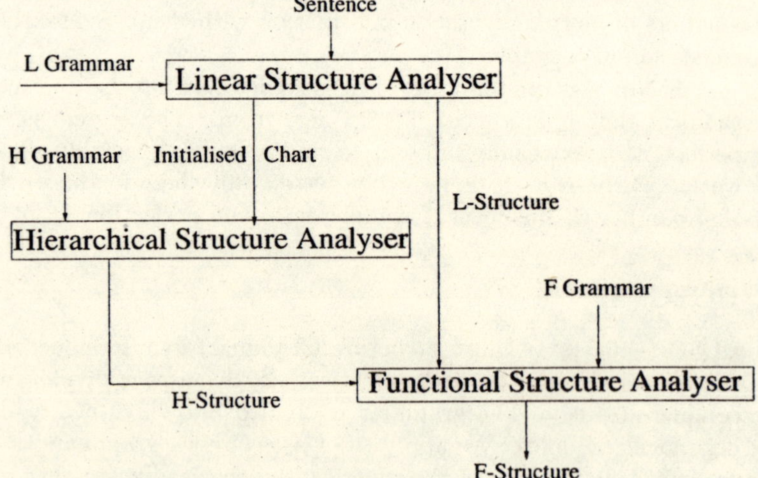

FIG 2.12 the UCSG Architecture

F-Structure depicts the assignment of functional roles to the various participants in a clause. The F part of the grammar provides constraints for role assignment. Functional roles should be so selected that role assignments can be made based mainly on syntactic information. We propose a set of functional roles motivated by the question-answer point of view. We employ a combination of top-down and bottom-up strategies for role assignment. The subcategorization frames associated with verbs provide the top-down expectations and the surface case markers associated with the nouns provide the bottom-up information. This should remind you of our discussions on paaNini's grammar system above. Any set of role assignments that satisfy all the F constraints simultaneously gives a valid F-Structure.

Each clause in a sentence corresponds to one atomic predication. It is a general principle of syntax that participants of a clause do not cross the clause boundaries except in so far as they are specifically licensed by syntax. Knowing the clause structure therefore greatly helps the functional structure analysis since functional structure analysis can then be localized to the respective clauses. The F part of the grammar can be specified for a single clause only and the F grammar becomes simpler and easier to write. Functional role assignment becomes essentially local to a clause. In UCSG we obtain the hierarchical structure of clauses and the clause boundaries before we attempt functional structure analysis. We show that clause structure can be determined before and without applying the functional structure constraints. H-Structure analysis logically precedes F-Structure analysis in UCSG. An independent H level analysis that is done before and without the aid of F level constraints sets UCSG apart from all other grammar formalisms.

We observe that there are strong constraints on the sequences of verbs and certain clause boundary markers called sentinels. We exploit these constraints to identify clauses, to determine the hierarchical nesting of clauses and even to determine the clause boundaries, although only partially. H-Structure depicts this hierarchical structure of clauses. The H grammars for different languages show only parametric variations even across positional and relatively free word order languages. The grammar of clause structure is highly language invariant. Hence the name Universal Clause Structure Grammar.

Further, we observe that the atomic units at both hierarchical structure and functional structure level are groups of words (chunks) rather than individual words. We therefore propose that all potential word groups be identified first and both hierarchical structure analysis and functional structure analysis be carried out on sequences of word groups rather than on sequences of words. This reduces the effective length of the sentence and increases the efficiency of parsing. The L part of the grammar provides constraints for group formation. We show that the L grammar constraints in both positional and relatively free word order languages are primarily constraints of linear position. Hence the name linear structure.

Functional dependencies can span across several clauses due to nesting of clauses. These dependencies have got something to do with the hierarchical structure of clauses but they have nothing to do whatever with *distance* - long or short. The concept of linear distance is irrelevant here. We get rid of the problems of long distance dependencies by working from whole to part instead of working from left to right. We determine the clause structure first and then analyze the functional structure clause by clause. We start from the main clause and go recursively into the nested clauses. We pass on information and expectations about displaced, shared and missing participants down the hierarchy of clauses. With this, functional structure analysis of a clause becomes practically completely independent of the functional structure of any other clause in the sentence. There will no longer be any long distance dependencies. Thus long distance dependencies, which require special mechanisms in other grammar formalisms, are a non-issue in UCSG.

In UCSG we work from whole to part rather than one end to the other. We know the hierarchical structure of clauses and clause boundaries before we attempt to analyze the functional structure of individual clauses. In all other grammar formalisms sentences are processed linearly, say, left to right. At any point in this process, decisions are taken based only on the information gathered from the part seen so far. We have really no idea of what lies ahead but for certain expectations which can be built based on what we have already seen. Working from whole to part has the advantage that we always have a global picture of what we are doing before we fill up the minor details. This has been the traditional wisdom in all branches of engineering. For example, maps are always made from whole to part.

We show that all potential word groups in a sentence can be obtained using finite state machine power in linear time. We also show that hierarchical structure analysis can be done using a very small number of context free grammar rules in cubic time - cubic in the number of verb groups and sentinels, which is typically much smaller than the number of words in the sentence. Finally, we show how the localization of functional structure analysis to the local domains of the respective clauses makes parsing in UCSG highly efficient on the whole.

In conclusion we see that the UCSG formalism has several merits. Firstly, we see that the division of work into three independent modules helps to discover, and hence exploit, what is common between a relatively free word order language like Telugu and a positional language like English. UCSG is equally well suited for parsing positional languages and relatively free word order languages. In fact even cross serial dependencies as in Dutch can be handled. Secondly, we get an elegant solution to the problem of long distance dependencies. Thirdly, grammars can be written more easily than with other grammar formalisms. Fourthly, we note that efficient parsers can be written. Lastly, and most importantly, the division of labour into three modules that have a very close correspondence with the three aspects of structure of human languages, will hopefully offer new and useful insights into the nature of our languages.

UCSG grammars have been developed for English and a few Indian languages and applied for machine translation between English and Indian languages. The UCSG system for English has been extended to a wide coverage robust partial parsing system by combining the basic architecture outlined above with statistical parsing techniques. The approach holds promise since grammars can be developed without need for a parsed training corpus. See references given in the bibliography for more on UCSG.

Partial Parsing

Although a lot of work has gone into developing syntactic parsers, it has not been possible to achieve high performance on unrestricted texts. Full syntactic parsers also have many limitations: 1) exponential solution space with the attended computational inefficiencies, 2) large and complex grammars 3) greater need for semantic and pragmatic contextual knowledge which are not easy to provide 4) need to tackle long-distance dependencies, and 5) accumulation and multiplication of errors. Given these, there has been an increased interest in wide coverage and robust but partial or shallow parsing systems in the last deçade or so.

Shallow parsing is the task of recovering only a limited amount of syntactic information from natural language sentences. Most of times shallow parsing is restricted to finding phrases in sentences, in which case it is also called chunking. Chunking is simply finding syntactically related non-overlapping group of words. It is the task of dividing the text into syntactically non-overlapping phrases. Here by non-overlapping we mean one word can become a member of only one chunk. Chunks are also referred to as *word groups* to distinguish them from *phrases*, a terminology that has come to acquire a different specialized connotation in linguistics.

For example, the sentence "He reckons the current account deficit will narrow to only # 1.8 billion in September" is parsed as follows:

[NP He] [VP reckons] [NP the current account deficit] [VP will narrow] [PP to] [NP only # 1.8 billion] [PP in] [NP September].

Note that the PP-Attachment ambiguities have not been resolved yet, nor are the thematic roles identified.

Developing computational grammars is a challenging task. There are broadly two approaches to development of grammars - the linguistic approach which depends upon hand-crafted rules, and, the machine learning approach where grammars are learnt automatically from a training corpus. Developing hand-crafted grammar rules is a very slow, tedious and difficult task, requiring substantial knowledge and skill on the part of the linguist. Automatic learning of grammars requires, on the other hand, a large, representative, parsed training corpus, which is often not available. Perhaps only a good combination of the two approaches can give us the best results with minimal effort.

While several grammars and parsing systems exist for English and other major languages of the world, Indian language are lagging far behind. There are hardly any substantial computational grammars for any of the Indian languages. Parsed corpora are also not available and hence machine learning approaches cannot be applied right away. How then do we develop wide coverage grammars and robust shallow parsers with minimal time and effort? Only an ingenious combination of linguistic and statistical methods with judicious bootstrapping may help us develop large scale computational grammars with minimal time and effort. Such efforts are currently underway and hopefully we will have at least partial parsing systems in Indian languages soon.

2.2.6 Semantics

Semantics is the study of meanings - meaning of words, of sentences and of discourse units. The very purpose of language is communication - communication of information, intentions, feelings, attitudes. Natural language understanding aims at recovering these information, intentions, feelings and attitudes from the linguistic message that is encoded as temporal sequences of sounds in speech and as linear sequence of symbols in the written text. Natural language generation aims at encoding given information, intentions, feelings and attitudes as linear sequences in speech or text form. Translation, summarization, categorization, information retrieval and all other applications require understanding the meaning of the text to achieve human-like performance. Semantics is thus at the very core of language technologies. In fact it would be proper to view all other aspects as steps towards understanding the meanings. If we cannot understand the meaning, there is only so much we can do. Attempting any language technology application without trying to understand meanings will be like driving a car with the eyes blind-folded. You can of course drive but only at a big risk.

But semantics is a difficult area. No one knows exactly what we mean by meaning. No one really knows exactly what we mean by understanding. Philosophers have been thinking on these topics for centuries. Now that these questions have become pertinent to development of technologies, scientists from a variety of other specializations have also been working on semantics and proposing new ideas. A lot of new ideas have come up over the last 60 years. But that does not mean that the problems have been solved. Given the nature of the problems and issues, it would be apt to say that we know today almost only as much as we knew centuries ago. In fact many of the ideas tried out by technologists are superficial and the real problems have not even been addressed properly.

No wonder then, that most of the applications today do not even incorporate a semantics component in any serious measure. There is even a claim that a lot can be done without going for any in-depth linguistic analysis. And practical experience does show that in some tasks high performance can be achieved by only a very superficial analysis provided large scale training data is available and the right methods are used for learning from this data. For example, text categorization systems achieve 95% plus performance by using raw words as features, without need for any dictionary or morphological analysis, let alone syntax or semantics. Human beings are also far from perfect and in some tasks it is possible to achieve performance comparable to or even some what better than human performance without need for in-depth linguistic analysis.

It would be wrong, however, to conclude that machines have reached or are approaching human levels of intelligence. Given suitable, data, sets of features to use, a method to compute and weigh the features and a classification method, automatic techniques exist for performing classification in an optimal way as defined by some given criteria. Human beings can also do this, although they may take more time than computers or commit mistakes while computing, but they can also do much more. Machine learning today is largely restricted to generalization from examples. But we human beings can 'learn' even new methods of machine learning. We learn to identify discriminative features, we learn to weigh them and we learn the optimization criteria and methods. There is no comparison between machines and human beings. High performance is achievable only in some restricted tasks under suitable assumptions. This does not mean that machines can understand the meaning of texts nor does it mean that understanding meanings is not necessary.

In the section on syntax, we said form follows function and hence knowing the structure greatly facilitates understanding the meanings. We even said the structural descriptions produced by a syntactic analyzer can be viewed as rough descriptions of meaning. This is not to say that meanings directly follow from syntactic analysis. Sentences and discourse segments that have similar structure may have widely varying semantics. Look at these two sets of sentences, due to Katz:

```
SET-1:

1. There is a fire in my kitchen

2. My kitchen is in my house

3. Hence, there is a fire in my house

SET-2:

1. There is a pain in my foot

2. My foot is in my shoe

3. Hence, there is a pain in my shoe
```

Sentences in natural language do not show up their underlying logical structure explicitly in their surface form. Making logical sense out of sentence and discourse structures is a complex task. Formal logics help us in eliminating ambiguities and representing meanings in a precise way. However, obtaining logical formulae from natural language sentences is tough. In fact we have only shifted the burden of semantics to the process of mapping given utterances into logical formulae.

Meaning, Reference and Truth

Meaning, reference and truth are different but related concepts. There are several theories about how we make sense of the world, inferring meaning. Is the meaning of a word the object it refers to? How do we deal with words that denote objects that do not exist at all in the physical world? Should we talk of mental objects? Do words have meanings at all or is it we who attribute meanings to words? There are several theories. Here we just list the general theories of understanding without getting into details:

- Attribution Theory: we need to attribute cause, that supports our ego
- Constructivism: we use constructs as perceptual categories
- Framing: mental combinations that affect perception

- Schema: mental structure to organize and interpret the world
- Symbolic Interaction Theory: we derive meaning around symbols
- Objectification: we simplify complex things into concrete images
- Story Model: We piece together complex situations into stories to build understanding
- Speech Act Theory: Speaking is acting. Meaning is context-dependent

There are also more specific theories about inferring meaning:

- Attention: How we pay attention to things around us
- Belief: What and how we believe
- Understanding ourselves: How we perceive ourselves
- Discomfort: How we handle discomfort
- Understanding others: How we make sense of other people
- Attribution: How we attribute cause

From this it should be clear that what exactly is the meaning of meaning is itself a big and difficult question. One should not, therefore, expect computer programs at this point of time to correctly identify meanings and behave like human beings. NLP is difficult. Do not fall for false claims of success.

Indian Theories of Meaning

There is an ocean of knowledge on meaning within the Indian tradition. There are several schools of thought and continuous scientific development of ideas for several thousand years now without gaps. It is unfortunate that there are separate worlds and people of one world know nothing about the other. That things are in Sanskrit and we do not know Sanskrit is not an acceptable excuse. Can we say today that we do not know English and so we do not care for anything that is published in English? Can we go ahead and re-publish ideas known for centuries as our own new discoveries? Indians are learning English because they think that is where knowledge is. If knowledge is in Sanskrit it should be equally natural that seekers of knowledge try to learn Sanskrit.

Indian theories of meaning make a three tier distinction in how meanings of words are to be considered *abhida, lakshaNa and vyanjana* gradually moving from literal to indicative or suggestive and metaphorical.

The discipline of *s'aabdaboodha* is all about meaning of words. Here we dig deep and provide a very detailed picture. Consider the simple verb *go*. Going requires somebody to go, somewhere to go and somewhere to go from. It is the act of going that is implied. Thus s'aabdaboodha *defines* the verb go as *an activity that is favourable for the dis-association of an object to its current location and re-association of that object to another location.* Every word is defined with such great detail. It becomes possible to derive the meanings of complex constructs through a series of logical deductions.

There is also a great scientific debate, going on for the last few thousand years in India, on whether the meaning of a sentence (or an utterance) can be constructed from the meanings of the words it is made up of or not. These are all largely unknown in the western world. It is taken for granted that syntax is useful for semantics and so much of time and effort is spent on syntax before the basic question of its utility for semantics is answered.

Meanings of words apart, our interpretation and understanding is what finally matters. In that sense meanings are in our minds. Somebody is a freedom-fighter or a terrorist depending upon how you look at it and which side you take. The same thing can mean different things to different people in different contexts. The same thing also changes meaning as you get better and deeper understanding. There is a limit for purely symbolic and objective consideration of meanings.

There is a lot that has been done in semantics but there is still a lot more that needs to be done. It is beyond the scope of this book to get into the depths of semantics. We will only look at selected linguistic phenomena with examples.

Attachment

There are some areas which lie at the boundary between syntax and semantics. Attachment of prepositional phrases and subordinate clauses is one example. Resolution of anaphoric references is another. To a small extent these problems can be tacked from the point of syntax but by and large they belong the realm of semantics. Syntax cannot take us too far. Consider the following well known example:

```
I saw a man on the hill with a telescope
```

The prepositional phrase *on the hill* may modify the verb, or the object. Accordingly we get two different meanings - the seeing action took place on the hill (compare: I ate an apple on the hill) or the man was actually on the hill when he was sighted. Similarly, the prepositional phrase *with a telescope* can modify either the verb or the man or the hill. Perhaps the telescope was used as an instrument for seeing or the man was carrying a portable telescope in his hand or a big telescope was mounted on the hill on which you saw the man. In any given sentence, one of these possibilities or the other may look more natural and some possibilities may even look odd. Look at many different examples and you will see that all the possible ways of attaching the prepositional phrases are appropriate for some example or the other. Syntax can provide some general biases but it cannot tell us exactly how to attach prepositional phrases. This is largely a problem of semantics.

If large scale training data is available one could think of using statistics to find out which way of attaching may the most likely for the given sentence. Words may be replaced with concepts using an ontology and the hierarchy of concepts exploited to make better judgements. You can think of mounting a telescope on a hill but a hill on a telescope makes no sense. Why? because you have never come across any such thing in your life. Based on the language experience and real world experience you have so far, such a thing looks impossible. A man carrying a telescope is imaginable - perhaps a telescope can be built which is small, lightweight and hence portable. Even if you have never seen a telescope in your life, you can make certain judgements intelligently. We do not know exactly how. How then do we build machines which can behave like us?

Consider the following sentence:

- I saw a man who was reading a newspaper while watching TV
- I killed a man who was reading a newspaper while driving my car

Was the man reading the newspaper while watching TV or was it that I saw such a man while watching TV? Who was driving my car? The problem of attaching subordinate clauses is similar to the problem of prepositional phrase attachment. These are largely problems of semantics and hence not easy to solve.

Quantification

Terms like *all, every, each, some, a* are *quantifiers* - they are used for expressing quantitative aspects through language. Consider the sentences:

```
1a. A man saw every dog
```

```
1b. A man saw each dog
```

The first sentence means that one particular man saw all the dogs whereas the second one permits an interpretation where different dogs were seen by possibly different men. That is, we may start looking at the dogs, one by one, and for each, find out which man saw that dog. We say "each" has *wider scope. Identification of the correct scope of quantifiers* is essential for understanding the meaning of natural language sentences.

The scope of quantifiers is specified by the particular quantifiers used as also by syntactic structure. Features such as definiteness, voice, position in the sentence seem to affect the relative scope of quantifiers. Think carefully about each of the following examples and see what kinds of interpretations they permit:

```
2a. A man saw every dog
```

```
2b. Every dog saw a man
```

3a. Every dog saw a man

3b. A man was seen by every dog

4a. Every dog saw the man

4b. The man saw every dog

4c. Each dog saw the man

5a. Who saw every dog?

5b. Who saw each dog?

6. There is a dog that saw every man

You may find at hard to lay down hard and fast rules but you can surely observe some general tendencies and preferences. Based on such observations, we may conclude that the general hierarchy of scope of these quantifiers could be:

$the > each > wh_terms > every, all, some, a$

Syntactic structures such as prepositional phrases and relative clauses can also affect scoping. Consider:

7a. The kitchen in every house had a stove

7b. The kitchen that was in every house had a stove

Negative markers appear in different positions in sentences and give different meanings. They also interact with quantifiers. Hence, they can be studied in terms of scope phenomena. Consider:

8a. Not every boy likes Mary

8b. Every boy does not like Mary

8c. Not every boy likes some girl

9. Every representative from some countries
did not speak at the meeting

As you can see things can become quite confusing when several quantifiers are used in a sentence. Like other problems in semantics, determining the exact scope of quantifiers is not very easy. It would be instructive to study quantifiers and scoping phenomena in your own language. You could consider examples such as the following Hindi sentences:

10a. `har aadmi kutte se pyaar kartaa hai`

10b. `har aadmi eek kutte se pyaar kartaa hai`

10c. `har aadmi kisii kutte se pyaar kartaa hai`

10d. `har aadmi kisii na kisii kutte se pyaar kartaa hai`

10e. `har aadmi eek na eek kutte se pyaar kartaa hai`

Modification

Nouns represent objects and we use adjectives to qualify these objects and specify their properties or attributes. Adjectives may specify additional, special, unusual, unexpected properties or otherwise modify the basic meaning of the noun in many complex ways. Here we are looking at the problems and issues associated with such qualification or modification. Here we shall use the terms qualification and modification interchangeably in this general sense.

There are two major issues:

1. What modifies what?
2. What is the semantic relationship between the modifier and the modified?

It must first be noted that although we may say nouns refer to objects and adjectives modify the nouns, nouns can act as adjectives and modify other nouns. Thus we need to talk about noun-noun modification and adjective-noun modification.

Noun-Noun Modification:

Consider the following examples:

1. `Water Meter Cover Adjustment Screw`

2. `Computer Software Development Training Institute`

We understand "water meter cover adjustment screw" as the "adjustment screw of the cover of the meter used for measuring the flow of water". What kind of a "meter"? "Water Meter". Thus "water" modifies "meter". "Cover" is a part of the "water meter". Thus "cover" is modified by "water meter". What kind of a "screw"? "Adjustment screw", not fixing screw. Thus "adjustment" is the modifier and "screw" is the modified. "Water meter cover" as a whole modifies "adjustment screw". Similarly "computer software development training institute" is an "institute that trains people in developing computer software". "Training" what? "Computer Software Development", not just "Development". You can think of many more examples of noun sequences such as these. Try to analyze and see what modifies what and how exactly you can say that.

How do we know all this? We use our common sense and world knowledge. We *know* that "water pump" is a pump used to pump water and "cast iron pump" is a pump made up of cast iron. Cast iron pump does not pump cast iron. nor is a water pump made up of water. It is only world knowledge and common sense that can tell this difference. Computers do not have world knowledge or common sense. Hence the challenge.

Not all sequences of nouns are cases of modification. In

The cat was hungry. So I gave the cat food

"cat" does not modify "food" (although elsewhere it can). What I gave is "food" and to whom I gave food is "cat".

In spoken language, we use prosodic cues such as stress to indicate modifier-modified relationships. Thus we can understand that "steel mill" is a mill for manufacturing or rolling steel and "steel beam" is a beam made up of steel based on the stress pattern. Written language is an impoverished version of spoken language and naturally the problems are harder.

No simple solutions exist to find what modifies what in all cases. There are some general preference tendencies in language and we can exploit them to make guesses. For example, given three nouns N1, N2 and N3 in sequence, N1 modifying N2 is more preferable to N2 modifying N3 and N1 modifying this combined group. We can also use statistical clues based on the analysis of a large and representative corpus.

Finding the nature of semantic relationship between the modifier and modifies is also tough. In "fan blade" blade is a part of the fan. In "rubber ball" rubber is the material of which the ball is made. In "Bush administration" Bush is the head of the administration. In "Maruti car" Maruti is the company that manufactures the car. In "ink pen" ink is the material used to fill the pen with for writing. In "Akash missile" Akash is the name given to the missile. In "Delhi declaration" Delhi is the place where some important declaration was made. In "1999 bombing" 1999 is the time when the bombing took place. These are not easy for a dumb machine to understand.

Adjective-Noun Modification:

Some adjectives are "intersective" in nature. These adjectives restrict the sense of the modified objects. Thus "red balls" are all those balls which are red. Balls which are not red are excluded. All red balls are balls. They have all the common properties of balls. Additionally, they are required to be red in colour. You can understand "red balls" by making a set of all balls and a set of all red objects and finding an intersection. Red balls are exactly those objects which are balls and which are red in colour. The set of red balls is smaller in size than the set of all balls (or equal in size in the extreme case where all balls are red and there are no balls of any other colour). Intersective adjectives are thus easier to understand.

However, not all adjectives are intersective in nature. You cannot understand "slow trains" by making a set of all trains and a set of all slow moving objects and finding the intersection. A set of all trains makes sense but a set of all slow objects cannot be made. A slow train may actually be far faster than a fast snail. Slow and fast are relative. We cannot make sets of all slow objects or all fast objects. So are adjectives like large, small, bright, dull, etc.

A "toy gun" is not a gun in the first place. An "alleged murderer" may not be a murderer for all you know. "Average marks" may not be treated as marks because marks may have to be whole numbers while the average may turn out to be a fraction.

Note that apart from adjectives, proper names, possessive nouns, possessive pronouns, past and present participles can all act as modifiers. There can be several modifiers in sequence and what modifies what can be ambiguous. All the sense ambiguities of words add up to the problem. Does "old ladies hostel" mean a ladies hostel that is old or a hostel for old ladies? Is "light red ball" a ball which is light in weight and red in colour or a ball which is light red in colour?

Note that all comparative adjectives are intersective in nature. Comparison is with respect to some specified thing and thus relative things become absolute. Thus in "logs heavier than 100 Kg", we can make a set of all logs and a set of all objects heavier than 100 Kgs. Interestingly, superlatives are non-intersective. You cannot make a set of "largest objects" to interpret "largest dog in the pound".

Word Sense Disambiguation

A word can have more than one sense. The sense in which the word is used can be determined, most of the times, by the context in which the word occurs. The word *bank* has several senses out of which *bank* as a financial institution and *bank* as a sloping land bordering a river can be easily distinguished from the context. Distinguishing between the senses of *bank* as a financial institution and *bank* as a building housing such an institution is more difficult. The process of identifying the correct sense of words in context is called *Word Sense Disambiguation* (WSD). Homonymy and Polysemy must both be considered. Word sense disambiguation contributes significantly to many natural language processing tasks such as machine translation and information retrieval.

Many words have more than one sense. Here are some more examples:

The focus of research in WSD is on distinguishing between senses of words within a given syntactic category, since senses across syntactic categories are more easily disambiguated through POS tagging techniques. Many researchers have focused on disambiguation of selected target words although there is some recent

Sense Definition
readiness to give attention
quality of causing attention to be given to
activity, etc. that one gives attention to
advantage, advancement or favor
a share in a company or business
money paid for the use of money

Table 2.1: Senses of the word *interest - noun*

Sense Definition	Example
not easy - difficult	it's hard to be disciplined
not soft - metaphoric	these are hard times
not soft - physical	the hard crust

Table 2.2: Senses of the word *hard - adjective*

interest in unrestricted WSD.

WSD systems often rely upon sense definitions in dictionaries, features of senses (for example, box-codes and subject categories present in Longman's Dictionary of Contemporary English (LDOCE)), entries in bilingual dictionaries, WordNet etc. Dictionaries and other sources do not always agree on the number and nature of senses for given words. For some tasks the fine granularity of senses as given in some dictionaries is not required or may even be counter productive and so methods to merge closely related senses have been explored by some researchers.

Both knowledge based and machine learning approaches have been applied for WSD. Glossaries of senses present in dictionaries are helpful. For example, the sense definition which has the maximum overlap with the definitions of the context words may be taken as the correct sense. Machine learning techniques such as Bayesian learning, decision lists, and decision trees have been used. Machine learning methods require a training corpus. Clustering techniques have been used to group cases with same sense together where labelled training data is not available.

Choice of the right features is often more important than the

Sense Definition	Example
function as something	serves as yard stick to
provide a service	dept. will serve select few
supply with food/means	serve dinner
hold an office	served as head of department

Table 2.3: Senses of the word *serve* - *verb*

choice of techniques for classification. A variety of features have been used, including bigrams, surface form of the target word, collocations, POS tags of target and neighboring words and syntactic features such as heads of phrases and categories of phrases in which the target word appears. Some researchers believe that lexical features are sufficient while others have argued for combining lexical features with syntactic features.

Not all words in the context are helpful for determining the sense of a target word. Syntax can help in identifying relevant parts of the context, thereby eliminating noise. Verb-object, subject-verb and noun-modifier relationships can be used. The role of various kinds of lexical and syntactic features have been studied in isolation as well as in various combinations. Ensemble techniques have been proposed to combine the results of different classifiers using different sets of features.

Some of the crucial issues such as the precise definition of word senses and granularity of sense distinctions have not been explored very well. WordNet and other available lexical resources are usually taken as the basis for fixing the possible senses of a word. Word sense disambiguation using purely linguistic methods will be very difficult. Recent studies have shown that fairly high performance can be obtained if sufficient training data is available. Sense tagged data, however, is not readily available. Thus automatic generation of sense tagged data has become a major question.

Resolution of Anaphora

Look the following examples (from Graeme Hirst):

```
1a. Bill Thought that John would laugh at him
```

```
1b. Bill Thought that John would laugh at himself

2a. When Sue went to Nadia's house for dinner,
    she served sukiyaki augratin

2b. When Sue went to Nadia's house for dinner,
    she ate sukiyaki augratin

3. Give the bananas to the monkeys
   although they are not ripe
   because they are hungry

4. Smoking gives one cancer
```

Who is "him" in 1a above and who is "himself" in 1b? Who served sukiyaki augratin and who ate? What are the two "they"s in 3 above? Who is this "one" in the last example? Words like "him, himself, they, one" refer to some body or something mentioned before. They are *references* to objects found elsewhere in the text. The objects referred to are called *referents* or *antecedents*. Resolving references, that is identifying what refers to what, is an important problem in linguistics and NLP.

Because we find it too monotonous and boring to say something like "cows give milk. Cows have four legs and two horns. Cows eat grass. Cows are domestic animals. Cows ..." we say "cow" once or twice and then onwards we start referring to this cow as "it". Pronouns have the main purpose of standing in place of nouns and referring to them. Pronouns are abbreviated forms of nouns, abbreviated in terms of their information content, that is. Thus "he" refers to any single male human being. This pronoun contains this much of information but the last piece identifying the exact person is missing. In fact any situation where there is an abbreviation of information, even ellipses, can be considered as a case of reference.

Modern linguistic theories provide a set of principles that apply to references. Anaphors such as "himself" must be bound in the local domain and so we know "himself" in 1b must be John. Pronouns such as "him" will not be bound inside the local domain and so it cannot refer to John in 1a. Since no other possibility exists we may conclude that "him" is Bill. But the principles provided in the linguistic theories are far from adequate to resolve all references in natural language. In fact the other examples given above cannot be solved with the application of linguistic theory alone. Of course the reference and the referent point to the same object and hence must share all grammatical and semantic properties. Thus agreement in gender, number and other grammatical features will be useful. Grammar alone will not be sufficient, semantics is essential as well. We understand sentences like 3 above only because we know that only fruits an be ripe or otherwise and only monkeys can be hungry, not the other way around. Pragmatic knowledge that it is usually the host who serves and the guest who eats helps us to understand 2a and 2b. Of course guest can serve, and host eats too. In 4 above "one" must be understood as anyone who smokes. No straight forward algorithms exist. We must combine grammatical, semantic and pragmatic knowledge with common sense. We can at best make good guesses.

It is possible to refer to parts of objects mentioned before ("the cover"), to sets of objects ("the longer ones"), to specific items of an ordered set ("the former", "the latter", "the third"), and in fact to any object that is semantically related to the referent in some way ("the choice of colours"). World knowledge as well as knowledge of the context are essential to resolve the references. Look at the following examples:

```
1. I drove by our house in my car

    a) The windows were dirty

    b) I saw my father's car. The windows were dirty

    c) I saw my father's bicycle. The windows were dirty

    d) The windows were dirty. The front door was open
```

Resolving anaphoric references remains one of the most fascinating and challenging tasks today.

Concluding Remarks

It is unfortunate that linguistics, like other disciplines, has redefined itself to address mostly problems of a superficial nature to the near total exclusion of the most important and crucial aspects of language. Areas like phonetics, phonology, morphology and syntax form the "core" of linguistics today while semantics is largely forgotten. Some even may call it "extra-linguistic"! Think of language without meaning! There are three factors that may be responsible for this. Firstly, there is growing professionalism and one is forced to address only manageable problems since successful results and solutions are expected. Secondly, real problems are often hard and there is no incentive for taking up real, hard problems. In fact the very complicated nature of the real problems often drives professionals away. Lastly, there is a rise and even dominance of empiricism. Language Engineering is nothing but this empiricism based on large scale corpora and quantitative methods. If we can get good performance in Information Retrieval, or Text Categorization or Search Engines by doing only the most superficial analysis of language, why bother to get deeper? Many superficial problems can be and have been solved. Real problems will remain. Application orientation is of course very useful - applications must drive theory as also test and prove theoretical ideas and hypotheses. But undue importance given to short sighted areas where immediate uses can be found, is harmful to the true development of human knowledge.

This is certainly not to say that there is no work going on in semantics. You will find a large number of groups working actively on various aspects of semantics in many parts of the world, if not so much in India. However, in the twentieth century, in contrast to earlier days, the choice of research problems and the way we go about doing research has changed a lot. We select areas which are doable, areas where we can publish papers or develop products. We do not select a problem because it is important to solve it. Knowledge and scholarship per se are not valued, only the show of knowledge is. In the process many fundamental questions remain unanswered. We make assumptions and go ahead. Once we have come a long way off, it becomes difficult even to remember those assumptions and appreciate that what all we have obtained is subject to our assumptions being true. Go back to the definition of NLP, NLU and NLG, go back to the discussion on question-answering systems and check for yourself where we stand today. Ask basic questions. Do words exist? Do words have meaning? Can we define the meaning of words precisely? What exactly do we mean by context? What exactly do we mean by sense of a word? Can we derive the meaning of a sentence from the meaning of the words and the structure of the sentence? Can we derive the meaning of a text in terms of the meaning of the sentences it is made up of? Suppose the answer to some of these questions turns out to be no. Don't you think a whole lot of all the work we are doing will become irrelevant and useless as far as NLP is concerned?

2.2.7 Pragmatics

Pragmatics is the study of the aspects of meaning and language use that are dependent on the speaker, the addressee and other features of the context of utterance, such as the following: a) The effect that the following have on the speaker's choice of expression and the addressee's interpretation of an utterance: Context of utterance, Generally observed principles of communication, The goals of the speaker b) Programmatic concerns, such as the treatment of given versus new information (including presupposition), deixis, speech acts (especially illocutionary acts), implicature, and the relations of meaning or function between portions of discourse or turns of conversation.

2.2.8 Other Areas of Linguistics

We have only touched some of the areas of linguistics that are perhaps more directly relevant for NLP. There are several other interesting and useful areas. Phonetics and phonology deal with the physical and logical levels of basic sound units that make up the words of a language. As such they are very much relevant for speech technologies. Psycholinguistics addresses questions relating to how humans process language and use experimental methods to build and test hypotheses. Sociolinguistics is a rich field concerned with social aspects of language. Language is related to social status, power and politics. Historical linguistics is concerned with linguistic genetics and language change over time.

Language policy is important as it has direct implications for the people. Should the primary education be in the mother tongue or in some other language? The three language formula in our country is a example of language policy implementation. Teaching language is another aspect that is closely related other areas of language and linguistics. Language teaching requires methodologies and techniques different from those required for teaching, say, mathematics or science. There are even language games that can promote effective language learning. To know the importance of language try to spend one day, just one day, without speaking, listening, reading or writing! That would be extremely difficult.

2.3 Corpus Based and Statistical Approaches

At one point of time, experts used to specify what is right or acceptable and what is not. Grammars used to be prescriptive in nature and students could be punished for not following the rules. This strictness was considered essential for maintaining the purity and standards. After all language is for communication and we cannot effectively communicate if we all do not follow a set of commonly accepted protocols and standards. Looseness and lightness of thought about language is really more dangerous than careless use of language. We often hear people say that grammar is not important and as long as they can communicate with others, that is good enough. But one must remember that we cannot communicate effectively unless we take language a bit more seriously. A large number of day to day problems at home or office can actually be traced to communication problems arising from laxity in the use of language. Carelessness about language is harmful. Effective communication is not possible unless language is taken seriously. Language and communication skills are essential for all walks of life and it is generally true that those who have come to the top are good communicators. Do not take language lightly.

The way we look at language has changed over time. Today linguists believe that what people actually use is the real language. If all of them make a mistake, it is better not to call that a mistake but a basic property of the language itself. The idea is not to introduce looseness of thought about language but to focus on developing descriptive grammars rather than prescriptive ones. Grammars must describe language as native speakers of a language actually use.

In order to take this view seriously, we need to base our linguistic studies on carefully collected large scale real life data. Such collections of linguistic data are called corpora. We cannot afford to sit down, meditate and make a list of different types of sentences and assert that these types cover almost all the major types used by people. Linguists have a great tendency even today to think of different types of constructs etc. How can we be sure? Studies show that what experts initially think is often falsified when we look at real data. Our power of imagination is not good enough when it comes to generating linguistic data. Concocted examples are often quite unrealistic. Linguists often come out which strange and bizarre constructions that may never occur in real usage while many important constructs we actually use regularly may be ignored altogether. If a system works well on a large and representative corpus, that would be more dependable than saying that the system performs very well on a thousand different types of constructs, carefully selected by expert linguists. Corpus linguistics uses corpora as the basis for all investigations, hypothesis generation, testing and validation.

Corpora are useful, why, almost essential for developing language technology applications. Corpora are used to build lexical resources such as word lists, dictionaries, thesauri and ontologies. Statistical techniques are available for automatic or semi-automatic development of lexical databases, morphological analyzers, POS taggers, syntactic parsers etc. Corpora are used for training in machine learning algorithms. Corpora are also used for testing and validation. Many of the language technology applications possible today owe their existence to the availability of large scale corpora, affordable storage and computing power and the advancements in machine learning techniques.

In this section we shall take a brief look at different kinds of corpora and techniques for developing, managing and using corpora for language engineering applications.

2.3.1 Corpora

A corpus is a large and representative collection of linguistic data, carefully collected according to prescribed criteria. It is understood that the data are in electronic and machine processable form. A library housing a collection of printed books is not a corpus. It is not of much direct value for the language engineering applications - machines cannot read or process printed books easily. Linguistic data can be at various levels and we can think of text corpora, speech corpora, corpora of scanned images of texts etc. The terms "large" and "representative" are qualitative but are intended to be objective and not entirely subjective. Some degree of objectivity can be introduced by having prescribed criteria. For example, if a text corpus is intended to be used for building dictionaries, there must be a reasonable degree of coverage of all the words of the language in the corpus. If we also need to look at sentential contexts in which different words are used, say for determining the senses of words in different contexts, then various possible contexts must be covered. Qualitative criteria such as these can be translated into more precise quantitative criteria. Yet, what is large enough and representative enough are big questions that are not easy to answer in all cases. The only assurance is the that a corpus is carefully collected with the intention and hope of covering the full range of variabilities of concern.

It is important to realize that what is large and representative enough for one kind of application is not necessarily good enough for a different use. There is really nothing like an all-purpose corpus. One must not assume that just because a large corpus has been used, the results and conclusions are universally valid and what works well here will also work well elsewhere. The size and nature of a corpus callas for careful consideration with regard to the particular application on hand.

Nonetheless, large corpora have often been found to be useful for a variety of uses, often unintended and unforeseen at the time of collection. A striking example of this is the WordNet - a collection of English words grouped based on semantic similarities and interconnected in various semantic dimensions of relationships. WordNet was initially developed with psychology in mind but it has been used very extensively in a variety of NLP tasks and applications. It is therefore important to be careful and be as general and open as possible and include as many dimensions of variability as practically possible, while developing a corpus. Corpus development is a time consuming and costly process and every care should be taken to ensure that what is done once can be used for many different applications.

Let us get back to the question of how large is a large corpus. We have seen the growth rate curves for types against tokens for several major Indian languages - refer to Figure 2.5 above. The distinction between Dravidian languages and Indo-Aryan languages is striking in this figure - there are many more word forms (types) in Dravidian languages than in the other Indian languages. While 150,000 to 200,000 word types should be giving a very good coverage for northern languages, Dravidian languages such as Telugu spoken mainly in the southern parts of India require a much larger number of word forms. And, more importantly, the available corpus is not sufficient even to get a clear idea of how many words are there in the language. The morphology of these languages is so rich, no one so far has an exact idea how many different word forms are there in the language. We have mentioned earlier that there can be as many as 1,80,000 different types arising from a single verb root Telugu.

What this shows is that techniques based on these corpora which work well for Indo-Aryan languages may not be applicable to Dravidian languages. For example, it would be possible to simply list all forms of all words and use this for dictionary based spelling error detection and correction system for Hindi, Punjabi or Bengali but such an approach cannot not be expected to produce comparable performance results for say, Telugu or Kannada. It would thus be not proper to make out right comparisons of performance of language engineering products across these classes of languages. The inherent complexity of the languages must be factored in when making any comparative judgements of performance.

If a 3 Million word corpus is insufficient for Telugu, would a 10 Million word corpus be big enough for a specified purpose? Let us see. A corpus of 225 full books adding up-to about 30,000 pages and 9.25 Million words has been developed for Telugu. The corpus includes a variety of topics and categories - newspaper articles, short stories, novels, poetry, classical and modern writings etc. The growth rate curve of types against tokens for the total corpus of Telugu now amounting to about 12 Million word is shown below. The curve still does not show any clear signs of saturation. There are about 21,00,000 types in this corpus and yet many of the possible types have not occurred even once in this corpus. If we build a large corpus, we should expect to see more new types unseen so far.

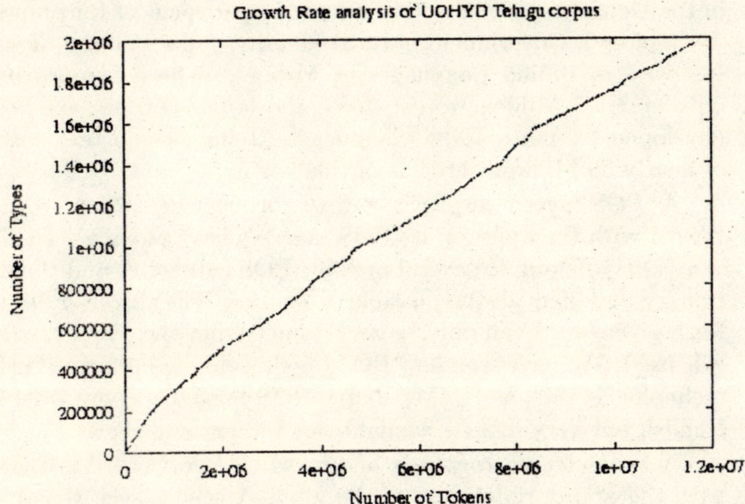

FIG 2.13 Type-Token Growth Rate Analysis

One must be very careful in developing and using corpora for statistical approaches to NLP. One study has shown that nearly 35% of words used in a standard newspaper in English are not available in a good printed dictionary and similarly, a large percentage of words listed in the dictionary are never used in the newspaper. Systems which give good performance on one corpus have often been found to fail on other corpora. Corpus provides an extremely useful data resource for all our investigations but one must be careful in coming to conclusions

Text Corpora

Types of Text Corpora:

A *plain text corpus* is simply a collection of electronic text documents. The collection may be organized in files or folders and directories. Documents usually contain headers which include meta-data such as title, author, publisher, year of publication, and other relevant fields. Several text corpora including hundreds of millions of words are now available for English. Plain text corpora in all the major Indian languages were developed with the support of the Department of Electronic (now Department of Information Technology), Government of India and distributed by the Central Institute of Indian Languages at Mysore. These corpora have only about 3 Million words. Recently, larger corpora are being developed for many Indian languages. Telugu has a text corpus of nearly 38 Million words as of this writing.

A *POS-tagged corpus* is a text corpus where each word is tagged with the appropriate POS tag. We have already seen that words may belong to several possible POS categories and the dictionary only lists all the possible categories. The correct POS tag for a given word can only be ascertained from the context where it is used. We have seen how POS tagging can be performed using technologies such as HMMs. Large POS tagged corpora exist for English but very little is available for Indian languages.

A *sense-tagged corpus* is one in which every word is tagged with the appropriate sense of the word. We have seen that POS tags can disambiguate between gross differences in meaning. To get a finer distinction among word senses, we need to get into *word sense disambiguation* (WSD). WSD systems need sense-tagged corpora for training. Only limited sense tagged corpora are available even for English. The WSD problem remains largely unsolved today but if large scale sense tagged corpora could somehow be generated, it may be possible to develop generic high performance WSD systems.

A *parsed corpus* has sentences that have been syntactically analyzed or parsed using a suitable grammar formalism. The tree structures or other kinds of descriptions of syntactic structures are explicitly shown in the corpus. A parsed corpus can be used, for example, to automatically learn grammars using statistical techniques. Small scale parsed corpora are available for English. As we have already seen, there is no computational grammars or parsers for Indian languages as yet.

Full syntactic parsing has proved to be difficult and many times we resort to shallow or partial parsing. We may just group words into phrases or chunks. Thus a shallow-parsed corpus will explicitly depict some aspects of syntax but not in full. There is hope that large scale *shallow parsed corpora* can be developed for Indian languages using a judicious combination of linguistic and statistical approaches.

Parallel corpora, including texts from one language and equivalent texts in another language, have been found to be very useful for a variety of applications. Both monolingual and bilingual applications can benefit from a parallel corpus. Dictionaries, morphological analyzers, POS taggers, WSD systems, machine translation systems can all benefit from parallel corpora, especially if there is a good one-to-one correspondence between the text units in the two languages. When such correspondences are weak, we prefer the term *similar corpora.*

Since the units of texts in the two languages in a parallel corpus may not match one to one in a very straight-forward manner, we need to *align* the corresponding units of text, be they sentences or chunks or words. A parallel corpus becomes very useful once it is aligned. Statistical techniques for alignment exist but for generating high quality training corpora, some manual effort is inevitable.

Developing Text Corpora:

Text corpora can be developed by typing in printed texts, using OCR or through speech recognition. OCR and speech technologies are far from perfect, especially for Indian languages and the only workable method is to key in texts as of today. Of course one may also make use of texts already available in electronic forms such as newspapers. This involves downloading as well as format conversion since many web pages in Indian languages today are not encoded in any standard text encoding standard such as ISCII or UNICODE. It can be expected that fairly large quantities of plain text corpora will become available soon for the major languages of India. A more critical question is whether these corpora are balanced. It is often not possible to develop corpora based on pre-set criteria and pre-selected genres simply because not much is available in those genres. You will find any amount of material on literature but hardly any on scientific and technical domains. Thus there is a tendency to put together whatever is available and call it a corpus. Such corpora may not be balanced and must be used with great care.

Indian languages are characterized by rich morphology and relatively free word order. Hence sequence based techniques such as HMMs may not be the most suitable for POS tagging of Indian language corpora. Also, since there are so many aspects that go into individual word tokens, the design of the tag-sets is itself a very complex task. Too gross a classification (such as into the basic grammatical categories) may not be good enough and too fine grained a classification would make POS tagging heavily dependent on morphology. If there are 1,80,000 word forms derived from a single verb root in Telugu, should we have so many tags then? That would not make much sense. Perhaps a hierarchical tagging scheme where we can work at various grain sizes in stages may be a good idea. POS tagged corpora are not yet available in a big measure in Indian languages today.

There are no computational grammars and hence no syntactic parsers for any of the Indian languages. The question of a parsed corpus therefore does not arise. Similarly, we do not have a clear idea about the number and nature of word sense distinctions that may have to be made. There are no dependable sources for word senses and dictionaries vary quite widely. There is no sense tagged corpora. We have a long way to go.

When we say so and so thing does not exist, we mean large scale, properly designed, thoroughly tested, proven, publicly available solutions do not exist. There may be some half-hearted, short-sighted, ad-hoc, hoch-poch implementations and student projects here and there. What is the use of such toy, demo systems?

Corpus based approaches require a number of tools for development, maintenance and usage. For example, a KWIC concordance tool locates lines containing a given word so that we can get an idea about the usage and range of senses for that word. There are tools for formatting, verification and validation and for analyzing in a variety of ways. Tools for alignment of parallel copora are also being developed. Several such tools have been developed specifically for Indian languages by various centres in India. Now tools exist for decoding any unknown font for converting the texts into a standard character encoding scheme such as ISCII or UNICODE. These tools will help accelerate the development of corpus based technologies for Indian languages.

Speech Corpora:

There is an increased interest in speech technologies in recent times in India. Unlike in the case of text, simply recording and digitizing speech will not constitute a corpus. That is not of much use. A speech corpus needs to be segmented and labelled at the level of sentences, words and sub-word units such as phones. This latter job is more complex, more time consuming and more tedious than just recording and digitizing. Also, since a speech signal is a composite of speech message, speaker's voice, environmental and system noise etc., a careful technological consideration of a variety of factors is essential to build a useful speech corpus. Even simple things like the microphone used, the location and direction of the microphone with respect to the speaker's mouth and the recording room conditions can be critical factors. While several centres are working on speech technologies in India, publicly useable speech corpora are not yet available for any of our languages.

Speech corpora meant for speech recognition are generally recorded under conditions similar to the conditions where the recognition system may finally be used, say in an ordinary office room or at a railway station. Speaker independent systems require speech data from a large number of speakers of different age, sex, speaking rates and styles etc. Spontaneous speech, natural, continuous but carefully articulated speech of cooperative speakers, or just read speech may be recorded depending on need. For speech synthesis purposes, data from a single speaker or a few selected speakers (one male, one female, for example) are recorded under noise-free conditions as in a studio. The future lies in speech. we will surely see more and more of speech technologies in future.

2.3.2 Statistical Approaches to Language

We may have difficulties in accepting a statistical orientation for human languages. We feel languages are rule governed and things are not a matter of chance or probability. How can simply some numbers characterize something so complex yet highly structured object as language? How can we interpret numbers and make sense out of them? Language manifests regularities and follows rules, either it is OK or it is not OK, where is the question of gradations? Everything must be either right or wrong, either true or false, either zero or one. Where does probability come from?

Linguistics is all about possibilities. The principles and rules of linguistics rule out the impossible combinations and allow valid combinations. The aim is to build theories and models so that all and only valid structures can be accepted.

We must immediately realize that the notion of probability includes the notion of possibility. If something is impossible it will have a probability of zero, else a non-zero value between zero and one. Thus nothing is lost in moving from possibility based view to a probability based view. In fact we gain a higher degree of control because now we can handle gradations of possibilities - from the most likely to the least. Thus at a ideological level, there need not be any concern in applying statistical techniques to human languages.

Then we must realize that languages do show gradations. It is not all a matter of yes or no, true or false, right or wrong, zero or one. Let us see some examples of gradation in language. We have nouns and we have verbs. Nouns are things and verbs are actions or states. Simple, right? Not quite. We also have things that are partly 'nouny' and partly 'verby'. Look at the following examples:

```
1. He saw the accident. He fainted.

2. He saw the accident and he fainted.

3. After he saw the accident, he fainted.

4. After seeing the accident he fainted.

5. On seeing the accident he fainted.

6. At the sight of the accident he fainted.
```

FIG 2.14 Gradations between Nouns and Verbs

Here *saw* is clearly a verb and *sight* is clearly a noun. *seeing* is in between - it is a gerund, a verb that acts like a noun, it fills the thematic roles that are normally taken by nouns but it shows up its expectations about objects etc. Seeing requires something to be seen and somebody who sees. Thus *the accident* which is the object of the verb initially, has gradually changed into the object of the prepositional phrase indicated by *of*. *After* is a preposition but it is also a subordinate conjunction. In comparison, *on* can only be a preposition. We have gradually moved from a verby structure to a nouny structure. There are gradations in language. This is just one example to prove this point.

In fact lexical categories are not completely rigid and fixed - they vary in usage. Although we may say initially that nouns are objects and adjectives are attributes of such objects, languages permit use of nouns as adjectival modifiers. In fact adjectives can also function as nouns. In *the poor envy the rich*, the "poor" stands for the poor people and "the rich" stands from the rich people. Thus even at the level of lexical categories, things are not very hard and fast.

If basic aspects such as lexical categories can show variations and gradations in usage, so will all the complex structures at higher levels of analysis. Grammaticality of sentences is not always a simple yes/no questions. Syntacticians are familiar with the "question mark" judgements by native speakers of a given language. It is very difficult to formulate purely linguistic rules for part-of-speech tagging for positional languages such as English. Our treatment of semantics should make it amply clear that problems in semantics are much more insidious and nebulous. It would not be easy to develop rules for word sense disambiguation purely based on linguistic constraints. Although languages show elaborate structure, it is not true that everything is completely rule governed.

Recent studies have shown that even small babies use statistical methods when they learn to speak and understand language. The linguistic inputs the child gets are too few and too imperfect for kids to learn symbolic rules. On the other hand, statistical decision rules based on probabilities can be obtained even from small scale and imperfect data and gradually refined and revised as more and more data becomes available. Contrary to what many linguists believe, statistical techniques seem to have psychological reality too.

Linguists are usually enthused by the quick identification of a few prominent rules that can account for a major part of linguistic phenomena. But as you expand the scope and look at more and more data, rules gradually give way to sub-rules and then to exceptions and finally things become too unwieldy. The 80-20 rule is largely true with human languages - 80% of the data can be handled with just 20% of the effort but the remaining 20% require much more effort. This rule applies recursively and it becomes harder and harder to cross beyond a level. Such saturation of linguistic approaches has been clearly observed in many applications. Statistical approaches based on large and representative data have many times crossed the point of linguistic saturation and hence the interest in these statistical approaches.

It is also not true that purely statistical approaches always work very well. Machine learning has largely been limited to generalization from examples and there are limits on generalizability. Often data required becomes too large to be practicable. The engineering challenge is to use a judicious combination of linguistic and statistical approaches to achieve the maximum possible with minimum effort

There are several ways we can integrate linguistic and statistical approaches in a hybrid architecture. Statistical methods can be applied first and linguistics used later as a filter to rule out combinations that are impossible. Alternatively, linguistic methods can be applied first and statistics used later only for rating and raking the possible outputs. Linguistics aims to deal with all and only valid constructs and it if often very difficult to take care of both these requirements at the same time. There may be several right answers but the wrong answers can be simply too many. How do we rule out all of them? So it makes sense to relax one of these constraints initially. For example, a linguistic method which captures all valid structure but does not necessarily bar all invalid structures is often much easier to construct. If inputs can be assumed to be correct in most cases, an assumption that is generally valid in many applications, we can use the linguistic module to analyze all inputs without worrying about their validity, and then apply statistical methods to rate, rank and if required filter out unacceptable combinations. Apart from these loosely-coupled architectures, we can also think of tightly integrated architectures. Linguistics often forms the main device for identifying the features to be used. Statistical methods can then be used for feature weighting, dimensionality reduction, etc.

2.3.3 Machine Learning

In Machine Learning approaches, a set of training data is given and the machine "learns" a general rule or builds a model for performing the intended task. The learning is automatic - there will be no manual intervention. If the training data is good and effective learning methods are used, good models can be learnt.

Machine learning methods are basically techniques for generalization from Examples. A typical way of using such machine learning techniques is to automatically group together similar objects or to classify objects into different classes or groups based on the similarities and dissimilarities. Thus the notions of *class* and *similarity* or *dissimilarity* are fundamental. Sometimes the term *distance* is also used to indicate a measure of dissimilarity. Distance can be quantified in many ways. Think of the road distance, the rail distance and as-the-crow-flies distance between two points. In any case distances are expressed and quantified in terms the values of one or more *features*. Thus each object is represented as a *vector of n features* if we are working with n different features. Each such feature vector can be mathematically viewed as *a point in n-dimensional space*. Think of distances in this n-dimensional space. If good features and appropriate distance measures are used machine learning techniques can learn effective decision rules for classification of given objects.

For example, to classify words as OK or not-OK in a spelling error detection system we may use the probability of a word starting with a given letter, the probabilities of two letters occurring next to each other (also called bi-gram probabilities), the probability of a word occurring before or after another given word etc. as features. These features can, for example, make a good guess that the string "abnidella" is unlikely to be a valid English word without consulting a dictionary.

Thus machine learning is a purely data driven approach. The greatest merit of this approach therefore is its generality and adaptability. All we need to migrate to a new language or a new application is to provide appropriate training data in that language or for that application. The machine unlearns and relearns to automatically to adapt to the new situation. Migrating from one language to another using a linguistic approach, on the other hand, would necessitate extensive manual exploration of the new language structures and properties.

Machine learning can be *supervised* or *unsupervised.* In supervised learning, a set of labeled training data is given and the machine learns a general decision rule which can be used for classification of new data items. In unsupervised learning, a set of unlabeled training data is given and the machine learns to group similar data items into clusters so that new data items can be placed into the right clusters. The number of clusters may or may not be known beforehand.

We describe here a selection of machine learning techniques briefly. The purpose is to give an exposure to the basic ideas. Interested readers may consult books on machine learning and pattern classification for an in-depth exposition.

Regression as Classification

Regression analysis is a statistical technique for investigating and modeling the relationship between variables in a system. When there are more than two variables in the system, the term multiple regression is employed. Regression is often used as a modeling technique where the value of one of the selected variables, called the response variable, is determined by the values of the other independent variables, also called the regressors. The modeling process basically involves determining parameters of the model, i.e. the weights of the regressor variables. The model itself could be linear or non-linear in the parameters. Regression distinguishes the response variable from the regressors and is thus generally considered to be a non-symmetric technique.

Multiple Regression can also be used as a two-class classification tool. The regressor variables are the feature vectors extracted from the training data. Since we are using regression for classification rather than for modeling, no particular feature is selected as a response variable or expressed in terms of the other features. We posit a separate decision variable, whose value is determined by the class the instance belongs to. The method is thus symmetric in the features. We give below the formulation of the Multiple Linear Regression as a classification technique.

Suppose there are k features. Let x_{ij} denote the ith observation of feature x_j where i = 1,2,...,n and j = 1,2,...,k. Let y_i be the ith observed value of the decision variable. Then

$$y_i = \beta_0 + \beta_1 x_{i1} + \beta_2 x_{i2} + ... + \beta_k x_{ik} + \varepsilon_i \tag{2.1}$$

where the parameters β_j, j = 0,1,2,...,k are called regression coefficients and ε_i are called error terms or residuals. The regression coefficients are the parameters in the model. Note that the equation is linear in the parameters. The aim is to estimate the values of these parameters from training data. In matrix notation, we have

$$\mathbf{y} = \mathbf{X}\ \beta + \varepsilon \tag{2.2}$$

where $\mathbf{y}$ is an n×1 vector of observations, $\mathbf{X}$ is an n×p matrix of feature values, where p is $k + 1$, β is p×1 vector of the regression coefficients, and ε is an n×1 vector of error terms. We may estimate the values of the parameters $\hat{\beta}$ using the least square method. That is, we wish to minimize

$$S(\beta) = \sum_{i=1}^{n} \varepsilon_i^2 = \varepsilon'\varepsilon = (\mathbf{y} - \mathbf{X}\beta)'(\mathbf{y} - \mathbf{X}\beta) \tag{2.3}$$

The least squares estimators must satisfy

$$\frac{\partial S}{\partial \beta}|_{\beta} = -2\mathbf{X}'\mathbf{y} + 2\mathbf{X}'\mathbf{X}\hat{\beta} = 0 \tag{2.4}$$

which can be simplified as

$$\hat{\beta} = (\mathbf{X}'\mathbf{X})^{-1}\mathbf{X}'\mathbf{y} \tag{2.5}$$

$(\mathbf{X}'\mathbf{X})^{-1}$ exists provided the features are linearly independent.

In order to determine the parameters, we need to know the value of the decision variable on the left hand side of the regression equation. Since the decision variable is not a feature in the system but an additional variable introduced to indicate the class for the purposes of classification, the value of the decision variable can be chosen arbitrarily subject to the following constraints. In order to ensure adequate separation between the two classes, the values for the two classes must be clearly separated. Also, the choice of the values for the decision variable influences the range of values for the parameters - the value chosen must result in reasonable ranges of values for the parameters, avoiding overflows and underflows in the extreme. Finally, choice of symmetric values for the two classes in the two-class case makes the decision rule and thresholding for rejection simpler. In practice the values are decided after a bit of experimentation with the actual data on hand.

For the two-class classification problem, we may use differential features - actual value of each feature is calculated as the difference between the values of the feature for the two classes. Values of the decision variable for the two classes are chosen symmetrically around zero and the parameters are estimated from the training data. A test sample can then be classified as belonging to class C1 or C2 depending upon whether the value of the decision variable is positive or negative. It is possible to reject a point if the value of the decision variable is too close to zero, say, closer than a specified threshold.

Classification performance can be specified in terms of Precision and Recall, or using some combined measure such as the F-Measure:

$$Recall = \frac{Ok}{Total} * 100 \tag{2.6}$$

$$Precision = \frac{Ok}{Total - Unknown} * 100 \tag{2.7}$$

$$F = \frac{2PR}{P + R} \tag{2.8}$$

where *Ok* is the number of test samples that are correctly classified, *Unknown* is the number of test samples that are not classified and *Total* is the total size of the test data. There is usually a trade off between Precision and Recall and a single combined measure is therefore useful for comparison. F-Measure is one such measure. The definition shown here gives equal weightage for Precision and Recall.

We have outlined a general method for supervised two-class classification using Multiple Linear Regression. The method is conceptually simple and based on sound theoretical foundations. The method is symmetric in the features. Although matrix inversion is required for estimating the values of the parameters, once the model is built classifying objects is very efficient - only computation of the linear regression equation and checking the sign of the decision variable are required. The technique is thus highly suitable for two-class classification problems with a reasonably small number of features.

Techniques also exist for validating the adequacy of the model for a given problem and for evaluating the relative significance of the various features (which can be used for feature selection).

We will illustrate the use of regression as a classification tool for identifying language from small text samples in section ??? below.

Nearest Neighbour Classifiers

One of the conceptually simple and practically quite effective classification methods is based on the notion of nearest neighbours. Once a collection of objects have been placed in a space of possible feature values, objects of the same kind tend to group together provided the features used are appropriate. Birds of the same feather flock together. If you can identify the type of the surrounding birds, you can guess the type of the bird on hand quite accurately. This is the basic idea behind nearest neighbour classification.

The feature values are computed and the k nearest neighbours are determined using a suitable distance measure. The value of k can be either simply assumed to be some small number, say 5, or the best value of k can be experimentally determined after trying out several values. The categories of each of nearest neighbours is checked and the object on hand is assigned the same category as the category of the majority of the k-nearest neighbours. Note that all the k-nearest neighbours may not be equally distant from the candidate object. To take the distances of the neighbours into account, distance-weighted decision rules have been proposed. Also, the k-neighbours may or may not show a clear majority. Several advanced ideas have been proposed to improve the classification performance.

Note that each time we need to classify a given object, the k nearest neighbours will have to be computed. This involves computing the distances to all the objects in the collection. Therefore this technique is an instance based classification technique.

Nearest neighbour classification techniques work quite well in many application areas and are widely used.

Bayesian Learning Theory

Bayesian Learning is a probabilistic approach to inference based on the assumption that the quantities of interest are governed by probability distributions and the optimal decision can be made by reasoning about these probabilities together with observed data.

In corpus based approaches, probabilities are estimated by counting the frequencies of favourable cases and all possible cases and taking the ratio of the two. For example, the number of documents belong to a given category divided by the total number of documents would give the probability that a document belongs to the specified category. Thus the probabilities we are talking here are empirical probabilities.

$P(X)$ denotes the probability of some event X. $P(X, Y)$ denotes the joint probability of both the events X and Y occurring together. $P(X|Y)$ denotes the probability of X given that Y has already occurred. It is thus a conditional probability. $P(X|Y)$ can be computed as $\frac{P(X,Y)}{P(Y)}$. Similarly, $P(Y|X)$ is $\frac{P(Y,X)}{P(X)}$. Since $P(X, Y)$ and $P(Y, X)$ are the same, we can combine these last two equations to get

$$P(X|Y) = \frac{P(Y|X)*P(X)}{P(Y)}$$

This is known as *Bayes Theorem.* To understand Bayes Theorem let us replace X by "disease" and Y by "symptoms". Then we get:

$$P(disease|symptoms) = \frac{P(symptoms|disease)*P(disease)}{P(symptoms)}$$

We are interested in computing the probability that a patient has a particular disease given the symptoms he has. For example, we may wish to compute the probability that a patient has viral fever given that he has head-ache. There is usually no direct way to compute this probability. Head-ache can be because of viral fever or many other possible causes including teeth pain or eye stress. Bayes Theorem expresses this probability in terms of other quantities which are usually easier to estimate. Look at the right hand side of the equation. It is possible to estimate the probability of observing given symptoms given that a patient has the specified disease. The fraction of the times a patient suffering from viral fever has head-ache gives the probability of observing head-ache given viral fever. This probability is called the *likelihood*. The other term in the numerator is called *prior probability*. Probability that any patient has a specified disease is simply based on the knowledge of how rampant that disease is at the given place and time. If viral fever is rampant, this knowledge will and should influence the final diagnosis. Since this knowledge exists even before the doctor examines the patient and notes down the symptoms, it is called prior knowledge. The diagnosis will be based on the combination of likelihood and prior knowledge - any one of them is not as good as the combination. The diagnosis will be correct to the extent that the symptoms are observed in patients with the given disease and to the extent that the disease itself is rampant. The denominator gives the probability of observing the symptoms without regard to any specified disease. If head-ache is a very common symptom then you will be less sure of your diagnosis based on this symptom. On the other hand, if yellow urine occurs quite rarely, then using this symptom to diagnose, say, jaundice, would be more safe. The probability on the left had side of the equation is called the *a posteriori probability*- it is the probability obtained after suitably refining the prior knowledge based on the observation of specified symptoms. The beauty of Bayes theorem is it combines all these aspects into a single equation, based on sound mathematical theory, yet very practical for estimating probabilities of interest.

Note that a diagnosis is usually not made based on just one symptom. When we say "symptoms" in the equation above, we actually mean one or more symptoms. The probabilities are thus joint probabilities of observing all the given symptoms simultaneously. What is the probability that the patient has jaundice given that he has yellow eyes, yellow urine, liver enlargement, nausea and weakness?

In Bayesian Learning methods a maximum *a posteriori* (MAP) probability is computed using the Bayes Theorem. We use Bayes Theorem to estimate the probability of each of the possible classes given the observed features and select the class for which this posterior probability is the highest. Note that the denominator on the right hand of the equation will be independent of the class, and hence it can be ignored as far as the aim is to find the class with the maximum a posteriori probability.

In some cases, the prior probabilities of all the hypotheses are assumed to be uniform and hence bracketed out. This assumption of uniform priors is questionable and has led to criticism of the Bayesian approaches.

Bayesian method requires the estimation of joint probabilities of all the features for each category. In order to simplify this, independence is often assumed. That is, the conditional probability of a feature given a category is assumed to be independent of the conditional probabilities of other features given that category. A Bayesian classifier that makes this independence assumption is termed a *Naive Bayes Classifier.* The Independence assumption is rarely valid in real world. Yet the method works quite well and is used in practice.

Probabilities are numbers less than one and multiplying probabilities makes the numbers smaller and smaller. Form an implementation point of view, therefore, it is useful to take logarithms. Logarithms also convert multiplications to additions.

In order to understand how Bayesian learning actually works, let us apply this to the Text Categorization problem. The basic idea is to use the joint probabilities of document terms and categories to estimate the probabilities of categories given a document. To categorize a test document d_j as belonging to a category C_i, the maximum likelihood is first estimated over all categories:

$$P(d_j|C_i) = \sum_{w \in d_j} log(P(w|C_i)) \tag{2.9}$$

Here w is a word or a term occurring in a given document. The basic idea is that words occur with varying frequencies in documents of different categories. No single word may be good enough to make a decision but the combined effect of all the words in the document collection may be good enough to give correct classification.

The prior probabilities of each category Prior(C_i) are evaluated as the ratios of the number of documents in category C_i to the number of documents in the total collection.

Finally, the posterior probabilities of each category are calculated by adding the log likelihoods to the log priors.

$$P(C_i|d_j) = log(P(d_j|C_i)) + log(Prior(C_i)) \tag{2.10}$$

A test document is assigned the category with the maximum posterior probability. To minimize misclassification errors due to narrow differences, a threshold value can be used to include a reject option. Performance can then be measured in terms of Precision, and Recall. In order to capture the Precision-Recall trade-off in a single quantity, a combined measure such as the F-measure can be used.

Unsupervised Learning: Clustering

When we have training data where the instances are not labelled for their correct class, we can still try to group the instances based on their similarities and dissimilarities. Similarity or dissimilarity is measured in terms of features and a suitable distance measure. What we do is to group together instances that are similar and hence close to one another. The idea is to group instances into clusters such that the intra-cluster distances are smaller and the inter-cluster distances are larger. This is kind of unsupervised learning is called clustering.

There are several interesting clustering algorithms but we shall sketch only one of them here - the K-Means Clustering Algorithm. The idea is simple. Let us say we have set of instances and we wish to group them into K classes. K is assumed to be known. We start by arbitrarily picking up K items from the given set of instances and treating them as the representatives of the K clusters to be discovered. Now the distances of each of the instances to these K cluster centres are computed and each instance is assigned to the cluster it is closest to. Once this is done, the centroids of the clusters are recomputed and they will become the representatives of the K clusters for the next iteration. The process is repeated. It can be observed that with each iteration, instances which are similar tend to get grouped together and after some iterations, no instance changes over to another cluster. A stable grouping of instances has been obtained. Even if the initial choice of the K representatives was not very good, because we assign instances to nearest clusters and recompute the centroids, we can hope to see natural clusters being formed.

Markov Models

Definition: Consider a system which may be described at any time as being in one of a set of N distinct states, $s_1, s_2, \ldots, s_N$. At regularly spaced discrete times, the system undergoes a change of state (possibly back to the same state) according to a set of probabilities associated with the state. We denote the time instants associated with state changes as $t = 1, 2, \ldots$, and we denote the actual state at time t as q_t. A full probabilistic description of the above system would, in general, require specification of the current state (at time t), as well as all the predecessor states. An example of Markov model is shown in the Figure 2.15.

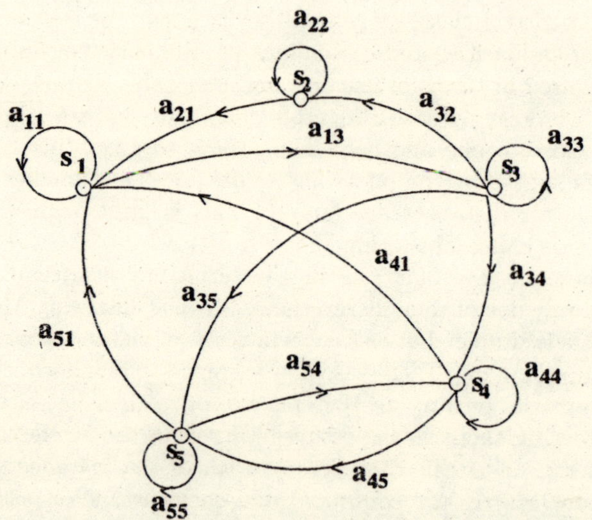

FIG 2.15 A Markov chain with 5 states with selected state transitions

For the sake of mathematical and computational tractability, following assumptions are made in the theory of Markov models.

The Markov assumption: It is assumed that the current state always depends only on preceding state. This is called the first order Markov assumption and the resulting model obtained is called first order Markov model. In this case of a discrete, first order, Markov chain, the probabilistic description is truncated to just the current and the predecessor state, i.e.,

$$P[q_t = j|q_{t-1} = i, q_{t-2} = k, \ldots] = P[q_t = j|q_{t-1} = i] \qquad (2.11)$$

However generally the current state may depend on past $k$states and it is possible to obtain such a model, called a kth order Markov model by defining the transition probabilities as follows.

$$\begin{aligned} P[q_t = j|q_{t-1} = j_{t-1}, q_{t-2} = j_{t-2}, \ldots] &= \\ P[q_t = j|q_{t-1} = j, q_{t-2} = j_{t-2}, \ldots, q_{t-k} = j_{t-k}] & \qquad (2.12) \end{aligned}$$

In any case we only peep a limited distance into the past history. Hence this assumption is also known as the *limited horizon* assumption.

State transition matrix A is:

$$A = \begin{bmatrix} a_{11} & a_{12} & \cdots & a_{1j} & \cdots & a_{1N} \\ a_{21} & a_{22} & \cdots & a_{2j} & \cdots & a_{2N} \\ \vdots & \vdots & \cdots & \vdots & \cdots & \vdots \\ a_{i1} & a_{i2} & \cdots & a_{ij} & \cdots & a_{iN} \\ \vdots & \vdots & \cdots & \vdots & \cdots & \vdots \\ a_{N1} & a_{N2} & \cdots & a_{Nj} & \cdots & a_{NN} \end{bmatrix}$$

where,
$a_{ij} = P(q_t = j|q_{t-1} = i) \quad 1 \leq i, j \leq N$

The state transition coefficients will have the properties:

$$a_{ij} \geq 0, \quad \forall i, j \qquad (2.13)$$

$$\sum_{j=1}^{N} a_{ij} = 1, \quad \forall i \qquad (2.14)$$

The stationarity assumption: It is also assumed that state transition probabilities are independent of the actual time at which the transitions take place. Mathematically,

$P(q_t = j|q_{t-1} = i) = P(q_{t+l} = j|q_{t+l-1} = i)$.

The above stochastic process could be called an observable Markov model since the output of the process is the set of states at each instant of time, where each state corresponds to a physical (observable) event.

Examples: Consider a simple 3-state Markov model λ of the weather. Assuming that once a day (e.g. at noon), the weather is observed as being one of the following:

state 1: Rainy(R)

state 2: Cloudy(C)

state 3: Sunny(S)

Let the A matrix be

$$A = \begin{bmatrix} 0.4 & 0.3 & 0.3 \\ 0.2 & 0.6 & 0.2 \\ 0.1 & 0.1 & 0.8 \end{bmatrix}$$

We could now compute the probability of any given sequence under the model. For example, the probability of the sequence: $O = (S, S, S, R, R, S, C, S)$ can be computed as follows:

$$\begin{aligned} P(O|\lambda) &= P(S, S, S, R, R, S, C, S|model) \\ &= P(S|S, S, S, R, R, S, C)P(S, S, S, R, R, S, C) \\ & \quad \text{(by cond. prob. rule)} \\ &= P(S|C)P(S, S, S, R, R, S, C) \\ & \quad \text{(by I order Markov property)} \\ & \quad \vdots \\ &= P(S)P(S|S)P(S|S)P(R|S)P(R|R) \\ & \quad P(S|R)P(C|S)P(S|C) \\ &= \pi_3 a_{33} a_{33} a_{31} a_{11} a_{13} a_{32} a_{23} \\ &= (1)(0.8)^2(0.1)(0.4)(0.3)(0.1)(0.2) \\ &= 1.536X10^{-4} \end{aligned}$$

where we use the notation $\pi_i = P(q_1 = i)$ to denote the initial state probabilities. Here we have assumed π to be 1 but in general the π values can be specified for each state.

Hidden Markov Models

So far we have considered Markov models in which each state corresponded to an observable (physical) event. Such a model is too restrictive to be applicable to many problems of interest. In the case of Hidden Markov Models the observations are probabilistic functions of the states i.e., the resulting model is a doubly embedded stochastic process with an underlying stochastic process that is not observable (hidden), but can only be observed through another set of stochastic processes that produce the sequence of observations.

A Hidden Markov Model is a finite set of states, each of which is associated with a probability distribution. Transitions among the states are governed by a set of probabilities called transition probabilities. In a particular state an outcome or observation can be generated, according to the associated probability distribution. It is only the outcome, not the state, which is visible to an external observer. The states are "hidden". Hence the name Hidden Markov Model.

Urn and Ball Model: Assume that there are N glass urns in a room. Within each urn there are a large number of colored balls. We assume that there are M distinct colors of the balls. The physical process for obtaining observations is as follows. A genie is in the room, and according to some random process, he (or she) chooses an initial urn. From this urn, a ball is chosen at random, and its color is recorded as the observation. The ball is then replaced in the urn from which it was selected. A new urn is selected according to the random selection process associated with the current urn, and the ball selection process is repeated. This entire process generates a finite observation sequence of colors, which we would like to model as the observed output of an HMM.

It is clear that the simplest HMM that can respond to the urn and ball process is one in which each state corresponds to a specific urn, and a (ball) color probability is defined for each state. The choice of urns is dictated by the state transition matrix of the HMM. Thus HMM is characterized by N urns containing colored balls, M distinct colors of balls and each urn having a (possibly) different distribution of colors.

Elements of a Hidden Markov Model:

An HMM is characterized by the following:

1) *N*, the number of states in the model. Although the states are hidden, for many practical applications there is often some physical significance attached to the states. In the urn and ball model, the states correspond to the urns. Generally states are interconnected in such a way that any state can be reached from any other state. We denote the set of states as Q and the state at time t as q_t

2) *M*, the number of distinct observation symbols associated with a state, i.e., the discrete alphabet set. The observation symbols correspond to the physical output of the system to be modeled. For the urn and ball model observation symbols were the colors of the balls selected from the urns. We denote the set of symbols as *V*.

3) The state transition probability distribution $A = a_{ij}$, where,

$$a_{ij} = P(q_{t+1} = j | q_t = i), \quad 1 \leq i, j \leq N \tag{2.15}$$

with the state transition probabilities satisfying the constraints

$$\begin{aligned} a_{ij} &\geq 0 \\ \sum_{j=1}^{N} a_{ij} &= 1 \end{aligned}$$

4) The observation symbol probability distribution in state j, $B = \{b_j(k)\}$, where,

$$b_j(k) = P\left[v_k | q_t = j\right], \quad 1 \leq j \leq N \quad 1 \leq k \leq M \tag{2.16}$$

and satisfying the following constraints

$$\begin{aligned} b_j(k) &\geq 0 \\ \sum_{k=1}^{M} b_j(k) &= 1 \end{aligned}$$

5) The initial state distribution $\pi = \pi_i$, where

$$\pi_i = P\left[q_1 = i\right], \qquad 1 \le i \le N \tag{2.17}$$

satisfying the constraint $\sum_{i=1}^{N} \pi_i = 1$
The entire model λ can be denoted as : $\lambda = (A, B, \pi)$

A complete specification of an HMM requires specification of two model parameters (*N* and *M*), specification of observation symbols, and the specification of the three probability measures *A*,*B*, and π. For convenience, we use the compact notation

$$\lambda = (A, B, \pi) \tag{2.18}$$

Given appropriate values of *N*,*M*,*A*,*B*, and π, the HMM can be used as a generator to generate an observation sequence $O = O_1 O_2 \ldots O_T$ (where each observation O_t is one of the symbols from *V*, and *T* is the number of observations in the sequence) as follows:

1. Choose an initial state $q_1 = s_i$ according to initial state distribution π.

2. Set *t=1*.

3. Choose $O_t = v_k$ according to the symbol probability distribution in state s_i, i.e., $b_i(k)$.

4. Transit to a new state $q_{t+1} = s_j$ according to the state transition probability distribution for state s_i, i.e., a_{ij}.

5. Set *t=t+1*; return to step 3) if t < T; otherwise terminate the procedure.

The above procedure can be used as both a generator of observations, and as a model for how a given observation sequence was generated by an appropriate HMM.

Three Basic Problems:

1. Given the observation sequence $O = (O_1, O_2, \ldots, O_T)$ and a model $\lambda = (A, B, \pi)$, how do we efficiently compute $P(O|\lambda)$, the probability of the observation sequence, given the model?

2. Given the observation sequence $O = (O_1, O_2, \ldots, O_T)$ and the model λ, how do we choose a corresponding state sequence $Q = (q_1, q_2, \ldots, q_t, \ldots, q_T)$ which is optimal in some meaningful sense ("that best explains the observations")?

3. Given the observation sequence $O = (o_1, o_2, \ldots, o_T)$, how do we adjust the model parameters $\lambda = (A, B, \pi)$ to maximize $P(O|\lambda)$?

Problem 1 is the evaluation problem, namely given a model and a sequence of observations, how do we compute the probability that the observed sequence was produced by the model. We can also view the problem as one of scoring how well a given model matches a given observation sequence. For example, if we consider the case in which we are trying to choose among several competing models, the solution to problem 1 allows us to choose the model which best matches the observations. Enumerating all possible state sequences and then computing the probability of observing the given sequence using that state sequence is computationally too expensive. There are two algorithms called the *Forward Algorithm* and the *Backward Algorithm* which can do the same computation more efficiently.

Problem 2 is the one in which we attempt to uncover the hidden part of the model, i.e., to find the "best" state sequence. We need to use some optimality criterion. There are several reasonable optimality criteria that can be imposed, and hence the choice of criterion is dependent on the intended use for the uncovered state sequence. The solution to this problem two is given by *Viterbi Algorithm.* In the case of POS tagging, we could model states as POS tags and words as observation symbols. POS tagging would then correspond to identifying an optimal state sequence using this Viterbi algorithm.

In problem 3 we attempt to optimize the model parameters so as to best describe a given observation sequence. The observation sequence used to adjust the model parameters is called a training sequence. The training problem is a crucial one for most applications of HMMs, since it allows us to optimally adapt model parameters to observed training data. The *Baum-Welch Algorithm* provides a method for doing this. This is basically a parameter re-estimating technique. Instead of simply computing empirical probabilities from training corpora, we can start with an initial model and iteratively refine the parameters as we get to see more and more training data. The Baum-Welch algorithm is actually an application of the EM algorithm.

We avoid the details of the algorithms here. The algorithms are readily available and can be easily accessed by the interested readers.

Other Techniques in Machine Learning

There are many learning techniques and many of them have been applied to language technology problems. Decision Trees and Decision Lists can be learnt automatically from training data. Several techniques exist to classify objects where the decision boundaries are non-linear. Support Vector Machines (SVMs), which are based on the principle of structural risk minimization, have been explored widely in recent times. Neural networks and genetic algorithms have been applied. Computational Learning Theory has started providing answers to fundamental relations between the training data size, the classification accuracy levels and the associated confidence levels. Machine learning is a large and fascinating field of study in itself. Interested readers will find many good books and other reference materials.

2.4 Technology Development in Indian Languages

India is a land of One Billion people - about one sixth of the whole world. Our civilization dates back to many thousands of years. India is a land of many religions, many cultures and many languages. A life time is not sufficient to get even a glimpse of everything that is Indian.

The Language Scene in India:

The language scene in India is quite unique. Most of higher education is imparted through the medium of English. Most people prefer to send their children to English medium schools. The quality of books and teachers in local languages are generally considered to be inferior, there is relatively little scientific and technical material available in these languages and scope for gainful employment are relatively less. English is the language of choice in business, medicine, law and even the government, although there are efforts to encourage the use of our own languages. In other non-English speaking countries, people use their own language for professional communicating among themselves and use English only to deal with outsiders. In India all business and professional transactions across the country are done in English. English has a greater role than our own languages.

The situation described above is actually true more of urban areas than in villages. A majority of Indians live in villages. Recent surveys show that a vast majority of our population do not know English and those who know a bit are not comfortable in the usage of English for day to day communications. The figures vary from 85% to 95% of the population. Thus a vast majority of our people are deprived of the direct benefits of all the modern information technology. People cannot be expected to know English, have typing skills and all the technical expertise required to use computers for retrieving relevant and useful pieces of information from the Internet or whatever. Indian language technologies, especially with voice input and output would go a long way in empowering people by providing them access to information.

Many people speak their own mother tongue at home but use English for everything else. With each generation, there is a slow decay in the use of our languages. Your grand parents were well read scholars, your parents studied your language up to high school and were able to read and write, you can speak but you cannot read and write, and your children will perhaps find it difficult even to speak your own language fluently. Language is a mirror of human life. Languages are also treasuries of human civilization. Everything that we know today is encoded in language somewhere. Everything we have learnt over the last thousands of years is hidden somewhere in our languages. As the languages slowly go into oblivion, so do these vast treasures of knowledge - knowledge of medicine, knowledge of astronomy, of mathematics, of mythology, of human values, of traditions and customs. Technology development for Indian languages has the potential to slow down and perhaps even reverse this trend, at least to some extent.

Almost all of the commercial and business transactions are

done in English not only for interacting with people abroad but even within the country. A large part of government and legal transactions are also performed in English. Almost all of the higher education is in the medium of English. Thus centres of power and money do not often see any great urgency for Indian language technologies. Private companies in Information technology sector recruit only those who know English. Companies need people who know English to interact with their foreign counterparts and it is easy to find people who are good in the relevant skills as also in English. Since everybody in the companies knows English, even the thought of using other local languages never arises. Groups trying to promote Indian language computing complain of lack of market. It is only recently that the importance of local language computing is getting realized more and more and Government of India has started promoting Indian language technologies in a big way.

The three language formula has worked well in some cases but has not worked very well in others. Nevertheless, a large number of people know two, three or even more number of languages. This is a kind of natural multi-lingualism, very different from the kind of multi-lingualism you will find in countries that are essentially mono-lingual. You will find that more or less free mixing of several languages is very common. Many documents are required to be in more than one language. With so many languages in use, correctly identifying the language used is itself an critical step in many language technology applications.

Although there are many languages and people from one part of the country sometimes feel almost like foreigners in other parts of the same country, it is not true that there are any serious language barriers. People have been travelling all over the country from ancient times and nobody has complained of language barriers. People know that everybody does not speak their language and there is a sense of tolerance, cooperation and understanding. *Learn more languages. Earn more friends* is the motto. Commonness of social culture, traditions and linguistic features also helps. Media and increased travel and mixing of people have helped too. English and Hindi act like national link languages. Thus there are no serious language barriers for simple day to day communications. However, it is still difficult for a vast majority of the people to use computers, access information from the Internet, etc.

Technology for Indian languages is developing fast and hopefully people will be able to overcome these problems soon.

We have heard people, especially from other countries, saying that India has one language called Hindi and about 20 or so dialects. Our own elders and policy makers often think that there are about 20 languages and hundreds of dialects. The fact is that there are about 150 different languages spoken in India, of which 22 have been given constitutional recognition and are considered to be the major languages. The status of languages is closely related to power politics and there are always fights to get higher and higher status for one's own language. Scientific analysis, however, is not based on power politics but on sound linguistic principles. Dialects are regional or social varieties of a given language - they all share a great degree of commonness in terms of vocabulary, grammar, pronunciation etc. If you hear somebody speaking a different dialect, you may find a few words, expressions, accent etc. a bit strange or even incomprehensible in the beginning but overall, it is your own language and you understand almost everything without difficulty. If the differences are so much that a person knowing one language cannot understand the other at all, we will have to consider them as separate languages. Although drawing the dividing line between language and dialects is a bit tricky, linguists have devised robust and reliable techniques for deciding if two varieties are dialects of the same language or two different languages. There is hardly anything common between Hindi and Kannada, for example, not even the words, and so it would be completely unacceptable to consider Kannada as a dialect of Hindi or the other way around. A Kannada speaker can understand the different dialects of Kannada but not Hindi, unless he or she has learnt Hindi. Kannada and Hindi as as distinct as English and French are. After careful studies, linguists have come to the conclusion that there are about 150 different languages spoken in India today. These are not dialects of one another. People coming from monolingual countries naturally find it difficult to accept this high degree of variation within a given country but those who know India well will have no difficulty. A survey conducted about 20 years ago showed that every 8 to 10 km we find some noticeable change in language, food, dress, customs and traditions etc. India is a land of great diversity.

Indian languages encompass four language families - the Indo-

Aryan, the Dravidian, the Tibeto-Burman and the Austro-Asiatic. Some of these languages have extensive literature going back to as early as 9th century AD. (The level of maturity seen in these early works prove beyond doubt that the languages must have been highly developed over many centuries before. Since we have not been able to locate any of the earlier works, we will have to go by the earliest available works to date our languages.) Many languages also exhibit a very rich oral 'literature'. The major Indian languages are among the most widely spoken languages of the world. We have an extraordinarily systematic and scientific linguistic tradition for more than 2000 years now. Phonology, Morphology, Syntax, Semantics, Logic, Pragmatics have been studied extensively over the past several thousand years. It is a challenge even to make a survey of all the works and the various schools of thought that have originated, grown, changed and evolved in India over a continuum of thousands of years.

With such a rich, varied, ancient and systematic and scientific background in human languages, we Indians should have been world the leaders in language technology. Instead, we are lagging far behind not only the western languages but also the languages of the far east. We are still struggling to use computers as type-writers - "type, compose and print"! The idea here is not to belittle the commendable work being done by many groups across the country. The point is, compared to what we could have achieved and what we should have achieved by now, what is actually achieved so far is meager.

We have stated above that there are about 150 different languages spoken in India. This is what linguists generally believe - we do not even have as yet an exact list of our languages. It takes a tremendous amount of effort to analyze each of these languages and the large number of dialects associated with each of them and study the vocabulary, the morphology, the syntax and the semantics. A majority of the recent work, especially in terms of technology, are limited to the 20 or so major languages.

Even in these major languages, resources available for technology development are scarce. Electronic dictionaries are becoming available only recently. There is no concept of a thesaurus in many languages. There is no computational grammar for any of these languages even today. Even the morphology has not been analyzed in enough depth and detail. It is not easy for an automatic system to say whether a given sequence of symbols is a valid word in a given language or not. In fact we do not know exactly how many words are there in many of our languages. There are no good spell checkers as yet in many of our languages.

The least that somebody would expect in today's times is a collection of texts in electronic form. Such a large and representative collection of texts, called a corpus, has immense value for statistical and linguistic analysis and for developing technology at all levels right from dictionaries and spell checkers to intelligent information retrieval, automatic categorization, automatic summarization and automatic translation. Unfortunately, even large plain text corpora are not yet available in may languages. Only about 3 Million word corpora are available for most of the major languages. These corpora have not be thoroughly proof-read and hence are not very dependable.

There are relatively few web-sites and web pages in Indian languages. Most of them are not indexed by search engines because standard encoding schemes are not followed. Some sites use pictures instead of text. Many use font-encoded pages and either depend on local availability of fonts at client side or dynamic font technology and plug-in's. Most of the newspapers, magazines and books will be in electronic form at some point of time or other during production but most often in completely non-standard, proprietary and secret encoding schemes and are thus useless for any further processing or analysis. In most cases, the electronic forms of the documents are never archieved.

Speech technologies are especially important for a country like India with many languages and high levels of illiteracy. There are again certain characteristics of Indian languages which are quite distinct from English. For example, stress is relatively less important and other prosodic features such as duration are more significant. Aspiration is a contrastive feature. A deeper understanding of characteristics of our languages is essential and technology developed for other languages cannot be simply borrowed. There is a lot of quantitative work that needs to be done. Very little has been done so far. We do not even have large speech corpora.

However, things are changing fast. There is a much higher degree of understanding and appreciation of the language technology issues at all levels. There is definite trend towards standardization. Several serious large scale efforts have been initiated. There is a corpus of about 35 Million words for Telugu today. Automatic text categorization systems have been developed. Language identification across Indian languages is now possible. OCR systems have started appearing for Indian scripts. Major initiatives have been taken in machine translation and speech technologies. Search engines specialized for Indian languages have been developed. There is progress on Information retrieval and extraction systems as well. There is hope that Indian language technologies will develop very fast over the next few years.

However, we should add a word of caution to our note of optimism. Whatever has been done so far in terms of technology development is largely ad-hoc, hoch-poch, untested, unfinished and essentially unusable. Specifications are not written down. Systems are not designed carefully. Instead we jump to implementation right away. Bench mark standards and standard test data are lacking. Standard testing and evaluation metrics, methods and tools are absent. Developers themselves double as testers. Training is done on test data and testing is done on training data. Even false claims are made at times. Standards are not respected. Peer review is discouraged. Teams are not built. There is too much of unnecessary competition. Everybody wants to do everything. A dozen groups are working on speech synthesis and each group develops its own text normalization techniques. Why cannot one group take up one small item like this, do a good job of it and make it available for all others to use? If there are competing ideas and there are enough people and resources to try out the various possibilities, then competition is good. Duplication of effort for want of coordination, lack of team spirit or due to ignorance is not welcome. Everybody wants to do big things and the foundations and ground realities are neglected. Everybody talks of all these issues and everybody wants to be the leader - 'you come and work for me' is the attitude. We cannot go on like this for ever. If we have achieved so little compared to what we could have, these are the reasons.

Apprehensions and lack of trust with regard to Intellectual Property Rights are perhaps another major set of reasons for the current scenario in India. Researchers are not fully aware of IPR issues, external support is inadequate, legal protection is poor, IPR is a costly issue and everybody is confused. Should we give out our products for free or should we transfer the technology to a company or should we sell them ourselves? In many cases there are no companies which are ready to take a technology and take it further. There are agents and traders looking for ready-made products which they can directly sell and make money but there are often no companies that are capable of absorbing a technology in the true sense, making a product out of that and market and maintain the product. Technology absorption requires substantial technical expertise and research capabilities. There is always a fight, right inside our own minds, whether we should give our products for free or make money out of it. Should we give out the source code? Should we take a patent? It makes no sense to take only an Indian patent. Getting a US patent takes a lot of time and money. Who wants to work with lawyers? There is a dilemma between use and misuse. There is a fight between putting the products of research into good use for the benefit of the people and preventing misuse and exploitation by unscrupulous elements. In the end a lot of good work done remains unknown and unused.

We have the capability. We can be world leaders. Only we must learn to rise above politics and personal ego and get more professional. We must learn grow beyond funds, power, name and fame and start looking at research from research point of view. We can then certainly achieve the status of global leadership in language technologies.

The Nature of Indian Languages:

Another reason for the relatively slow progress of Indian language technology is the very nature of our languages. Indian languages are characterized by several unique features that make them very different from other major languages of the world. Thus the technologies developed for English or Japanese cannot always be borrowed in a more or less direct fashion and applied to our languages. This is a double-edged sword. There are some nice properties of Indian languages which we can exploit and build simpler, more elegant and more efficient solutions. There are also certain characteristics that make Indian language processing more complex. Hence a clear understanding and appreciation of the salient characteristics of Indian languages is very essential. Here we give a brief sketch of some these salient characteristics.

Ours is primarily a oral culture. Vast amounts of knowledge

has been passed on from generation to generation, for thousands of years, only through the word of mouth. An exceptionally elaborate system was used to ensure that the knowledge so transmitted does not get corrupted or influenced by local conditions. If every copy of a traditional text were to be destroyed, nothing will have been lost - there are people who know the whole stuff by heart and the book can simply be written down again. Even after writing came into use, writing was looked down upon - you write it down only if you are not capable or confident of retaining it in your memory. It is said that we normally use only a very small part of our brain's capacity and our ancestors believed more in their own mental abilities than in external physical devices. Today the first thing we do is to take a photocopy. Copies lying in our bookshelves do not constitute *our* knowledge. Our knowledge is what we have in our finger tips. To this day, many of our tribal languages have no script. But they do have a very rich oral 'literature'. Thus not everything we have is available in written form. The greatest scholars in India have always been "illiterate" and they preferred to remain so even after writing became possible. The western notion of illiteracy is thus not applicable to India. Illiterates are not necessarily uneducated or ignorant.

This book, however, is focussed on computer processing of written texts. We shall therefore start with a study of our writing systems and the text processing environment. Our aim here will be to a get a feel for the nature of Indian languages and issues in technology development for Indian languages. We shall briefly survey a few selected technologies.

2.4.1 The Text Processing Environment:

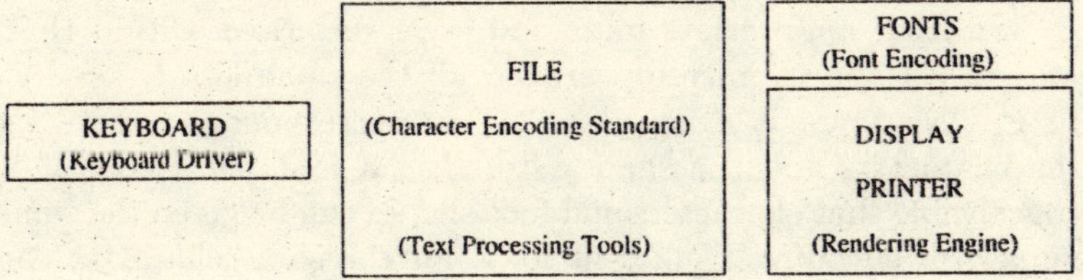

FIG 2.16 The Text Processing Environment

When you type in some text from a computer keyboard, a piece of software called the *keyboard driver* checks which keys are pressed and sends out corresponding numerical codes. The text editing software converts these codes into a possibly different set of codes corresponding to the character encoding scheme used. A character is a letter of the alphabet, a punctuation mark or a symbol such as '#' or '+'. For example, if ASCII is the character encoding scheme used, the upper case letter A is coded as the number 65. What is actually stored in a text file is just this number 65. All the software programs 'know' how to deal with this number 65. For example, a text editor would display it as the letter 'A'. A sorting program would know that 'A' comes before 'B'. If we are using the ISCII character encoding standard, the 1991 BIS standard (IS 13194:1991), and you type the character 'ka', the number 179 will be stored. UNICODE is yet another character encoding scheme - it specifies how exactly texts will be coded into numbers and stored in a text file. ASCII is suitable for languages using the English alphabet. ISCII can be used for Indian Language texts, including English. UNICODE is intended to be useful for all languages.

A character encoding scheme specifies how texts in a given language are encoded and stored in files. Presumably, all the text processing operations operate on this known, public, established standard. Note that the emphasis is on storage representation, not on how the characters appear when displayed or printed.

Words are simply linear sequences of letters. Writing on paper as well as displaying on the computer screen and printing through a computer printer are simple processes where the appropriate font shapes are selected and placed one next to the other in a left to right fashion by a piece of software called a *rendering engine*. By selecting appropriate fonts and style variations within that, we can get the various appearances of the same letter, say 'A'. In English there is a near one to one correspondence between the characters and the shapes stored in a font file. Thus it is conceivable that characters and font shapes can be given the same numerical encoding. Different fonts for the same character can also be given the same numerical encoding. The encoding for the letter 'A' is 65 irrespective of which font is used for display. It is the rendering engine which actually constructs the appropriate images on the computer screen or in a print-out as required.

A character encoding scheme specifies the character set, imposes a default collating sequence on the characters in the set and maps these characters to numerical codes. Text files simply contain these codes. Only when displayed or printed by a rendering engine using appropriate fonts will you start seeing the content of such text files in a readable form.

Things are different in Indian languages. The very notion of a character is different. A thorough understanding of the basics of characters and character encoding schemes is invaluable. Let us start by looking at the alphabets.

2.4.2 The Alphabet

English uses an alphabetic writing system. There are 26 letters in the alphabet and all words in English language are simply sequences of these 26 letters. Knowing A-B-C-D is not enough to read English - you must also learn spellings. Spelling rules are quite arbitrary. If P-U-T is put why is B-U-T but? One letter is used to give different sounds and different letter combinations are used to give the same sound: (f*a*t - f*a*te, m*e*t - m*e*te, k*i*t - k*i*te, p*u*t - b*u*t, *c*ase - *c*hess - *c*ess), (meet - meat - mete, bore - boar). Bernard Shaw once remarked that "fish" can be spelled as "goat" in English, by borrowing the 'g' for the 'f' sound from 'rough', 'o' for the 'i' sound from 'women' and 't' for 'sh' from 'station'!

Spelling based alphabetic writing systems necessitate an additional level of processing in many applications. For example, a Text-To-Speech system must have the rules to map the spellings to sounds so that texts can be read out correctly.

On the other hand, every nursery kid in India starts by a systematic study of phonetics, the science of sounds. The equivalent of the alphabet chart, called *varNamaala* shows a systematic and scientific classification of different sounds in the language. Since sounds are largely universal and language independent, the chart has the same structure for all languages. The written shapes differ but the overall scheme is the same. There are only very minor deviations from language to language. Let us look at a slightly abstracted version of such a chart so that it will be applicable to almost all Indian languages:

varNamaala

a	aa	i	ii	u	uu	e	ee	ai	o	oo	au
	M	H									
k	kh	g	gh	ng							
c	ch	j	jh	jnya							
T	Th	D	Dh	N							
t	th	d	dh	n							
p	ph	b	bh	m							
y	r	l	v	s'	S	s	h				

FIG 2.17 The "Alphabets" of Indian Scripts

Note how vowels and consonants are clearly separated. First come the vowels, then the consonants. First the back vowel 'a', then the mid vowel 'i' and finally the vowel 'u' produced by lip rounding. The 'a' vowel is the most basic and one of the simplest vowel sound in any language of the world. Short and long vowels are paired nicely. The diphthongs 'ai' and 'au' come towards the end. The first line ends with the semi-vowels 'M' and 'H'. The consonants come in two parts, first 25 of them are grouped into 5 rows of 5 columns each and then the rest are listed. Each row stands for a place of articulation and each column a manner of articulation. The rows represent velars, palatals, alveolars, dentals and labials, systematically moving from the throat towards the lips. The columns represent unvoiced-unaspirated, unvoiced-aspirated, voiced-unsapirated, voiced-aspirated, an finally the nasals. The second part includes the semi-vowels, liquids and fricative sounds.

Such a nice phonetically based orthographic system makes our languages free of spellings - what we write is what we speak. The child only learns the shapes of the letters and how they combine to depict complex sound clusters. Reading and writing then come naturally.

There are of course small deviations and variations from language to language and script to script but our aim here is to discern the simplicity and beauty of this scheme. A lot more can be said about our varNamaala but we shall avoid digressing too much into those issues. It is believed that Lord s'iva himself gave the sound system to mankind through his Damaruga and that is how we human beings got this great gift of speech. The s'iva suutras form the basis for all of our grammars. Readers are urged to explore these further.

2.4.3 The Script Grammar

Another unique characteristic of Indian languages is a grammar at the level of scripts. We can talk of grammatically valid an invalid sequences, which is not the same as valid or invalid spelling. A word which is not spelled correctly in English could still be conceived of as a possible proper name or abbreviation or acronym or a domain specific term. On the other hand, a sequence that is ungrammatical can never occur in any language, even in the future, not even as an acronym or proper name.

English and many other western languages use an alphabetic writing system. Any word is simply a (linear) sequence of the letters of the alphabet. Thus words have spellings. Spelling rules may be highly regular or quite irregular and largely arbitrary as in English, forcing us to remember the spellings of all the words. On the other hand, ideographic languages such as Chinese and Japanese use pictures to depict meanings. In contrast to these, Indian languages use a syllabic writing system.

Speaking and listening come naturally whereas writing and reading come much later. Written language needs to be taught and learnt. Not all are capable of reading and writing - there are illiterates. In fact language *is* speech - writing is an artifact. It is noteworthy that Indian scripts are based on sound units. There are really no spellings at all.

Indian scripts are directly based on phonetics - the units of orthography exhibit a more or less one to one correspondence with the spoken sounds. The units of orthography are essentially C*V syllables (more accurately called *aksharas*) where C denotes a consonant sound and V a vowel sound. C* segments are also allowed and hence the term 'syllable', although often used, is not accurate. We shall use the term *akshara*. Aksharas are the atomic units of writing. Parts of an akshara do not necessarily constitute valid linguistic units.

Since aksharas are of the general form C*V or C* and there can be several consonants in consonant clusters, the total number of possible aksharas is very large. There are examples of consonant clusters consisting of as many as five consonants (example, *kaartsnya*, Sanskrit). If all possible five consonant clusters are allowed, we get more than 2 Billion aksharas, assuming about 35 consonants, about 15 vowels and three vowel modifiers!

Of course all these mathematically possible aksharas may not occur in any given language and all those that can occur do not occur equally frequently. Studies have shown that about 5000 aksharas cover more than 99% of all words in all the major Indian languages taken together. Even five thousand is a large number - we cannot possibly treat them as atomic units. Can we have 5000 keys on a type-writer or a computer keyboard? Typing in, editing, storing, processing, displaying and printing of Indian languages all seem to be much more complex. Methods used for western languages are not suitable.

Five to ten thousand aksharas are all that we use frequently but to ensure completeness, we need to be able to represent every possible akshara while ruling out all invalid ones. It is clearly not feasible to give a separate symbol to each of the possible aksharas. That would make the orthography too complex to be practicable. It would make a lot of sense to consider consonants and vowels as basic units an compose aksharas out of them. Consonants and vowels are reasonably small in number, about 40 consonants and about 15 vowels in all. However we need some more issues relating to orthography to be taken into consideration before we come up with a good scheme.

Pure consonant sounds cannot in general be pronounced independently, they need the help of a vowel sound to pronounce. Of all the vowels we can think of 'a' (as in English word 'but') is the simplest, the most frequent and the most universal vowel sound. In fact 'a' and 'm' sounds are so basic that these are the sounds babies learn to speak first in almost all languages. It is no wonder that the word for mother is based on 'a' and/or 'm' sounds in most languages of the world. So when we learn the basic alphabet, the varNamaala, as kids, we are told to read out the consonant sounds with the help of the 'a' vowel. Consonants combined with vowels are more frequent than pure consonants and consonants combined with 'a' vowel are generally the most frequent. It therefore makes sense to consider consonants with an implied 'a' vowel as basic units and explicitly remove the implied 'a' vowel only when needed. In this scheme, a symbol called *halaMt* meaning consonant-ending is explicitly added to obtain a pure consonant. One may of course argue that we can treat pure consonants as basic and add the 'a' vowel as and when needed. Without getting into debates on which of these methods is really superior, let us adapt the former scheme for our purpose here. Every consonant has an implied 'a' vowel sound in it.

Of course consonants may combine with vowels other than 'a' and we need to specify the particular vowel in such cases. It will be assumed that the implicit 'a' is removed and the specified vowel is used in its place. We also need a mechanism to distinguish between a consonant sound with an implied 'a' vowel followed by another different vowel such as 'i', from the case where we need the combination of the consonant with the 'i' vowel sound - ("ka-i" is different from "ki"). Further, the written shapes for vowels occurring independently in their own right and vowels that combine with consonants to form single aksharas are substantially different in many scripts. Given these two factors, it makes good sense to distinguish between independent vowels and vowel sounds that combine with consonants. The latter are called vowel *maatras*.

Finally, we also have a couple of semi-vowels, namely 'm' and 'h' (called *anusvaara and visarga* in Sanskrit), which can be appended to the vowel sounds occurring either independently or with one or more consonants. In some languages we also have a half-anusvaara. These are called *vowel modifiers.*

The only other mechanism we need is to allow a pure consonant without automatically combining it with following consonant to form a cluster. This occurs relatively rarely as in the case of English and other foreign language words when written in our scripts. A simple escape mechanism is provided - use two halaMts in sequence to terminate the akshara and prevent combination with following consonants if any.

Now that we have all the required ingredients we can start defining aksharas very precisely. Note that the basic units of akshara construction are consonants, vowels, halaMt, vowel maatras and vowel modifiers. Note also that not all possible sequences of such building blocks are valid. For example, vowel maatras can only post-modify consonants, they cannot occur before or independently. You can have only one maatra, not more than one. Thus there are valid and invalid sequences. We are ready to give a grammar, a grammar of scripts that accepts *all valid aksharas* and *only valid aksharas.* Any sequence which is invalid can never ever occur in any language. The grammar is *complete*, it is not a sample. Every one of the billions of possible valid aksharas is handled. There is no compromise. Here is the grammar:

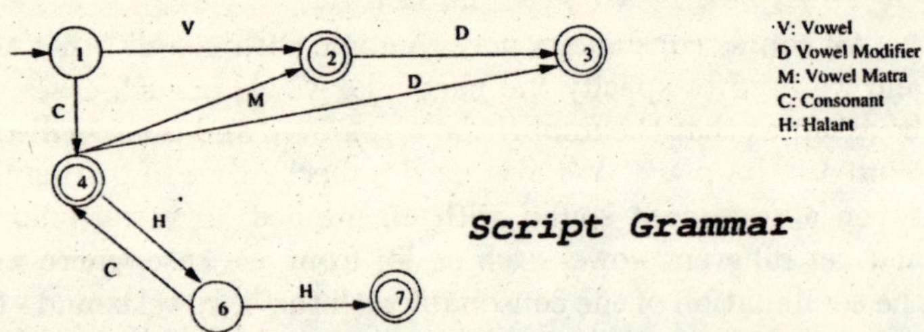

FIG 2.18 Script Grammar for Indian Languages

This extremely simple grammar is complete and consistent. It allows all valid aksharas, potentially infinite in number, without regard to their frequency of occurrence in any particular language or domain. It is primarily based on sound units and hence universal and language independent. We have a common grammar for all languages and all scripts. What an excellent solution!

Note that the grammar specified here is a Finite State Machine. It is the simplest kind of grammar we can think of and the most efficient. All aksharas in a given word can be identified in a single scan in linear time. The grammar can be used to identify invalid aksharas as a kind of spell-checking process, to break a word into its constituent aksharas and for other similar purpose.

The script grammar is sometimes given as phrase structure rules but one must recognize that the power of Context Free Grammars is not required. Finite State power is sufficient. Thus giving phrase structure rules can be misleading.

Although the above grammar for scripts is well accepted, there could be alternative schemes. For example, we may treat consonants as pure consonants without any implicit vowel. This would make the halaMt unnecessary but 'a' vowel needs to be explicitly shown where needed. This would also eliminate the need to assume that the implicit 'a' is removed when a consonant combines with some other vowel.

Also note that this grammar is not entirely phonetic based. If it were, we would not be treating vowels and vowel maatras as separate elements since they represent the same phonetic items. But remember that our purpose here is not to do a phonetic transcription of speech, our purpose is to develop a grammar for scripts. In terms of written symbols, many Indian languages show substantial variations in shape - independent vowels and vowel maatras look very different. Our choice here is not vary bad then. Vowels and vowel maatras look different and we need some mechanism to distinguish between the two.

2.4.4 Fonts, Glyphs and Encoding Standards

The same letter 'A' may appear differently on the computer screen and in print-outs depending upon which 'font' is used. In lay man's terms, fonts are different styles of writing characters. A font file specifies the exact shapes of characters and the various shapes are given numerical codes. Within a given font it is often possible to show finer variations such as size, boldface, italics, underline, strike-through etc. The figure below shows some examples of English fonts and variations within these.

A A A A A A

FIG 2.19 English Fonts

In Indian scripts, the number of aksharas is very large and it is also not practicable to have one font shape for each akshara. Just as aksharas themselves were composed of more basic elements such as vowels and consonants, font shapes need to be composed of more basic elements. However, the primary aim here would not be phonetics or grammaticality, the primary aim would be ease of composition. A font should be designed to have a small number of basic shapes from which all valid aksharas can be easily composed. Such basic shapes used to define fonts are called *glyphs*. Here are some examples of glyphs and how they combine to form full aksharas:

అ ఆ ఇ ఈ ఉ ఊ

ఋ ౠ ఎ ఏ ఐ ఒ ఓ ఔ

అం అః

క ఖ గ ఘ ఙ

చ ౘ ఛ జ ౙ ఝ ఞ

ట ఠ డ ఢ ణ

త థ ద ధ న

ప ఫ బ భ మ

య ర ల ళ వ శ

ష స హ క్ష ఱ

FIG 2.20 Telugu Script: Vowels and Consonants

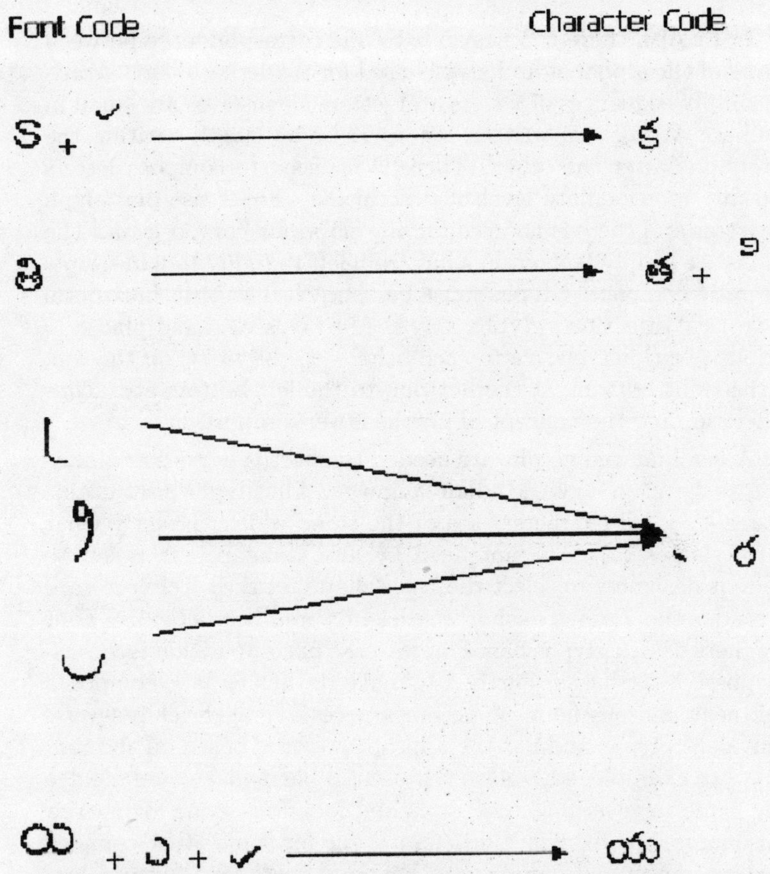

FIG 2.20 Contd. Glyph to Character Mappings

The shapes we use in defining a font should be selected based on the simplicity of their being composed to obtain combined shapes for displaying full aksharas. The shapes are quite different from script to script. The script grammar, on the other hand, was based on phonetics and the aim was to develop a simple and efficient grammar to define all valid aksharas in a language independent manner. From this, it should be clear that there may not be any one-to-one correspondence between glyphs used in defining fonts and the elements of which the script grammar itself was developed. Different scripts look differently and hence the fonts and the glyphs of which these fonts are made of, also differ.

In English there is a near one to one correspondence between letters of the alphabet and glyphs used for rendering them. Words are simply sequences of letters and letters themselves are small in number. Words are written left to right by simply writing the letters one after the other. There is no need to compose letters into any intermediate level of description. Fonts use one glyph per letter and there is no need for any elaborate composition. The glyphs are simply laid out in a line from left to right. Indian scripts are more complex. Glyphs must be composed in both horizontal an vertical direction - glyphs may need to be scaled and placed in various positions relative to each other - to the right, on the top, to the right-bottom, at the bottom, to the left-bottom etc. Thus understanding the concept of glyphs is very important.

A few hundred glyphs are needed to effectively render all possible aksharas in a given Indian language. The glyphs are variable in size - not all characters are of the same width. Exactly what set of shapes to use is not fixed by any standard. It is left to the font designers to select the basic shape set they feel necessary to render the various aksharas efficiently and aesthetically. Font designers design glyphs based on the ease of composition into various possible aksharas. Further, to make the aksharas so composed look neat and aesthetic, it becomes necessary to develop several equivalent glyphs and use the appropriate ones based on the context. For example, a glyph to represent a particular vowel maatra may come in several shapes, sizes and locations - one for narrow consonants, one for wide consonants, one for some other complex combination of consonants, etc. Different fonts for the same language may, and often do, differ in terms of the glyph sets they employ. Fonts also vary in terms of the position in the code table, that is, what numerical codes are given to each of the glyphs they encompass. *Each font uses a possibly different set of glyphs and positions them in possibly different ways in the code table.* In fact there is no glyph encoding standard. There is even some opposition to the idea of developing a glyph encoding standard fearing that such a standard may curtail the creativity of font designers in producing aesthetic fonts.

This total lack of standardization at the level of glyphs and fonts has far reaching consequences. For example, simply selecting a piece of text and changing the font can render the text junk. Fonts have been treated like pieces of art and they remain proprietary, non-standard and incompatible with one another. Of late there is some realization that standards are useful if not essential and there is hope that some sort of standards will develop and get widely accepted. Tamil is perhaps the only language where there has been a great deal of effort in overcoming teething problems of this kind and standards have been developed and widely accepted, although keeping only Tamil language in mind.

In fact many commercial software vendors have promoted the use of their own proprietary, non-standard and secret fonts. Texts typed from these software are encoded in terms of these proprietary fonts, rather than in terms of any standard character encoding scheme. A large number of electronic texts in Indian languages have been encoded in proprietary fonts and thus not directly useful for any language technology application. Text typed in through one commercial software is often not useable in another software. A great deal of time, effort and money goes into developing inter-conversion tools between different fonts. Perhaps India could have been in a much more advanced state today if standards had been respected and commercial companies not allowed to take the whole country for a ride. In spite of the fact that almost every publisher is using electronic typing and composing of some kind or the other, developing even plain text corpora in Indian languages has been such an arduous task. It is only very recently that corpora crossing 30 Million words have started appearing at least for some languages.

2.4.5 Character Encoding Standards

In alphabetic writing systems such as English, there are a small number of letters which can be directly encoded in a character encoding standard such as ASCII. Letters of the alphabet, along with other special symbols such as punctuation marks, numerals, parenthesis, quote marks etc, are called *characters*. A character encoding scheme specifies the allowed set of characters and places them in a particular order. This order defines the collating sequence. Usually collating sequence is so selected that sorting in alphabetical order becomes straight forward. Each position is given a numerical code and the characters are represented inside computers by these numbers. Thus the character 'A' is represented as number 65 in ASCII. Since there is a one-to-one correspondence between letters and glyphs, fonts can also use the same numerical codes for placing the corresponding glyphs. Thus 'A' can be represented as 65 in ASCII character encoding standard as also in any of the fonts. This makes the whole scheme very simple and neat. The encoded text remains the same irrespective of which fonts are used.

We need a character encoding scheme for Indian languages too. But we must first understand what we mean by a character. Aksharas are the basic units of writing but there are too many of them. We cannot encode each possible akshara by giving it a numerical code. We must get into more basic units and encode them. Thus aksharas will need to be composed of more basic units. The script grammar we have seen above forms an excellent scheme to define a character encoding standard.

Any character encoding scheme for Indian language scripts must ideally define a script grammar and implement it by specifying the numerical codes for the consonants, vowels and other symbols used in the grammar. In spite of the fact that the number of valid aksharas is potentially infinite and practically very large, a script grammar makes it possible to encode texts using a fairly small number of different codes. The texts encoded in such a scheme would be a sequence of such numeric codes. The appropriate units of reading, displaying, printing and otherwise manipulating Indian languages are aksharas, not individual symbols such as vowels, consonants, maatras etc. It is straight forward to synthesize aksharas as also to break running texts into sequences of aksharas using the script grammar. Aksharas are the atoms of Indian writing systems. Any method that attempts to directly deal with sub-atomic units such as vowels, consonants and maatras are to be rejected as they are fundamentally flawed. Such designs result in improper and unacceptable breaking of aksharas. How often do we see a consonant at the end of one line and the associated maatra in the beginning of the next line!

ISCII

ISCII is a National Standard for character encoding of major scripts of Indian languages. A brief description of the ISCII character encoding schemes given below. Refer to the 1991 BIS standard (IS 13194:1991) for more information.

India is a multi-lingual country. Of the major languages, Urdu, Sindhi and Kashmiri are primarily written in Perso-Arabic scripts, although Devanagari script is also used. Sindhi is also written in Gujarati script. All the remaining languages are written in 10 different scripts, all of which have the origins in the ancient braahmii script. These scripts are Devanagari, Gurumukhi (Punjabi), Gujarati, Oriya, Bengali, Assamese, Telugu, Kannada, Malayalam and Tamil. Many of these languages are written in more than one script. Sanskrit is written in almost all the scripts. Also, a given script may be used for writing several languages. Sanskrit, Hindi and Marathi are all written using the Devanagari script. The association between languages and scripts is not one to one. People who come from the west often have difficulties in understanding this situation.

All the 10 braahmii based scripts have the same phonetic structure. Linguists have also shown that India is a linguistic area and thanks to great similarities and commonness in the cultural and social settings across India, Indian languages have many things in common at various levels of linguistic description ranging from the aksharas through word and sentence structure and meaning to expressions and idioms. There is a unique blend of similarity and commonness, along with distinctive and contrastive characteristics. It is therefore most appropriate to have a common script code for all the 10 braahmii based scripts, as indeed ISCII does.

We have seen that the varNamaala for Indian languages is a very systematic and scientific organization of the basic sounds - the vowels and the consonants. We have also seen that units of writing are aksharas and there is a script grammar that defines the valid aksharas in a simple and efficient manner. The script grammar is common to all the ten braahmii based scripts. ISCII takes advantage of these facts and encodes 15 vowels, 38 consonants, 3 vowel modifiers, a nukta symbol to indicate alternative forms of certain selected consonants, thereby forming a slight superset of all the elements used in these ten braahmii based scripts. These are placed in the code table in such a manner that correct sorting is automatically obtained for ISCII encoded texts. Since the total number of items to be encoded is less than 128, ISCII has chosen to use the second half of the ASCII table, retaining the first 128 codes as they are. This makes mixing of English and

Indian languages, a very common phenomenon in India, trivial. Thus ISCII includes all of the basic ASCII characters without any change.

Using a common script code for different scripts makes transliteration between these scripts trivial. What we encode are the sounds and the sounds are the same in all languages although the shapes used in writing these sounds may be very different. It must be noted that transliterating texts from one script to another is very common in India. The very nature of the language situation in India makes this necessary. We use words from other languages but write them in our script. Transliteration also makes it possible to 'read' texts in a language we do not know. Actually, because of the linguistic and social similarities, we can understand other languages to some limited extent provided we can 'read' them by transliterating the texts into a script we know. In ISCII transliteration is trivial - the encoding is exactly the same in all scripts and all we really need to see the text in another script is to simply render the same text in the required script. Note that the flip side of the coin is that there can be no multi-lingual (multi-script) plain text in pure ISCII. Language and/or script can be indicated only using annotations or markup.

ISCII encodes sound units and sound units are largely common across the languages of the world. It is therefore conceivable that ISCII can be extended to encode all languages of the world. What is common to different languages of the world is the set of sound units. Really nothing else is so universal. The ISCII scheme would perhaps be the best scheme for developing universal character encoding scheme for all the languages and scripts of the world. If we can do it for so many diverse languages and scripts of India, why not for the whole world?

Although the ISCII standard is now almost 14 years old, it is not very widely known or used. Commercial companies have promoted their own proprietary font encoded texts and very few of them have even export-import facilities to ISCII. ISCII is not a registered standard and is not supported by many Operating Systems and Web Browsers. ISCII only defines the character encoding scheme, it does not provide any standards for glyph encoding, nor does it provide a set of compatible fonts. This makes it necessary for application software to handle all issues of keyboard drivers, ISCII-to-Font mapping and rendering. Perhaps this is the main reason why ISCII has not picked up as much as it should have done and we see proliferation of non-standard and proprietary schemes even today.

The ISCII standard does recommend keyboard layouts for different scripts under the name *INSCRIPT*. The inscript keyboards are well designed and reasonably efficient once you learn trying in inscript. Nevertheless, there are different views and again we find a proliferation of several keyboarding schemes. Some find it more convenient to type in Indian scripts using the Roman transliterations. There are again several roman phonetic schemes. Thus one who is proficient in typing in a particular scheme will find it difficult to use anther. Not all software vendors support all the available schemes.

ISCII standard specifies the script grammar. The ISCII standard however uses phrase structure rules instead of the simpler Finite State Machine notation. It must be made clear that finite state power is sufficient, we do not need the power of context free grammars. It should also be noted that ISCII standard only 'specifies' the grammar of scripts. It is the duty of the software systems to 'enforce' this grammar and allow only grammatically valid aksharas. Many of the commercial software packages do not enforce the script grammar properly and the texts you create using such software will be ungrammatical. Often there will be multiple spellings (sequences of encoded bytes) for the same word. What you see and what is stored in the file will be different. Processing such texts will be unnecessarily more complex than needed.

ISCII is based on the script grammar we have seen above. Consonants are assumed to have an implicit 'a' vowel in them. This scheme gives a one byte code for 'ka' and two byte codes for 'ki', 'kii' etc., making the text processing algorithms a trifle bit more complex than would have been otherwise necessary. Vowels and vowel maatras are encoded separately although they represent the same sounds - a deviation of the basic philosophy that what we speak is what we write. However, this design makes it easy to distinguish between a consonant followed by a vowel from a consonant that combines with a vowel sound to form a single akshara.

ISCII makes a super set of sounds over a set of languages. This is theoretically objectionable as each language has its own characteristic set of sounds (phonemes) and foreign sounds cannot be included. However it makes a lot of practical engineering sense to develop a common scheme when the commonness overwhelmingly shadows minor differences.

ISCII also errs by including special sequences and separate codes for minor variations in shapes of certain rendered characters. Fonts specify how exactly the characters appear when displayed or printed, a non-issue as far as character encoding schemes are concerned. We should not be concerned with allographs, with minor variations in shapes of rendered characters that do not change the word in question. As a character encoding standard, ISCII should have worried only about encoding characters and not about fonts or rendering.

It must be understood that there can be no multi-lingual (that is multi-script) plain text in ISCII since the codes are same for all scripts. Sounds are the same in all languages and thus ISCII carries no information about language or script. Attributes are essential to explicate language and script. The best way to handle variations is to use attributes. The best way to encode attributes is to use open, public, visible XML style attributes, not invisible control characters. ISCII attempts to specify some of the commonly used attributes. Attributes are application specific and open ended. It would have been much better for ISCII to provide a general scheme for annotation rather than attempt to specify attribute and extension codes. The attribute and extension codes specified in ISCII standard are not uniformly followed and software vendors make their own non-standard extensions and modifications. They even use "prohibited" codes. Government of India has come out with a very good standard for character encoding. However, the standard has not been enforced or widely accepted and properly used. We could have saved a lot of time, effort and money had we simply respected the ISCII standard from day one. If a standard is imperfect, we may work towards bringing out a revised and improved standard. We cannot use that as an excuse for not using the standard at all. An imperfect standard is better than no standard at all.

A plain ISCII document has no explicit indication of language. Given the multi-lingual nature of our country, automatically identifying language from small text samples is therefore very important. Think of a text containing Sanskrit verses and explanatory notes in Marathi or Hindi. Everything is in Devanagari script, possibly in the same font but a spell checker operating on such a document needs to know which parts are in Sanskrit and which parts are in Marathi or Hindi.

UNICODE

With increasing globalization, the need for handling various languages of the world is becoming more and more important. UNICODE has come out of the desire to handle all languages of the world in a uniform way. It aims to provide a separate code space for each language. There is however, a bit of confusion between languages and scripts and sometimes code spaces are assigned to script-wise rather than language-wise.

UNICODE for Indian languages is based on (an older, outdated version of) ISCII - each language has a separate code space but the codes mainly differ only in terms of the starting offset. Thus the foundations for script coding remain identical to ISCII and the main difference is only the use of two bytes for each character, the first byte indicating the language and the second byte being the same as in ISCII. There is really no major change at all. Texts become larger due to the use of multi-byte characters but this is not such a crucial issue. ISCII makes transliteration between Indian scripts trivial and it is quite straight forward to do this in UNICODE too. There was no multi-lingual plain ISCII text possible but with UNICODE the language/script identification is built in.

We still have some teething problems in using Indian languages on computers. It is not always easy to do even simple things like searching and sorting. Part of the reason for this is the proliferation of proprietary and non-standard technologies by commercial companies. Also, ISCII is not a registered standard, and it is not directly supported by operating systems, browsers etc. There are no standard ISCII compatible fonts and standard mapping tools between ISCII and the fonts. While things have been improving of late, UNICODE is slowly becoming more popular. UNICODE has provision for fonts with embedded the mapping rules. Thus it will be easier to render UNICODE texts for display and printing purposes. With improving system level support, some of the teething problems can be avoided or overcome. UNICODE is likely to be widely supported by many operating systems, Browsers and other standard software. Although there are many problems and issues yet to be sorted out with UNICODE and related fonts for Indian languages, UNICODE is slowly picking up and may become the dominant encoding scheme. Some think switching to Unicode is inevitable. For some time at least ISCII and UNICODE will co-exist as standard character encoding schemes for Indian languages. Migrating from ISCII to UNICODE will anyway not be much difficult.

From Characters to Fonts:

We have seen that many commercial software packages encode documents in their own proprietary font encodings. A font encoded document is really not text at all. Fonts are made up of glyphs - graphic shapes which have no one-to-one correspondence with any appropriate level of linguistic description. A glyph can be a full vowel or a consonant but it can also be part of a consonant, a consonant combined with a particular vowel maatra, just a vowel maatra or any other arbitrary unit that is designed purely for the sake of graphical composition and rendering into aksharas. A dot that appears in the middle of some aksharas in Telugu could be a glyph. How can we interpret or process documents encoded as sequences of such arbitrary symbols? Even basic operations such as searching and sorting cannot be performed on such documents using standard tools. Glyphs do not correspond to aksharas or to more basic elements such as vowels ans consonants, glyphs cannot be placed in a collating sequence that permits natural sorting. Font encoded documents are not texts at all. You may be able to type, compose and print documents using a proprietary commercial software but you cannot use such documents like normal texts in other languages.

All texts, Indian language texts included, must be encoded in some character encoding standard such as ISCII or UNICODE. But unlike in the case of English, an ISCII encoded text cannot be directly displayed or printed because ISCII encodes texts in terms of sound units, not shape units required for visual rendering. ISCII is designed for the ears, not eyes. We have already seen that fonts are made up of glyphs and glyphs may not have one-to-one correspondence with the elements of the script grammar on which ISCII is based. This necessitates that we posit a level of processing that translates an ISCII encoded text into a selected font for the purposes of display and printing. It must be emphasized that fonts are required only for display and printing. There is no other role for fonts. All processing is best done on a character encoded text, not on a font encoded document. For example, if you want to develop a spell checker or a grammar checker, an automatic summarization system or a text categorization system, character encoded texts can be processed in a uniform and efficient way while font encoded pages will be idiosyncratic to specific fonts used and thus not generic and universal. If you just change over to a different font tomorrow, all your programs may fail.

Texts must be encoded in a character encoding standard based on the script grammar and the glyphs in a font do not necessarily correspond to aksharas or to the basic elements of which aksharas are built. Aksharas are too numerous for a one-glyph-per-akshara design. *Thus converting from a character encoding such as ISCII or UNICODE into and from a given font encoding is an additional step that is essential for Indian languages.* However, there is as yet no 'standard' way of mapping from ISCII into various fonts - there is no standard 'grammar' to specify this mapping. There are very few free fonts and most software vendors have their own proprietary fonts and ad-hoc methods of mapping if any. Some have used table-look-up, some use context free grammars and some use ad-hoc pieces of code. These solutions are usually not complete or consistent. Often a poorly designed commercial software can be crashed by simply typing in a particular sequence of characters which the system is unable to process.

Given this situation, most commercial vendors of Indian language software have chosen to store texts directly in terms of the font encoding scheme for their own, mostly proprietary, fonts, rather than using ISCII which has been in existence for over a decade as a National standard. This makes it difficult to take texts typed using one software and use it on another software system. In fact simply selecting a block of text and changing the font can render the block junk. No standard text processing algorithms can be run on such documents. Searching, sorting, spell checking, dictionary look up, frequency analysis, and all other text processing applications will have to be tuned to work with specified fonts and the same processes cannot be guaranteed to work correctly with other documents or documents encoded in other fonts. Commercial softwares are also often extremely slow because they try to directly work with the text as it would be finally rendered. *Font encoded texts are not texts at all by any standard.* They are at best suitable only for displaying on the screen and printing on paper. It is completely unacceptable to encode texts in any scheme other than National or International character encoding standards such as ISCII or UNICODE. We need to grow beyond using computers merely as type-writers. Of what use is a text which is encoded in some non-standard, proprietary, secret system of codes? Vast amounts of texts in Indian languages are being developed for some purpose or the other and in most cases the documents are in electronic form at some stage or the other. All this effort goes waste when it comes to re-using these texts for any research and development activity.

Thus there is a need to develop a simple, uniform and efficient scheme for mapping ISCII encoded pages into a selected font for the purposes of visualization. The scheme should be provably complete and consistent. It should be easy to adapt the scheme developed for one font for other fonts with minimal effort.

Converting from ISCII to font is best done at the level of aksharas. ISCII defines the script grammar and texts can be easily broken into aksharas using this grammar. Each akshara must then be mapped to the appropriate glyph sequence. Note that there is no grammar for fonts and hence mapping from font encoded documents back into ISCII would be a bit more complex. In the case of complex scripts such as Telugu, a non-deterministic solution requiring search may be necessary. In any case, it would be much better to map between ISCII and fonts rather than attempt to map directly from one font to another. Direct font to font converters are ad-hoc solutions, not generic, one-time, re-usable modules.

Things are changing slowly now. Standard text editors are becoming available. People have started demanding more. Text processing applications will get widely used. Ministry of Information Technology, Government of India, is a voting member of the UNICODE consortium and can influence decision making in UNICODE. UNICODE is still in the making. It has hardly come to be used for Indian languages in any significant way. This is the right time to understand all the issues carefully and take the right steps in the right direction.

Issues in Character Encoding Standards:

There is a lot of confusion regarding character encoding standards and their relation with fonts, keyboard drivers, rendering engines etc. People think in terms of what they see on the computer screen or on a printed paper. Seeing is not believing when it comes to encoding standards. The reality is not what appears on the screen but what is actually stored in the file. We have already seen that ISCII encodes sound units and thus an ISCII document is independent of language and script used, let alone fonts. What we see on the screen is not the main concern here. We must think in terms of what is stored in files and how to process such text files. The following points are included here to clearly bring out the major concerns in designing character encoding standards for Indian languages.

- Since character encoding schemes deal with scripts, inherent properties of scripts must be part of character encoding standards themselves. They cannot be relegated to the level of fonts or software implementations. One such issue is the script grammar. There are other important issues as well. For example, Telugu and Kannada scripts differ from say, Devanagari script in terms of how consonant clusters are represented. To represent a C1C2 cluster, Devanagari uses a half C1 and a full C2 shapes whereas Telugu and Kannada would use a full C1 and a half C2 shape. The best place to make this assertion is at the script level.
- Further, although the relation between languages and scripts is not necessarily one-to-one and character encoding schemes worry about scripts and not languages, there are certain basic properties of scripts in relation to languages that use them and such properties must be mentioned in the standard. For example, in Hindi the last consonant in a word is taken as a pure consonant even without any explicit halaMt whereas in Sanskrit it is not so.
- Any character encoding scheme for Indian languages must include a grammar of aksharas. ISCII standard already does so. Characters *are* aksharas.
- Every software developed for Indian languages must include and enforce the grammar of aksharas. Aksharas are atomic

units of our writing systems and aksharas cannot be arbitrarily split at any cost. Operating systems, text editors and word processors, web browsers must all treat aksharas as indivisible atomic units. As of today, this is not so. You might have seen pages of text where a consonant appears at the end of a line and the associated maatra appears in the beginning of the next line!. You will also find components of a single akshara separated by spaces. Web browsers are not yet ISCII-aware and UNICODE-aware browsers are only beginning to come. It is not enough for a browser to 'know' UNICODE, it must have the grammar of aksharas built-in too. Checking for ungrammatical aksharas must be an integral part of every software. Most commercial softwares today do not check or enforce grammaticality at akshara level - they permit ungrammatical combinations to be typed in, they do not necessarily show this up in rendering, and hence it is not possible to check and correct these mistakes manually by looking at the screen. What you see on the screen is not what is stored in the document file. No wonder some of the text corpora developed using such softwares is full of errors.

- Every software system must support all grammatically valid aksharas. Completeness is essential. Good character-to-font mapping schemes need to be developed.

- It is also not correct to split words at arbitrary akshara boundaries. Hyphenation rules will have to be developed for Indian languages so that justification of texts in narrow columns etc. can be done properly. This is especially important in Indian languages since the average length of words is much larger than in the case of English.

- A font developer may choose his own set of glyphs and place them anywhere in the font code table according to his own needs. There is no real need to enforce a glyph encoding standard. However, every font must be accompanied by a mapping system that can map every grammatically possible akshara onto the corresponding sequence of glyphs and vice versa. In case any special rules are required for selection of glyphs or for correct rendering, they must be included as part of the package. It is not sufficient to give just the font file. The mapping system must be provably complete, consistent and computationally efficient in terms of storage and processing time. No grammatical akshara must be incapable of being used because of font, mapping or rendering limitations.

- Of course if glyph encoding standards can be developed and accepted and used, issues of compatibility between fonts and character to font mappings can be taken care of once for all.

- The over all user experience depends on all the components of a text processing environment and their inter-compatibility. Character encoding standards, fonts and rendering engines must all be developed carefully to provide the appropriate user experience on the whole. Quality of rendered texts depend on the fonts, the glyph sets used in the font, the mapping rules used and glyph selections made, and the details of the rendering engine. However, *character encoding is not directly concerned with the appearance of rendered texts at all. Decisions on character encoding issues should never be taken based solely on how rendered texts appear to the eye. Character encoding has nothing to do with aesthetics. All issues relating to character encoding standards must be based solely on how the texts would be coded and how text processing algorithms would treat these texts.* Will there be one or several 'spellings' for a given word? Will a default sorting algorithm sort words in the same order as in a dictionary? How can we design simple, efficient and uniform sorting methods that can sort texts in different languages? If we carry out a type-token analysis on a corpus will frequencies of words get counted correctly? What about other statistical analyses such as n-grams or Markov analysis? What happens when we transliterate texts from one language to another? The 'spelling' of words is thus the only important aspect that should dictate character encoding issues.

To give a specific example, whether 'kSa' should be encoded directly in a character encoding standard such as ISCII or UNICODE should be decided solely on whether dictionaries treat 'kSa' differently from the cluster formed from the consonants 'ka' and 'Sa'. Are there two different words, otherwise identical, one using 'kSa' as a single unit and the other using a cluster of 'ka' and 'Sa'? That 'kSa' appears differently on the screen is no reason to argue for a separate code. One should not also go by what is given in primary school text books. The purpose there is to teach the children to read and write. If something looks a bit different, it is useful to point that out and teach it as a separate entity. When it comes to usage on a computer, the fonts and the rendering engine can be and must be designed to give you exactly what you want to see on the screen and in printed matter even if 'kSa' is not encoded as a separate 'character' in the character encoding scheme. There is no need to compromise on what the users really want to see on the screen and in print-outs - users shall see exactly what they like to see in rendered texts. But this does not require separate encoding of alternative shapes. Encoding need not be and should not be compromised. Users can still see exactly what they wish to see.

- It is important to clearly distinguish between basic characters and special symbols. Basic characters are those that form the words of a given language, as found in a dictionary and in various inflected forms in running texts. Basic characters dictate the 'spellings', the sorting order and so on. Special symbols such as the currency symbols, religious symbols, symbols for playing cards, symbols used in music etc. may have to be carefully incorporated into character encoding schemes but every care must be taken to avoid proliferation of multiple 'spellings' for words. As a specific example, currency is indicated in Kannada by simply writing 'ruu.' the standard way. Adding a new special symbol will make it possible to write the same thing in two different ways. This is highly undesirable. New symbols must be added with great care. Multiple spellings must be avoided at all costs.

- While we agree that sounds are more basic than written symbols, arguments about sounds must not be carried too far. The items in the varNamaala are just names of the corresponding characters which are abstract in nature. 'a' is the name of a vowel sound rather than an accurate representation of any vowel sound, just as 'ef' and 'em' are names of the consonants 'f' and 'm' respectively in English. Character encoding schemes are used only for writing and what we write is at best an attempt to approximate what we speak, even in Indian languages. Minor (allophonic) variations in pronunciation cannot be and need not be depicted in the writing system. We need to make a distinction if and only where the variations are significant enough to confuse one word for the other. If there is no ambiguity, there is no need to show the variations in the orthography. *Character encoding schemes must not be concerned with allophonic variations.* A character encoding scheme is primarily concerned with scripts and orthography, not with pronunciations or meanings. As a specific example, in Kannada there are no vowel sound as in the English word 'cat'. In Telugu, this particular sound does occur in speech but is not distinguished from the normal 'a' sound (as in the English word 'but') in writing. This does not introduce any ambiguities. There is no confusion as to which word is meant. Hence there is no need to introduce a new character corresponding to the vowel sound as in 'cat' as far as native words are concerned. Adding new character codes will only add to the confusion and the proliferation of spellings. The primary goal is to write words of our own language, not words of foreign languages! We are we so much worried about accurate depiction of 'cat', 'cot' and 'caught' in Indian scripts?

Some consonants such as 'ka' and 'Da' have significant variations in pronunciation in some languages and we usually put a dot underneath these characters when writing on paper. We can take care of these variations by adding a separate code called the 'Nukta'. Whether to encode these variations or not is primarily a question of whether these are allophonic variations or linguistically significant variations. However, one must also keep in mind the possibility that these variations have already been encoded and depicted in the scripts by convention in the past.

- ISCII has already been extended to include the vowel sounds as in the English words 'cat', 'caught' and 'cot' as distinguished from the normal 'a' sound in Sanskrit and other Indian languages. These sounds may not be used in native words - they are used only for transliterating English and other foreign language words into our languages. They are useful for distinguishing between cases like 'cat', 'caught' and 'cot' when transliterated into Indian scripts. If we have to accommodate these new codes at all, we must at least do it uniformly for all Indian languages. We must uniformly add these new characters AYE and AWE into the UNICODE code table for each of the Indian languages and add annotations saying that these characters shall be used only for transliterated foreign words and they shall never be used for native words.

We must however be careful to understand that ordinary users may not read or follow the annotations in code tables and other documentation associated with standards. They just use whatever suits them from the set of available codes. Thus there is always an element of risk of proliferating multiple 'spellings' for words. This would surely happen for quite some time, since many languages already have well established conventions. In Kannada, for example, we write 'kyaat', 'byaank', and 'myaap' to depict the English words 'cat', 'bank' and 'map'. Different languages have different sets of conventions. Some of these have been in use for a long time and well stabilized. While we may hope that in future people will shift over to the new characters provided, there is no guarantee that the intended shift will take place completely. Hence decisions to add new characters must be taken with utmost care. If something can be avoided, not adding it is the best.

- It will be a good idea to place all special symbols in a separate code space rather than duplicate them in the code table for each language. Also, the space available within the code tables for specific languages may not be sufficient to incorporate all the required special symbols. Punctuation marks, diacritics and many special symbols are used in all or most languages and are therefore best treated independent of any specific language. ISCII does not disturb the first half of the ASCII table and thus at least the basic punctuation marks etc. are uniformly available for all languages.

- We will have to live with multiple standards. ISCII and UNICODE will co-exist. Other standards such as those for Perso-Arabic scripts may also need to be integrated. Inter-compatibility amongst the various standards is therefore a very important consideration. The various standards must develop and grow together. Migration is costly and time consuming.

- One possible idea is to use ISCII as the internal base for all softwares for Indian languages and provide export/import to/from UNICODE for compatibility during the transitional period.

- It is advisable to use a standard keyboarding scheme such as INSCRIPT. There are however, several keyboarding schemes in popular use. It is alright. It must be ensured however, that the keyboard layouts and the drivers are complete and consistent with respect to the character encoding scheme used. There should not be any character which cannot be typed in! Software systems must strive to provide for all popular schemes and make the schemes easily adaptable or customizable by user himself.

- Only a small number of aksharas with three consonant clusters are in frequent use in Indian languages. Consonant clusters with four or more consonants are relatively rare. Care must be taken, however, to consider clusters required to write texts transliterated from some foreign language. It is pragmatic, nevertheless, to allow splitting of consonant clusters with more than, say, three consonants. We may take a uniform national level decision to invariably split consonant clusters with more than three consonants by introducing an extra HalaMt. A uniform policy of this kind would go a long way in ensuring compatibility between software systems and text documents prepared or processed using them. This would drastically reduce the set of grammatical aksharas too.

- A small set of fonts suitable for headings and running texts must be made freely available for all Indian languages. We are currently in a ridiculous situation where if you buy a computer in India you automatically get A, B, C, D but not 'a', 'aa', 'i', 'ii'. There is no harm if special and fancy fonts are developed and sold on commercial basis but a small set of free fonts must be freely available to all and available for free. Fonts without character-to-font mappings are of no use - the fonts must be readily useable on any platform, with any software whatever.

- There are now few UNICODE compliant fonts for Indian languages. Unless urgent steps are taken to develop free UNICODE fonts, we will not be able to take advantage of the technological developments. It is also ridiculous to ask each user to buy commercial fonts for a price. A small set of UNICODE compliant fonts must be developed and made available freely.

- It is neither fair nor economically sound to insist that all Indians use software compatible with any one commercial vendor. All issues of standardization must be made very carefully so that they are applicable across hardware and software platforms. This is very important when developing software tools and even more so when developing fonts, since there are several different technologies used for specifying font shapes (Ex. ttf, metafont, open-type.

- Revising the UNICODE standard is all the more critical since the UNICODE consortium does not allow characters to be deleted or their primary properties altered as a matter of policy and principle. A mistake committed once will stay for ever. It is better to go slow on contentious addition of new symbols.

- A character encoding scheme automatically specifies the default sorting order - words get sorted in the order of the numerical codes used to represent them. Hence every care must be taken to ensure that the positions alloted for the various characters and special symbols give us the correct sorting order. However, we need not go too far on this - universal sorting algorithms exist and the sorting order can be easily specified through map files to meet our exact requirements even if the default sorting order is not acceptable.

Sounds are more basic than orthography (the writing system). We learn to speak words much before we start reading and writing. Speaking is learnt naturally, writing - with conscious effort. Sounds are basic, natural, intrinsic properties of a languages. Orthography is an artifact. Not all are able to read and write - there are illiterates too. Orthography is at best an approximate mapping of the sounds that we use in a language onto a graphical format, even in Indian languages which are basically phonetic in nature. Character encoding schemes are best designed based on the structure of sounds in a language rather than based on the way words are written. The varNamaala reflects an arrangement of characters based on the nature of sounds. ISCII is based on this principle too. Since the sounds are more or less the same in all Indian languages, ISCII uses the same code space for all these languages. UNICODE, on the other hand, places each Indian language in a separate code space. However, UNICODE is not completely opposed to idea of proving a common code space as can be seen from the following quote from the UNICODE Technical Documentation:

"Duplicate encoding of characters is avoided by unifying characters within scripts across languages; characters that are equivalent in form are given a single code. Chinese / Japanese / Korean (CJK) consolidation is achieved by assigning a single code for each ideograph that is common to more than one of these languages. This is instead of providing a separate code for the ideograph each time it appears in a different language. (These three languages share many thousands of identical characters because their ideograph sets evolved from the same source.)"

Why not then a common code space for all Indian languages? UNICODE for Indian languages is still on its way, it is not already firmly established and so widely used that changes would do great harm. There is no harm in incorporating significant changes in the way UNICODE is developing. In fact this is the right opportunity to correct any mistakes of the past and improve upon the present. All efforts must therefore be made to set further development of UNICODE on the best path.

- Fonts must also include punctuation marks, diacritics and other special symbols as required. As of today, many fonts do not provide even the basic punctuation marks. Thus users are forced to switch to English even to insert a comma or a quote mark. Since size and other parameters of fonts do not map one to one between English and Indian language fonts, there are problems associated with this need to switch languages merely for using punctuation marks.

- Any new standardization attempt must give careful thought to local standardization and 'rationalization' efforts already implemented or currently being debated and discussed. People should not feel that we are going back-wards. In some cases the reform processes may have been completed and well accepted conventions established and uniformly followed. In some cases, we may actually be passing through the processes of change. The guiding principle in all cases must be to respect the present and move towards the future, rather than dogmatically stick to what was only used long ago. At the same time, it would be prudent to carry along the legacy as long as they are still in vogue. We must however be careful to add annotations stating that these characters and symbols are provided only for backward compatibility and shall not be used for current writing.

- Every care must be taken to ensure that basic characters as well as special symbols are placed in the code table in corresponding positions across various Indian languages so that transliteration remains simple. At the same time placement in the code table must also ensure correct sorting order.

- Englishmen may not even think of writing Kannada words using the English alphabet but it is much more natural for Kannada people to write English words in Kannada script. Transliteration is commonplace in Indian languages. We freely write Sanskrit in many different scripts. Some languages are written in more than one script. We often write

English and other foreign words in our scripts. Musical compositions of Saint tyaagaraaja are written by Kannadigas in Kannada script and by the Telugu people in the Telugu script so that they can learn and sing these compositions. Transliteration is a basic operation that must be accounted for. All efforts must therefore be made to ensure straight forward transliteration across Indian languages. Yet, if there is a clash between the requirements of a given language and the needs of easy transliteration to or from other languages, the basic needs of the given language per se must have the final word. After all the code space for a language is primarily meant for that language.

- While transliteration among Indian languages is very important, 100% fidelity in transliteration among Indian languages may not be possible. What would happen if the source language uses a particular character that the target language does not have at all? Should we create artificial characters just to make a language compatible with other languages? What do native speakers of that language do with such unknown symbols? Arguments about transliteration must not be carried too far.

- Some Indian languages have their own numerals. These are in regular use in some languages while in others they are not used these days. A careful decision must accordingly be taken. Roman numerals must be permitted in any case.

From these discussions, it must be clear that there are confusions and unresolved issues. Users must learn to live with confusions and imperfect solutions for some time. All the teething problems are being addressed and hopefully we will be able to use Indian languages on computers as simply and as easily as English.

2.4.6 Romanization

We have seen examples of Sanskrit, Hindi, Telugu and Kannada words written using the Roman alphabet. The unique multilingual environment in India makes it necessary to write one language using the script of another language. Sanskrit is often written in the scripts of local languages. For example, the verses from bhagavadgiita may be given along with the commentaries written in Telugu language, both of which are written in the Telugu script for the benefit of the Telugu knowing people. Now that English has become a very important link language, it also becomes necessary to write Indian languages in the Roman script. English newspapers carry advertisements of Hindi movies. The movie names etc. are naturally written in the Roman script. Thus there is a regular, routine need for writing Indian languages in the Roman script, not just for those special meta occasions when we are talking about languages per se. An Englishman may never even think of writing English in Kannada script but it is natural and essential to write Kannada in the Roman script.

However, there seem to be no serious concerted effort to come up with a good standard, widely accepted scheme for Roman transliteration. There are several schemes but most people use some ad-hoc scheme of the r own creation. Let us understand the nature of the task first.

It must be recognized at the outset that English is an alphabetic writing system based on the 26 letters of the alphabet and spelling rules while Indian scripts are phonetically based and syllabic in nature. Even if we were to count the basic units such as vowels and consonants instead of full aksharas, we find that the numbers are larger than the 26 letters we have. One common solution is to use diacritic marks but this scheme is inconvenient for direct use on the computer. Typing in diacritic marks from the computer keyboard is not convenient. Another common solution is to mix lower case and upper case letters. In English capital letters are used for proper names and acronyms as also to mark the beginning of a sentence. Here we need to use capital letters instead for denoting retroflex consonants etc. Multi-byte equivalents are also required as there are more symbols in Indian scripts than 52. We need to handle long and short vowels, aspirated and unaspirated consonants, retroflex sounds, etc. Based on these ideas, several schemes have been proposed including the iTRANS scheme and the Rice University scheme.

The worst part of the story is that people use completely ad-hoc transliterations without consistently sticking to any one scheme. Each person seems to have his/her own standard. Newspapers need to transliterate Indian languages into Roman on a daily basis but each time it is left to the whims and fancies of individual journalists and editors. Advertisements are worse. It takes a substantial amount of time, patience as well as knowledge of the language concerned to understand these transliterations. The problem is complicated by the fact that there are many languages and we need to perform language identification as well.

There are several issues in the design of a good Romain transliteration scheme. Some systems are case sensitive while others are not. Thus mixing of upper and lower cases has its own merits and demerits. This mixing also makes the text look a bit awkward as upper case letters generally appear bigger. Some researchers have worried about storage space and suggest the use of upper case letters even for long vowels. The IIT(Kanpur) group has taken this idea of economy of representation to the extreme and they propose highly unnatural mappings such as 'w' for the 'th' sound as in 'thesis' and 'x' for the 'd' sound as in 'Daddy'. A few bytes might be saved but the texts now look really ugly and difficult to read. Also, keying in letters of different cases requires frequent use of SHIFT or CAPS-LOCK keys. Some use 'aa' for long 'a'. Then we might expect that the same logic be universally applied and we use 'ii' for the long vowel sound as in 'feet' and 'ee' for the long vowel sound in 'ate'. However, while 'ee' is frequently used in English spellings, 'ii' is never used. Some argue that we must use those sequences which are more natural and frequent in English while others are upset that English spellings should form the basis for writing Indian languages. English spelling rules are ghastly and English phone set is different from the set we use for our languages. English spellings cannot answer all our concerns. Yet readability is important too. Any scheme that is systematic and uniform is more likely to be accepted and picked up easily compared to ad-hoc schemes. Why should Romanization of Indian scripts be ad-hoc just because English happens to be ad-hoc? In the long run, people will find it easier to get used to a systematic, uniform scheme than a hoch-poch scheme based on a foreign language. Should English knowing people decide things for Indian scripts or should we keep Indians speaking Indian languages and knowing Indian scripts as the base? Some have proposed the use of special symbols such as the colon to suggest vowel lengthening but others say special symbols will interfere with processing of such texts. Whether we use special symbols or not, there will always be a need for an escape mechanism so that literal interpretations can be permitted. Some are worried about single or even round trip transliteration among various scripts. With the increasing use of multi-lingual and multi-script documents, problems will only increase. It is high time a well thought out standard is prepared and brought into widespread use.

In the absence of a single widely accepted and widely known transliteration scheme, in this book we have avoided taking a strong position based on any one ideology and used what we consider a fairly simple and straight forward scheme in this book. It is generally acceptable to add a 'h' to indicate aspirated sounds and use capitals for retroflex sounds. Long vowels have been indicated by doublets. Proper names and sentence initial words are not capitalized.

2.4.7 Spell Checkers

Spell checkers form one of the most basic technologies for any given language. It may be surprising then, that good spell checkers are not available for many Indian languages even today. Let us see why. We take examples from Kannada language. We start with general issues in the design of spell checkers.

Spelling Error Detection and Correction

A spell checker is a computer program that deals with the detection and correction of spelling errors in texts. An ideal detector should pin point all and only those words in the text that are wrongly spelled. An ideal corrector should automatically correct all such errors. In practice, neither detection nor correction can be perfect. Most practical spell checkers do not even attempt to automatically correct spelling errors - instead they only offer list of suggested alternatives for the user to choose from. The user has several options: he may select one of the suggestions provided by the system, he may direct the program to accept the specific instance or even all instances of current spelling in the text, he may direct the system to add this "new" word to the custom dictionary, or he may choose to edit the word manually.

A good spell checker must detect all or most of the spelling errors and at the same time minimize false alarms. It must offer either the single *right* suggestion or a small set of suggestions for correction in which the *right* suggestion is included. The suggestions offered must be ranked and the *right* suggestion must occur in the top of the list in most cases.

A good spell checker may be required to handle loan words, split and merged tokens, archaic usage, dialectal variations, accepted cases of spelling variations, colloquial forms, domain specific terminology, acronyms and abbreviations, proper names etc. Clearly no practical spell checker can be expected to handle all these cases perfectly.

Most practical spell checkers work one word at a time and hence cannot even detect *real word errors* - mistakes that result in some other valid word in the language, as against *non-word errors* - mistakes that result in an invalid word. For example, most spell checkers will not find anything wrong in the sentence "One plus one is tow". Catching real word errors requires context based processing. Ideally, full syntactic parsing, semantic and pragmatic analysis may be required. The context must somehow be brought to bear to decide whether there is any spelling error or not. Both the textual context in which the word occurs and the situational context and topic of the discourse are important. Practical spell checkers are far from ideal.

Detection and correction can both be done using dictionaries and morphology and other linguistic tools, using statistical techniques, or using a combination of both. In a dictionary based approach, a word not found in the dictionary is considered to be due to a spelling error and other words from the dictionary which are *close to the input word in terms of spelling* are given out as suggestions for correction. In a simple statistical approach, the probability of a particular alphabet/word sequence in the language is used instead as the basis. Interested readers may look at a survey paper by Karen Kuckich for a variety of techniques for detection and correction of spelling errors.

A large dictionary is also not necessarily the best. A large dictionary includes many infrequent words which may be confused for other words with a real-word spelling error. A user who wanted to type 'leave' actually types 'lave' by mistake but the system quietly accepts this as a valid word form!

What is a spelling error?

All through the previous section, we used the term *word* to mean simply a sequence of alphabets separated by spaces. Thus a word is seen here from the perspective of its spelling rather than from the perspective of pronunciation or meaning. The mapping from spelling to meaning is mostly arbitrary.

In languages like English, the mapping from spellings to pronunciation is also quite ad-hoc. The same alphabet gives rise to different sounds in different contexts and the same sounds can be realized using a variety of spelling combinations. Thus spellings have to be learnt and carefully remembered and people naturally tend to make mistakes. The origin of spelling errors can thus be cognitive. Of course phonetic and typographical errors are also possible.

Indian scripts, on the other hand, are primarily phonetic in nature - the orthography reflects the phonetics to a large extent. Thus *there is really no such thing as spelling.* Nevertheless, there is scope for mistakes of a variety of kinds and techniques of spell checking can be applied just the same.

All sequences of vowels, consonants, maatras and vowel modifiers are not valid aksharas. Thus it is not possible to have an isolated maatra, an akshara beginning with a maatra or an akshara with more than one maatra. The script grammar specifies valid combinations. Thus one level of checking for correctness is built into our scripts.

One common mistake in many Indian languages is the use of an aspirate for the corresponding non-aspirate or vice versa - is it *saMbaMdha* or saMbhaMda (relationship) ?. Modern Indian languages have many words borrowed from Sanskrit. While Sanskrit uses aspirates and non-aspirates distinctively, the distinction may be inherently less prominent or absent in the native language and hence the confusion. There is large scale hyper-correction: *aadhi (first, orginal) s'aMkara, vidhyaa (knowledge) gaNapati.* Most of the sign boards you see have one or more mistakes. These are all cognitive errors.

Phonetic errors are also not inconceivable. *aDugemane* (kitchen) is quite often pronounced and written as *aDigemane. huDugi* (girl) often becomes *huDigi.* Non-initial vowels appear to be less important. Frequent and regular usages like *huDgi* especially in the spoken variety only substantiate this view. Even *huDagi* may be acceptable. This results in variations in spelling. Word initial *ha* is often pronounced as *a* - *aasana* (seat or chair) for *haasana* - the name of a place. One may become conscious of this error and may even resort to hyper-correction. These effects in pronunciation can be reflected in orthography leading to spelling errors.

Typos are also possible for typed text although it is possible to design editors that disallow right away certain invalid combinations of symbols. For example, an editor may prevent an accidental second maatra for a consonant. Nonetheless, it will not be possible to prevent typos in all cases.

Further, there are often variations in spellings, some of which may be more acceptable than others for specific purposes and thus spelling error correction can be viewed as more of a *normalization* effort. In Kannada, the spoken and written varieties of language are quite distinct (example - barutteene vs. baruttiini (I come)) Dialectal variations also exist. There are loan words whose native sounds cannot be represented directly in orthography. There is no phonetically accurate way to write *bank* in Kannada and naturally new conventions have come to use. A common rendering is *byaank.* There is no representation for the 'fa' sound and a convention that has come to widespread use is to write two dots (a special kind of nukta) below the 'pa' letter - as in *kaapi* (coffee). However, these conventions are not followed uniformly in all cases thus leading to variations in spelling. The half consonant 'ra' in consonant clusters as in *muurti* (image/idol) is written in Kannada as a special symbol called *arkaavattu* and is written by convention after the latter consonant in the cluster. However, in recent writings, the default method of writing consonant clusters with the 'ra' consonant is used quite often instead of the 'arkaavattu'. In Telugu, words are split at arbitrary points and very often the same author writes the same word in two different ways within a single page. In effect, there are many variations. Normalization is highly desirable where the texts are intended to be subjected to automatic language processing tools. Otherwise there would be difficulties in searching, sorting and many other such processes.

Normalization is not to be confused with standardization. Standardization is a sensitive issue. We do not mean defining one or the other alternative form as the standard and imposing it on everybody. That is not the point. The idea is two fold. Firstly, a spell checker must provide options for the user to normalize the given texts as per his/her requirements. If a user wants all colloquial forms to be replaced with formal varieties, a spell checker can be designed to assist in the process. A user must be able to specify which dialects are to be accepted and which ones are to be treated as errors and substituted. Many of our languages have a long history and there are archaic forms and modern forms. If a user desires that he better avoid archaic forms, a spell checker must assist him/her in that. Secondly, unwanted variability in the text can be reduced by normalization of spellings. This will be very useful for text processing applications in Indian languages. Spell checkers for Indian languages can and must be much more than the usual spell checkers for other languages.

Spell Checking in Morphologically Rich Languages:

Although English has a rich and complex system of derivational morphology, inflectional morphology is quite simple and straight forward. Most spell checkers for English therefore store the derived forms directly in the lexicon and apply rules of morphology only for a few cases where the rules are simple and highly productive. This approach is practically feasible and reasonably efficient for languages such as English.

Morphological analysis and generation in Indian languages is quite an involved and complex task. Often there are six or seven levels of affixation, there being several possible affixes at each level Thus *tiMduhaakiddanu* ((he) had eaten) can be analyzed as

tinnu	i	haaku	i	iru	id	anu
Rt:(eat)	pt-part.	asp.aux.	pt-part.	Perf.	Pt	m,sl,p3

In languages such as Kannada, a verb root may give rise to several-hundred thousands of complete words. Dravidian languages, especially Kannada and Telugu, are among the most complex languages of the world, comparable only to languages such as Finnish and Turkish. A verb form may include several aspectual auxiliaries, clitics, particles and vocatives, apart from tense, gender, number and person suffixes. A word in Kannada often corresponds to a whole phrase in English. Thus 'although (I/we/you/he/she/it/they) had certainly wanted to come' would be just one word in Kannada - roughly 'baraleebeekeMdukoMDiddaruu'. Inter-word saMdhi and compounds add to the problem. It is practically not feasible to store all forms of all words in the dictionary. A detailed morphological component is essential for developing a good spell checker for languages such as Kannada.

In order to detect spelling errors, every word in the text has to be morphologically analyzed and checked with a dictionary. Only then can we accept all and only the valid words and flag the others as erroneous. Spelling errors may occur in the roots, in the various affixes or in the internal saMdhi that glues these parts into the whole word. Once the source of the error is found, appropriate suggestions for correcting that part may be generated using a variety of techniques. Finally, the morphological generator would be called to put together the correct parts to re-build the complete word form. Thus 'hugaLannu' will be analyzed as 'hu + gaLu + annu' (noun + plural + accusative), 'hu' corrected to 'huu' (flower)', and then the correct form 'huugaLannu' generated. Similarly, 'huugalannu' can be corrected as 'huugaLannu'. Complexity increases if there are multiple errors in a word. However, multiple errors are relatively less frequent.

The block diagram below gives the overall structure of a typical spell checker for a morphologically rich language such as Kannada. The techniques used here can also be applied fruitfully for other languages. The morphological analyzer and generator can be implemented in the *Network and Process model.*

As we have seen, morphological analysis and generation are complex processes and the performance of current systems is not very high. We may therefore wish to apply hybrid techniques. Type-token analysis is performed on a large and representative corpus and the most frequent word forms are identified. A suitable threshold can be determined which optimizes the spell checker performance in terms of both false alarms and missed detections. High frequency word forms can be directly stored in the dictionary and morphology applied only in those cases where the word is not listed in the dictionary. There are many advanced techniques for spell checker design. Interested readers will find good papers.

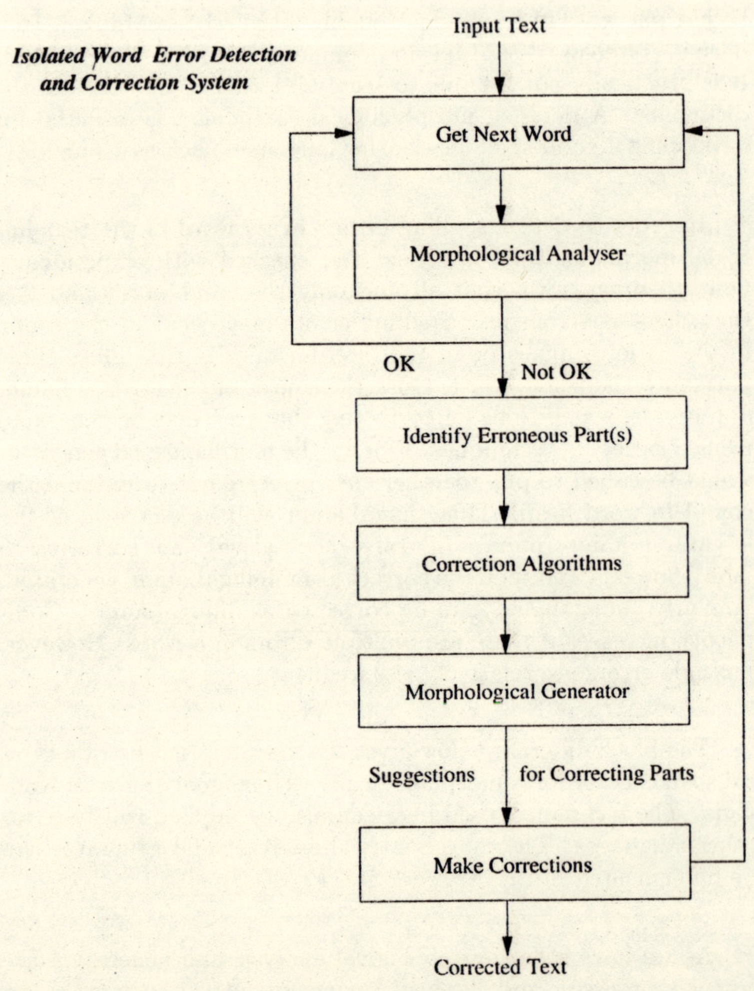

FIG 2.21 A Typical Dictionary-Morphology based Spell Checker

There are no bench mark data for testing and evaluating the performance of spell checkers in many Indian languages. Most of the spell checkers available today have not been thoroughly evaluated.

2.4.8 Optical Character Recognition

An Optical Character Recognition (OCR) system converts a scanned image of a text document into electronic text just as if the text matter was typed-in by somebody. Scanned images are much larger in size compared to corresponding text files. The statement "A picture is worth one thousand words" is literally true here. Texts occupy less storage space and less network bandwidth when sent across a network. Converting images into texts makes it possible to edit and process the contents as normal text. OCR systems are therefore very useful.

OCR systems can be used to convert available paper documents into electronic texts without typing. Since OCR engine can be run day and night on several computers parallelly, we can generate large scale corpora with less time and effort. OCR engines can also be used for a variety of other applications. OCR systems have just started appearing for Indian scripts. Most of the current OCR systems for Indian languages are designed only for printed texts and perform well only on reasonably good quality documents. Research work is going on for handling hand-written documents. Handling old manuscripts is more complex. The paper or other base materials used would have deteriorated, coloured and noisy. Also the character shapes used may be more complex and quite different from the shapes used in modern digital fonts.

System Overview

An OCR system typically contains three stages: preprocessing stage, recognition stage and post-processing stage. Binarization, separation of image regions into textual and graphical regions, multi-column detection and skew correction are some of the major tasks performed in preprocessing phase. Separation of text into glyphs, characters, words and lines, and recognition of individual glyphs are tasks of the recognition stage. Post-processing comprises combining the recognized glyphs into valid aksharas and words, spell-checking, etc. Optical character recognition is a vast field and there are a large number of alternative technologies at every level. The following paragraphs sketch some of the simple techniques that have been effectively used in OCR. The treatment here is not intended to be comprehensive or suggestive of the best or recommended methods. OCR is currently an active area of research and the interested readers will find a vast body of literature giving more technical details.

Preprocessing Stage

Binarization: refers to the conversion of a scanned gray level image into a two-tone or binary (pure black and white) image. A binary image is appropriate for OCR work as the image document contains only two useful classes of data — the background, say the paper, and the foreground, the printed text. It is common to represent the background paper colour by *white-coloured* pixels and the text by *black-coloured* pixels. In image processing jargon, the background pixels have a value of 1 and the foreground pixels have a value of 0. Binarization has a significant impact because it provides input to every other stage of an OCR system. All pixels darker than a threshold are mapped to pure black and the rest of the pixels are mapped to pure white. Several strategies can be used for binarization to achieve desired performance on different types of scanned documents and scanners. Global, percentile based and iterative methods have been applied to identify the best threshold.

Skew Detection and Correction: stages deal with improper alignment of a document while it is scanned. The usual effect of skew could be that the lines of text or no longer horizontal but at an angle, called the *skew* angle. Documents with skew cause line, word and character breaking routines to fail. Skew also causes reduction in recognition accuracy. Skew detection and correction can be done by, say, maximizing the variance in horizontal projection profile.

Text and Graphics Separation: refers to the process of identifying which regions of the document image contain text and which regions contain pictures and other non-text information that is not relevant to the OCR system. Horizontal and vertical projection profiles can be used for such separation as well as for many other preprocessing operations (see below). A horizontal profile is obtained by counting and plotting the number of text or black pixels in each row of the image. A vertical profile is obtained by counting the black pixels in each column of the image. Horizontal profiles show distinct peaks that correspond to lines of text and valleys that result from inter-line gaps. A line of text is revealed by a peak in the horizontal profile whose width is approximately the font size. A graphic object, in contrast, is much larger. The actual shape of the peak is also different because of higher density of black pixels in a graphics block. Thus, the profile shapes discriminate between text and graphical blocks.

Multi-column Text Detection: can be done using *Recursive X-Y Cuts* technique. It is based on recursively splitting a document into rectangular regions using vertical and horizontal projection profiles alternately.

The use of horizontal and vertical projection profiles for all the major preprocessing tasks minimizes system complexity and allows faster processing of documents.

Recognition Stage

Line, Word, Character and Glyph Separation: is a very important task as the recognition engine processes only one glyph at a time. Word and glyph separation are the key steps. In one recent successful system, word segmentation has been done using a combination of *Run-Length Smearing Algorithm (RLSA)* and *Connected-Component Labelling.* Words are combined into lines using simple heuristics based on their locations. The performance of RLSA in accurately segmenting words is very high on good quality text but drops in the presence of complex layouts and tightly packed text that is sometimes seen in magazines. A variety of zoning techniques have also be used. Words can be decomposed into glyphs by running the connected component labelling algorithm again. The method is conceptually simple and glyph separation can be very accurate.

Recognition: There are broadly two approaches to recognition *template matching* and *classification based on features.* Direct matching rarely works but refined template matching algorithms can actually give fairly good recognition performance. One such template matching technique that has been used very successfully is based on the notion of *fringe distance* where the distance between two images is a function of the distance of each black pixel in one image to the nearest black pixel in the other image. A database is created from standard glyph shapes and any new glyph image can be matched against the templates stored in the database and the reference template that matches best could be given out as the recognized output.

The two images need to be scaled and normalized before such a comparison can be made. We may use a *linear scaling* algorithm that uniformly scales all parts of the image to the required size. Linear scaling is fast but suffers from problems with complex shaped glyphs at large font sizes and with small glyphs at small font sizes. *Non-linear normalization* can improve performance by selectively scaling regions of low curvature. Punctuation marks, which are easily distorted because of their small sizes, are usually handled separately. For example, heuristics based on *location and stacking* can be used to handle these punctuation marks.

There is a large variety of features that can be used to discriminate between various glyphs, a large variety of distance measures to compute the distance or dissimilarity and a variety of classification techniques to finally classify a given glyph assign a class label. Interested readers will find more details in the published papers.

Post-processing Stage

Assembling Glyphs into aksharas: is much more challenging than it appears in the case of Indian scripts. For example, in Telugu script, glyphs can be scaled and placed on top, to the left bottom, directly below, to the right bottom or to the right side of another base glyph. The glyphs may not be recognized in the same order in which they are required to assemble aksharas correctly. Glyph shapes may be same but distinctions may have to be made based on relative size and relative location. The end result of this complex assembly process is the text encoded in a suitable character encoding scheme such as ISCII or UNICODE.

Spell-Checker: OCR works glyph by glyph and there can be errors of omission and commission. The kinds of errors made by an OCR engine are quite different from the kinds of spelling mistakes we make when we type from a computer keyboard. Statistical approaches are generally preferred for building spell checkers for OCR systems.

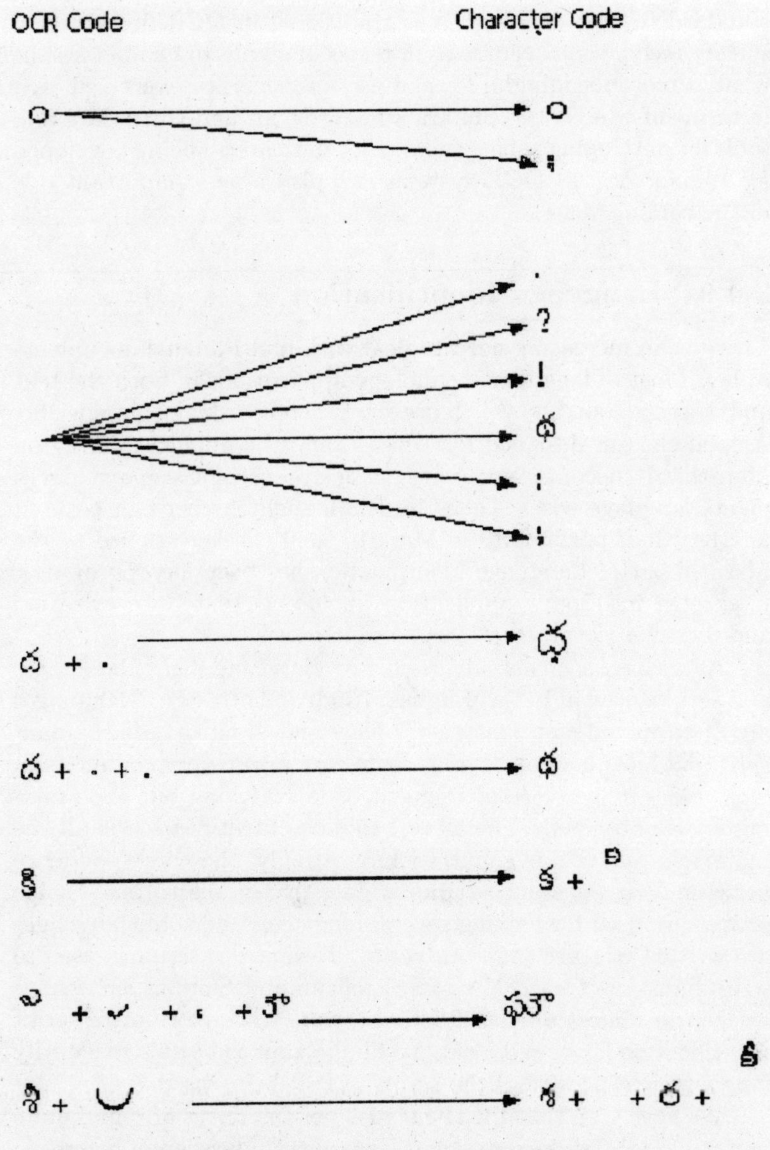

FIG 2.22 Assembling Glyphs into Aksharas

OCR systems, like other systems in language engineering and NLP, need to be tested against standard benchmark data and standard test procedures. It is traditional in OCR literature to specify recognition accuracies in terms of glyphs or characters but what is more meaningful for end users is accuracy expressed, say, in terms of words. Benchmark standards, ground truth data and tools for developing such ground truth data are all being developed for Indian scripts. OCR systems can play a very important role in the coming years.

2.4.9 Language Identification

There is an increasing need to deal with multi-lingual documents today. Most of language technology applications in both the text and speech domains are, however, inherently language specific. A spell checker designed for Hindi cannot be applied directly on Marathi. It becomes necessary, therefore, to first segment documents language-wise. Then the Hindi spell checker can be used for the Hindi parts and the Marathi spell checker applied to the Marathi parts. Language Identification has been incorporated or integrated into many applications including Text Categorization and Text Retrieval.

As we have seen already, there are a large number of languages and scripts used in India. English, Hindi and other local languages are often mixed as a matter of policy and practice. Mixing Sanskrit and local languages in a single text is also very common. In most cases it is a case of frequent code switching but code mixing is also observed. Therefore Language Identification is all the more relevant in our country. Interestingly, the correspondence between languages and scripts is not strictly one to one - some scripts are used for writing several languages and some languages are written in more than one script. Devanagari script is used to write Sanskrit, Hindi, Marathi, Konkani and Sindhi. Sanskrit is written in almost all the different scripts. Therefore mere script identification is not sufficient. It is important to be able to identify language irrespective of the script or font being used.

We have seen that ISCII encodes texts in terms of sound units and a plain ISCII document has no explicit indication of language. Automatically identifying language from small text samples in ISCII texts is therefore very important. It may also be noted that switching to UNICODE will not solve the problem - UNICODE provides code spaces for scripts, not necessarily one for each language. Devanagari script is used for several languages including Sanskrit, Hindi, Marathi, Nepali and Konkani. The Bengali script is also used for Assamese.

Instead of viewing Language Identification as a document segmentation problem, it is possible to take the somewhat simpler view of classifying a given small segment of text into one of the given set of languages. Language Identification can be viewed as a generic machine learning problem, a supervised classification task in which features extracted from a training corpus are used for classification. Any of the machine learning techniques can be used.

In the last decade or so, corpus based Machine Learning approaches have become predominant in language engineering over the Knowledge Based approaches which use explicit rules handcrafted by domain experts. Recent research on Language Identification has been limited almost exclusively to Machine Learning approaches.

A Machine Learning system is expected to be generic and it is understood that training is based only on the intrinsic properties of the data, as expressed through a set of "features". Extraneous indicators such as clues from scripts or fonts used, header information or explicit markup tags in the document structure cannot be used.

The basic idea is that each language uses a unique or a very characteristic alphabet, and the letters of the alphabet appear with surprisingly consistent frequencies in any statistically significant text. In addition, the frequency of occurrence of sequences of two, three, four and more letters are characteristically stable within, but diverse among different natural languages. The most frequent 3-grams, 4-grams etc. have been used for language identification. A crucial part of the recognition system is the identification of the set of most distinctive, most frequently encountered sequences of characters (that is, bigrams, trigrams, etc.) that can be associated with each language. Distinctiveness implies that the frequency of a letter combination for a given language should be high relative to the frequency of occurrence in other languages.

In alphabetic writing systems such as those used for English and other European languages, a character is simply a letter of the alphabet (or a punctuation mark, a digit or other special symbol), which is typically represented as a single byte in a character encoding scheme such as ASCII. Researchers dealing with such languages have naturally chosen a byte as the basic unit of text. Features such as n-grams are defined in terms of bytes. Indian scripts are not alphabetic but rather syllabic in nature. Aksharas are the atomic units of writing - individual bytes have no significance in Indian scripts. Texts are to be treated sequences of aksharas.

Some researchers have used lists of frequent words to distinguish one language from the other. Comparing with stored lists of frequent words can be very effective for language identification. Our experiments using word lists with Indian Languages, not described here, also confirm this point. However, there are several objections to the use of lists of words, affixes etc. As test samples become smaller, chances of finding full words reduce. In small samples, words may be cut and storing lists of full words will be of no use. The most frequent words are usually closed class grammatical words such as determiners, prepositions and conjunctions and carry little semantic information. Small text samples exacerbate the bursty nature of texts where such closed class words surround pockets of less common words. It is these less common words that may in fact be more useful for language identification between certain languages than the small function words. Which words to include in a word list is therefore an open question. Lastly, statistical features such as n-grams in any case include the information contained in small, frequent words, affixes etc. Given these facts and the desire to build generic, trainable language identification systems, machine learning approaches that depend solely on features extracted from data are preferred.

A number of language identification systems have been built for various language groups of the world. Despite its great relevance, Language Identification had, however remained a largely unexplored area for Indian languages. Recently, Multiple Linear Regression has been successfully applied to develop high performance pair-wise language identification among the major Indian languages. An F-Measure of 98% plus has been achieved for Indian languages when test samples were about 10 aksharas in size and the performance went up to nearly 100% when the sample size was increased to about 25 aksharas. Note that aksharas are appropriate units of text for Indian scripts, not bytes. Experimental results also corroborate this claim.

Texts are treated a sequences of aksharas. The script grammar is used to segment texts into aksharas. Aksharas are smaller units than full words. The number of frequently used aksharas is also smaller than number of words. The number of distinct words is of the order of hundreds of thousands whereas aksharas in common use are in thousands. Studies have shown that about 5000 aksharas account for more than 99% of all words in all the major Indian languages. Thus the size of the training corpus required will be much smaller if we use akshara based features. There is no need to talk in terms of words or morphemes.

Monograms, bigrams and trigrams of aksharas can be used as features. We may also consider positional features - word initial, word medial and word final n-grams may be distinguished. It is useful to use differential features - n-grams that occur frequently in one language but not in the other can be extracted from a corpus and listed in a table.

A two level feature extraction process may be followed. In the first level, text corpora are used to extract akshara level monograms, bigrams and trigrams. Only the most frequently occurring and differential features are retained. The result is a set of tables for each pair of languages. The tables simply list the akshara level monograms, bigrams and trigrams that occur frequently in the first language but not in the second, and vice versa. The frequencies themselves are not stored. After this step, full corpora are never used again.

In the second phase, training samples are extracted randomly from the corpora and used for estimating the parameters of the regression model. A training data set consists of random samples containing only a small number of aksharas. Since the features are defined in a differential manner, the actual feature values are obtained by simply counting the occurrences of these features in the training samples. For example, all possible trigrams are extracted from a training sample and each is checked in the feature tables obtained in the first phase. The value of the trigram feature for language L1 is the total number of these trigrams found frequently in L1 but not in L2. Thus the feature values are all integers.

Note that the feature values are not computed directly and solely from the training samples. Instead, they are expressed in terms of the prior knowledge obtained from corpora as encapsulated in the tables obtained in the first phase. Since all we need is plain text corpora and small corpora are sufficient, this two-stage feature extraction is feasible and practicable. The features so extracted can be expected to be more robust and more reliable than features extracted directly from small training samples.

If we are using the MLR technique, the parameters of the regression equation are estimated from the training samples randomly extracted from the corpora. Then testing can be carried out on test data, also extracted randomly from the rest of the corpus. Each sample is analyzed into aksharas and the differential feature values are obtained. The value of the decision variable is computed and the sample classified accordingly. The performance is measured in terms of Precision, Recall and F-Measure. Experiments may be conducted to ascertain the effect of number of training samples, size of training samples, size of test samples, relative significance of features in various combinations etc. Experiments can also be repeated for purposes of cross-validation.

Experiments can also be performed with different values for the threshold in order to explore the trade-off between Precision and Recall. When encountered with the task of identifying the language of a small piece of text, it is possible to initially look for a high-precision, low-recall solution and reduce the threshold value iteratively in case identification fails until a solution is obtained.

The differences between the within-language-family and across-language-family cases may be explored. We can see the degree of "closeness" between various language pairs. Hindi and Punjabi may show up to be closer than, say, Oriya and Punjabi. When we need to recognize languages that are closer to one another, we may need more sophisticated features or larger data to get the same level of performance. This idea can be extended further to study other kinds of variations among languages or language families as also to uncover universal, language-invariant features in a quantitative way.

Note that machine learning methods are completely generic and hence the same program can be used for identification between any two languages - all that we need is suitable training corpora and a few minutes of time to retrain the system on the new training data. We do not need any word lists or other linguistic information about the languages being distinguished. This generic nature and adaptability is the most important merit of machine learning techniques. Linguistic approaches, on the other hand, normally require careful linguistic study for each language under consideration and hence a lot of time and effort. Machine learning techniques can be adapted to new languages within minutes and without any manual effort.

2.4.10 Others Technologies for Indian Languages

Machine translation has been taken quite seriously in India and a lot of progress has been made. Major focus has been laid on translating between Indian languages, exploiting the commonness of these languages along the linguistic and cultural dimensions. Recently, there is also an increased emphasis on translation between English and Indian languages. While demonstration level systems have been built, there is a long way to go before machine translation can be applied in real life situations.

There is some scattered work on Information Retrieval, Information Extraction, Text summarization, Text and Web Mining, etc. Strong, focussed, long term efforts are rarely seen.

There is an acute paucity of lexical resources including plain and annotated corpora, parallel corpora, dictionaries, thesauri, WordNets etc. Greater emphasis is being given to development of lexical resources and hopefully things would be much better soon.

In spite of being a country with many languages, high degree of illiteracy and basically an oral tradition, speech has taken a back seat. Only a couple of centres have been active in speech for a long time. There is now a realization that the future lies in speech. There is even some thought on speech based cross-lingual information access and speech-to-speech translation. Closer integration of NLP and speech technologies is the need of the hour.

2.4.11 NLP and Sanskrit

There is a common misconception that Sanskrit is the best language for NLP. What does this mean? Should we stop using all other languages and start using only Sanskrit for everything? That would not make much sense. Many people would surely want to learn Sanskrit but not for the sake of giving up their own mother tongue, not because computers would start demanding Sanskrit.

It is also not true that Sanskrit is a lot more amenable for automatic processing by the computer. True, Sanskrit has an extremely systematic and scientific way of dealing with all aspects of language starting from the alphabet through words, phonetics, phonology, morphology and syntax to semantics and proper interpretation of meanings. Yet all this is designed for intelligent human beings with common-sense, not for dumb machines. A substantial degree of common sense and world knowledge is required to process and understand any language for that matter and perhaps it is only more so in the case of Sanskrit. We have seen for example that compounds are very common in Sanskrit and interpreting compounds often requires human intelligence. It is also very common to leave out portions that we can fill up ourselves. Sanskrit statements are often highly elliptic. Handing ellipses is still a very difficult task for computers. Further, if one were to look at Sanskrit as it is actually used, you will very often find highly abstract and cryptic statements, calling for expert interpretation and explanation from a Guru. Knowing the literal meanings is of little use. If you come across the statement *You are That* what sense will you make out of this?

Yet knowing Sanskrit may perhaps help in two ways. Firstly, modern Indian languages have a lot of things borrowed from Sanskrit and partly or wholly assimilated into them. Knowing Sanskrit helps one to get a deeper insight into the structure and meaning of words and sentences in our languages. One can start understanding the beauty of language in a better way. We will get to know how different languages have adapted, assimilated, developed and grown in their own ways. We can begin to understand and appreciate even those languages which we knew nothing about. You become a bit more broad minded. Secondly, and much more importantly, knowing Sanskrit helps us to get a more scientific and systematic way of dealing with language at all levels. Sanskrit not only has an excellent grammar, one that is hard to find fault with, there is a whole science of grammar of which the Sanskrit grammar is just an instance. It is not the Sanskrit grammar itself that is so very important, it is the underlying science of grammar that is crucial. The same is true of phonetics, phonology, morphology and semantics. Linguists cannot afford to be ignorant of Sanskrit.

A whole ocean of knowledge exists in Sanskrit on almost all

aspects of language, meaning, logic and understanding. However, simply knowing Sanskrit is not sufficient to make full use of all this knowledge. Today we are unable to leverage this wealth of knowledge and experience not just because the number of people who know Sanskrit is less. This is due largely to the very nature of these traditional knowledge sources. According to Indian tradition, knowledge was not meant for all - in fact every effort was made to ensure that knowledge does not reach the hands of the "un-deserving". (If everybody is taught how to make bombs you know what happens. There are no "right" hands for bombs - if you are "right" you will not need a bomb at all. The only hands interested in bombs are the "wrong hands") It is foolish to publish all knowledge and then worry about it boomeranging back on you. Hence Gurus were extremely choosy about whom they will teach and how much they will teach. Knowledge was meant only for those who are extremely serious - those who consider seeking knowledge as the main goal of life and those who are adjudged to be capable of correct interpretation and proper application of that knowledge for righteous purposes. Given these, it was expected that a seeker of knowledge should search for the right teacher (guru) and learn from him. Knowledge was not "pushed" onto everybody, one had to seek and "pull" knowledge with effort. Public knowledge was thus limited. An extremely cryptic style is followed - often in the form of suutras (aphorisms, formulae). It is the nature of the tradition that commentaries are written on the original texts to make them easier to understand and commentaries are written on such commentaries! To this day, getting an in-depth understanding of these works requires spending years of your life with a guru. The number of serious students within the Indian tradition is steadily decreasing and so it is becoming more and more difficult even to find a good guru. Added to all this is the difficulty in communicating with traditional scholars in a parlance that make sense to a modern language engineer. Further, the original purpose of these works were very different from the purposes for which we wish to use them today. By and large, this wealth of traditional knowledge has remained dormant and largely unused. Our future lies in our past.

2.4.12 Epilogue

We have noted that developments in technology for Indian languages has been painfully slow and the major reasons for this include non-availability of large scale data resources and slow development of basic tools and technologies, partly due to inherent complexity of our languages.

Language technology issues are not widely known or appreciated in India. These technologies are not part of the curriculum and trained manpower is in short supply. It is also not easy to motivate people to work in this area. Lack of adequate manpower is one of the main reasons for the slow progress.

There is a great apathy towards standards and good engineering practices. The number of people working on language technologies is so small and there is so much work to do that there is a great tendency to take short cuts. In many cases there are neither any written specifications nor design documents. Researchers get down to writing code straight away. There are no benchmark data or established standards for testing and evaluation. There are no separate teams for evaluation and the developers themselves double as evaluators of their own software. At times training is done on test data and testing on the training data. Thus results claimed by researchers cannot always be taken on the face value.

Partly due to lack of standards and proper engineering practices and partly due to the feeling that there is so much to do but not enough hands, researchers tend to take "big" ideas and try to become Jack of all. As an example, there are many teams working on Text-to-Speech systems and each team develops its own text normalization tools. Would it not be better if each team takes up one small idea at a time and does a thorough job of it so that everybody can just take and use that one small module? These are matters of perceptions. If you are doing TTS and Machine Translation then you are doing some big thing but if you are developing a good dictionary or a morphological analyzer that is not going to catch anybody's attention in a big way. Most teams try to develop everything from scratch on their own rather than team up with others. This may be partly due to lack of mutual trust and understanding. As a country, we have the potential to become world leaders in language technologies. But we need to learn many basic lessons first.

2.5 Conclusions

By now you will have realized that NLP is a vast and highly inter-disciplinary subject. It is not possible to cover everything in detail in a single book. The purpose of this book is only to give you an initial idea about the nature of problems and issues, kinds of approaches that can be and have been taken, some idea about the current status and challenges yet to be overcome and some general idea about the shape of things to come. Each of the topics covered here is a vast subject in itself and the readers interested in pursuing any of the areas in more depth will find many good books and research articles. We have seen that although a great deal of progress has been made over the last five decades, many of the core problems remain unsolved. There are many interesting and useful applications and there is a lot that needs to be done. If this book helps beginners to get interested and to kick start serious explorations and research, it would have served its purpose.

We have been looking at NLP both as an independent field of study and in the context of Information retrieval and other closely related applications. We will get back to IR in the next chapter and look at some of the advances that are being made in that field.

Chapter 3

Advances in Information Retrieval

Information Retrieval is all about efficient storage and retrieval of documents. The idea is to retrieve documents which are relevant to a user at a given point of time for a particular purpose. The document collection may be very large. Thus IR deals with efficient storage, indexing and matching techniques.

In this chapter we will look at some the recent advances in the field of Information Retrieval. We begin with a brief historical sketch and then give the basic IR model. Then we look at various directions of development of the IR field. The idea of Intelligent Information Retrieval will be introduced and the need for deeper linguistic analysis will be highlighted.

3.1 A Brief History of Information Retrieval

Initial explorations of text retrieval systems from small collections of scientific abstracts, legal and business documents etc. began in the nineteen sixties and seventies. Foundations of Boolean and vector-space models were developed. During these early days, documents were studied and brief descriptors or lists of index terms were manually prepared for each document.

During the eighties, large scale document databases started appearing. *Lexis-Nexis, Dialog and MEDLINE* are noteworthy examples of such databases. The need for efficient retrieval from large collections was increasingly felt. This gave a big push to IR research and development.

During the nineties, focus shifted to searching FTP-able documents on Internet (example: *Archie, WAIS*) and searching the World Wide Web (example: *Lycos, Yahoo, Altavista).* Organized competitions such as *NIST TREC* were held. Recommender systems (example: *Ringo, Amazon, NetPerceptions*) appeared. Automated text categorization and clustering systems were developed. Large scale information extraction systems started appearing in the 2000's. Google's innovating ideas such as the back link based page ranking are noteworthy. Current interests include retrieval from rich media documents and cross-lingual information retrieval. There is an increasing cross-fertilization and integration of related technologies including speech.

Currently indexing is performed automatically on full texts Manual processing is slow, costly and may be inconsistent. On the other hand, while automatic processing can be very fast, it lacks the commonsense and human judgement of manual methods and can therefore be somewhat inferior in quality. The challenge today is to keep the superior speed factor and yet achieve near-human performance through automatic methods.

It is clear that IR today is closely related to many other disciplines. It interfaces with Database Management systems, Library and Information sciences, Artificial Intelligence, Natural Language Processing and Machine Learning. Database Management systems focus on structured data stored in tables and efficient processing of precisely defined queries expressed in a formal language such as SQL. The syntax and semantics of the data as well as the query are clear. Recent trends towards semi-structured data such as XML brings it closer to IR. Library and Information Science has focused on the human user aspects such as human-computer interaction, user interfaces and visualization. Effective categorization of human knowledge is a primary goal. Citation analysis and bibliometrics are focus areas. Recent work in digital libraries is bringing library science closer to computer science and information retrieval.AI has focussed on representation of knowledge, inference and intelligent action. Recent work on web ontologies and intelligent information agents brings it closer to IR. NLP is essential to move from superficial treatment of documents and queries to deeper, meaning based approaches. Word Sense Disambiguation has a direct impact. We have seen that IR systems can be viewed as a kind of natural language Question Answering systems. Supervised and unsupervised learning techniques help us to group together similar documents and thereby facilitate effective IR. Further developments in IR will clearly be related developments in all these various disciplines.

3.1.1 From The Library to the Internet

Within the domain of the library, one of the main tasks is the manual classification of books according to a specified classification system so that relevant books can be easily accessed by users. Often only limited parts of the documents such as titles, front and back matter, table of contents etc. are used for the purpose. Full text indexing is not feasible in manual methods. Human beings have commonsense and manual classification can be claimed to be superior in quality. However, to err is human and human errors do creep in at times. Automated systems can guarantee consistency.

The arrival of the World Wide Web around 1993 spurred a substantial increase in the already immense world of Internet. The size and scope of the Internet today has reached mind boggling levels. As the volume of information available on the World Wide Web went on increasing, the need for efficient ways of locating requisite information on the web was increasingly felt and this gave rise to the first search engine Yahoo (http://www.yahoo.com) and later many others such as Altavista, Infoseek, Excite, Hotbot, Lycos, Webcrawler and Google. Search engines follow the standard technique of using a spider or crawler to create and update a database or an index of web pages. The task of creating an index is made complicated by the large size of the data as also the highly dynamic nature of the web, lack of any centralized control and the heterogeneity of the document types and formats. Today IR means retrieving relevant documents from very large collections such as from the web. Full text indexing is taken for granted.

3.2 Basic IR Models

In *ad-hoc retrieval*, the most common view of IR, an unaided user expresses his need through a short query. The IR system matches the query against the documents in the collection and returns the documents that match. The returned documents may be given in a ranked order. The document collection is fixed and a one time indexing on the whole collection is performed to create and store an index. Matching is performed on the index, not on the original documents. Each time a user issues a query, a match operation is performed and the results returned. *Document Filtering* provides an alternative view. Here the query may be considered fixed and a stream of documents need to be checked. The query expresses what exactly a particular user wants or does not want. Documents are filtered out accordingly. There is no scope to perform indexing of the whole collection of documents since the collection is not available beforehand and documents keep coming. Here the decision is usually Boolean - include or exclude a document. Ranking is also conceivable. *Routing* is also similar to filtering except that the documents filtered in may also have to be routed to different agencies. If nothing is mentioned, ad-hoc retrieval is usually taken as the the default mode.

3.2.1 IR Models

An IR model must specify four things:

- Document Representation
- Query Representation
- Definition of Relevance
- Matching/Retrieval Function

The simplest way one can think of matching documents and query is to perform direct *keyword search* - search for the given query string verbatim in the documents and return the documents that contain the given query string. This is too rigid. *Computer* will not match *Computers* or even *computer* if the search is case sensitive. So some kind of *soft match* may be introduced. Even with that extension the search is too rigid. Suppose you want documents containing the words *Sun, Moon, orbit, eclipse* but not necessarily all at one place and not necessarily exactly in the order given. It would then be helpful to consider documents and queries as unordered collections of words. This is called that *bag-of-words* representation. A *bag* is an unordered collection of items just like a set, only multiple occurrences are allowed. Some early systems used pre-specified sets of index terms. Current systems tend to prefer full text indexing. It is also possible to exploit structure of documents and meta-data (such as URL, title, anchor string, author and other meta tags, font sizes, capitalization and position in the document). Thus the HTML/XML structure in hypertext documents could be made use of.

The Boolean Retrieval Model

The Boolean model is based on set theoretic principles. Here documents are treated as sets of keywords. Note that a set is an unordered collection of items. Frequency of occurrence is not relevant. In a set an item is either present or absent. Items cannot repeat. Queries are treated as Boolean expressions of keywords, connected by logical operators such as AND, OR and NOT. Brackets can be used to explicate scope or for over-riding the default scope of operators. Thus we could search for:

```
(Hotel && (Three Star || Five Star)) && !Sheraton
```

Any given document will either match or not match. There are no partial matches. There are no ranks.

The Boolean model is simple, easy to understand and use, clean and efficient. It is possible to strictly enforce which terms should or should not be present. Boolean models were quite widely used at one point of time. However, these models are very rigid. AND means ALL and OR means ANY. All matched documents will be retrieved - there may be too many or too few, there is no way to control the number. This is especially problematic when the document collections are very large, as in the case of the Internet. It is difficult to rank the matching documents. It is difficult to express complex requirements. Ideas such as query reformulation and relevance feedback are difficult to incorporate. Because of all these factors, Boolean models are no longer the preferred retrieval models for IR.

The Vector Space Retrieval Model

The vector space model treats documents as bags of words - unordered collections of terms, repetitions allowed, so we can talk of frequencies. Documents as well as queries are treated as vectors (arrays) of features. Each term (a word, a phrase or other similar entity) is a possible feature. Features are given numerical values. Thus feature vectors can be geometrically visualized as points in n-dimensional space or as vectors connecting the origin to these points. The spatial similarity between such vectors is used as a metaphor to define the similarity between documents and queries. Retrieved documents are ranked based on the degree of similarity.

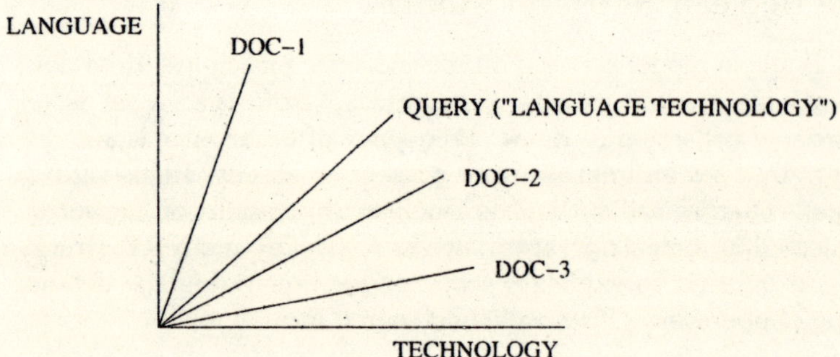

FIG 3.1 The Vector Space Model in Two Dimensions

There are several issues in the design of a vector space model. How do we determine which terms in a given document are important? What about word sense? Should we take the surface form of words or the root forms? What definition of word do we use? How do we take care of multi-token words, compounds, idioms and phrases? What is the relationship between the importance of a given term for a given document in relation to its importance for other documents in the collection or for the whole collection? How exactly do we compute the similarity between a query and a document? In the case of a large hyperlinked and highly dynamic collection such as the world wide web, what exactly is the collection and what are the effects of the hyperlinks, formatting information and meta data available? There are no perfect answers to all the questions but we will be able to give some ideas as we proceed.

Vector space models based on the bag-of-words representation ignores syntax (word order, phrase structure, proximity, and more) and semantics (word senses, scope of quantifiers and negation, anaphoric references, synonymy and other kinds of relationships between words and between words and concepts). "Restaurant" will not match with "cafe". "PRC" will not match with "China". But "Bat" as in cricket may match with the mammal called bat. "Apple" will treat the apple fruit and the Apple computer without distinction. Vector space models lack the tight control that Boolean models permit. Given a query "A B", vector space models may prefer a document containing A frequently but not B, or B frequently but not A, over documents that contain both A and B but less frequently. Is this what we really want in all situations?

In spite of the fact that there are still many open questions, vector space models have worked fairly well in practice, especially for large collections such as the web. They are simple, based on principles of mathematics and statistics and amenable for efficient implementations. They are more flexible than Boolean Models - partial matching is allowed and the retrieved documents can be ranked and ordered. The vector space model based on the bag-of-words representation is the mainstream approach in IR today.

3.2.2 Term Weighting: tf-idf

It may be argued that the number of times a term occurs in a document is a stronger indicator of its semantic content as compared to mere presence or absence of terms. Thus feature values can be taken as *Term Frequency (TF)* rather than as Boolean. An *inverted index* can also be maintained, giving for each word, the frequencies and the positions of the word for each document. The inverted index makes it easy to locate documents containing particular words or phrases. Thus if the terms *Batting, Bowling, Fielding, LBW, Run Out, Boundary, Catch, Run* etc. occur frequently, we may think that that the document must be related to Cricket.

One cannot be so sure that the document is about football if the word *goal* appears frequently because the word goal can appear in many different kinds of documents with different meanings. Similarly, if some words, say, *important, however, also, re-*

cently, although, change etc. occur frequently in some document, we may not be able to say much about the semantic content of the document. In fact these words may occur frequently in many documents on a variety of topics. Hence it makes sense to look at the number of different documents in the collection in which a particular term appears. If a term occurs in many, or almost all the documents, it is less useful as an indicator of any particular topic. The *Inverse Document Frequency (IDF)* is the ratio of the total number of documents in the collection to the number of documents in the collection in which the specified term occurs.

The term frequency is often dampened - $\sqrt{tf}$ or $1 + log(tf)$ is used. This is because a document containing a term more often is more significant but may not be by as much as the frequency itself suggests. If a term occurs once in d1 and thrice in d2, d2 is surely more significant than d1 for the given term but may not be really three times as significant. Also, there are length effects. A large document and a small document should not be treated on par. The occurrence of a rare term in a small document is perhaps more significant than the occurrence of the same term in a large document. Thus the tf values are often normalized for length by dividing them by the size of the document or, perhaps better still, by the frequency of the most frequent word in the document. Another formula that has been proposed to refine the raw tf is $0.5 + (0.5 * tf)/(max_t f)$.

Since the total number of documents in a collection may be large, it is usual to squash the raw idf value also by taking logarithms.

The product of Term Frequency and Inverse Document Frequency, abbreviated as *tf.idf*, is one of most basic term weighing schemes. In fact tf.idf is a class of term weighting schemes. There are several combinations, some of the commonly used ones are shown below:

Term Frequency	**IDF**	**Normal- -ization.**
n: natural: tf	n:natural: idf: $\frac{N}{n_i}$	n:no norm.
l: log: 1 + log(tf)	t:log($\frac{N}{n_i}$)	c:cosine
a: augmented: $0.5 + \frac{0.5*tf}{max\_tf}$ max_tf: freq. of the most frequent term in the doc.		

Various schemes of tf.idf weighting are denoted using the labels in the above table. Thus ltc.ann refers to logarithmic terms frequency, logarithmic idf and cosine normalization for the documents and augmented term frequency, plain idf and no normalization for the query terms. Weights for terms that do not occur in a given document can be taken as zero.

These tf.idf schemes consider both the local and global effects of term frequencies. They are simple and effective, they are widely used.

However, such schemes for term weighting are ad hoc and lack a proper mathematical basis. Schemes based on term distribution probability models have been proposed. Some of the commonly used schemes are based on 1) Poisson distribution, 2) two-Poisson model and 3) Katz's K-Mixture model.

The terms in the query are usually taken to be equally weighted but it is conceivable that users specify the relative weights of the query terms. There will still be no logical connectives and the matching algorithms will continue to be statistical. It is not easy for users to think of appropriate ways of weighting the query terms and hence this idea is difficult to use.

3.2.3 Similarity Measures

How do we quantify the similarity between two vectors? We have seen that directions between the two vectors can be taken as a measure of similarity between the two vectors. (Sometimes it is more convenient to talk in terms of dissimilarity rather than similarity. Greater the *distance* between two quantities, higher is the dissimilarity. Hence the name Distance Measures.) It is usual to measure the Cosine of the angle between the two vectors rather than the angle itself. The cosine will be 1 when the two vectors coincide and 0 when they are completely disjoint (orthogonal). The cosine measure is given by:

$$cosine(\mathbf{q}, \mathbf{d}) = \frac{\sum_{i=1}^{n} q_i * d_i}{\sqrt{\sum_{i=1}^{n} q_i^2} \; * \; \sqrt{\sum_{i=1}^{n} d_i^2}}$$

It is appropriate to normalize the lengths of all vectors to 1. Otherwise, longer vectors (corresponding to longer documents) would have an unfair advantage and the corresponding documents tend to get ranked higher than the shorter documents. If the vector lengths are all normalized to 1, the denominator becomes 1 and so the cosine is simply the dot product of the two vectors. It can be shown that the cosine measure and the Euclidean distance produce identical rankings.

3.2.4 The Probability Ranking Principle

If the user does not find many relevant documents in the first page of returned results, he is often willing to look at the next page, thereby trading Precision for Recall. The *Probability Ranking Principle* states that *ranking documents in order of decreasing probability of relevance is optimal.* Retrieval is viewed as a greedy search where at each step we try to identify the most relevant document yet to be retrieved and finally rank the obtained documents in decreasing order of relevance. This assumes that the documents are independent. A clear but extreme example of the violation of this assumption is when there are duplicates in the collection. If an ambiguous word such as *capital* is included in the query, an optimal system may be expected to retrieve and present the documents so that the user sees this ambiguity but the PRP principle would give documents that are maximally relevant for either of the two senses of the ambiguous word. Further, relevance is difficult to quantify and measure accurately. At best we make good estimates. It may be worth looking at the variance of these estimates and prefer those decisions with lower variance.

3.2.5 Performance Evaluation

As we have already seen, Precision is the percentage of relevant documents in the returned set and Recall is the percentage of all relevant documents in the collection that is in the returned set. However, most IR systems produce a ranked list of returned documents and a case where the last three of the ten documents returned are relevant cannot be equated with the case where the first three out of ten are relevant. Most users scan the returned documents from top to bottom and would like to see many relevant documents right at the top. Thus by measuring the precision at several initial segments of the ranked list, one may obtain a good impression of how well the system ranks relevant documents. We may therefore measure the *Precision at specified cutoff levels* such as 5, 10, 20 or 100 from the top. By considering all the documents above a relevant document and computing Precision and then by averaging all such Precision values for each of the relevant document retrieved, one gets an *uninterpolated average Precision.* This average Precision will be 1 if all the relevant documents are at the top of the list. Documents further down in the list are also considered and Precision for relevant documents beyond the returned list is taken as zero. Therefore this quantity actually indirectly measures recall. On the other hand *interpolated average Precision* is more directly based on the Recall. Precision values are calculated for each specified levels of Recall and then averaged. In the case of the widely used 11-point average, for example, Precision is measured at Recall levels of 0%, 10%, 20%, 30%, 40%, 50%, 60%, 70%, 80%, 90% and 100%. One point to note is that if the Precision value at any Recall level is lower than a Precision value at a higher Recall value, the higher value is used. This is based on the idea that if the Precision is increasing, people will be willing to go down further. This process is called interpolation. Curves which show the variation between Precision and Recall are called *Precision-Recall curves.* Average Precision is one way to compute a combined measure indicating the trade-off between Precision and Recall. the F-Measure is another commonly used combined measure. The F-Measure is given by

$$F = \frac{1}{\alpha\frac{1}{P}+(1-\alpha)\frac{1}{R}}$$

where α gives the relative weights for Precision P and Recall R. If equal weightage is given for the two, then

$$F = \frac{2*P*R}{P+R}$$

3.3 Towards Intelligent Information Retrieval

Let us now take stock of where we stand, where we would like to go, and how to get there. We start by recapitulating what we have already seen.

Let us define a typical IR task: given a corpus of textual natural-language documents and a user query in the form of a textual string, to find a ranked set of documents that are relevant to the query. As we have already seen, the most common approach is to view documents and queries are bags of words and represent them as feature vectors where each feature corresponds to one word. Similarity between feature vectors is quantified in terms of the orientations of these vectors. Performance is measured in terms of Precision and Recall.

Intelligent IR, on the other hand, requires that we consider the syntax as well as semantics of documents and queries, we adapt to users based on direct or indirect feedback and learning, and we take care of authority and dependability of documents. An ideal information retrieval system is one that can perform like a human assistant. This is really the software grand challenge. Obviously, we are far from such an ideal. Let us now see what kinds of improvements and enhancements can be or have been made in the field of information retrieval.

Mere presence or absence of keywords is clearly too naive a view of a document. Can we say *I have a bad head ache* and *Now I am free from head ache* mean the same thing and both match the query *head ache* equally well? Is *India beat Australia* same as *Australia beat India*? Can we equate *I like Govinda's movies* and *I like Govinda's movies as much as I would like a burning stove if I were sitting on it*? Most current IR systems continue to use the bag-of-words representation while examples like this clearly show the inadequacies of such a representation.

There are several way we may think for improving this basic model of IR. We can try to take into account the meaning of the words used. *Match* may mean a cricket match or a matrimonial match or a match box and only when we are able to disambiguate the correct sense of the word can we be sure that we are looking at the right document. We may try to take into account the order of words in the query. A full syntactic analysis may be carried out. We may try to adapt to the user based on direct or indirect feedback. We may try to take into account the authority of the source.

We have already seen that many of the NLP tasks are inherently difficult in themselves and performance of current systems is limited. Thus full syntactic analysis is not only time consuming but also limited in performance - current grammars and parsers fail on a significant percentage of cases. Unrestricted WSD systems are still at a research level. The real challenge, therefore, is to integrate the best of available NLP technologies with IR models without sacrificing the simplicity and efficiency of IR models. We will explore below some the ideas and techniques that have been used to build better IR systems.

3.3.1 Improving User Queries - Relevance Feedback

A big question is how do we assess the relevance of a retrieved document for a given query? Relevance is a subjective judgment and may include being on the proper subject, being timely (recent information), being authoritative (from a trusted source), satisfying the goals of the user and his/her intended use of the information (information need), etc. Relevance is not an yes/no question, we may have to deal with degrees of relevance. No single document may be very relevant but a set of them could together be. Evaluating the relevance of a document for a given query is thus a very complex task and we need to make some simplifying assumptions in practice. For example, we may use the simplest notion of relevance that the query string appears verbatim in the document. A slightly less strict notion could be that the words in the query appear frequently in the document, in any order (bag of words).

Instead of looking for improving the performance of retrieval for given queries, we may invert the problem and see how the query itself may be improved so that performance is maximized. This makes sense because it is not always very easy for a user to specify exactly what he wants as a query. An ideal query is one that expresses the user's requirements precisely in relation to the documents in the collection. But finding an ideal query is difficult unless we already know exactly what the documents in the collection contain. We may therefore start with a good guess and hope to improve after we see some results. We make the assumption that documents which are relevant to a given query are similar. Therefore a query can be improved by making it closer to relevant documents retrieved and farther from the irrelevant documents retrieved. Thus by looking at the returned results and judging them as relevant or otherwise, we may obtain an improved query. More terms from the relevant documents retrieved can be added and weights for the terms can also be adjusted based on the frequency of occurrence of those terms in the relevant and irrelevant documents. Usually performance increases substantially with just one iteration but if required the process can be iterated upon. This process is called *Relevance Feedback*. Which terms to add and how exactly to adjust the weights are the important issues.

Instead of interactively improving the query, one may assume that the top few (say, 20) hits are all actually relevant and automatically improve the query without asking users to judge any retrieved documents. This technique is termed *Pseudo-relevance Feedback*.

3.3.2 Page Ranking

Retrieving the documents that best match the given query does not necessarily give us the best overall performance. There are a very large number of documents on the Internet and too many of them may match equally well. Simply listing a large number of relevant documents is not very good. How do we help the users then? We should use not only the terms in the documents and queries for matching and ranking the documents, but also some general measure of goodness of various documents. It would be nice if we could somehow compute authenticity or dependability of documents but there is no simple way to do that. What search engines such as Google do is to instead use the popularity of the documents as a measure of goodness. If many people are looking at a document perhaps there is something important or useful about it. But how do we find out who is looking at which document and for what purpose? One thing that is clearly computable from the web of documents on the Internet is the hyperlink structure that links up various documents. We could look at the links going out from a given document but perhaps the links coming into a given documents from other documents is a better measure of its importance. Thus the rank of a page goes high if it is pointed to by many documents. Of course the documents that point to a given document themselves may or may not be very important. Also we must not allow people to deliberately manipulate these ranks by artificially creating a large number of dummy documents and make them all point to a given document to increase its rank.

Google works by looking at all the documents that point to a given document and weight these pointers by the ranks of those documents. Thus a document gets a high rank if it has many links coming from high ranked documents. Of course this definition is recursive but there is a simple iterative algorithm that keeps updating the page ranks. It is not easy to fool the system for long - even if dummy documents are created to enhance the page rank of some document, those dummy documents would soon get very low ranks as no other high ranked documents would be really linking to them. The web may appear to be a totally unorganized and uncontrolled mess but simple ideas like this can bring some order to the chaos.

The Google Page Rank (PR) computation formula is given below:

$$PR(A) = (1 - d) + d(PR(T_1)/C(T_1) + ... + PR(T_n)/C(T_n))$$

where T_is are citations of document A and $C(T)$ gives the total number of outgoing links from document T. Here d is a factor that specifies the relative importance of the current document to the documents which cite it.

3.3.3 Role of Linguistics

Stop Words

Words that seem to be useless for searching are termed stop words. These are mainly grammatical or function words such as articles, prepositions and conjunctions. Words such as *the, from, could* have important grammatical function in sentences but are unlikely to help us in retrieving relevant documents using the bag-of-words representation. Function words may be extracted from an electronic dictionary. Stop words are usually high frequency words and small in size. So we may also make an initial list of stop words by looking at the frequency and/or length. Eliminating stop words reduces the feature vector size. However, removing stop words has its own negative effects. How do we handle the phrase *when and where* if all these three words are eliminated as stop words?

Instead of using ad-hoc methods to remove some terms as stop words, we may try to measure the significance of words and then remove those with low significance. For example, terms with very low tf.idf values can be removed.

Morphology

The simple bag-of-words representation described so far would treat *compute, computer, computing etc.* as individual, unrelated words in their own right, although all these words are semantically closely related. A morphological analyzer can analyze full words into roots and affixes according to valid rules of morphophonemics. However, developing a full morphological analyzer is not always easy, especially for languages with a very rich system of morphology. We know that Indian languages fall into this category. Most IR systems take a short cut and apply simplified versions of analyzers called *stemmers*. Lovin and Porter stemmer are widely used for English. A stemming algorithm removes affixes according to some rules. Thus *compute, computer, computing* will all be reduced to *comput-*. Note that *comput* is not even a valid word in English! Stemming algorithms can reduce semantically unrelated words into a common stem. Thus *stocks and stockings* may both get reduced to *stock-* causing serious damage. Also reducing both *gallery and gall* to *gall-* makes it difficult for people to understand what is happening.

Phrases

If you are looking for *interest rate* you cannot simply go by documents containing the words *interest* and *rate* anywhere in them. Thus identifying phrases and treating them as single terms is important. However, identifying phrases is not as simple as it may appear. How do we take care of *interest rate*, *interest rates* and *rate of interest* as all meaning essentially the same thing? How do we distinguish between phrases and compounds? How do we distinguish between words that occur in sequence merely by chance with word sequences that have a unitary meaning? Handling phrases is much more complex than we may think. Most current IR systems follow a simple and crude yet quite effective method. They simply identify ordered pairs of words (called *bigrams*) that occur frequently and treat them as individual terms. Of course this is very restrictive - phrases with more than two words are not at all considered. Some systems have a separate phrase identification module and attempt more sophisticated techniques, similar to techniques used for identifying collocations.

Syntax

Since *Godse killed Gandhi* and *Gandhi killed Godse* mean very different things, the bag-of-words representation is too crude. A good IR system must really consider the relative positions of words and analyze the structure of sentences in depth. However, syntactic analysis is itself a very complex and challenging task. Most current parsing systems are limited in their performance. Also, attempts to use deeper analysis have given mixed results - performance does not necessarily improve. There is now an increasing interest in partial or shallow parsing systems. Wide coverage robust partial parsing systems are becoming available.

Word Sense Disambiguation

Words have several meanings and simply counting the frequency of the word *match* without knowing whether is is used to mean a cricket match or a matrimonial match or just a match box is no good. the role played by Homonymy, Polysemy and Synonymy is complex. If a query contains the term *house* and no word sense disambiguation is done, the system returns documents containing the term house in any of its senses including an ordinary dwelling place and a parliamentary house, thereby reducing the real Precision. At the same time, it may miss out other relevant documents that may use synonymous or similar meaning words such as 'residence' or 'home'. Thus Recall is also reduced. This shows how important it is to identify the correct senses of words in context.

Yet Word Sense Disambiguation is itself a difficult area of research and as of now, most IR systems do not bother to look at the meanings of words at all. We will look at a technique later by which word sense disambiguation is indirectly taken care of to some extent.

Anaphora Resolution

Pronouns are often discarded as stop words but they actually stand for some nouns. References are informationally abbreviated forms of the referents. The references and the referents point to the same thing - they must be treated as equals. Resolution of anaphoric references can therefore help in improving the performance of IR systems.

Discourse Segmentation

In large documents, the topic keeps shifting and the topics of smaller identifiable units such as sections and paragraphs may be more relevant than the topic of entire documents. For example, if you are looking for *Malaria* a paragraph in which the term malaria occurs several times could be more informative and useful to you than a large document in which the word occurs scattered all over, even if the total frequency of occurrence is higher. Discourse segmentation can therefore be useful.

Text Tiling

There are techniques for automatically identifying discourse segments within a text. One method, called *Text Tiling*, breaks texts into fixed size blocks and assumes that they are separated by hypothetical 'gaps'. A *Cohesion Scorer* measures the topic continuity across gaps. A *Depth Scorer* checks how low the cohesion of a gap is relative to neighboring gaps. Cohesion is relative. Finally a *Boundary Selector* finds the segmentation points. Once a document is segmented into discourse segments, we could think of performing IR on discourse segments rather than on whole documents.

Current views on use of NLP in IR are mixed. While the limitations of current IR models are well understood and the need for deeper linguistic analysis is accepted in principle, practical studies and experiments including NLP components have not consistently given better performance. This could be partly because of the nature and limitations of the NLP modules considered in these experiments. Even if speed is sacrificed to some extent, if we can show that accuracies can be significantly and consistently improved, then the role of NLP could be better appreciated. User perspectives matter a lot. Many users may be happy that they are able to get something useful from the Internet and not bothered too much about the low precision and recall of the current systems. As user expectations grow, and IR is applied for more serious and highly specific retrieval tasks, the need for moving towards more intelligent models would be felt more and more.

3.3.4 Latent Semantic Indexing

The bag-of-words representation treats words and phrases as isolated occurrences. In fact the co-occurrence of terms has a significant implication for the semantic content of documents. Co-occurrence also implicitly disambiguates words. For example, if the word *bank* occurs frequently with words such as *cheque, withdraw, deposit, balance, interest, etc.* then it indicates the financial institution sense, not the bank of a river. Latent Semantic Indexing (LSI) is a technique by which co-occurring terms are grouped together and treated similarly. LSI actually projects from the original n-dimensional vector space with n different terms onto a lower dimensional space such that co-occurring terms fall along same dimensions and non-co-occurring terms are projected onto different dimensions. The idea is that the *latent*, that is hidden, 'true' semantic space of possibilities is obtained from the surface representation where each term is treated as a separate entity and the semantic relationships between the terms are implicit. In the latent semantic space, a query and a document can have high similarity even if they do not share any terms, as long as the terms are semantically similar according to the co-occurrence analysis. LSI can thus be viewed as a similarity metric and an alternative to word overlap measures such as tf.idf. The latent semantic space has fewer dimensions and thus LSI can also be looked upon as a *dimensionality reduction technique.*

LSI chooses an optimal mapping among various possible mappings to a lower dimension. This is achieved by using a mathematical technique known as *Singular Value Decomposition (SVD)*. LSI is basically an application of SVD to the word-by-document matrix. The dimensions of the reduced space correspond to the axes of greatest variation. The idea is to capture as much of the variation in the data as possible. SVD can be viewed as a method to rotate the axes of on an n-dimensional space so that the first axis runs along the direction of largest variation, the second axis runs along the direction of the second largest variation, and so on. Thus SVD is similar to *Principle Component Analysis (PCA)*. PCA is applicable only to square matrices whereas SVD can be applied to any matrix. SVD is a least square method. SVD takes a matrix A and represents it as $\hat{A}$ in a lower dimensional space such that the "distance" between the two as measured by the 2-norm is minimized:

$$\triangle = \| A - \hat{A} \|_2$$

The 2-norm is for matrices what Euclidean distance is for vectors.

SVD, and therefore LSI, assumes normal distribution which is seldom true for term distributions. Also SVD can be slower. Hence the use of LSI is justified only when the performance improvements are very significant.

3.3.5 Meta Search Engines

With millions of pages being added to the World Wide Web every year it was realized that no search engine could possibly index all the information on the web and be reasonably efficient at the same time. The web is extremely large. To get an idea, consider these 1996 figures for the number of pages indexed by various search engines: Excite - 1.5 Million pages, Lycos - 19 Million unique URLs including ftps and gopher and Altavista - 166 Million pages. These look like toys by today's standards. Yet no search engine indexes all the available web pages. As the web keeps growing faster and larger this need would only become more and more apparent. While interacting with search engines, it was realized that the user who had a varied set of interests started gradually transcending a single search engine and was forced to submit and resubmit his queries to several search engines. This was a major bottleneck in World Wide Web searching and from this need for reducing the amount of user time spent in submitting queries to multiple search engines arose the concept of a meta search engine.

A meta search engine takes a user query and submits the query to many public domain search engines either in parallel or sequentially, collects results returned by each search engine and returns the compiled result to the user. Apart from this, a meta search engine may provide other facilities such as removing duplicates and filtering the results. Meta search engines are not intended to replace search engines - search engines are the service providers to the meta search engines. Search engines are likely to be increasingly used by meta search engines rather than by the end users directly. If Internet keeps growing at the phenomenal rate it is doing now, the amount of user time spent in locating relevant information will also keep growing. Hence we need to look for alternative architectures for searching and information retrieval from the web.

Meta search engines have several advantages over direct use of search engines. Unlike search engines, meta search engines can reside locally and can be customized or adapted to the needs of a specific user or a user group. A meta search engine can be linked to a local database so that web search can be replaced with local search in some situations and frequently downloaded pages can be locally archived. Advanced techniques for automatically building and adapting user models are of great interest. It has been seen that users generally restrict themselves to a particular subset of topics when they initiate a web search. This can be used to construct a user profile which should be extremely useful in search optimization. More detailed understanding of the user's needs becomes possible as the meta search engine is local and customizable. For example, you may specify whether you are seriously looking for an answer to a very specific question or you are generally exploring what all is available. Search engines treat each query as a fresh task and they have no idea of what you have already searched, what all you already know and what exactly you are now looking for. Meta search engines can be customized to work in the background mode so that user's time in waiting for results can be minimized. A meta search engine can monitor the network bandwidth dynamically and adjust the firing of the various search engines accordingly. Users need to learn a single query interface since the system automatically formulates the user's query as required by various search engines. The system can also learn statistical models of search engines and the pages they index so that it becomes possible to choose the right search engines for the right query. Such models can be used to predict, for example, the expected results for a given search. The meta search engine can "know", even before searching, that there will be too many hits and the query needs to be tightened up or that there may not be many relevant documents. Overall performance can also be optimized by choosing the search engines and firing them judiciously.

Users spend a lot of time trying to locate what they want from the Internet. Even with technology improvements and increasing bandwidths, effective bandwidth is getting offset by increasing resources and the number of users. On the whole availability of sufficient bandwidth will remain an imminent problem in many parts of the world. Meta search engines offer one good solution to saving user time.

There are several meta search engines in use. The Metacrawler and the Savvy search (http://www.savvy.com) are two such search services on the web. The Metacrawler utilizes several search engines to which it submits its queries. The service removes duplicates from the results returned and presents it to the user in a click-able format. The All in One Page (http://www.allone.com) is a meta search service which provides results from multiple resource applications which include gopher, Archie, HTTP and others.

Here we shall briefly look at a Meta Search Engine called *Personal Search Assistant (PSA)* developed by us sometime back. The PSA system has been implemented using CGI scripts written in Perl which run under the Apache Web Server. PSA is modular. Let us take a quick look at each of the major modules:

- The *Collector Module* submits queries to several search engines in parallel and collects the results in local files for further processing. It can be configured to look for specified kinds of information for focussed search, say URLs, email ids, or ftp sites relating to a given topic. It can work in the background. It monitors the network bandwidth and adjusts the parallel firing of search engines accordingly.
- The *Update Module* interprets the search results given by

different search engines, takes care of formatting variations, and updates one or more local databases. It may also initiate its own collection phase to refresh outdated database entries.

- The *Local Database Handler* interfaces with various modules in the system and allows the user to search, view and modify different parts of the various local databases.
- The *History Module* maintains logs of previous search operations. The log includes information such as search specific user login for the search, the search term/terms used, links followed by the user, links followed by others, search engine statistics for each search, the specific search engines utilized by the search, engine speed (= number of hits/time spent), number of search engine links followed and total number of times a particular search engine is chosen. PSA computes values of certain parameters including average search engine speed, search engine popularity and uses these values to make suggestions and recommendations to the user, for modelling search engines and for user modelling. The PSA history subsystem works during and after the collecting phase and interacts with the LDB handler to update the local database with the history details of a previous search. The history subsystem keeps track of search queries, formats in which they are submitted, who submitted them, how far the results were appropriate in relation to the search queries as perceived by the user and user preferences in following the returned links.
- The *Personal Agent* module uses these pieces of information to construct a user profile. The user need not spend any time on the global search phase as it can be a non-interactive, background phase. The user can interact with the local database at any time during or after the search is over.

3.3.6 Semantic Web

We have seen that one of the major issues in IR is the need to understand the documents in the collection. Instead of looking for more and more sophisticated techniques for unearthing hidden semantic information from plain text documents, why not think of embedding semantics explicitly into the documents themselves? That would give a big push to all automatic document processing systems including IR systems. The big question however is, how do we incorporate all this semantics into the documents?

Tim Berners-Lee, the inventor of the WWW (World Wide Web), URI (Uniform Resource Identifier), HTTP (HyperText Transfer Protocol), and HTML (HyperText Markup Language), says "The Semantic Web is an extension of the current web in which information is given well-defined meaning, better enabling computers and people to work in cooperation.". The Semantic Web provides a common framework that allows data to be shared and reused across application, enterprise, and community boundaries. It is a collaborative effort led by W3C (World Wide Web Consortium) with participation from a large number of researchers and industrial partners. It is based on the Resource Description Framework (RDF), which integrates a variety of applications using XML for syntax and URIs for naming. See Scientific American May 2001 issue for an interesting article by Tim Berners-Lee.

3.3.7 Information Retrieval is Difficult

IR is an inherently difficult task. Can you search millions of documents and accurately suggest the most relevant documents for a given query in a fraction of a second? In IR we are asking computers to do what we human beings cannot do. And we want IR to be fully automatic - there is no scope for human intervention. What makes IR difficult? There are three major issues:

- *Understanding user needs:* Understanding exactly what the user is looking for is not easy. Key words do not tell us what is the purpose of the current search, what all the user already knows, what all he has already searched or what level of abstraction would suit his level of knowledge and expertise. Social and cultural contexts are important. It looks strange that we set forth on a grand searching and retrieval operation without understanding exactly what we are looking for!

- *Understanding the Documents:* Unless you know exactly what the documents contain, what they pertain to and what all things they include, for whom it is written, what background is assumed etc., how can we say which documents will suit a given user's needs at a given point of time? We have already seen that understanding the meanings and intentions in a document is extremely difficult. So we go ahead and search documents without knowing what exactly they contain?

Efficient Indexing ad Searching: Computationally efficient indexing of extremely large and highly dynamic collections such as the world wide web is a technological challenge. Searching and matching in such large collections is also not easy. Clever use of data structures and algorithms must be combined with distributed and parallel architectures involving thousands of computers spread across the globe. Hardware may fail, network services may be disrupted, but search engines must deliver under all circumstances. Building in such a high degree of robustness and fault-tolerance are technological challenges.

Given all this, is it not a great thing that today's search engines are doing quite well, if not fully satisfactorily? The fact that people use search engines routinely shows that the today's IR technologies are useable and useful. Nevertheless, dissatisfaction is the starting point for innovation and design. We want IR to deliver more. Improvements in IR are likely to come as much from clever heuristics and tricks as from in depth linguistic analysis. Statistical analysis and modelling techniques are likely to play a major role too. We can expect greater cross-fertilization, synergy and integration of IR with other areas of language engineering.

3.3.8 Conclusions

Intelligent IR requires that we consider the syntax and semantics of documents and queries, we adapt to users based on direct or indirect feedback and learning, and we take care of authority and dependability of documents. Developing an information retrieval system that can perform like a human assistant has been dubbed as the software grand challenge. It is natural, therefore, that we have talked more of problems and broad ideas rather than concrete solutions.

On the one hand we feel the need for deeper linguistic analysis and NLP. On the other hand we want great speed and robustness. The challenge is to use deeper linguistic analysis without losing the advantages of speed, flexibility and robustness. Linguistic analysis is usually quite language specific whereas statistical techniques and machine learning algorithms can be adapted to a wide variety of languages without much manual effort.Linguists have been talking of universal grammars for a long time now but there do not seem to be any such universal grammars that can be used right away.

Developments in IR must be understood in the context of development in related fields such as Information Extraction, Text Categorization and Automatic Summarization as also NLP technologies such as WordNets, stemming algorithms, partial parsing systems and WSD. With the rapid developments in each of these fields and increasing synergy between the various areas, we can expect IR systems to become much more sophisticated in the years to come.

Document in Indian languages have slowly started growing. There are still some teething problems with regard to non-standard encoding schemes. We can hope that the Indian language content will grow fast in the near future. The need for indexing and searching pages in Indian languages will grow. The tools and techniques which have been been fine tuned for English do not necessarily work well for Indian languages. Richness of morphology would call for special attention. Being late has one advantage - we can gain from others' experiences and make a better design.

There is also a great need for indexing and searching pages not in, but on Indian languages and Indian tradition and culture. Multi-lingual and multi-media extensions will become increasingly important.

Bibliography

1. Akshar Bharati, Vineet Chaitanya and Rajeev Sangal, "Natural Language Processing: A Paninian Perspective", Prentice Hall of India, 1995

2. Andrian Akmajian, Richard A Demers and Robert M Harnish, "Linguistics: An Introduction to Language and Communication", The MIT Press, Second Edition, 1984

3. Baker C L, "English Syntax", MIT Press, 1989

4. Ben Gold and Nelson Morgan, "Speech an Audio Signal Processing",John Wiley and Sons Inc., 2002

5. Charniak E, "Statistical Language Learning", MIT Press, 1993

6. Christopher D Manning and Hinrich Shutze, "Foundations of Statistical Natural Language Processing", The MIT Press, 2000

7. Daniel Jurafsky and James H Martin, "Speech and Language Processing", Pearson Education, 2002

8. Douglas O'Shaughnessy, "Speech Communications - Human and Machine", Second Edition, Universities Press, 2001

9. D C Montgomery, E A Peck and G G Vining, "Introduction to Linear Regression Analysis", John Wiley and Sons, INC., 2001

10. George W Smith, "Computers and Human Language", Oxford University Press, 1991

11. Hopcroft J.E. and Ullman J.D., "Introduction to Automata Theory, Languages, and Computation", Addison-Wesley, 1979

12. Inderjeet Mani and Mark T Maybury (Eds), "Advances in Automatic Text Summarization", the MIT Press, 1999

13. James Allen,"Natural Language Understanding", Second Edition, Pearson Education, 2003

14. Lawrence Rabiner and Biing-Hwang Juang, "Fundamentals of Speech Recognition", Pearson Education, 2003

15. Michael G Dyer, "In-Depth Understanding", MIT Press,1983

16. Nigel Fabb, "Sentence Structure", Routledge

17. Ralph Grishman, "Computational Linguistics: An Introduction", Cambridge University Press, 1999

18. Richard Coates, "Word Structure", Routledge, 1999

19. Richard Hudson, "Word Meaning", Routledge

20. Richard O Duda, Peter E Hart and David G Stork, "Pattern Classification", John Wiley and Sons Inc., 2001

21. Richard Sproat, "Morphology and Computation", MIT Press, 1992

22. Roche E.and Schabes Y. (Eds), "Finite State Language Processing", MIT Press, 1997

23. Tom M Mitchell, "Machine Learning", The McGraw-Hill Companies Inc., 1997

24. The Unicode Standard Version 4.0, Addison-Wesley, 2004

Appendix 1: C5 Tag Set

1. AJ0 adjective (unmarked) (e.g. GOOD, OLD)
2. AJC comparative adjective (e.g. BETTER, OLDER)
3. AJS superlative adjective (e.g. BEST, OLDEST)
4. AT0 article (e.g. THE, A, AN)
5. AV0 adverb (unmarked) (e.g. OFTEN, WELL, LONGER, FURTHEST)
6. AVP adverb particle (e.g. UP, OFF, OUT)
7. AVQ wh-adverb (e.g. WHEN, HOW, WHY)
8. CJC coordinating conjunction (e.g. AND, OR)
9. CJS subordinating conjunction (e.g. ALTHOUGH, WHEN)
10. CJT the conjunction THAT
11. CRD cardinal numeral (e.g. 3, FIFTY-FIVE, 6609)
12. DPS possessive determiner form (e.g. YOUR, THEIR)
13. DT0 general determiner (e.g. THESE, SOME)
14. DTQ wh-determiner (e.g. WHOSE, WHICH)
15. EX0 existential THERE
16. ITJ interjection or other isolate (e.g. OH, YES, MHM)
17. NN0 noun (neutral for number) (e.g. AIRCRAFT, DATA)

18. NN1 singular noun (e.g. PENCIL, GOOSE)

19. NN2 plural noun (e.g. PENCILS, GEESE)

20. NP0 proper noun (e.g. LONDON, MICHAEL, MARS)

21. ORD ordinal (e.g. SIXTH, 77TH, LAST)

22. PNI indefinite pronoun (e.g. NONE, EVERYTHING)

23. PNP personal pronoun (e.g. YOU, THEM, OURS)

24. PNQ wh-pronoun (e.g. WHO, WHOEVER)

25. PNX reflexive pronoun (e.g. ITSELF, OURSELVES)

26. POS the possessive (or genitive morpheme) 'S or '

27. PRF the preposition OF

28. PRP preposition (except for OF) (e.g. FOR, ABOVE, TO)

29. PUL punctuation - left bracket (i.e. (or [ )

30. PUN punctuation - general mark (i.e. . ! , : ; - ? ...)

31. PUQ punctuation - quotation mark (i.e. ' ' ")

32. PUR punctuation - right bracket (i.e.) or])

33. TO0 infinitive marker TO

34. UNC "unclassified" items which are not words of the English lexicon

35. VBB the "base forms" of the verb "BE" (except the infinitive), i.e. AM, ARE

36. VBD past form of the verb "BE", i.e. WAS, WERE

37. VBG -ing form of the verb "BE", i.e. BEING

38. VBI infinitive of the verb "BE"

39. VBN past participle of the verb "BE", i.e. BEEN

40. VBZ -s form of the verb "BE", i.e. IS, 'S

41. VDB base form of the verb "DO" (except the infinitive), i.e. "DO"

42. VDD past form of the verb "DO", i.e. DID

43. VDG -ing form of the verb "DO", i.e. DOING

44. VDI infinitive of the verb "DO"

45. VDN past participle of the verb "DO", i.e. DONE

46. VDZ -s form of the verb "DO", i.e. DOES

47. VHB base form of the verb "HAVE" (except the infinitive), i.e. HAVE

48. VHD past tense form of the verb "HAVE", i.e. HAD, 'D

49. VHG -ing form of the verb "HAVE", i.e. HAVING

50. VHI infinitive of the verb "HAVE"

51. VHN past participle of the verb "HAVE", i.e. HAD

52. VHZ -s form of the verb "HAVE", i.e. HAS, 'S

53. VM0 modal auxiliary verb (e.g. CAN, COULD, WILL, 'LL)

54. VVB base form of lexical verb (except the infinitive)(e.g. TAKE, LIVE)

55. VVD past tense form of lexical verb (e.g. TOOK, LIVED)

56. VVG -ing form of lexical verb (e.g. TAKING, LIVING)

57. VVI infinitive of lexical verb

58. VVN past participle form of lex. verb (e.g. TAKEN, LIVED)

59. VVZ -s form of lexical verb (e.g. TAKES, LIVES)

60. XX0 the negative NOT or N'T

61. ZZ0 alphabetical symbol (e.g. A, B, c, d)

Appendix 2: Sample Sentences

Readers may find it instructive to work out these sentences (adapted from Terry Winograd and other sources) using the ATN grammar given in this book. A star indicates an ungrammatical sentence and a question mark indicates a sentences that some may consider ungrammatical. This list is not intended to provide a comprehensive coverage of all the important syntactic phenomena.

1. I slept
2. * I slept the baby
3. * The baby has been slept
4. * I slept him the blanket
5. * I like
6. I like you
7. * I like her a book
8. I bought her a rose
9. * I bought a rose her
10. I wrote a letter to my mother
11. * I ate an apple to my mother
12. I wrote a letter
13. I wrote
14. The wood was burned by the fire

15. The wood was stored by the fire
16. The fish have been caught
17. We gave them the fish
18. We gave the fish to them
19. ? We gave the fish them
20. Sita wanted to sing
21. Sita wanted Rama to sing
22. For her to argue would have upset him
23. Sita wanted to be entertained
24. There are three windows in this room
25. It was Rama who asked Lakshmana not to leave Sita alone
26. Did you catch a fish?
27. Which swimmer caught a fish?
28. Which fish did the swimmer catch?
29. What river was it caught in?
30. Whom did you want Rama to tell to catch a fish?
31. * In what river they fished?
32. Whom was the fish caught by?
33. By whom was the fish caught?
34. Whom was the fish expected to be given to?
35. An engineer reading the newspaper in the balcony got angry
36. They found the answer that they were looking for
37. Yesterday I ate a cake the likes of which I had never seen
38. The deity in whose image we were depicted was unknown to many
39. The windows broken in the scuffle have been replaced
40. I saw a baby being given a bath in the open
41. The fish that they thought you had told me not to bother with was very small
42. The horse raced past the barn fell

Appendix 3: ISCII Character Set

Code	Character Name
161	Vowel-Modifier caMdrabiMdu
162	Vowel-Modifier anusvaara
163	Vowel-Modifier visarga
164	Vowel a
165	Vowel aa
166	Vowel i
167	Vowel ii
168	Vowel u
169	Vowel uu
170	Vowel R
171	Vowel e (Southern Scripts)
172	Vowel ee
173	Vowel ai
174	Vowel aye (deevanaagari Script)
175	Vowel o (Southern Scripts)
176	Vowel oo
177	Vowel au
178	Vowel awe (deevanaagari Script)
179	Consonant ka
180	Consonant kha
181	Consonant ga
182	Consonant gha
183	Consonant nga

Code	Character Name
184	Consonant ca
185	Consonant cha
186	Consonant ja
187	Consonant jha
188	Consonant jnya
189	Consonant Ta
190	Consonant Tha
191	Consonant Da
192	Consonant Dha
193	Consonant Na
194	Consonant ta
195	Consonant tha
196	Consonant da
197	Consonant dha
198	Consonant na
199	Consonant na (Tamil)
200	Consonant pa
201	Consonant pha
202	Consonant ba
203	Consonant bha
204	Consonant ma
205	Consonant ya
206	Consonant jya (Assamese, Bangla, Oriya Scripts)
207	Consonant ra
208	Consonant Hard ra (Southern Scripts)
209	Consonant la
210	Consonant La
211	Consonant zha (Tamil, Malayalam Scripts)
212	Consonant va
213	Consonant s'a
214	Consonant Sa
215	Consonant sa
216	Consonant ha
217	Consonant INVISIBLE

Code	Character Name
218	Vowel Sign aa
219	Vowel Sign i
220	Vowel Sign ii
221	Vowel Sign u
222	Vowel Sign uu
223	Vowel Sign R
224	Vowel Sign e (Southern Scripts)
225	Vowel Sign ee
226	Vowel Sign ai
227	Vowel Sign aye (deevanaagari Script)
228	Vowel Sign o (Southern Scripts)
229	Vowel Sign oo
230	Vowel Sign au
231	Vowel Sign awe (deevanaagari Script)
232	Vowel Omission Sign (halaMt)
233	Diacritic Sign (nukta)
234	Full Stop (viraam, Northern Scripts)
235	Reserved
236	Reserved
237	Reserved
238	Reserved
239	Attribute Code
240	Extension Code
241	Digit 0
242	Digit 1
243	Digit 2
244	Digit 3
245	Digit 4
246	Digit 5
247	Digit 6
248	Digit 7
249	Digit 8
250	Digit 9
251	Reserved
252	Reserved
253	Reserved
254	Reserved

BIS Standard IS 13194:1991

Index

About the Author

Kavi Narayana Murthy obtained his bachelors degree in Mechanical Engineering from Bangalore University in the year 1983, Master of Technology in Artificial Intelligence and Robotics from University of Hyderabad in the year 1988, and PhD in Computer Science from University of Hyderabad in the year 1996. He has over 5 years of experience in reputed private and public industries and over 15 years of post graduate teaching and research experience at the department of computer and information sciences, University of Hyderabad. His research interests include Natural Language Processing and Speech Recognition. He has over 40 publications. He has traveled widely and delivered lectures in many prestigious academic institutions as well as industry. He knows several languages. His general interests include Sanskrit and Indian traditional knowledge systems.